An unusually comical tragedy.
An autobiography

Charles Edward Gerson

WHO ?

This book is written to provide information and motivation to readers. Its purpose is not to render any type of psychological, legal, or professional advice of any kind. The content is the sole opinion and expression of the author, and not necessarily that of the publisher.

Copyright © 2019 by Charles Edward Gerson

All rights reserved. No part of this book may be reproduced, transmitted, or distributed in any form by any means, including, but not limited to, recording, photocopying, or taking screenshots of parts of the book, without prior written permission from the author or the publisher. Brief quotations for noncommercial purposes, such as book reviews, permitted by Fair Use of the U.S. Copyright Law, are allowed without written permissions, as long as such quotations do not cause damage to the book's commercial value. For permissions, write to the publisher, whose address is stated below.

Printed in the United States of America.

ISBN   978-1-949746-32-7   (Paperback)
ISBN   978-1-949746-33-4   (Digital)

Lettra Press books may be ordered through booksellers or by contacting:

Lettra Press LLC
18229 E 52nd Ave.
Denver City, CO 80249
1 303 586 1431 | info@lettrapress.com
www.lettrapress.com

Table of Contents

Preface xi
Introduction xiii

Chapter One 1
    My parents get married and then
    the second coming of Christ, me.

Chapter Two 8
    My younger years and family in Philadelphia.

Chapter Three 25
    Heading for California, Indians & wipers.

Chapter Four 32
    Los Angeles, Pomona, Walnut trees & teen learning.

Chapter Five 39
    High school sports, L. A. County Fair, & Mexicans.

Chapter Six 53
    New friends, youthful talents, Hesperia, & jr. high graduation.

Chapter Seven 69
    School classes, gangs, the Golden Arches, & my broken cherry.

Chapter Eight 85
    Driver license, first car, Tuck and Roll, & a two dollar trick.

Chapter Nine 104
    Skinny dipping, back stabben, snow
    hooden, gangs, jail, and fuzzy moles.

Chapter Ten 140
    The whore mobile, Bar-B-Q's, fire & graveyards.

Chapter Eleven 149
    Beatings, painting, Snipes, and
    Munger, Bill the killer, me the hooker,

Chapter Twelve 177
    Four cherries, the Arizona flash & marriage.

Chapter Thirteen 182
    College, Heather, Holly, Cherokee, Mad Dog,
    the infamous hand squeeze, Max & a trampoline.

Chapter Fourteen 195
    Shoot the bro, film dad's ass, the scouts, one
    arm man, an operation, areola & phlegm.

Chapter Fifteen 211
    Twenty-one, age or cards, you're what, Peter,
    Paul and Mary, the Beatles, puke & a new job.

Chapter Sixteen 227
    Manicures, toe jobs, wigs and crawdads,
    poor Joe is dead, das boat, da moon & Elvis.

Chapter Seventeen 252
    Pee in a boot, stuck in a toilet, Water Beds,
    Cochise, XKE, Super Bowl & a horse.

Chapter Eighteen 286
    Linen, tee shirts, El Paso, green box, lymph
    nodes, Helmsly, The Osmands, & N.Y. Parking.

Chapter Nineteen 297
    Nineteen eighty-one, Aaron's flowers,
    bookie Cal, Caliente & horse stories.

Chapter Twenty..311
    The factory, the butts, Heather sprints,
    Mom drives & Barstow is a bitch.

Chapter Twenty-One..322
    The dog, the kid, the flying Heather, the
    salesman, the jerk, the dope & the divorce.

Chapter Twenty-Two 335
    The alcoholic bar tender, the good son bad son, she's
    split, pissin partners, the wedding & the garage goose.

Chapter Twenty-Three 351
    Moving north, tee shirts and mosquitoes, bench warmer,
    earthquakes, ADAPT, Yosemite, karaoke & rogue waves.

Chapter Twenty-Four..397
    Lost me, Tahoe, lesbians, slots, E.T.
    Gasping for breath & I feel better now.

Chapter Twenty-Five 408
    Docent, power, earthquake, jail,
    horses, Colorado River, & one arm.

Chapter Twenty-Six 425
    She's baaaaack, fortune tellers,
    Pocketfullofpesos, & the company is gone.

Chapter Twenty-Seven 435
    Dogs, alligators, Martha, marriage, & Elvis.

Yiddish Glossary 449
    Yiddish translation to English with a little humor to Follow.

Poem used with permission of Dorothea Grossman, author.
Copyright, nineteen ninety-five.

Contents

Written by: Charles Edward Gerson

Directed by: Charles Edward Gerson

Produced by: Charles Edward Gerson

And staring: Charles Edward Gerson

Please note; any mistakes you might find throughout this entire book are my brother, Mark's, fault!

Mom always liked me better, anyway!

This has been edited by so many friends, that if I listed them all, I would need to add another twenty-five pages, and we know that we don't need that. However, there are one or two whom I really need to acknowledge and thank for their unselfish free time that they have donated to me.

*Wally **Sherman**.*

***Joey** Palmieri*

(Both female)

Preface

I am far from either Stephen Hawking, who is probably the smartest person in the world right now or an Albert Einstein, with whom you may be more familiar. In fact, I am A D D in spelling, grammar and comprehension. Now, I am writing a book. Go figure! I asked an acquaintance of mine, an English teacher, to explain to me what a preface is. I had seen it in the five books that I have read since I was a pup, and she said this. She, being Wally (see, it already starts kind of weird and not to mention Joey, who also helped me, also of the same gender), said, "It usually gives a reason why you are writing the book."

My reason is to leave my unseen grand children and great grand children with names unknown, and faces un-seen, who I really am. I would think that the truth may be contrary to what they might have been told about me, but I need to set the record straight. Also, to let the world know (if I have this book published for human consumption) that there are stranger, more unusual, crazy, smarter, and much dumber people on our blue globe than they might think there are. Starting with me! Wally also said, "You might want to dedicate your book to someone."

So, I will dedicate it to my oldest friend who plays a large part in my writings. He recently took his own life. (Nancy, please contact me.) Raymond Eugene Hawkins. At the risk of seeming selfish, I want to share this dedication with my old friend. Although I have not taken my own life, obviously, (although it has crossed my mind a time or two.) but having gone through the crap from my children, the crap that I am still going through with the IRS, and a plethora of other things about which you will read as you dive into the works of a self-proclaimed author. I want to dedicate it to myself, as well. Let's make it a three-some and include my dad. (May he rest in peace.) He plays a major role in my life.

One more thing that Wally (the female) mentioned was that I could give a thank you to anyone who may have helped me write this five hundred plus page autobiography. There are a few minor awards such as my friend Joey, my cousin, Sandy, and my brother, Mark. I guess if I could mention the helpful ones I would think that I can mention the ones who could have really helped out but declined. That would have been my ex-wife, Heather. She has a memory that would put an elephant to shame. She could remember shit that I did years prior to when I did them and still have me on the carpet about them fifteen years later. She could remember what colors I wore to a dance and what I paid for the tickets, twenty years hence. I asked her to meet me in Las Vegas. It is about the same distance for both of us and kind of equal grounds. Not to mention, it would be nice to, maybe break bread, and catch up a bit. (I got her e-mail address from my cousin, Sandy.) All expenses paid by me. I had intended to ask her if she would collaborate with me on some things that she would remember much better than I. Things the children did and when they did them. Maybe dates and times we did things with friends and neighbors as they would come up in my writings. Stuff like that. She really has a photographic memory. However, she had no problem saying, "No." The reason I have added Heather and her answer at this time is to ask you, the readers, forgiveness to some of the times, dates and even some of the people mentioned. Although, all is true in this book, they may be off as much as three or four years, one way or another.

The one major thing that you need to know is that no matter how weird, unsettling, strange, off the wall, aggressive, non-flattering, stupid, offensive or extremely smart (not many of those, however), everything in this book, if not one hundred percent true, is based on one hundred percent truth. If I have offended anyone, I sincerely apologize. But that may have been the way the story needed to be told. There has been some exaggeration and humor added to make this book fun reading. Hell, I even laugh sometimes myself.

One other thing that you will notice is that I use a capital "L" with any form of the use of the word "Love". I really feel that if you use that word it should be strongly emphasized.

In retrospect, Gene, you and my father were my rock. My dad was always my ace in the hole. I wish you, Gene, Mom and Dad were still around to read this book. I would even give you three a copy, at no charge. (Maybe!)

Now, it's all about me.

Introduction

I am not sure why anyone would buy a book about someone they don't know, especially a nobody like me. I am neither a millionaire nor a movie star, a prophet, a poet, a politician (YUCK), or any kind of a celebrity or nationally known figure. Just a plain ole guy who has put in his 60 plus years on this planet, like so many of us, and basically has nothing to show for it! But I do appreciate the purchase as I really do need the money.

In 2005 I was told to retire by the cardiologist because my ticker wasn't ticking so well any more. I had no plans to do so, and I didn't have much money put away. The doc said, "The multitude of problems in business and a few other very personal family issues are causing you way too much stress" in addition to a guy named Hugh Stahl, who worked for the I.R.S., badgering me for past federal tax crap. So, after a major stress-caused heart attack, I am in the hospital looking up at a small box on the wall that shows a heart rate of 22 to 24 beats per minute and sometimes nothing for five and six seconds at a time. My GP (General Practitioner) by my side said "It's now or never. You're checking out. You need to make a decision. It's been six hours, and it won't be six more." I really didn't want an operation at that point in my life. I really thought it was OK to "check out." Right then and there, I really didn't see a lot for which to live. I had had a full life as you will read. The only possible reason to hang in there would have been for my kids. But they, for some unknown reason, abandoned me six years ago and won't tell me why. But the doc was very convincing. I made a quick call to my brother and asked him if things don't work out the way they are supposed to will he pull the plug? (Now-a-days, you have to have a plug puller so the doctor doesn't get sued.) Without hesitation he said, "YES." (He always thought that Mom liked me better than him so I figured that was his chance to get back at me.) So, now I am retired, complete with a pace maker, and to add insult to injury, unbeknownst to me the Internal Revenue Service (I.R.S.) was planning an all out attack on me for five years of back taxes, again. The stress I had in business was incidental to the stress I am having now. It seems like I am having a heart attack a week. If I live long enough to finish writing and to sell this book, at least you know that the proceeds from it will go to keep me alive or if the I.R.S. wins, Bush's war effort.

Now, that I think about it, it seems embarrassing that the richest country in the world has to come to me for money! In recent years the I.R.S. has let off famous-name movie stars for millions and millions of dollars, in back taxes. The government needs my few bucks to fight the war or whatever? Go figure! At least the movie stars and I have something in common; we all think we can entertain you.

I will begin the writing of this book. It starts way before I am a gleam in my daddy's eye. I hope I finish before I play frog (croak). But, if we both, you the reader and me the writer, get lucky, I'll finish, you can buy it, and I can make a buck. And . . . . you *will be* entertained!

To (almost) quote a line from a Steve Martin movie (Steve Who?), "I was born a *small* poor *Black* child." (*9 pounds and 3 ounces.*) Although, *Jewish*, I was born in *St. Joseph's* (*Catholic*) Hospital. Confusing? Wait, it gets worse. My grandparents on my father's side were from Russia and Poland. That Grandmother (AKA Bubba, Yiddish for Grandmother and not to be confused with a large black football player), was about five years older than my Grandfather (AKA Zada, Yiddish for Grandfather) when she got to this GREAT country and hated it. She refused to learn English or to get with any part of the American program. Why, I don't know. She just didn't.

My Zada was a very good-looking tall guy with a very easy going type of personality. In fact, one day his store was robbed and the only way anyone in the family knew it was robbed was because they read about it in the Philadelphia Inquirer newspaper. He even had neighbors who were black, and he talked to them! On the other hand, my Bubba, who was not a "ten" by any stretch of the imagination, didn't talk to anyone!

My grandparents on my mother's side were from England. That grandfather played frog (croaked) before I ever knew him, so I was named after him, "Charles." Naming someone after the dead is a Jewish tradition. (You would have thought that after 5000 plus years, we Jews would have thought of a more up beat and lively way of naming children.) Obviously, he must have been a GREAT man! I was born in Philadelphia, Pennsylvania. With my background, as you will soon learn, you would have thought *Transylvania* and not *Pennsylvania*. I guess my eye teeth were not long or pointy enough to qualify for Transylvania.

From birth *canal*, in '42 to cruising the Panama *Canal* in '05, my life, you will find, has been very different from yours. I have only three real regrets, one was cheating on my wife (the most beautiful woman, both in and out, I have ever known), gambling, (a problem I still have only to a much smaller degree), and the other was beating a six foot five kid (my oldest son) with a belt for way too long. To this day, it still haunts me on a regular basis. Stretching out to the other side, one of the greatest things, if not the greatest thing of my adult life, was winning the Sunshine Million horse race in partnership with my youngest son, Sean. That was a thrill that will last in my heart forever.

From playing hooky to being a bookie, a thief at 14, a straight "A" student until 16, a gang member, maybe even a killer from childhood to husband and fatherhood, I will fill a plethora of pages with adverbs and adjectives that describe me. Some of them are routine, some exciting, some crazy, and some a little unbelievable. But, all have a basis of one hundred percent truth. I will put them all together with meaning that will really tell you who I am and why I am writing this book. You have already bought it, so, I guess you will just have to keep reading to see why you have spent your money on a guy you don't even know.

Chapter One

Now in 2008 as I start this auto biography . . . **OH! Wait!** Let me tell you a funny story that just happened this last weekend (05/17/08) with my cousin Dottie just to prove how nutty my family and I are. (By the way, most of the names in this book have been changed to protect the innocent, embarrassed and the ashamed, not to mention keeping me from being sued). Dottie (my cousin who now lives in California) thinks she is a poet; some might call her "imagistic" because she thinks her poetry is full of images to her and to her audience as she speaks. I think she is a Beatnik (WHAT'S THAT!) type jazz entertainer. She reads something that she wrote and calls it poetry and people clap. Now, I am going to quote one of the poems she wrote and recited on the 17th. and then explain how nuts the whole thing is. Not the poem (that you will see for yourself) but the reason she belongs in my family tree. Here goes:

"Time now for a word about my father/a life long student/ of the occult and magic,/and worshipper of the Great Houdini/who famously tried to cheat death,/in this case by pulling pennies/out of my ear."

That's the whole poem. Go figure! Now, here's the real deal. Dottie's mother, Sadie, (everyone called her that except for the children in the family. We called her Aunt Shirley. All of my father's kin had two names: one for the adults and one for the kids. I think it was to make the family seem so much bigger so that it looked like we had our own little mafia. Except my Zada's brother, his name was Zalman, and with a name like that, who needs a second one?) who worked for the school system her whole life (maybe even longer). Knowing that, her daughter, Dottie, at a ripe young age, said that she will never have to go back to school again because her father (the magician) can make money just by pulling it out of her ears, will certainly undo a solid husband/wife relationship with the very strict school teacher. *Strangely enough*, Sadie's husband Ted (Dottie's father) passed away not long after this whole situation happened and daughter Dottie started back to fourth grade.

Now where was I? *Oh yea, my autobiography.* I hope I finish it by the time the world, as we know it, ends according to the Mayan calendar which is December 21st. 2012. There are many other well known collaborators, of whom you may have heard, that agree, such as H. G. Wells, Nostradamus, John (of the Book of John), Revelations in the Bible, etc. (Of course, they're all dead now just like the Mayans and don't have to worry about it). Sixty-five million years ago the dinosaurs went caput, so why not us? They were much bigger and stronger then us and could withstand much more abuse although they were much dumber. They would not have known how to handle the problems that arose. We, however, are much smarter but seem to be causing the problems, *but that's another book.*

My parents met in a Chinese restaurant by chance, at least that's the way the story goes. My dad Mike (Michael), later to be known as Uncle Mike to the kids and Myer to the adults, was on a date. My mom Lil (Lillian), later to be known as Aunt Lil to the kids and Lil to the adults, (she only had one name and you will find out why later) was also on a date at the same restaurant. (Not with each other.) Mike spotted Lil as she was on the way to the restroom. Instant Love!! He grabbed her as she walked by, threw her on the table right there in front of his date (hopefully, their food had not yet been delivered), and kissed her. Not exactly sure what happened to the other dates in the next few minutes, but the rest is history. I guess that is why my favorite food is Chinese, and my favorite part of sex is kissing. Go figure!!

My future mom and dad dated for a couple of years or so and then finally got around to getting married. Not a real big tzores (tzores, Yiddish for a big deal or problem). The idea of getting married was not a big deal but the wedding itself. Not a big wedding because no one had a lot of gelt. (Gelt, another Yiddish word meaning money, bucks, bread, geddes, cash, *get it?*) Not sure how old they were but I don't think Mike was 21 yet and Lil was about a year younger. After the not-so-big tzores (wedding), they came back to my Grandfather's house for the reception. (The Bubba/Zada, Grandmother/Grandfather's, house)

My Grandmother (Bubba sometimes known as Bubbie to the kids, *how unusual, two names*), the one who hated the USA, swore from the very first meeting of my future mom and all through the dating time and the engagement time and the wedding time that my mom to be was not Jewish. Bubba said she didn't look Jewish to her; *therefore, it was fact.* Many years later I found out that Bubba felt the same way about my Uncle Izzy's wife, Molly. (My cousin Joan had read this part of my book, before it was published, and told me that the same thing happened to her mom-to-be, Molly. Izzy and Molly are passed now, but I would have Loved to have asked them where they had their reception!)

For the entire time of my parents' relationship, there was nothing but arguing, yelling, complaining, (Complaining, a Jewish Grandmother complaining?) and resentment of my future mom from my Bubba and, of course, it involved all of my aunts and uncles to be. This was really hard for me to believe since I never saw my Bubba get out of her bed the whole time that I knew her. But we will get to that story when I am born. (That's kind of a weird statement! Could I be John Conner? That's for you movie fans, "The Terminator".) So, when my future mom and dad got to the house for the reception, Bubba does not let in Lil, my future mom. Obviously, Bubba is out of her bed at this stage in her life and giving full credit to the title of Jewish Grandmother. Sooooooo, Mike has to make a decision. Party without his new wife at the reception (if he was a lot like me, this is a very hard decision to make, as he is still a kid) or he can take his new bride away and show how much in Love he is and start to make a new life for them, starting now. So, much like his offspring to be, me, he must have had morals and stuck to his recently spoken vows, 'Till death do us part'. (Hmmmmm, party, wife, party, wife, party, wife@#$%^&*) He pulled out a knife, *just joking! He* grabbed the beautiful babe, took a hit of some Jack, said his farewells to all his relatives at the reception, got a phone number of a friend (from an uncle at the party) who lives in Chicago, and lit off for a world of challenges with $73.83 in his pocket, a beautiful new bride, a borrowed car, and an eight hundred mile trip in front of them. Dressed in a tuxedo, she in her bridal garb, married 3 hours ago at 3 o'clock on a Sunday afternoon heading for Chicago on December 23rd ! What the hell was she thinking at this moment? Talk about being in Love!!

The next few days of their life were never too clear to me. (Just about like *my entire life* has been.) My dad must have called the contact in Chicago and wound up in an Armour and Sons meat packing plant for a job. I actually have pictures of him on his job. (One of my sons who is not born yet has them in a scrap book that he will not give me because he hates me. I was right about a subject that we argued or something like that, but that is in chapter 7037. Bet ya can't wait!) I hope you are sitting down.

OH yea! Wait! I forgot to tell you, my Bubba and Zada, the grandparents who would not let my parents in the house after the wedding are VERY, VERY kosher. To make a very, very long, long explanation short, kosher means you never mix milk products with meat products. (My apologies to the "Orthodox Jews" who are reading this book) There are many other things, of course, but I will try to stick to the story line which has been violated a bunch already.

In a kosher house you have two sinks, two sets of dishes and silverware. The milk and meat products are never, never allowed to touch each other. If there is one MAJOR, MAJOR rule among the kosher laws that you MUST stand by and regard as the ALMIGHTYS LAW above all others, is that you NEVER eat PORK or shell fish. Now, try to picture this in your mind! I have pictures of my dad wearing a tuxedo (obviously the only clothes he took or had when he left for Chicago) shvitzing like a pig. (Shvitzing, another Yiddish word that means to sweat). He is standing in a very large room with a very large dead pig hanging in front of him, by its hind legs, after being scalded by, I think, very very hot water trying to burn the hair off its body before going through the next process to clean this anti-Semitic food for human consumption. It had to be no less than 125 degrees in that room. (In fact my dad told me he lost twenty five-pounds in the month that he worked there). My dad's job was to shave the remaining hair off the pig that was missed by the scalding water. Now, this is speculation of course, but if you remember, I mentioned that my Bubba was able to stand a few days ago and had no problem running off my dad and mom. I wouldn't put it past him to have sent a picture of himself like the one I have of him (in fact, it could be the same picture) shaving a pig to my Bubba even though she was his very KOSHER mom. (My Dad and I seem to have the same sense of humor. We think things are funny, but no one else does.) Now, being as religious as she was, seeing him shaving a PIG in a slaughter house in a tuxedo, may be the reason she never got out of bed again! I am not really sure how long my dad actually worked for Armour and Sons, but I do know he got promoted after a month or so. He went to the boss and complained about him being a Jew in a slaughter house and that he should not be in this capacity. He told them that he was a hard worker and should be in a management position. He did get moved up. Management, no! However he did get out of the heat.

Now, being in Chicago around prohibition, (I am guessing 1936 or thereabouts) my dad, being a full-fledged character and chance taker much like myself, and in need of money (much like myself) and certainly ready to get out of the food business, was approached by a relative who owned a taxi cab company. I believe it was the cousin of the uncle that recommended my dad for the highly acclaimed position in the slaughter house. However, this taxi cab company was a little bit different than most. It went from Chicago to Philadelphia non-stop, then back again with no passengers. Well, why, you ask? How did they make any money, you ask? My dad asked the exact same questions, and here is what they told him. Well, Mike, (or possibly Myer) I'll tell you how and why. We transport booze not people. We have a hollowed out floor board then we load up with our order and just drive it to our destination. It's just that simple. Are you in? "Whoa" Mike said, "This seems like very easy money." "Mike, I will even tell you something else. You don't even have to drive. Just ride shot gun (that is on the passenger side) and keep a look out for any cars or people who look suspicious." (No one mentioned that those people who they were talking about were the Feds with warrants, machine guns, and jail time.) Mike took the job, and although there were a few chases that were a little hair rising and not fun, the pay was very good and the pictures that were sent back to his mom and dad were much more appreciated. Well at least to his mom, Bubba! She was not exactly up on prohibition. However, Zada was, and the *non-speaking episodes* of my Bubba and my future mom, Lil, changed to my Zada, and his son, Mike, my future dad. "It's illegal." Zada said. "You will be killed", Zada said. "You will disgrace the family!" he said. "You are as bad as my brother, Zalman, the big time bookie," he said. "I have a legitimate furniture business and am trying to raise a family and trying to make a living, and you try to disgrace me and ruin me," he said. It just seems that someone in the Gerson family just has to be different than most other people. Thank God it went to me and not my brother. He would have hanged himself by now. The Gerson curse did transfer to both my boys and would, at least, be split so they could handle all the crap that was to come. I am sure it does ease the pain when it is divided.

As time went on, being in this type of business, (Running booze) it led to meeting other people in the same type of underworld environment. My dad actually knew and was friendly with Al Capone. (For you younger readers, Al Capone played for the Brooklyn Dodgers. They were a football team. For you older readers, you know I am full of shit.) They weren't bosom buddies but did have a mild relationship. I think what kept it mild was when Al asked my dad to go to work for him. I think my dad would have Loved to but to work for Al, you had to carry a gun and my dad didn't want to do it. Not sure if my mom had anything to do with that decision! Even though my dad would not carry a gun, he was known to shoot off his mouth a lot. Dad was pretty wild as I was told by many. He kept running the booze for quite a while until one day something happened.

Not sure where or when it was but during a regular run, the cab stopped at a traffic light. The traffic cop, directing traffic in the center of the intersection, (that was how they did it in those days. In fact, they still do it in New York City that way, I'm told) started to walk over to the cab, for what reason, they and certainly I, have no idea. When the cop got right to the door, the driver of the cab opened the door, hit the gas and spun the cop on to the pavement with great force. The cab never stopped until it reached its destination. My dad got out of the cab. That was the last day he ever ran booze. In fact, from that day on, he wouldn't even take a cab to go anywhere. "The trolley (What the hell is a trolley?) is the only way to go," he'd say. Not exactly sure what happened after that. I think Dad and Mom went home to his mom and dad (my Bubba and Zada) in Philadelphia. They must have resolved their differences between them. My dad finally got a real job with Bond Clothing Stores as a salesman. He worked for them for the next 25 years or so.

Now in 1942 the best thing since sliced bread came along. *Me*! I did lie about being Black in the beginning of the book, but I did weigh 9 pounds and 3 ounces and never stopped hearing about it from the moment I could hear and understand anything. How I completely ruined my mother's insides because I was so big. How she hemorrhaged and stretched beyond anyone's belief. She had excruciating pain that occurred throughout the pregnancy and all through the delivery and months thereafter.

Five years later, when my little brother was born, according to my mom, it was my fault he was so small at birth because of the damage I had inflicted on her during my birth. Because of what I had done to her insides, she did not have enough room for him to develop properly and so on and so on. Yes, this is the life of a good Jewish boy with a normal Jewish mother.

And so the story begins.

Chapter Two

Now, I can't remember too much at birth, (I was very young), in fact, I can't remember too much today but for a different reason. (I am very old.) It seems that one of the first things I do remember, as a very young child, is seeing a dog. Now, if you can hark back a few pages, I remember telling you that my life was a very confusing one. This dog may be one of the only normal things in my life. The dog was named Brownie. Guess what? The dog was Brown!

Now, I will get back to some of the confusing stuff. The first 12 years of my life I would like to remember more but can't. The next 12 years of my life I would like to remember less but can't. I grew up in the big city of Philadelphia. For some reason our family moved around a lot. I really never noticed it as a youth or even thought about it until many years later when living in California. It was brought up in conversation, and it did turn on a light in my head. Why did we move so much?

I can remember living in Philadelphia in an area called Logan on 8th Street in the same house with *my favorite* male cousin, Arnold, and his sister, Sharon. (I only had one male cousin). Why both families lived together I have no idea; we just did. My mom and his mom were sisters. His dad, Uncle Lou, (he only had one name because he was on my mom's side of the family) seemed to go to the race track a lot. I think he was some kind of a salesman that always seemed to be selling some kind of gimmick and or things that might rip off people. Kind of a hit and run artist and that afforded him the free time to go to the horse races. He was always nice to me, and I liked him a lot.

I remember one day, getting up very early in the morning. I think Arnold and I were about 5 or 6 ish and going out to the screened-in patio and coloring in our coloring books. He was great at coloring. I stunk! I was always outside of the lines. I used to get so pissed off at him. I could have killed him just for coloring inside the lines. (No wonder my life went the direction it took.) However, it is funny how things can change. As we got older, he would read the newspaper in the bathroom and leave it all messed up on the floor. I could never understand that, because he would read it while on the toilet. He went so fast while in there that he had no time to mess up the newspaper. From neatness in coloring to making a mess in the toilet in just a few short years! There is just no accounting for change. At least I never change. When I was young, I couldn't stay inside the lines while coloring. Now that I am old, I can't stay inside the lines while driving!

Speaking about being a five year old and not coloring-inside the lines as well as my cousin Arnold and then having a teacher write a note and sending it home with me as to my possible vision problem, my dad took me to the optometrist. He said I needed glasses. At first I thought that would be great. With the glasses I could color within the lines. I couldn't wait to get them. Finally, they were in. It took me a day or so to adjust to them. After a week I still couldn't color any better, but all the kids at school kept calling me four eyes and a few other things that I didn't like.

One morning, as I was walking to school, I threw the glasses down the gutter and went to school without them. When I got home and was at the table eating my dinner, my dad said, "Where are your glasses?" I said, "I couldn't find them this morning." He said, "You had them on when you left for school." I said, "I did?" He said, "Yes you did." "Then, I must have lost them at school." He was not a happy camper. Glasses cost a lot of money, and we were far from flush. He started to quiz me and as time went on, the quizzing got rougher and rougher. Pretty soon I was crying and afraid that I was going to get a beating for the loss. I finally broke down and told him what I did and why. The reason held no water. He said, "We are going to go and get them right now." "Right now" I said? "It's cold, dark, and I won't be able to see them and besides, they are down in the gutter with all that there is in a gutter." We put on our jackets and were off. I found the right gutter I think and I tried to reach in through the opening at the side of the curb but couldn't reach anything. So, Dad said he would take the manhole cover off and then I could reach in further as there would be more room. He did exactly that. The cover came off, and he put a flashlight to the bottom. I could see the glasses about five or six feet down. He held my feet and lowered me down as far as he could. I was crying now just about like I will be, when I get to be twelve or thirteen and a little fatter. (You will have to read further in the book to understand that.) I could not reach the glasses. He told me to wait here, and he would be right back. It seemed like three days went by, but had I had a watch, I probably would have counted off about ten minutes or so. That is if I could read it. I didn't have my glasses on. When he got back, he was carrying a rope. If I was a little older, I would have said SHIT. Not a rope, SHIT! He tied the rope around my waist and dropped me into the sewer like I was a yoyo. My hands were feeling around in the crap that was in there. No telling what was in there. He wouldn't give me the flashlight as he said he needed it to see to where he was lowering me. If I had been a little older, I would have told him, "Hell, that's where, HELL!" Finally, I had them in my hands and tried to yell, "Pull me up," but the tears had filled my yelling parts so I could only whimper. He yelled to me, "Can you see them?" Had I been a little older, I would have told him that I can't see them because I don't have my glasses. You have the flashlight! How could I see them? Then, all of a sudden my yeller worked, and I screamed, (like a scream from hell itself), the word "UP! UP!" He pulled me up, took the glasses from me and said, "If this happens again, I won't pull the rope back up, understand"? I did. We walked home. Mom saw what I looked like and said, "Mike, he's not coming into this house like that." I undressed outside. It must have been forty below. Shaking, I ran to the tub. This may have been the one and only time of my childhood that I took a bath without having to be told to do so, and enjoyed it.

Arnold (my cousin) was about a year younger than I was. We spent a lot of time together. In fact, we were so close that I think of him more as a brother than a cousin. I was more of a bully then he was. He was more of a goody goody kind of a guy and sometimes a pain in the ass. A lot like my little brother Mark.

One summer I remember walking home one day from the Choo-Choo Restaurant. We were about 9, maybe 10 years old. (That was a restaurant where you would order your hamburger or whatever, and it would be delivered by a Lionel Train on a track that was on the bar counter. It would stop in front of you, so you could take your food off the flat car, and then it would leave and come back later with the bill on the caboose.) Arnold and I got into it for some reason that escapes me now, but I nailed him with a right, and much to my surprise, he came back with a couple of his own punches. Soon, we were on the ground rolling around on the sidewalk and punching it out. I finally quit as he was getting the best of me. (My brother has a current day saying for losing a fight. It goes like this: I gave him the one, two punch, and he gave me the three, four and five. I am not sure why I am telling you this, but I am sure somewhere later in this story I will probably have to refer to it!)

While we are on the subject of food, one night my family, Mom, Dad, Mark and I were out to dinner at a fairly nice restaurant, and I must have been acting up. (Hmmmmm, me?) Not sure exactly what I had been doing but Mom, yes my mild, sweet, and Loving mother, got so pissed off at me, that when I reached for something on the table, she stabbed me with her fork. My arm was stretched out, and, as I looked at it, the fork was standing straight up in my arm and swaying back and forth, all by its self. I started to yell from the pain. Forget the humiliation! When dad looked at me with that look, I winced, shut my mouth, and just let the tears roll out from beneath my eye lids (Can Asians do that? Do they have eye lids?), and the blood drip from my arm. Thank God for pink linen napkins. It hardly showed on the table. Mark, on the other hand, was doing his best to keep from laughing his head off. He and I had the same facial look, only different. I think that was when I knew that Mom, Dad and Mark were a team and I was a loner. To this day, I think nothing has changed. I am still a loner.

I can remember in the winter, on the weekend when it had snowed all night, we, Arnold and I, would go to the kitchen early in the morning and open the back door. The snow would be packed all the way to the top of the door so that no one could get in or out. We would tunnel through the snow about six or seven feet and then up a few and got out. His mom would scream at us when she got up. "You kids could be buried alive if there was a collapse!" Like we cared!

One thing I can remember is that I was a fire bug.

Where I picked it up from, I have no clue. One morning, when living with my cousins, I went down the back steps. Under those steps was where my Aunt Sil (Arnold's mother) kept the trash cans. I lit a fire in the cans and proceeded to burn down the back steps to the house. Why and for what reason, I'll never know, but I did. I think that was about the time we moved to another place.

I also lived on Lancaster Avenue in Philadelphia. I think that is the street where the Philadelphia Zoo is. Speaking of the zoo, I don't remember much when I was a kid, but I do remember one time when I was all grown up and had my own family in California. I went back for a visit to Philadelphia. Arnold and Sandy (Arnold's wife) and my beautiful bride, (at that time) Heather, all went to the zoo. Now, Sandy is a piece of work. Probably the nicest lady you will ever know but may be a couple of fries short of a happy meal. Not in a dumb way but just a little naive. So, the four of us were walking around the zoo, and I saw two 500 pound turtles doing it. (Please don't ask me what doing it is.) That is a sight to see by itself. So, I asked Sandy to stand by the fence because I wanted to take a picture of her. She, of course, doesn't see the turtles, and I position her so that it looks like she is helping them. SNAP! A few days later, when she saw the picture, she almost had a heart attack. It's, "OH MY GOD! OH MY GOD! OH MY GOD! How could you do that to me???" You would have thought that she was actually part of the action!

Also, on Lancaster Avenue, there was a delicatessen called "Levitz Deli." My dad had a charge account there. My bother and I would walk there from either my Zada's store, or from wherever I lived near there and grab pickles. Sounds nuts? Well, it isn't if you're a kid. Now that I think about it, I don't know if my brother was with me or not. I would go there and find a barrel filled with kosher pickles floating around in the barrel. I would stick my arm in the barrel, and grab a pickle of my choice, and eat it. If I didn't like the one I chose, I would just drop it back in, before I took a bite, and fish out another one. Now, what determined which one I would keep or drop back in boggles my mind! But, as a child, I am sure I knew the difference. I would eat the one I wanted and say charge it to my dad. I would often take a TastyKake, as well. (TastyKakes, are a special kind confection that are only found on the East Coast and not unlike Twinkies in the west).

Now, this Lancaster Avenue really teams with variety. My dad would take me there to get my hair cut when we were at my Zada's house. The place was called Vince's Hair Cuts. Owned by guess who, Vince! This guy was totally different from any other hair cut shop I had ever been to before or since. After the hair cut was over, he would take a long stick match or two and burn my hair. He called it singeing. What the purpose was, I did not know then, and I still don't know today. I don't know if he had an inside desire to be a monk or what. It was scary because I could smell the hair burning. Not a nice smell. Fortunately, it had to do with fire so I could tolerate it!

Now, Bustleton Avenue I have no remembrance of that street. Not sure, if there is such a place. But if there is, it must be in Philadelphia. Maybe Bruce Willis knows of it!

Then there was Girard Avenue, on the second story above a dress shop is where I learned to drink coffee at a very young age. I remember coming down the very narrow stairway in the very early morning (way before my mom and dad where awake) to visit the two women who lived together and who owned the dress shop below. Now that I think about it, they may have been gay, but at my tender age, I didn't know what gay was. In fact, Johnny Mathis *is* my favorite singer, and I still don't believe he's gay. (Once again for you younger people, Johnny Mathis is another ball player, much like Al Capone was, just a different kind of ball.) I would knock on the door. They would always be up and have the coffee ready. I don't think I was four years old yet. They would sit on the bottom step with me and bring me my coffee. (I believe I called it cossee at that age.) It had about an inch of coffee as I recall and about three inches of milk and probably a half pound of sugar in the cup. This went on for a very long time. To this day, I still drink that crap. Just less milk and a lot less sugar. I wish I could say the same for my dad. But, that's in another chapter. Now for you Westerners, that is the way almost all grown ups in the East still drink their coffee today.

One morning, I awoke a bit earlier then usual and knowing that it was too early to start drinking "cossee," I found some matches on a counter. (Mom and Dad both smoked cigarettes). Mom and Dad were still asleep so I got my little brother, Mark and the matches. We sat on the floor facing each other, with our feet touching each others, as if to make a circle with our legs. In the middle of that circle, I got a couple of pieces of newspaper, crunched them together, and proceeded to make a bonfire. The paper caught fire, the carpet caught fire, and Mark almost caught fire. Not sure what woke Dad and Mom up, maybe Mark and me yelling "yippee" at the top of our lungs. I think that may have been when I found out what a belt was for, besides keeping up your pants!

I also lived in the Mayfair section of Philadelphia, on McKinley Street, where I cut my stomach in half. I bet you can't wait to hear that story. Now that I think about it, that was probably the first time that I started blaming things on the opposite sex. I still do it to this day, even if I know it wasn't "she" that did anything wrong. *It's just fun*! However, it does piss off some women.

But before I get to that story, I would like to tell you another one that is kind of funny. I was probably eleven. One summer it was very hot. *Philadelphia Hot!* A bunch of us kids would play outside in the hot sun. Playing whatever games kids played at that age including stick ball. The good humor man (someone who sells ice cream out of a truck) would come around two to three times a day to sell his ice cream and popsicles. Well, I was one of his best customers. I can't tell you how many popsicles I bought each and every day. I am sure it was at least ten or more. (Hmmmmmm, I wondered why Jewish kids seem so fat at twelve). One day, as I was playing, I had this terrible pain in my stomach. Really bad! I fell and couldn't get up. One of my friends went and called my mother to come out and to see if she could do anything. Of course, Mom went berserk, and panicked. I was crying loud from the pain, and she kept asking the other kids if they had hit me with the stick we were using for stick ball. (Remember the hit me with a stick thing, for a latter chapter. Mom just doesn't change.) They kept saying no, and she kept asking. Meanwhile, I'm lying on the hot asphalt ready to pass out. Mom ran in and called an ambulance and within thirty minutes, I was in emergency. Test after test after test. They were sure it was my appendix. For two days I could not eat or poop, just cry. Not to mention sleep. Nothing going in and nothing coming out, just pain. So, they scheduled me for surgery the next morning. Of course, the whole entourage was there. Cousins, aunts, uncles and, of course, Mom and Dad were there. As I was being talked to about the surgery, I started to feel better. The pain went as fast as it had come. I was joking with everyone, even the nurse, who was giving me the instructions. When the doctor walked in, I joked with him as well! The doc said, "This is not normal. The pain with an appendix problem does not just go away that fast." They stopped the surgery and started to ask me a lot of questions. After the interrogation they all agreed that the problem was frozen insides from all the popsicles I had eaten. Go Figure! By the way, I still have that little guy. No! Not that little guy. (Get your mind out of the gutter.) My appendix!

I was about eleven or more likely twelve and most of my spare time went to studying the Haftorah for my Bar Mitzvah, (You know, Boe, Ba, Beh, Hoe Ha, Heh and so on and so forth.) and just learning Hebrew in general. And of course doing my school work as well. (To my gentile readers, the Haftorah is something you learn to sing when you go to the *Mitzvah bar* to drink. Kinda like a Jewish Karaoke.) Try not to believe too much of what I write. (The Jews will understand and the non Jews probably don't give a shit any way.) At this point in my life, I was a fine student, just a little over weight. All Jewish kids, about twelve years old, are a little over weight and they seem to cry a lot. I just couldn't color within the lines in a coloring book as good as my cousin Arnold. In fact, I think that was what started the fight with him a few pages back. I knew I'd get back to that.

Anyway, one summer, this very pretty girl moved in about four or five houses down from me. If memory serves me correctly, her name was Ann. She was tall and had long dark hair. She would ride her bike around the neighborhood a lot, and I would watch her. I had never noticed a girl before. (Shit, I thought, I bet now I am going to start growing hair on my chin or elsewhere.) I would hang out by the curb so she had to ride by me when she rode in the front of our house. She wore shorts all the time. Not like the shorts girls wear today, but they were still shorts. She had some thing on her leg. It was brown, kinda tan-ish brown. It was driving me nuts for days. It was about three or four inches around. I thought that would be a good way to start a conversation with her. You know, "Hey you, what's that big ugly thing on your leg?" (Tact was never my long suit then and still isn't today.) I don't think I ever talked to a girl before, with the exception of a couple of school mates, on occasion and all my girl cousins. I have all girl cousins except for Arnold, and they certainly didn't seem like Ann. I also gave thought to jumping in front of her bike as she rode by. When she fell and while she was lying there bleeding I could ask her, "What's that thing on your leg?" Then, I can offer to fix her bike and be her hero. Naw, that's too simple. So, I figured she really liked to ride her bike, so I will ride my bike. I was a pretty good bike rider. (I got much better in California but that, again is another chapter.) So, I am riding around, and of course, showing off by doing jumps and going into skids, and of course, ignoring her. A couple of friends came over, and we were doing our thing but nothing seemed to impress her or at least she didn't seem to acknowledge us, in any way. (At age 67 now, some fifty plus years later, nothing has changed. I still can't impress a female.)

Night fell and the next day the same old thing started again. Well, at least for me. I started biking around after breakfast. Now, I hope I can describe the back of our row type houses because it is important that you visualize this. There was the street, then a side walk in front, a front yard, then the house, of course, then a small alley about 10-12 feet wide in back of the houses and then a small, unfenced grassy area for about 30 feet or so after the alley with tee-shaped metal poles at both ends of the grassy area, for hanging your clothes to dry after washing. Now, unbeknownst to me, Ann decided to play house that morning and not ride her bike. She strung a clothes line to hang clothes, not from the metal pole to the metal pole like a normal person would. NO, she decided to string it from the closest metal tee pole to the back of the house where the garage is and attach a very strong line to the garage door spring, stretching across the alley. Now, try to picture this in your mind, Joe cool, me, at 95 degrees in the late summer morning in my swim trunks and no top, riding my bike as fast as I can go. You already know I had worn glasses since I was five years old (near-sighted) and, of course, not having them on (to try and impress her), was doing about 105 miles an hour through the alley-way so she would see me at a very high rate of speed. I hit that clothes line like a freight train. Have you ever seen a hot knife touch a stick of butter? That's what that quarter inch horse hair clothes line did to my stomach. My bike went about fifty feet forward, and I went about ten feet backwards. The clothes line never broke! Not knowing what happened, I got up and looked at my gut, I saw this White line going from my pipic, (Another Yiddish word meaning belly button) around as far as I could see towards my back. As I told you before, all fat twelve year old Jewish boys cry a lot. I started to cry and ran home.

It must have been a weekend or Dad didn't have a job, but he drove me to the hospital. The whole time the deep gouge in my stomach never bled. It seemed at least an hour before there was any blood that I saw. But when it came, it came. The doctor told me that the reason there was no immediate bleeding for so long was that the force of the hit pushed the blood away from that area. The gouge actually went from my belly button around to the middle of my back. It was just a little bit higher then my belly button but just low enough to have missed the ribs by half an inch. Any higher, and I would have been in real trouble. The hospital wrapped me in twelve miles of gauze and sent me home.

I was lying in my bed. About four or five o'clock my mother said someone wanted to see me. Guess who walked in? Right, Ann. Great, just F—g, great! If there was someone I did not want to see at that time, it was Ann. How embarrassing! Being twelve and kind of fat, I thought about crying but didn't. In she walked-long dark hair, shorts and that thing on her leg. She said her name was Ann and asked me how I was feeling. She said she felt so bad because she had put the clothes line in the wrong place. She told me that she fixed my bike and brought it back to my yard. The fixing of the bike and returning it all somehow seemed so familiar, only different. But that was the beginning of me and women. I don't think I ever kissed her. But for the short time that I knew her, I think I matured a little in that department.

Another story from Mc Kinley Street happened when I was about eleven. Not too long before my family and I left for California. It was Christmas, and the snow was all around. As kids, the snow is always great! As adults, it is too damn cold! As religious as my Bubba and Zada were, that's how much my parents were not. Rebellious or just different, I don't know. My dad bought a big cardboard fireplace with a reindeer jumping over the chimney and put it up on the wall in the living room. My parents bought gifts for my brother and me, for each other, and for any one else they knew who had less than us. (My Dad was very generous.) In fact, one year, we opened the door at Passover time so Elijah could come in for his wine. (A Jewish tradition.) Instead, a stray horse walked in through the door. Dad tried to feed it while everyone else in the house tried to chase it out. Dad said it was good luck. It had four horse shoes. (They won!) Dad would put the gifts under the fake cardboard fireplace by the wall. We had a bunch of gifts stacked up all over. This had to be just a day or so before Christmas. I just happened to be looking out the front window, at the falling snow. A car pulled up in front. It was my Uncle Al (the Canter) and his wife Aunt Eva and shit, ZADA! I yelled out to Mom and Dad, and just like it would have been a sitcom on TV, I saw nothing but elbows and assholes moving at warp speed taking down, NO ripping down, the fireplace and tossing the gifts into the closet and running them upstairs to a closet with no regard for breakage or human sacrifice. I swear, just as the doorbell rang, the last of the stuff was gone, except for the White Chanukkah bush (Flocked Christmas tree) which I took and ran out the back door to Ann's house and dropped it on her lawn. Mom opened the door and in walked the Three Wise Men and all seemed well until Uncle Al took his and Zada's overcoats off and started to put them in the hall closet. You know, the one that had all the gifts. (Was it Ken Manyard, Hoot Gibson or Tim McCoy who always said, "Here we go again boys?") Hoot, who? Never mind you little kiddies. They were the new age "Three Musketeers." You know, "D' Artagnan and the boys". My dad grabbed the coats and took them upstairs. No one even questioned why. You see, there is a God after all! The men had their schnapps, (Schnapps, Yiddish for booze) (booze American slang for liquor) (liquor has something to do with (I am told), French sex) and the women had their conversation. In an hour or so they left. I can't even imagine what would have happened if I did not see them arrive and they had just rung the bell and my brother or I just opened the door and they walked in. It would have made the Holocaust look like a coming-out party.

One other thing that happened on McKinley Street was my introduction to music. I don't know how or when or why it came to my house or for whom it was, but there was a wind-up Victrola (record player). To this day, I have no idea why, but I would walk up and down the street (McKinley Street, of course) carrying and winding the record player and singing the two songs that were on a thirty-three and a third record. I remember the songs like it was yesterday. They were the "Bluebird of Happiness" and "Beautiful Dreamer." Now, I figure that at least 50% of all who are reading this book have no f—g idea of what the hell I am talking about. Record player/victrola ? Thirty-three and a third?? Do you know what? I am not going to tell you either. However, that was the start of my illustrious singing career that was not so illustrious but is still in effect today. Keep reading!

Starting out in my younger years, as you can see, there has not been a lot a constants in my life. But one constant I can remember and usually looked forward to, were Sundays. Our family and my dad's twin brother, (I swear they looked about as much alike as Glimpy and Mugsy from the Dead End Kids.) WHO? Their two sisters and one older brother with all families in tow would go to Zada's house for the day and evening. All the cousins would get together and play and tear up the place. Now that I think about it, I never knew what the grown ups did. Nor did any of us care. Hmmmmm! However, whenever I was in the kitchen, there was always someone at the table. It was like a feeding frenzy marathon. All day and all night! With the exception of my dad's twin brother, Uncle Jack, no one in the Gerson family was underweight. Oh yea' wait. At that time the only other exception was my brother. He was so underweight that all my relatives seriously thought that I was eating his food. I don't think Mark, my little brother, had eaten voluntarily for two or three years. He was usually forced fed by Mom. I am sure my mother knew it had to do with the way I kicked the shit out of her ribs during my birth.

My Zada had a three-story house on Girard Avenue right in the middle of all the schvartzas. (Schvartzas is what the Jews called the Negros back in those days. Today, we call them Schvartzas! Well, except for my good friend Frankie D., he calls them something else.)

Zada had a used furniture store with a basement so absolutely loaded with so much crap that my brother and I took an hour to crawl from one end to the other. On top of the basement was the store and store front at street level. On top of the store was the living quarters, a living room, a very long hall, kitchen, bath and the bedroom in the back overlooking the backyard (10 or 12 feet below) at street level. On top of that level was another floor with more rooms. That was where my Aunt Eva and Uncle Al, the Cantor, lived. (Cantor is a term for a Jewish person who sings at special times in a synagogue, and no one really knows what the hell he is saying.) (A Synagogue is basically a Jewish church.)

Now, as I had mentioned previously, all my aunts and uncles had two names, all but Aunt Eva.

So, we kids made up a name for her, *An Teva* instead of Aunt Eva. (Just a small adjustment of the "T") At that time it seemed pretty funny. Today, so so! But, An Teva had two other things about which all of us kids used to joke. Tits! Tits and more Tits! Huge Tits! I am not even sure we knew what we were looking at, at our ripe old age of ten-ish to maybe thirteen. She couldn't have been 4'10" if an inch. But, if horizontal, she was still the same height. She always wore a dress that resembled a mattress cover. You know kinda grey and white with a stripe pattern only a little different. Once, we saw her bra, oops! I mean brassier hanging over the tub. (There were no bras in those days.) The holder parts, (that's what we kids called them then) cups, were big enough to easily cover our heads. Huge! We would chase her all the time and make her run away from us. Sometimes, she would turn around and chase us and that way we could see her bounce and we could joke about them.

The back bedroom, where Bubba stayed, happened to be the room you needed to go through to jump off the roof or to climb down to get to the backyard. (You couldn't get to the back yard through the store level because of all the furniture in it, just like the basement.) All of us kids would want to do that, except for Dottie and Bernice. They were the older girl cousins. I guess they stayed with the grown ups and did what they did. To this day, like I said, I still don't know what all the adults did. I do remember Dottie being with us *sometimes*. Maybe she was a spy for the adults.

The kids that always attended Zada's every Sunday were Barbara and Joan. Twins! They did look very much the same, although, as I grew older, I could tell them apart easily. When we were older kids, I remember sometimes they would make a date and when the date came over to pick them up, the wrong one would go out on the date. I never did get a report as to what happened on the date. I guess they thought that I was too young for the good stuff. They also sounded alike, so they would talk to people on the phone who called for the other one. Even in later years, when the twins were visiting each other, their husbands would call for their wives and the wrong one would get an ear full that was not meant for her. They had four years on me, I think.

Their father was the oldest of Zada's offspring. His name was Irving or Irv to the adults and Uncle Izzy to the kids. His wife was Molly. (frequently called, "the horse's ass" by her husband Irv). Now Molly was a piece of work and had a couple of addictions as well. One was eating. She stood about six foot and weighed about 300 pounds plus. Uncle Izzy was about 5'5" and a little rolly-polly himself. (Actually, through my eyes, he looked a little like Yoda from Star Wars.) My brother must have taken after him since Mark's wife was three inches or so taller but not as heavy, comparably speaking. The other addiction Aunt Molly had was gambling. Horses to be specific! I won't get into a long dissertation about it, but she once got arrested for bookmaking out of her house. She had so many phones installed, so that she could make calls to HER bookmakers and find out the results from all the different race tracks where she bet, without tying up other phone lines. This way she could make her bets on time. She really wasn't a bookmaker and got off, but it cost Irv, her husband, thousands to defend her. I guess I have to confess. I must have taken after her. I have had an addiction to horses, betting on them, booking them, and owning them for 30 years or so. I was arrested for bookmaking twice! But, we will get to that later.

One thing that was really fun with Aunt Molly and Uncle Izzy were that all the cousins would go to their house often in the summer. Uncle Izzy had a nice, big house in Philadelphia (I guess he needed it big to have room for all the extra phones for Aunt Molly.) He was in business for himself, selling and fixing vacuum cleaners. Now that I think about it, I really think his store was a front for something illegal. That would fit in with the Gerson family. He was always the one who had money in the family. All the big functions would take place at his house. He even had a second house in Brigantine, New Jersey.

Anyway, at night, in the summer, when all the cousins were there, we would catch fire flies. Now, most of you who live here on the west coast probably have never even heard of them. They are small and very similar to a regular house fly, but they have a little light that glows and flickers on and off in the dark. I don't know what the real purpose is for them (maybe bat food), or the little light that flickers on and off, but we would catch them, rip the little light bulb off, and drop the fly on the ground. It would soon die, but the bulb would stay lit for awhile. We then would string the little bulbs together with needle and thread and make bracelets and rings with the glowing flickering little lights. We really thought it was cool. PETA would have shit a brick if they had known.

One other thing about my Uncle Izzy was that he only had daughters. So, every once in a while, he would ask me to go to the men's club (gym) with him to go swimming. But, they swam naked! I was always scared to go. Why, I am not sure, I just was. Hell, today, I would swim naked with women I don't even know!

The next kids in the group are Dottie and Bernice, daughters of Sadie, to the adults and Aunt Shirley to the kids. She is the second oldest female of Zada's offspring. She is the one earlier in this thing I am writing who had the magician husband, Ted. If I had to put any type of normalcy on any of the kids in this group at that time, it would have to be Bernice. You already know about Dottie and her poetry! So that leaves her out. Bernice married a doctor. They had a child with Downs Syndrome, and that relationship went down hill from there.

Then, there was Aunt Eva and Uncle Al. Uncle AL the Cantor. (Couldn't he have been Neil Diamond the Cantor?) They never had any kids. The rumor was that he devoted his life to God, and her, to taking care of her father and mother in this new world. I personally have my own opinion. I think that her tits were so big that they couldn't get as close as they needed to, to do it!

Then there was the oldest of the twin boys, about two minutes older. He was Jake or Jay to the adults and Uncle Jack to the kids. He had three names, I guess because of his skinny build. The three extra names kind of filled him out. His wife was Evelyn and was very beautiful. That's probably from where their daughters got it. They had three beautiful girls. The oldest was Linda, who today is married to a guy fifteen years younger than she is. She lives in an apartment building that houses the office where she works. She never has to leave her building. Now, there's a life for you! Makes you kind of wonder if she has ever seen the sun! Next, there was Phyllis who aspired to be a ballerina for years and now (I think) is a dance instructor. Then, there is the baby, Pauline, whom I don't have a line on except that she does not show up when I visit the East Coast. So, she is out of my will!

Uncle Jack died very early in life, age fifty to be exact! For some reason my dad, the other half of the twin thing, got it into his mind that he had only fifty years himself. So every day that he made it past fifty years old, he felt it was a gift. That may be the reason my dad had such a great attitude and outlook about life and people.

That brings us to me and my bro. We are the only two boys to carry on the Gerson family name. My younger brother of five years is Mark. Mark Fredrick Gerson, to be exact and to this day, sometimes introduces himself that way. My little brother was very thin. (I am sure it was because I kicked the shit out of my mom's ribs at birth, which I recently mentioned.) Actually, he was not very old yet, so not only was he not fat yet, he didn't even cry much, either. I was not thin. In fact, quite the contrary, and was constantly accused of eating my brothers portions of food at home. (Which I have already just mentioned) I really think the family thought it was true. He *was* really skinny. However, after his tonsillectomy, he gained about forty pounds in six months and I was exonerated.

Now for my mom's side of the family there was her father, Charles, as I have told you after whom I was named. His wife was Bessy, my mom's mom, who Arnold and Sharon, (my cousins) and my brother Mark and I referred to as Nana. There were many other relatives on that side of the family as well. One of them (I think it was the son of my Aunt June), was awarded the contract for all the plumbing in the construction of the EL (the elevated train in Philadelphia). From then on, most of my Nana's side of the family never seemed to associate with the Gerson side of our family much anymore. (I am sure it had nothing to do with all of the money that they made.) However, there was Aunt June and her beautiful collie. That was Bessy's (Nana's) sister. (Aunt June, not the collie)! For the most part, Mom's side of the family seemed to be pretty mundane so we will not be talking about them much. But three things stand out in my mind about my Nana.

One was that she lived in an area called Strawberry Mansion on 33rd. Street. I never saw any strawberries there. However, it could have been called Blackberry Mansion for obvious reasons. It was fairly far away from where we lived, so, when we went to see her we got to take the trolley. That, to a kid, was fun.

The second thing was that she always had a bunch of sucking (hard) candy at her house. Usually jelly filled. We would always fill our bellies and pockets before we went home.

But the best thing was the coal shoot to the basement. That was where there was a large metal plate on the sidewalk outside that you take off and the coal man dumps coal in it. The coal slides down a metal slide to the basement so you can shovel the coal into the furnace for heat. However, we (my brother and I) found a different use for it. It works just as well for kids to slide down. We knew Mom was not going to let us do it; so, we made a beeline for the cellar as soon as we said, "Hi", to Nana or stuffed our faces with sucking candies and before Mom gave it a thought. Man, was it fun, but did we catch hell all the time. Not for the danger but for the black and black and black soot that would be indelible on us for the duration of the stay. It would get on everything. We had to eat in the back yard and could not sit with the family when it was just talk time. We did miss out on a lot of stuff while we were there. Was it worth it? Yep! You bet!

Before we get to Chapter Three, I remember back when we were doing all the moving from house to house, there was a scrap book with my dad's picture on the front page of the Philadelphia Inquirer Newspaper. He had his leg up on a tank, in an army uniform, and the caption read, "Mike Gerson enlists and Germany surrenders!" What the hell was that all about? In later years (so I could understand), I was told that our family had a little pull somewhere and with someone. (Bookies, booze running, Al Capone, and the underground in general; of course, we had some pull with someone and somewhere.) Dad was able to keep out of the war for quite awhile. When Uncle Sam finally did get his hooks on him, it was three days later that Germany surrendered in forty-five. So friends of the family somehow got the paper to print the story and the picture. Dad was home in less than a week!

Speaking about the Philadelphia Inquirer Newspaper, we also had another head line story. It read, "The Mike Gerson family is the third family in Philadelphia to have a T. V.". (B. F. D.)

Speaking of T. V.'s, when my Uncle Izzy, (Irving to the adults) finally got one not too long after we did, he 'one upped" us. He had a magnifying glass about eleven inches square installed on a slider in front of his nine inch T. V. This way he could slide it up and back to make the images on the T.V. larger so that all of us could watch it from ten feet away. Now, try to imagine this: Ten to fifteen chairs set about ten feet away from this nine inch T. V. with all chairs filled at Texaco time. It was total chaos with everyone trying to inch up a little closer to see Uncle Miltey walk on the inside of his shoes. (You younger ones forget it. It would be way too hard to explain). But that is the Gersons for you.

Chapter Three

California or bust! Well, as a kid, I would take California; but as an adult, I'll take the bust! (Pardon the pun)!

As I have mentioned, as a youngster, I don't remember much, not even when we moved to California. I don't remember Dad or Mom saying, "Let's go to California." I don't remember packing. I don't remember saying goodbye to friends and family. Nothing, just nothing! Maybe I blocked it out of my mind because I really didn't want to leave Philadelphia. (Everybody wants to leave Philadelphia except me and Rocky and maybe Bruce Willis!) It seemed that Bubba died and then we were gone. I don't even remember taking anything. No clothes, furniture, our dog, nothing. It was 1954, and we were in a car going to the new world three thousand miles away with a Brown water bag hanging in front of the car. I do remember a lot of the relatives, especially Aunt Eve and Aunt Shirley, warning my dad about the Indians out there. "Be careful," they said. "They can still attack from the hills. It is unsettled country." It's the wild, wild West. Beware and be careful!" The Indians, the Indians, the Indians! I was thinking that my dad would not carry a gun to work for Al Capone but could he be packing now!

I can't remember much of the trip out to California, but we made it in five or six days, as I recall. I do remember stopping at a Motel Six one night. I even think it might have cost us six dollars. (Where does the time go?) My brother and I slept in one bed and Mom and Dad in the other.

Now, I am sure you have seen this movie before. Everyone has at one time or another. Sometime in the middle of the night (unbeknownst to us we were on the train track or within ten feet of it, maybe less), it seemed like a train came through and just like the movies, our beds started to move and bounce for at least five minutes. The seven billion car train kept coming and coming and coming! As I said before, I can't remember much of our trip, but I do remember one major pissed-off father that night. After all he had just paid dearly for this beauty we were in. If I am correct, I believe that is a buck fifty each, and it included breakfast. Try and get that deal today! So, after a good night sleep, (hmmmmm) and a hearty breakfast, we gassed up (probably twelve cents a gallon) and went on our way again. My dad, the happy-go-lucky person that he was, was so glad to leave that I believe he gave the motel a one-finger wave good bye.

While we were driving through the Western part of the country, I remember seeing a sign that read, "Watch out for falling rock." I asked Dad what it meant, and his reply was, "That "Falling Rock" was a small Indian child who was lost." So, if you see one, let him know, and he will call the tribe so they can go get him." I guess a nineteen sixty "amber alert." I believed him.

I do remember going through Albuquerque. When Mom or Dad would say "Albuquerque" we (Mark and I) would say "Where's a turkey?" We thought that was pretty funny. However, when we got there, it was raining so bad that the police were directing traffic in many areas. We had to go into this one area where the street dipped down about fifteen feet or so and was flooded to a depth of maybe three feet. The police were letting one vehicle, at a time, go through, with four-wheel drive or if it was a pickup truck, without question, and giving the option to others if they thought that they had a chance to make it. Everyone was going through nice and slow and seemed to be having no problem until it was Dad's turn. So, Mr. Philadelphia, with his four-door (not to be confused with four-wheel) family car and not much experience in flooded ditch situations, when the police asked him if he wanted to try it, of course, he said, "YEP! (That was Dad's cowboy talk. We were in New Mexico.) "Not a problem officer," he said. We were up kinda high and had to go down a slight grade through three feet of water and then back up the grade on the other side again. The whole trip couldn't have been sixty-seventy feet, tops. At the top of the ditch, on the other side, there was a slight grade downhill, in order for us to resume our drive. Now, Dad, being a little different than most, (again, much like myself) decided to do this fast and get it over with. So, he gunned the engine down the grade, hit the three-foot flood like a brick wall, made a big enough wave, (you could have surfed on) that the water came back and flooded the engine. The car died. Twenty-eight thousand cars went through and not a problem until us. Great! Just Great!

Here we are, stuck in the middle of a three-foot pool and a bunch of cars waiting to go through. We were blocking them all. I can see the police waving the tow truck over to tow us out. Meanwhile, I saw a little water seeping in through the bottom of the doors, just a little. I did the wrong thing. I mentioned it to Mom. She immediately started to panic. She had already started ragging on Dad for going too fast into the water and now, she started yelling that we were all going to drown. She was screaming at the top of her lungs, "Help! Help! Help! We are all going to drown! Help!" My dad, I can see, is ready to deck the broad, although he would never hit a woman. But, I am sure; the thought had crossed his mind. He's yelling, "Shut up!" She's yelling, "Help," and Mark and I are laughing our asses off. In fact, we ask Mom if it is ok to open the window and go swimming. She yelled, "Don't you dare! We will all drown." My brother and I knew that the water was not even close to the window but we wanted to get Mom going more. (We did that a lot in later years) We were like that.

Finally, the tow truck came and started to push us out of the water. Seems like all is going to be fine, right? Wrong! These are the Gersons. Kinda like the Griswalds, with Chevy Chase in the movie picture, "Vacation". We got pushed out to the top of the ditch and now have to go down the slight grade to continue on our way. But, and I say but, at the bottom of the slight grade, about two hundred feet or so, is a right turn that we must make. We start going down the slight grade, picking up a little speed. Dad goes to hit the brakes to slow down for the turn. Guess what? No brakes! Nothing, nada, zilch. So, we go straight and straight take us into a gas station aiming for the pumps. No engine, no brakes, and Mom yelling at the top of her lungs, Mark and I, are having the greatest time of our lives. Somehow, Dad manages to turn the wheel enough to run into some hay bails that were there, and the car stops. Mark and I are laughing our butts off. Mom's yelling in a major panic, and Dad says, "Anyone hungry?" We're gonna love California!

We left the car at the gas station and had the attendant dry off the spark plugs and the brakes. Then, we walked a block or so in the rain to a restaurant to have some food. Dad and Mom had something much stronger! Well you would think that things would end there, but not for the Griswald's. Oops, I mean the Gersons. Bellies full and a full tank of gas, we were off again to the Promised Land and a new start. However, about fifty miles later, the windshield wiper motor gave out. So, I jury rigged a string that ran from the right windshield wiper through the inside of the car to the left windshield wiper that I had to physically move from side to side which, in turn, made the wipers move from side to side. This did the job but created two problems. Water constantly came into the car through the wind wings (for you youngsters, ask your grandparents what wind-wings are) as they had to be open to let the string slide back and forth.

The second problem was that after ten minutes or so, my arms got tired. We either had to stop the car for a bit, which caused us to run later than we planned, or to switch seats with Mom so she could do it for awhile. Either way, it was a real problem and to be perfectly honest with you, the wipers did not do the best job. But, we did muddle through. Thank God dad was prone not to drive fast. In later years he did drive on the sidewalks, but he did it slowly. (I think that had something to do with a taxi cab job he once had!) Finally, we stopped for the night (not at hotel six!) and ordered a windshield wiper motor. By noon the next day, it had been installed, and we were on our way again. However, Mark had a full-time job rubbing arms for the next twelve hours. He was not a happy camper.

Practically, from the very first state we drove into after leaving Pennsylvania (probably West Virginia or the like), my little brother had seen a cow. Remember, we lived in a cement world, Philadelphia all our lives, (Maybe a few cabal stones here or there) and to see a real live cow, that many people take for granted, was something special. A real cow! Wow! From that first cow seen by my little brother, Mark, it started a chain reaction of, "I want to stop and pet a cow." Remember, he was only seven, maybe only six and change, then. Every time he would see a cow, and there were plenty of them, state after state after state and pasture after pasture after pasture, everyday the same thing! I want to pet a cow. Hell, it reached a point where I wanted to deck the little bastard! It was driving Mom and Dad nuts, also. This was going on for almost a week. Finally, Dad said, "Ok, we will stop soon, and you can pet a cow." Now, I don't know how many of you have driven across the United States, or for that matter, driven across any state. For those of you who have, how many times have you seen a sign or billboard advertising a multitude of strange things, like, "Stop, fifty miles ahead, a two-headed snake!" "Don't pass this one, the only five-legged deer in captivity." "See a real Indian dance that will bring rain." "Live baby dinosaurs ahead," and so on and so on. Well, unbeknownst to any of us, my dad had seen a sign that said, "See Brahma Bulls for free." So, my dad told Mark that we would stop soon so he could pet a cow. (Remember what I said about Dad's humor?) We drove for a while and low and behold, we stopped and got out of the car. My brother was ecstatic with joy and had a smile from ear to ear and then some. He was so happy he almost pissed his pants. "Where are they, Dad? Where are they?" he said. There was a sign that read "Brahma Bulls here" and a fenced area about fifty by fifty and about five feet high. We walked over to it. Mom had a perplexed look on her face, and I wasn't sure what was going on myself. Mark was yelling, "Hurry, hurry, Dad, hurry!" We got to the fence. Dad looked over it and then proceeded to lift Mark up and sit him on the top of the fence so that he could see the cows. Mark's big grin in a second, turned to tears as the bulls ran into the fence, horns first, at about warp speed and almost knocked Mark off the top of the fence. Then, they hit the fence a second time and a third time. In less then thirty seconds the tears were flowing at a rapid rate and the yelling started. Only, it wasn't, "Let me see the cows." It was "Take me down! Take me down I don't like cows. Take me down, Dad, take me down!" Dad's ears seemed to be failing as the descent that my brother was wishing for was nowhere to be found. "Dad, down, I don't like cows! Take me down, Dad, take me down." Dad's hands and arms seemed to be frozen in place. But, then the boss got into the act. "Mike, take him down! He's scared." Mom said. (No shit!) By this time, I am laughing so hard I can't even say, "NO Mom, he's loving it." (That wasn't a Mac Donald's saying in those days.) In fact, I was laughing so hard that major tears were rolling down my cheeks, so much so, that Mom thought I was crying as well, and told Dad that *I* was frightened also, "so please take mark down." Dad obeyed, and we never heard the word cow again. However, every once in a while, Dad would look back at me, in the back seat, and smile. Now that I think about it, my father won't ride in a cab any more. I wonder if Mark has ever petted a cow again. I do know that when he has a steak, he has it not only well done, but butter flied well done as well. I think he is burning cows (Brahma Bulls) in effigy!

So, the trek continues. On to California! We are now entering the place where all my relatives said we would be, the Indian laden mountains and desert where the attacks are to be certain. A place called Arizona. A place where cows seemed to disappear and horses appeared. (A thing I am sure my little brother was very happy about.) Trading light colored people for light brown-colored people and water for hot air! Man, was it hot! Being from Philadelphia, where it can get very hot there, also, but there you sweat like a pig in 90 to 100 degrees with 100 degrees humidity and go in and take a shower. But, here, it was a dry heat. WHAT? A dry heat! Ever hear of that? (I was twelve and would hear that for the next fifty plus years of my life.) It was at least 110 maybe 210, and no sweat on my body. WHAT? That's right, no sweat. However, I was sitting in a pool of water in the back seat of the car. (Thought I'd seen a Brahma Bull!) Mom is ready to pass out but needs to stay alert and watch out for the Indians. Mark is watching out also just to make sure there are no cows around. All of a sudden Dad says, "The car is over heating." But, by us being very intelligent people from the East Coast, Dad had thought ahead and bought a burlap water bag prior to entering this God forsaken land. But when he bought it, no one told Dad where to hang it. So, being the smart person that Dad was, he hung it in front of the car so that it would get the wind as we drove and kept cool for later use. (Sure made sense to us city dwellers.) However, being the city slicker that Dad was, the bag blocked the wind from entering the engine through the front grill, therefore, over-heating the car not once but several times as we drove on. Finally, after several over-heatings in a few hours, someone, (probably me, light bulb went on) said, "Lets move the bag to the side of the car and see if the wind will blow through the front grill and maybe keep the engine cooler so we won't over-heat as much." It worked. So, do you think Dad would say, "Good thinking son." No, he just slapped me on the back of the head (which he would do on a regular basis) you know, the zets, (Zets, slang for a light slap) and said, "Why didn't you think of that earlier?"

Sooooo, as we drove on, we were seeing a lot of red rock in the mountain formations. Mark and I kept asking to stop and to get a few of the red rocks. We wanted to carve them with our new pen knives that our relatives gave us when we left, for protection from the Indians. So far, we did not get a chance to use them to defend ourselves. Dad finally gave in, stopped, and got a few of those red rocks. Carving we did! There was red dust all over the car, on our clothes, in our noses and eyes. This, of course, started a yelling contest between Dad and Mom. "Had to stop, heh, Mike?" she'd say. He'd say, "The kids needed something to do; they were bored." Mom said, "You could have stopped to see a cow instead." (Mark's eyes opened wide. red dust and all!) Obviously, tempers were starting to wear thin from the very long trip. After all, a long trip in Philadelphia is about twenty miles, and now, we had gone somewhere near three thousand.

When we finally stopped for the night, our black and grey car became a chameleon and was now black and red. Can't exactly remember where we had stopped for the night, but the next stop was Los Angeles, California.

Now, being a child, the last thing I was concerned about was where we were going to live. I never gave it a thought. I figured that's what parents are for. Hell, I was still wondering why we left Philadelphia and all my friends and relatives. I was even a "straight A" student there. Boy, will that change soon. So, we move into what I thought was an apartment building with eight connecting units. There were four units upstairs and four downstairs. The units were actually perpendicular to each other and kind of formed an "L" shape. We moved into the top right and if I stood on the porch and leaned over the banister a bit, I could see into the living room of the last apartment on the top floor. In reality, we moved from one cement city to another one, I thought! And so, my California life begins.

Chapter Four

We only lived in L. A. for about six or seven months and then moved around the end of nineteen fifty-four to Pomona. (How unusual, moving!) But those few months were filled with growing pains. Unlike the book "Portnoy's Complaint" where the teenager shot out light bulbs with his orgasms, I didn't shoot out light bulbs, but I did learn how to masturbate. Another invaluable thing I learned was to cheat on tests, lie to Mom and Dad, beat up my little brother, learn that there are Catholics in the world, and that there are some places that the colored people (today called Blacks or Afro Americans) do not out-number the white people. If you had seen my kindergarten class picture, you would have seen forty-two Black heads and three white dots. One of those white dots was me.

I soon met the kid next door. He was another twelve year old Jewish kid named Bobby. Bobby, being twelve and Jewish, of course, was a little fat. He probably cried a lot, too, but I didn't see him do it unless he got hurt or something like that. When he got hurt, he really screamed loud.

Let me clarify the crying thing about fat Jewish twelve year olds. It may sound silly to a non-Jew or to a Jew who doesn't really want to hear it, but we, at twelve get insulted easily and that happens a lot, either by someone else, usually our parents, or even by ourselves by something we do or say that may be stupid and we know it but don't want to admit it, so we cry. Also, at twelve and thirteen for some unknown reason, we seem to be over-weight as well. I am sure it has nothing to do with our Jewish mothers. This crying thing seems to go on for a year or so but seems to stop about age thirteen or fourteen. I guess because we become a man!

Anyway, where was I, oh yea, Bobby! Bobby and I became really good friends. We went to the same school and synagogue together. We became very close. Now, on the bottom floor of our apartments, Bobby told me that there was a kid named Barney. He was fourteen and had a bunch of freckles, was skinny and Catholic. Bobby said that his parents told him that he was not to play with Barney much because he was Catholic. Now, I know this is going to sound stupid to some of my readers, but, I said, "What is Catholic? I had never met one before. I asked Bobby. Are they bad people that they have out here in the West, like the Indians?" Bobby told me that Catholics were a different religion. "Catholics are a different religion?" I said. "Oh, like some of the schvartzas in Philadelphia. Some of them are of a different religion also." Bobby said, "Yes, but they are black, and we *never* associate with them, either." Man, was I confused. Anyway, as time went on, I should have listened to what Bobby's parents had said and not associated with Barney but not for the same reasons.

I wound up meeting Barney, and we became very close. My parents didn't see why we shouldn't be friends with anyone. So, as time went on, Barney, Bobby and I became very tight. Although we had to sneak around sometimes because of Bobby's parents, we didn't want to let on that Bobby and Barney were becoming good friends as well. Somehow, Barney always had a way for all of us to meet; a plan, a scheme, a way around every obstacle so we could always be together. He seemed to be a little ahead of us, but we didn't seem to notice it at the time. I guess it was about mid-summer when we had become friends.

On Saturdays I would put Mark, my little brother, on my bike and ride to the Baldwin Hills Movie Theater. It was about a mile or so from our place. This was religious! Every Saturday! *You need to listen to this.* My dad would give us each a quarter. Twenty-five cents, one fourth of a dollar, US currency and for that we would get a hot dog, Coke and admittance to the movie theater. We're talking twenty-five cents here. The show had two full-length features, twenty cartoons, two serials and a Yo Yo contest or some kind of a contest where we could win a prize. Twenty-five cents! I always thought Dad was great for letting us go every Saturday until Barney told me that that was just his way of getting me and my brother out of the house so he and my mom could be alone for five hours. I thought Barney was crazed. What the hell could they possibly do in five hours alone! I dismissed his accusations.

Now, if you remember, I mentioned that we had just moved from one cement city to another cement city. Boy was I wrong! Certainly, as I would realize later, that is waaaay off at least in 1954. But, in the eyes of a twelve year old, fat Jewish cry baby, that was how I saw it. Although we did live in Los Angeles, it was on the border of Culver City in the Baldwin Hills area. Baldwin Hills area actually did have hills and not too far from where I lived, maybe a mile and a half to two miles away. Hard to remember exactly, it was so long ago, but on the top of Baldwin hill there was a dam. Don't really know if it was a working dam, (if there is such a thing as a working or non-working dam) but never-the-less some sort of a dam. There was water in it and a six-foot high chain link fence that ran all around it with signs that read, "KEEP OUT." Now, to three kids, it really read, "TRY ME." When the three of us went there (Barney, Bobby and I), we could see different types of diggings and holes in the ground that we thought were either caves or mines or both. (Months later we found out that the dam was a reservoir. *City boys*!) To twelve and thirteen year old boys, is this a gold mine of fun or what? How do we get over the fence and into the dam to explore? Hmmmm, all we had was ourselves. So, we figured that we needed some kind of a ladder or something to raise us up over the fence. So, Barney said, "Let's go home and come back tomorrow and bring the right tool." Bobby looks at me, and I look at Bobby, and we both say, "Tool?" Barney just smiles! We went home.

The next day we started out on our new adventure to the dam. Barney, as we are walking, says, "It is in my pocket" and, of course, the twelve-year old fat Jews have no idea what he has in his pocket that will lift us over a chain link fence. We finally got there and Barney says, "Let's find a safe place so no one can see us." We don't want to get caught. Now, doing stuff like this is brand new to the twelve-year old fat Jews. They have been brought up to be quiet, peaceful, reserved normal people. Barney, (I am sure it has nothing to do with him being Catholic), seems to have many years of experience on us. It's almost like he is twenty-five and not fourteen. So, like little Indians, we creep all stooped over and walk around the fence until Barney says, "Here, right here, this is a good place. No one can see us from here." We said, "Good, now let's see this ladder you have in your pocket." Barney pulls out what looks like a tool. (See, Jews do not know much about tools. Our parents teach us at a very early age to use the phone to call someone for help so we don't get our hands dirty or injured so we can grow up to be doctors or lawyers.) Barney said he will just cut our way in with these wire cutters. PANIC strikes! The Jews are immediately in a panic.

Cut the wire! Cut the wire! That is damaging other's property. We can't be a part of that. It's not right to destroy other's property. Barney calls us chicken and said that our parents pay taxes for this fence so it is partially ours and proceeds to cut through the wire fence. Bobby and I don't know what to do. Run home? Tell the cops? But being who we are, the two fat Jews (Hmmmm, that could be a good name for a singing group), who need their leader, follow Barney through the cut fence and say, "Now what do we do?" Barney said, "What did we do this for, the cave right?" So we start heading for the cave. Both Bobby and I were scared shitless, but we followed. Finally, we found the first cave. It wasn't really a cave when we got there. It was a kind of a short, mining hole and rock quarry. It was about eight or nine feet wide, fifteen feet deep and at about a forty degree angle from top to bottom. Kind of a cave, I guess, but more down and sideways into the hill. It was all rocks. The rocks were about a couple of inches around and very smooth. So now we had a natural made fort in the Baldwin Hills. How cool was that! Barney said that the fence was probably to keep out little kids from drowning in the dam, but we should bring our bathing suits tomorrow and swim. Bobby and I had that look again! So, we hunkered down in our new fort/cave and just talked for a while. After a while Barney said, "I am not waiting for tomorrow. It's hot, and I'm going swimming now!" Wait! "You don't have a swim suit!" Bobby said, "I have my underwear and that's good enough." The follow-the-leader fatties, without much hesitation, went in as well. Somehow, no one ever seemed to have found the hole Barney cut into the fence. Well, at least as long as I lived there. So, we had a great fort for all summer with our own private swimming hole and plenty of places to go hiking right into the fall.

One time, when we three were there, we decided to get naked and slide down the rocks from top to bottom and see what it felt like. Whose idea this was I can't remember, but I do remember, it was fun. Why, I don't know. It just was, and we did it often.

Sometimes, I find it difficult to write this book and don't know why I put in certain things, but I guess it is because it is all true and definitely different. Here is just one of those things.

One day, just Barney and I were in the fort; I don't remember why Bobby wasn't there, but it was just Barney and me. Barney said, "Do you jerk off yet?" "Huh! What's that?" I said. "You really don't know what it is?" "No, what is jerking off?" Barney said, "It is fun and if you want, I will show you how to do it. In fact, I will do it for you the first time, but I have to touch your dick." I said, "Touch my dick! Why? What could you do with my dick that will be fun?" He said, "Watch and I will show you." We had been sliding down the rocks in our underpants, so he didn't have far to reach. Barney started to play with me and after a while my dick started to get bigger. I said, "How did you do that and will it get smaller like it was?" Barney said, "No problem" (He would have said, "No problemo" but, the Terminator hadn't been made yet and Arnold, at that time, was only my cousin.), and continued to play with it. A little while longer he started to stroke it up and down, and I could feel something happening. I didn't know what, but something! It did feel nice. The more he stroked it, the better or stranger it felt. I wasn't sure which one it was, but it didn't matter. It was a feeling I had never felt before. Then, all of a sudden, this shit shot out of me all over the place. Gush after gush and I felt really good! I think! I got kinda scared a bit. It was so strange but good. I guess it might be similar to a girl having sex for the first time and breaking her maiden, a little painful, yet a really good feeling of pleasure! "Barney", I said, "that was great! Where did you learn that?" "From a book," he said. Shit, and I read the Haftorah! Maybe I should become Catholic. (In retrospect, I wonder if a priest or two ever got hold of him. A bunch of that stuff came out in the 90's and who knows. He could have been one of those who was molested and got a million dollars in settlement. Shit, I knew I should have kept his phone number.) I can't wait to tell mom and dad what you taught me. Barney said, "NO! That's not a good idea. We are not supposed to know this stuff until we are married. Then, I think the wife is supposed to teach us how to do it." "How about Bobby, can we tell him?" "No, it is our little secret! I only want to do it to you, OK?" "I guess so, but I can't wait to do it myself." Barney said, "If you can find a girly magazine and look at it at the same time you do it, it is even better." "Great, where in the hell can I get a girly magazine? (Wait, what the hell is a girly magazine?)" So, now only you, the reader, know one of my inner most secrets. Please don't share it with anyone. Again, much later in years, I wonder which way Barney went. A/C or D/C?

Barney, Bobby and I stayed friends throughout the summer and most of the fall. Then, Bobby moved away and left me to deal with mister knowledge (Barney) all by myself. But, with school starting and me in a crash course to learn three years of Bar Mitzvah lessons in six months, I was pretty busy. So, learning more stuff from Barney (bad or good) was at a minimum, and I learned rapidly how to masturbate myself! But ever since then, I have had a deep respect for Catholics.

When Bobby and his family moved out of his apartment, an older couple moved in. Mom and Dad made friends with them right away. They seemed to get close fast. Later, I found out that he was the architect for the Travelodge Motels. Every once in a while Mom and Dad would tell me to watch over Mark (my little brother) for about five or six hours as they were asked to inspect one of the hotels. *What was that all about!* I am sure Barney would have shed some light on the subject had I asked.

One day Mom got sick and had to go to the hospital. She was there for a week or so. Not sure what was wrong, but I think it was female stuff. Dad had no insurance so it took a large toll on our finances. Even with this burden, Dad managed to buy a four bedrooms two bath, ranch house in Pomona, California. The selling price, I think, was nineteen thousand nine hundred dollars. He bought it on the G. I. Bill at that time (for which Dad's seven days in the army qualified him), and the down payment was not much, if any, and the payments were ninety-five dollars a month.

Every Sunday, we would drive to Pomona and see how much construction had been done on our new house. Little by little, we saw the house being built. At first, it was really fun. After a while it did become *not so much fun* for Mark and me. The only thing that kept us from trying to think of a way not to go was the fact that there were walnut trees on the property. Mark and I would either pick them or find them on the ground and take them home. We would put them on the window sill and let the sun ripen them for a couple of weeks. Then we would sell them to the neighbors. Hmmmm, new houses are good!

I remember going to Baldwin Hills once in November. I went alone for some reason. I think it was to kind of say good bye to our fort and the good times I had spent there with my friends. I was soon to move, in early December, to our new house in Pomona and probably not have time to go there again. Once again, I don't remember how or why, but I set the whole Fuckin hill on fire. (Maybe my destiny was to grow up to be a monk!) When Mom and Dad read about the fire in the paper the next day, they told me that I couldn't go back there to hike, play or ride my bike anymore because it was dangerous. I, of course, obeyed! The only person I told about the fire was Barney. By telling him, I think it was my way to finally be on his level and be accepted by him. (You know, I am almost a teenager and know everything now, class.) Now, as luck would have it, the back lots at the Culver City Motion Picture Studios burnt down in the next few weeks. The studios were not far from the apartments where we lived. It was not me that caused the fire, but Barney always had that look when he saw me!

Well, that just about concluded my family's six months stay in the big city of Los Angeles. We moved shortly after the fires to Pomona, which at that time was a pretty classy area, with all new ranch homes and new schools and shopping centers.

I will always remember Barney, as many years later, after my divorce; I affectionately named my right hand Barney!!!

Chapter Five

We moved to Pomona from Los Angeles. The schools were on different half-year schedules. So, my dad and mom chose to hold me back instead of putting me ahead a half year. Believe it or not, the exact same thing happened when we moved from Philadelphia to Los Angles. Had we gone straight from Philadelphia to Pomona, I would have graduated one year earlier. What were my parents thinking or did they know something about my intelligence that I didn't??

As I said many pages earlier, I did not remember much up until twelve and way too much after that. Well, you have already gotten the drift with the Barney thing, at twelve and a half, so hold on because when I get into high school, my life really starts to turn to shit.

I am not sure, but when we finally moved into the Pomona house on Barjud Street (Loved that name), it was about the middle or end of December. (By the way, when I finally had children, I wanted to name a boy Barjud after the street where I lived and a girl Jardene which I thought would go well with Barjud. However, my wife had something to say about that!)

Now, my birthday is January 23rd, and I needed to have my bar mitzvah about that time so I could be a man. Jews, at or around the age of thirteen, have a special ceremony called a bar mitzvah. We automatically become a man. It just shoves you from childhood to manhood just like that! Can we smoke? NO! Can we drink alcohol? NO! Can we vote? NO! Can we talk back to our parents? NO! Can we drive? NO! Can we have a credit card? NO! Can we join in on adult conversation? NO! Can we get laid? NO! Can we quit school? NO! Get the picture? We just become a man! My dad will still whack me with a belt when he thinks I need it, slap me on the back of my head (zets) whether he thinks I need it or not, and still tell me when I am to eat, shit and go to school. A man, FEH! (Feh is a Yiddish term that means "no good" or "who needs it.")

Now, to become a man, we have to go to Hebrew school for about three years to learn to read, write and speak the Yiddish language. We learn the special things we have to do during this special time. We partake in many activities at the synagogue (Jewish church) that give "the already men" a break from what they regularly do and so on and so forth, at the same time we are learning what we are to do in life. (My dad once tried to go to the synagogue on Christmas Day. It was closed for business!) The men (over thirteen) wear a funny little cap called a yarmulke. (Most pronounce it "ya-ma-ca.") Now, if you go long enough to a synagogue, you will notice that these hats actually have a reverse growth pattern. Yarmulkes are all made the same size, just in different colors. When you are a young child, they seem to be too big for your head. When you are very old, they seem to be a lot smaller. Some men (the really older ones like forty-five and up) just wear a regular hat and that is fine. It is hard to see the Rabbi in front while sitting in the back, over the hat. "Rabbi" A Rabbi (from where they got this name Rabbi I will never know), A Rabbi seems to be the head guy. He even has his own parking space with his name on it. Rabbi! (You can usually tell if he is liked or not by the kids. Sometimes the kids will paint a "T" at the end of his name.) He is like a priest, an elder or even the head monk, etc. etc. etc. (Is more than one Monk called Monkies?) He runs the place. He gives sermons, tells stories on the holidays, and selects people to call other people who have not paid their dues for the year. But, in actuality, he pretty much does what his wife tells him to do. Let me explain something. When the gonads are cut off a male horse, that's called gelding! In the Jewish religion, it's called marriage. Now, where the hell was I? Oh yeah.

I had to have my bar mitzvah in about a month or so, so I am on a crash course. I had little training in the language when in Philadelphia and little or less in Los Angeles in what to do and when to do it. The singing of the Haftorah was the real problem. It is about an hour of singing in Hebrew with no words and no music anywhere. You have to know when to come in at the right time and when to shut up as well. You intermingle with the Rabbi, the Cantor and other people in the synagogue. This is all done in a harmonic parallel with everyone. It was all on a really large record called, a thirty-three and a third which I was given to study and to memorize. One month to memorize an hour of Yiddish singing of which I didn't even know the tune. Shit! Oh yeah, I had to go to school, at a brand new school, as well, and try to make friends and keep up my grades. This is way too much to ask of a twelve year old. Maybe that's why when it is all done, I will be a man! Go figure!

Now, I didn't even know where the synagogue was and with whom I was going to work. You know, the Rabbi. To make a very long story short, in thirty days or so, I did very well and became a man who still can't do shit! However, there is a reward for all this. There is a bar mitzvah party, and all of my new friends (most from the synagogue whom I really didn't know) were to come. They brought me gifts. We drank lots of soda and ate candy. There was also music from the fifties being played. Most of the parents of my friends were all there as well. They were not drinking soda!!!!!

Now, I could dance a little because of my all girl cousins. They would ask me to dance when we were together so that they could tune up for American Bandstand in Philadelphia. They were always going. I went once or twice, but I would rather stay home and eat candy. So, this girl at my party asked me to dance with her, and I did. She was kind of cute but a little heavy. Like I should talk! I probably still cried more than she! We danced a few times and then we started to play some games. Everybody wanted to play spin the bottle. The girl who had asked me to dance was really pushing it. I knew of the game but had never played it because you had to kiss a girl. That just didn't seem like too much fun. So, we made a rule that we had to go into the closet to kiss so no one would be embarrassed if they didn't want to actually kiss. You were not allowed to tell if you didn't. Now, I am just thirteen and almost one of the youngest ones there with the exception of my brother and his friends who were invited. They were not allowed to play with the grown ups. (You know us men!) Every boy had their bar mitzvah and in those days, the girls didn't really have one. It was optional if they chose to, but not pushed. So, we started playing and guess who spins and gets to kiss me? Yep! It was the fat chick who had asked me to dance a few times. Little did I know that she liked me and had planned it. A few others knew about it as well. So, I am starting to shit my pants as we walk to the closet. I really don't want to kiss this chick or any others, either. So, I figure that I will give her a really quick peck, and I'm out of there. She had other plans! We got in the closet, and she said to me, "It is your birthday, and I have to give you a really good kiss for it." "Why? I said? Can't you just say you did and we are out of here?" Well, in between the "of" and the "here," I was attacked by her mouth. She made Mick Jagger seem like Tweety Bird. She planted a big one on me, and I didn't know what to do. This is not like I kiss my mom or dad. This is different. She wouldn't let go. It seemed like I was in the closet for two days. She finally let go to get air, I guess I said, "Wow!" I wasn't sure if I was happy or mad. She asked me if I liked the way she kissed. Knowing only the way my mom and dad kissed me, I said, "It certainly was different." (That was possibly the first and the last time in my life that I showed any diplomacy.) But, I think I liked it. She was happy! This should have been a lesson that I should have learned and remembered. Tell a Jewish female it's good, and you will never get an argument, no matter what it is about. Go Know! So, know I am starting to become a sex maniac. Between Barney teaching me a thing or two and knowing that this chick likes kissing me, I figure I am ready for marriage. I AM MAN!!

So, that was my first kiss, and I can't remember who it was or what she even looked like. (Probably grew up to be Marilyn Monroe.) A lot of years have gone by so it's hard to remember things like that. I don't think she ever kissed me again. Sounds like most of the Jewish females that I have met in my life. Kiss and run! It must have been the closet that turned her off. I am sure that it wasn't my vast kissing experience and technique!

Now the pressure was off as my bar mitzvah was over, and I could concentrate on my school work. I liked school. I always got good grades.

So, now we are in our new house. I have my own bedroom and am working on getting some girly magazines. I'm in sixth grade. It was the second half of sixth grade, and I met a guy named Eugene. We all called him Gene. His dad's name was Othar. He must have come from the same place as my uncle Zalman! Where do these people get these names? (Can you imagine if they were, not only Jewish but black as well!) SHIT! Gene and I hooked up and became very good friends. We finished sixth grade and were inseparable through the summer. We did a lot of swimming every day for four or five hours in the local public pool. We rode our bikes all the time and spent time at his house and mine eating. Summer went very fast. In fact, as much as I liked school, I didn't want to go back because I was having so much fun. Gene was just thirteen, also. He didn't come from Philadelphia! Born locally I think. Fullerton, Ca.

When school started in September we were seventh graders in the first year of a three-year stint in junior high. Gene and I both had the same homeroom and the same English class. The teacher was Mrs. Tacamori. (I could tell by her name that she definitely wasn't Jewish.) As a matter of fact, Gene wasn't Jewish either. (Now that I think about it, he was Catholic. I wonder if Barney ever got hold of him.) As I found out later, very few people in California were Jewish. This, alone, was a very new experience for me. Mrs. Tacamori was the toughest teacher I ever had. She was Oriental. (They didn't invent Asians yet.)

We also had choir together. Although I can't remember that teacher's name, I still can remember what she looked like. She was beautiful and very young for a teacher so I thought. Probably the reason I still remember her was that she would call all of us kids up to the piano. We would gather around and sing as she played. Most of the kids would look at the sheet music she gave us. I found a way to get close enough to be able to look down her blouse. She wasn't real large. I couldn't really see much, but it gave me something to think about when I couldn't get my magazines.

As much as we all liked our glee club (choir) teacher, that was how much Gene and I didn't like Mrs. Tacamori. In fact, Gene and I made up a song about her. The words and the tune I still remember. The tune was to "The Toreadore Song". We sang: "Torey adoory, sit on the floory, spit on Tacamori, that's what she's for." Today, it sounds pretty dorkey, but then it seemed to fit the bill. So, whenever someone tells you that fifty years later you won't remember a thing, they are wrong! Two things that will always stick with you are hate and tits!

Gene and I were pretty even in school. We did the same things and got the same grades, "A's". I was a little more adventuress than he, and he was certainly more reserved. Of course, I had the training from Barney. We went to a school named Emerson Junior High. We went there for one year. While we were attending Emerson, a brand new school opened. It was called John Marshall Junior High. At the beginning of the next school year, we started at John Marshall as eighth graders and were the second graduating class from there as ninth graders.

When we moved to John Marshall from Emerson, we thought we had dumped Mrs. Tacamori. Well, that lasted about a minute until we entered our English class. Gene and I had gotten the same English class again. When we walked into the class, guess who we saw? Yep, the Oriental chick, Mrs. Tacamori. We looked at each other and could have died. The good part was, we both took choir and again had Miss Little Tits. (Being of Jewish decent, this was saving me money on magazines and I liked it.) So, a pretty uneventful year went by. Just hitting the books, kind of getting into cars, and trying to figure out what everyone thought was so important about chicks. (Besides tits!)

Now, living in Pomona, it is home to the Los Angeles County Fair. This fair ran from the end of September to the beginning of October. About two weeks, maybe sixteen days. I am sixty-six years old as I write this part of my book. Until now, I have never seen a bigger and better fair and have never had a better hot dog on a stick! The L. A. County Fair was what everyone looked forward to and waited patiently for. The schools even gave out admission tickets to the students for one free admission to it. As I remember, we went from summer vacation to school for a few days and then the fair opened.

Man, I'm telling you, that's what it's all about! The fair! This fair had everything you could imagine, everything! It had candy cotton, dogs on a stick to die for, a dozen restaurants featuring everything from pizza and hamburgers to filet mignon steak, free stages with dancing, singing and magic entertainment; an amusement park with everything new and scary to ride on or to fall off of and even to throw up from. You could throw a dart or toss a bean bag. You could even jump on a trampoline for free. There was a horse race track so you could bet on horses. There was a live stock area where they not only had an auction but had contests to figure out which cow is fatter than the others, which bull had a bigger dick, which sheep were furrier than the next, and which chickens would lay more eggs than you could imagine. They had building after building that displayed pigeons, pictures, gardens and water falls, makeup and beauty supply displays. So much shit that you had to come back three times to see it all. Now that I think about it that may have been the plan! Admission, admission, admission!

Well, most of us who lived in Pomona were not rich. It wasn't Beverly Hills or the like so a free admission from the school usually did it for most of us. Now, as I started to grow up, you know, the Barney thing, the fat chick kissing me thing and a few other things that I just kind of drifted into and of course now being a man, I needed to continue on this path that is quickly accelerating the old me to a new me. I could ask Dad for some money to get into the fair a second time, but when we moved to Pomona, a few months after Mom had another operation, that left us pretty broke. So, I figured I needed to kind of do things myself if at all possible. I talked to Gene about going to the fair a second time and he said great. He liked the fair as much as anybody. The difference with him was he had money and could pay for the admission and food when inside.

We picked a night and a place to meet at the fair. His dad dropped him off and I walked. It was only a couple of miles and the weather was fine. Now I am at the gates and do not have enough money to get in. What do I do! The whole fair had a chain link fence around it. (Where are Barney and his tool when you need him?) There has got to be a hole here somewhere. I started walking and looking and soon I saw a bunch of guys sneaking in. I walked over towards them and followed them in. When I got through the fence and was in, I was going to tell them thanks, but before I got to talk, one of them grabbed me by the throat and said, that if I tell anyone about the break in the fence, they would kill me. I said mum is the word. I was scared shitless. (Anyway, Jews don't fight. They think, and trust me, I was no Mohammad Ali. I couldn't even beat up my weak cousin Arnold.) They had an accent and were very brown, Mexican, I think. This would play a big roll in the up and coming years of my life. But for now, I gave it very little thought. I escaped with my life and was in the fair free. Now to find Gene!

I found Gene and we had a great time. Killed three or four hours and went home. His dad picked him up and asked if I wanted a ride and dropped me off as well. I actually went back a few more times that year. The price was right! I, of course, checked first for Mexicans as I entered the free admission entrance. I told Gene about it at the risk of losing my life. He opted to pay, and he did meet me there a time or two more. As I look back now, I do see a big difference between him and me, but then we were pals. Close pals!

Summer came fast and school was out. Good by eighth grade. Hooray I said! Thought I'd never say that. I seemed to have slipped from a straight "A" student to a "B" kind of guy. My parents were really upset. I really Loved school. I am fourteen and quickly approaching fifteen. At fifteen and a half it is driver's license (permit) time. In September, when school starts, I will be in ninth grade and a senior. Macho, big shit, chai-cocked! (Chai cocked (pronounced high cocked) is Yiddish slang for big deal.)

As summer vacation started I began to swim a lot more and lose a little weight. Now, I am about five foot eight, maybe nine and about one hundred and ninety pounds. Not a pleasant sight if you are looking at me, but I think I am great. I probably lost 20 pounds through the summer and gained an inch or so.

As I entered the ninth grade and to be the second graduating class from John Marshall Junior High, I think I am big shit. To keep this self-imposed status, I need to play sports. Actually, a little late, as most of the REAL big shits, started in seventh grade and had worked up in the last two years to that status. Pitchers, quarterbacks, pole vaulters, cheerleaders, etc. etc! But being a Jew, sports are not what we normally do. How often do you see a professional star that is a Jew? NEVER! The Jews own the teams which the professionals are on.

Getting into sports is a little weird for me. I discussed it with my mom and dad. They had a fit! Sports! Sports! You can get hurt. Hit with a ball! Hit with a stick! Knocked on the floor and get scraped up! Stepped on, knocked over, lose an eye! (Who mentioned Red Rider B. B. gun?) "Stick with your singing. That's nice for a Jew. Look at Neil Diamond. He did so well as a cantor. Yes, singing." "Ok Mom, OK." The next day I talked to Gene who also talked to his parents about sports. His intentions were different than mine. He wanted to play sports because he liked sports. Me, I wanted to be a big shit on campus. At this time I was still not interested in girls (but I had started to notice them) so who the hell am I trying to impress? Gene said his mom said it was fine. He was going to go out for track and field. I said to Gene, "You can get hurt! You could get hit with a stick! You could get hit with a ball! You could lose an eye!" Gene said, "Not in track." "Are you sure??" MOM!!!

The next day I enlisted for the track team. You have to imagine this. A five foot eight fat Jew trying to figure out what event to do. The closest I ever came to doing anything physical was putting on my shoes and carrying my school books. What can I do? Pole vault? Yeah right! Lift this body up into the air ten feet or so with a stick. Even if I could, I promised Mom no sticks! So that's out. High jump! Yeah, right again! I am so fat I can't jump a puddle in the street when it rains. That's out. I thought the long jump, but realistically, anything where I have to lift my body up more than two inches is out of the question. Gene suggested the shot put or a running event. Why didn't I think about that? So I signed up for shot put and the fifty yard dash. Now, I am a stud! Big shit on campus!

The first weeks of school we did nothing as the football guys were playing. But when the baseball guys started to practice, we did too. Now the shot putt was not so bad. You would have to lift some weights and learn how to spin around and not fall down from being dizzy. The weight-lifting part was a little tough. I was not a strong child. You don't get muscles from eating baloney sandwiches and matzos. (Matzos, a Jewish cracker that is very large and made without taste. Feh!) I did try the running of the fifty yard dash, which I had thought would be a cinch, was a bitch. The coach made me run around the whole track. That's a quarter of a mile! A quarter of a mile! What happened to the fifty yard thing? Fifty yards coach, fifty yards. He said it is a part of the training, just like the weight lifting. You are not going to lift weights, are you? You are throwing the shot putt. You won't be running the quarter of a mile, but it is part of the training. Let me tell you, running a quarter of a mile is a schlep! (Schlep, a Yiddish word meaning a long tough journey.) The good thing about it was that in training, all of the guys had to do it. The bad thing was, I was always the last guy to finish. At the beginning sometimes I didn't finish! So, in gym class, and after school, I ran. And ran! And ran!

Now let me tell you a very funny story. Not that this whole book hasn't been one, but . . .

During gym class we would do whatever the current sport was. During football season we would play football. During basketball season we would play basketball. Get it! But when it rained, we could not go outdoors to play anything. Not even dodge ball! So, we would stay in the gymnasium and play a game. The name of that game right now slips my mind and probably for good reason. But it could have been called, "Beat the hell out of Charlie" for good reason. We did have to dress in our gym shorts and tee shirts, as usual. We would line up in a circle, all facing each other. Across the way we all could see the face of the guy directly across from us. We had to put our hands behind our backs with our fingers out stretched and palms up as if to grab something. The coach would walk behind us and put a rolled up shower towel in the hands of one of the guys.

Let me explain the towel thing. This towel was wrapped in a very special way so as to be about a foot long and hard as a rock. Maybe harder! The guy that received it from the coach was to do the same thing, walk around behind everyone, and put the towel into the outstretched hands of a guy. Any one of his choice! The difference, this time, is (now that the coach is out of the picture) that the guy who receives the towel in his open hands was to chase the guy who dropped it into his hands, completely around the outside of all the guys, and try to beat him with the towel on his butt until he gets back to the spot that was now open. The guy now with the towel, who just beat the guy, has to drop the towel into the hands of another guy. He is now the one to get beat around the circle until he gets to the open spot for safety. If you are a fast runner, you can outrun the guy with the towel and maybe only get hit once, if any. If you were not so fast, (a fat Jew) you were in trouble! Guess what! Right, I was in trouble.

There were a few overweight guys in the class, but I was the target most of the time. Sometimes I would come home with welts on my ass. The words "pray for rain" were not in my vocabulary. I was always told that the Jews are the chosen people. This time I could have relinquished that thought! Now, between the beating I took in gym on rainy days and the running of the track daily, combined with the lifting of weights, a huge weight loss occurred from all of this crap. Believe it or not, I wound up breaking the school record for the fifty yard dash when track and field time came at the end of the school year. Isn't it funny how the Lord works in mysterious ways! Stud was I!

Now, during all of this stud stuff, I was still in choir. We were a pretty good group of voices. Gene and I, alone, had three years of singing experience each, by now. I suppose many others had also. There was a singing competition in San Diego. Choirs from all over the state were invited. I couldn't wait because I had never been out of the area. This is really exciting for me. Gene had been to San Diego many times to see his much older sister, Jeanne, aka, Neeneepoo, who was married at the ripe age of blackjack. (Twenty-one for you non-gamblers) and was now twenty-three. (Does that make Gene an oopsy?)

The choir practiced the same songs over and over for three months and then finally went to San Diego for the contest. All of us were high for this as we knew our stuff. Prepared, confident and happy! The bus ride down there went way too fast. We were there in three hours, I think, and did not stop except once to go to the bathroom. I saw almost nothing. I did see the sea. The ocean! Most kids would be happy about this and, for the most part, the kids on the bus were fascinated with it. Not me!

Let's hark back to my tender years of about seven or eight for a second or maybe even younger. My Grandfather, Zada, had two brothers, Zalman and Mike. Zada, Zalman and Mike. Where the hell does Mike fit in here? Anyway, Mike had a wife named Gerti. How Jewish of her. If she had been a gentile, her name would have been Gertrude, I expect. (Why is it that Jews have these funny names?) Well Gerti and Mike owned a couple of hotels in Atlantic City, New Jersey, right on the board walk! How the heck they wound up with hotels on the board walk is beyond me. No jobs, just hotels. In fact, they owned a Russian restaurant with a violinist and Russian dancers in downtown Philadelphia, as well. I am sure it had nothing to do with the brother named Zalman, the big time bookie in Philadelphia, or the bootlegging that Mike was doing himself.

In the summer my mom, my very little brother and I would live there in one of the hotels. My dad would commute to Philadelphia on the weekends from whatever job he had working at that time. Now that I think about it, I never remember him having a job. Most kids can say, "My dad is a fireman or a milkman or a salesman." Hmmm! So for most of the summer my bro and I would swim or sit on the pier with a string and a hook on it and catch fish and, occasionally, a Hammerhead shark. Mom Loved that when we caught the Hammerheads! Year after year after year, almost until we moved to California! However, there was one thing my brother and I looked forward to at the end of each week when Dad came home for the weekend.

On Saturday we were allowed to go in the diving bell. Yep, there is such a thing. (Or at least was.) We would pay a quarter each (big money at that time), and we would get into this big round metal thing with about five or six port holes in it. We would be lowered down to the bottom of the ocean and stay there for a while. Fish would swim by, and we could see crabs and shells and plants. We were there for about ten minutes or so. Don't know if there was air pumped in or there was enough in it to breathe until we returned, but when you are small, you don't even think of that kind of stuff. Breathing, that comes naturally. It was really cool. We would tell our friends when we got back to school, and they were envious of us.

Another thing that took place during the summer was playing a game called, "Knuckles." My brother and I had made some friends who did the same thing as we did in summer, spend it in Atlantic City. So we all would play "Knuckles." I really don't remember how it was played, it's been awhile, but I do remember what happened to the losers. Depending on how many points you lost by, each of the winners would take the deck of cards and smack you on the knuckles, as hard as they could, and as many times as you had lost by the same amount of points. Often we would bleed, and as it got closer to my twelfth birthday, cry as well! Our mothers didn't like us to play Knuckles. We really didn't understand! Today, as we speak, I have this arthritis problem in the knuckle area on my right hand.

While I am here in Atlantic City, I might as well tell you one more thing, and then I will get back to the San Diego singing stuff.

I was very young and small. Mom and I were the only ones in our room in the hotel in Atlantic City just off Steel Pier, (Steel Pier was a famous amusement park with many attractions and rides) and there was a hurricane. A big hurricane! This was probably about 1944 or thereabouts. We were on the second floor so the story goes. The hurricane raged for hours. My mom saw household appliances floating passed the second story window. She was really shaken. Mom was holding me in her arms (a very good move, by the way!), waiting for Dad to come and protect us. The power lines were down and visibility was non-existent. Dad finally makes it, parks the car, and tries to come to us from the parking lot. My mom could see the power lines down and yells to dad out of the window, "Don't come up! You will be electrocuted." Dad shows no fear and continues his trek through the downed lines to the hotel. (Dad was a lot like me, or maybe, I was a lot like him. He didn't think much either.) He finally makes it, and we are all together. Safe, I don't know, but together. Our hero! (I had a girl friend once that used to call me *her* hero, but that is another chapter and probably for another reason.) Finally, the water subsides and the world comes together again.

At one time Steel Pier had some of the biggest attractions on the East Coast. It was later destroyed along with many houses by a hurricane. Now that I have mentioned "Steel Pier", when my dad was very young, he worked on it. He dove from a one hundred foot tower into a very small amount of water. (Dad said it was only about six inches, but we kind of discounted that.) Dad also said that he was a lion tamer. People who know me, say I'm nuts! But the fact is, Dad had scars on his legs from the animals reaching out and scratching him in close calls. But Dad would say, "It was from the animal that was in bed with him at night!" Now, back to reality! Where was I? OH yeah!

So, we arrive at the performance center where there are so many buses that we had to walk a couple of blocks just to get to the auditorium where we were singing. Everyone is in a special colorful robe or special type of gown or dress. It was really great to hear so many voices in one place. I was very impressed! I found out later that there were fifty-eight schools competing. We were the 20th or so to sing. We had to sit through a lot of the other schools as they sang their two songs. Most were very good. Now, it was our turn. Our instructor led us up to the stage and gave the sheet music to the orchestra leader. It was to me, like being in a movie. Every one's eyes were on us. (not to mention a reward to be handed out to the best schools.) Out of the fifty of us on stage, there was one girl who had a solo part. What if she was so good and someone spotted her and she landed a part in a movie or wound up on Bandstand, or maybe even a play! I could say I knew her. Awesome, just awesome! Shit like this can't happen in Philadelphia! Our leader puts his arms up, music rod in hand, the down beat, and the music starts. This is our big moment! We knew we were going to be in the top five if not win it!

What the hell is that? That's not our music! That's not the song we learned! That's not what we practiced for three months! What the hell is going on? Our illustrious leader brought the wrong F—g sheet music! The wrong sheet music! The wrong sheet music!!! We had to forfeit and leave the stage and return to our seats and listen to the other 30 or so schools sing and look at us and snicker and stare at us as if we were idiots. How humiliating! (Had I still been thirteen and a little fatter, I would have burst into tears.) I never heard anybody say a word for at least an hour. When I did it wasn't very nice as they looked at our EX leader. Some of the girls were crying.

The ride on the bus home was the longest three hours I had ever experienced. Our leader tried to apologize to us, but most of us weren't hearing it. The only good thing that came from it was that everyone somehow got an "A" in the class.

Now, in January of fifty-seven, I turned fifteen. It should have been like my name was Johnny, and I won the gold banjo from the devil. But my name is Chuck, and I just lost my soul to him, instead.

Chapter Six

I had been living on Barjud Street in Pomona with my family now for about two years or so. I had not made a lot of friends in the track of homes where I lived because of my friendship with Gene. We pretty much did everything together. When we were not together, I had plenty of other things to keep me busy like school work, taking my little, pain in the ass, brother with me when I went somewhere, or going to Hesperia. Where?? Hesperia!

When, why and how I don't know, but my dad got a five acre piece of land granted to him in Hesperia. Hesperia is about fifty miles south of Barstow. Barstow?? Barstow is about one hundred and fifty miles south of Las Vegas. It was all desert (like most of California was at that time), and the only thing that was required to keep this piece of property was that in a five-year time period, my dad had to put a dwelling on it. Any dwelling! It did not have to have water. It didn't have to have electricity. It did not have to have anything, just four walls and a roof. So we, the family, would go there every four weeks or so and plan what to do with the land. Now we were big, hi-cocked land owners in Hesperia. As I have said, Fifty miles south of Barstow. Now, at that time, Barstow was thought of as the arm pit of California and we were fifty miles further away from it. No wonder they gave it to us. So, when we were there we, my brother and I noticed that there were a lot of birds, rabbits and lizards. We rationalized that they were utilizing our land without permission. We needed to do something about it.

We asked Dad if we could have a B. B. gun and a twenty-two rifle. The B. B. gun would be for Mark and the twenty-two for me. I can't tell you the resistance we received. You would have thought we had asked for anthrax so that we could eradicate the schools where we attended. Jewish parents are something, aren't they? I bet Barney would have gotten the guns in a hot New York minute! We pleaded our case for months that we just wanted to target shoot. Finally, after talking ourselves blue in the face, we were rewarded with the WEAPONS. Ah Ha! Now, to just put this slow progression into perspective, just a few months ago I was in a choir and now I have weapons of mass destruction in my hands.

The routine was, we would go to Hesperia. Mom and Dad would go off to have a drink, lunch and smooze with the other locals and to see what they were going to do with their land and leave us alone for a while. We would set up a target against a tree (Yucca, of course) shoot a couple of B. B.'s and a couple of twenty-two bullets into it and then go off on a hunt for wild animals. In the next two or three years I can't tell you how many birds, lizards and rabbits we killed. It was great! (PETA who?) Dad eventually got sick and never built the shack so we lost the grant and the five acres. Not a problem. It is only worth about eight hundred thousand now! That's American by the way! The Lord giveth and the Lord taketh away. My brother still has the guns!

Right around this time (age fifteen) a guy named Bill moved in about six or seven houses away from us and across the street. Had I been a little wiser, I would have checked for three sixes on the back of his neck. Bill was a really great-looking guy but real small. He was only about five-five or so. We made friends and palled around together for the next five years. Between him and Gene, it was like Doctor Jeckel and Mister Hyde. Bill was number one in my transition of good to evil. He, within three months, had me smoking cigarettes and from there it went down hill. Bill was like, I said, a great looking guy and all the chicks hung around him at school. He must have known Barney because he knew everything about girls. Everything! He used to tell me things that didn't make sense. I would relate them to Gene. He would say that's not possible, and I would agree. When I first met Bill, the only thing that I saw about him that I didn't like was that he smoked. But that only lasted three months.

After a few months or maybe just weeks, I told Bill about my addiction with girly magazines. He never asked why, and I never mentioned why. One day he said, "Let's go and get some girly magazines." I told him that I had no money. Dad was starting to get ill and cash was in short demand. He said that I didn't need any cash. I asked him how that worked. He said, "We just cop them." "Cop them. What's that?" "Don't you know anything? We steal them." "Steal them! What if we get caught?" "We won't get caught. I have been doing this stuff for years." "Are you sure?" "Yea, just follow me and watch." It was like any good sense my parents taught me was out the door. First, guns, then smoking, and now stealing! What next? Knocking off a bank? Shit! I'm only fifteen!

So, we go to a liquor store. Bill walks up to the magazine rack and picks up a Sports Illustrated magazine or something like that and looks at it. He sees the clerk looking at him. The clerk sees that Bill is not reading the dirty magazines so the clerk turns away. Bill, at that time, bends over and puts the magazine back on the rack and on the way up grabs a Playboy magazine and puts it to his chest, turns and walks away. Before I knew it we left with the magazine. How cool was that! What an education I am starting to get in a short period of time.

Now, to shift gears! When my family moved to Pomona, there was an extra bedroom. Dad made it into a bar. Hawaiian style! We had surf boards hanging on the walls and leis draped on doors and pictures of beaches and neon lit signs with beer stuff, waterfalls, and scantily clad women on them. He always had the bar stocked with booze. Vodka, bourbon, scotch, tequila and so on. If they made it, it was behind the bar. I had been sampling the stuff for two years or so. Now, being the goody-goody that I was, I did not go crazy. But, when a bottle did seem to be a little low, I put a little water in it and then started on a new bottle.

Every year Dad would have a New Year's party. At the stroke of midnight, all who were still there, the men, had a tequila drinking contest. Every two minutes they would shoot a shot of tequila with or without the lime and salt. The choice was theirs until the last one standing was the winner. No prize, just bragging rights for the next year. At thirteen, I might add, and a man now, I was allowed to join. The first year I couldn't stand the stuff. It not only smelled bad, it taste bad and on top of all that, I couldn't even spell it. But, as the year went on, and I was doing my sampling through-out it, I did better the next year. When I was sixteen, I won the contest and never looked back!

Switching gears once more, one day I was with Bill. He said, "Let's go see Roger." "Who the hell is Roger?" I had been in this track of homes for two years now and Bill just a few months, and this guy knows everybody all ready. Ok, let's go see Roger. Now, Roger, if you met him today, you would call him a geek! Not good looking, long greasy hair, skinny and pimples! Feh! But Roger's dad had been divorced and remarried, and the new step-mother, much younger, was a knock out! That's probably why Bill made friends with Roger. Figured he could get into her pants when the old guy, Roger's father, is gone.

Now, this Roger was a real character. Right out of a Mickey Splaine or a Damon Runyon movie. He had a brother five years older, and two very, much younger, step brothers by the new mom, about two and four years old. Roger smoked like a fiend and had no interference from his parents. Bill did also. Roger's dad was probably consumed with the new bride to notice anything. Roger played guitar and really stunk. Although he thought he was f—g Elvis! (By the way, again for you younger readers, Elvis was one of Santa's Reindeer who passed away and Rudolph took over.) He didn't play like Elvis. He didn't have a great guitar like Elvis. He didn't have hair like Elvis, and he certainly didn't look like Elvis. But, he thought he was as good as Elvis. However, about fifty years later, I did meet another guy named Bill who sounded more like Elvis than Elvis. But that is in chapter 794730-6. Just another chapter for which to hold your breath! Now, Elvis (Roger) and I became pretty good friends. We palled around a lot. I was splitting my time between Gene and the terrible duo.

Roger, Bill and I, for the most part, walked to and from school together. If the weather was good, we would walk. John Marshall Jr. High was only a mile, maybe two, from our houses. When we left our track of homes, we had to go through a field that was used for growing hay in the summer. As it got towards maybe April, the growers started to cut and bail the hay. On the way home from school, sometimes we would stop and put a few bails around in a circle. Then, put another row on top of those bails so the bails had some height. We would put one bail in the center on the ground and open it so we could lie in the hay and smoke our cigarettes. That way we couldn't be seen smoking.

One day, on the way home, we did it as usual. We were lying around talking shit when I looked up into the sky and saw something that didn't make a lot of sense. I pointed it out to Bill and Rog, and they couldn't believe their eyes. Way up high, at about the angle of 1 o'clock to us, there were three round circles in a triangular form. Like a pyramid tilted at a small angle. They were the size of a nickel with about a dimes worth of space in between them. Three of them! We watched with amazement for maybe five minutes or so, and then, with the speed of nothing from this planet, in unison, they sped away, never to be seen again. That was the first time and the only time that I have ever seen a U.F.O. To this day I will swear that there are U.F.O.'s.

Now, while we are on the hay subject, I was all by myself one day. I think it was a Saturday. Not sure if I was on my hourly lunch from my job at the Texaco station (which will come into play shortly) or another reason, but I was having a smoke in my hay fort. It was time to go. I got up, brushed myself off, jumped over the top bail and I headed away from the hay circle. (AKA, the UFO spotting area.) I must have walked a couple of hundred feet by now and for some reason, I turned and looked back. OH SHIT! The whole field was on fire. I must have not put my cigarette out good enough! It was totally out of control, and it couldn't have been two minutes. I didn't know whether to run away, which might cause suspicion, or walk towards it to create the illusion that I was concerned and surprised, or what to do. So, with two thirds of my fortitude missing (Bill and Roger), I ran like hell. Never to smoke in the field again! To this day, I will never understand my relationship with the flame.

I was a pretty big TV fan as a kid. One of my favorite shows, if not my favorite, was Davy Crocket. Now, I know many of you have no clue about who in hell I am talking about and I am not going to tell you, either. My Grandfather,s brother, Zalmon, had a son who sold hats. Now, there's a job! He sold hats in the western United States. That was his territory, I think. Although his family had plenty of money, he somehow was one of the cheapest assholes that ever walked the earth and single handedly helped give a bad name to Jews! So, every time he was in the area where we lived, he would come over and stay with us for free instead of taking a motel room. He usually stayed two or three days at a time. This went on for years. Never asked if we would like to go to dinner on him or can he take the kids (Mark and me) to McDonalds or if he could pay for the room or whatever. Never an offer to pay for anything. Just, "I will be there for a few days, is it OK?" My mom and dad were givers and never expected anything from anyone, especially family. So with them, I guess it was ok.

One time he came over and brought Mark and me each a hat. This was the only time it ever happened. Now remember this guy never brought shit for the family for years, nothing, and he was loaded. This was a big deal. You will never guess what the hat was? A Davy Crocket hat with a detachable tail! A coon skin cap just like Davy Crocket wore! My brother and I were in hog heaven. This may have been the best gift I had ever gotten. Better than the Red Ryder B. B. gun, in the movie, "Christmas Story." A real coon skin cap! WOW! His name was Hymie, son of Zalmon. (Sounds Sci—Fi to me!) Now, as I think about it today, me being from Philadelphia, the hat could have been made out of a Koala Bear for all I know. (Hey Bruce, do they have Koala Bears in Philadelphia?)

While I am on the subject of TV, one of the best shows that kept me glued to it was the Mickey Mouse Club. I don't know anyone who didn't watch it. Most of the guys watched it for the same reason that I watched it. Annette Funicello. Was she a great actress? No! Was she talented? No! Did she seem friendly? No! But did she have big tits? OOOOH YEA! If I knew the term "getting your rocks off" then as I know it today, that was why we watched the Mickey Mouse Club. I think the girls watched it for some guy named Bobby. The reason I bring Annette up now is that she will come into play at a later date in my life, and also to reflect a little on her tits!

The school year went on, and Dad got sicker. I felt I had to help make money for the family so I took a job at the Texaco station at the end of the housing tract where we lived. I worked weekends and nights after school. I think I made eighty-five cents an hour and a commission when I sold a quart of oil, a fan belt or a tire. This was my first job and an experience in sales for which we Jews are supposed to be good. I can't tell you how much un-needed oil I sold! That's probably why Texaco is so big now. I may have single handedly put them on the map!

Dad continually got sicker, but I remember when he was ok, years before, he smoked Lucky Strike cigarettes. When I was very young and still in Philadelphia, he would give me two dimes. I would go to the cigarette machine, put in the two dimes, and pull the knob, and a pack of Lucky's would come out. I would take them to Dad. He would shake the pack and two pennies would fall out. He would give them to me. (Eighteen cents for a pack of cigges)! I am not sure if my brother was around yet but if he was, he wouldn't get shit! I was obviously the favorite son he thought. Today, he still thinks that's true.

It got to a point that Dad could not go to work. He had cancer of the larynx and was going to have Cobalt treatments soon to cure the cancer. Dad was a salesman for Bond's Clothing and obviously couldn't sell. Hell, he could hardly talk! Things got pretty bad financially after a while. I can remember going to school in the morning and when I opened the door to go out, a bag or two of groceries would stop me from swinging open the screen door. This would happen often. Dad and Mom had a lot of friends. Like I said, they were givers and I guess it was time to get something back. Their house was always open to anyone who was in need of food, company or a drink. So much so that in fact, sometimes, even in the good times, our own family suffered on occasion becuse Dad was way too giving.

Two of Mom and Dad's friends were the Rasmusuns. They were Mormon. (I believe the correct term for them would have been, "Jack Mormons".) They would have the head of their church come over every two weeks and say a prayer over Dad. By coincidence, each and every time he left our house, we would find a fifty dollar bill on the floor or under a lamp or in the bathroom.

Now while all of this was going on, I still felt helpless, even though I was working and trying to help out. I wanted to quit school and get a real job, but Dad said, "Absolutely not." Fortunately, I had good friends like Bill and Roger. They would help me COP some stuff that I sold at school for a profit so that I could buy a little food for the house at times and take care of some of my lunches in school. Besides Bill and Roger teaching me to smoke (so I could be cool like them), I started to let my hair grow and put grease on it. The pimples came all by themselves.

Now, even though Dad was sick, at this point, Dad was not totally bed ridden. He just couldn't work. I was quickly approaching fifteen and a half and in those days, you could get a driver's permit at that age. That's all I needed was a weapon bigger than my twenty-two.

Dad had a Studebaker. He was teaching me how to drive. He would take me out on a back road behind our track of homes, later to be called Magazine Road, and even later to be called Guts Road. (Chapter 763 and 799) Now, I really don't know if all Jewish dads or for that matter, any dads, teach this way, but Dad's Studebaker had a stick shift. Every time I stalled it, I got a slap on the back of the head (more commonly known in the world of Jews as a zetz) and was called stupid. This would have been ok, I guess, except for the habit that started. Not only when I stalled the car but when I did something that Dad thought was wrong, I got a zetz. Sometimes it was so hard that it knocked my head into the steering wheel as I was driving. I started to feel like a ball in a pin ball machine. Then, he wanted to know why I couldn't see the turn or the center divider. This driving stuff can't be all that's it cracked up to be, can it?

Anyway, I finally went for my driving test and written test after months of physical abuse. I passed the written test with a 90 and that was fine. Then, when I got into the car with the driving instructor to take the driving part of the test, the instructor said, "Why is your head so swollen and your eyes so red?" I didn't know if I should just tell him the truth or ask him to hit me as I drove!

Now, I am a big deal, at the wheel. In those days you could drive anytime and anywhere with a permit as long as you had an adult with you. (Someone over eighteen) For the next six months I begged to go to the store to get their smokes, groceries, and gas. Wherever Mom and Dad were to go, I was available to drive them. Five days before, I wouldn't have accompanied them to the morgue! Now, I have to work on them to buy me a car. In six months I will become a monster. My own car!

It is now time to graduate junior high school and to start the summer. Gene got his driver's permit, also, and from what I could tell, Bill and Roger will never get theirs. Where Gene and I had a really good family life, Bill and Roger didn't. They just seemed to be out of sorts with their parents. Bill didn't have a mom, and Roger came from a divorced environment. But we all graduated. Even Bill and Roger!

Gene and I spent a lot of time riding our bikes again throughout the whole summer. We also did well in track and field and were very happy about that. As I had mentioned, I did break the school record for the fifty yard dash. (However, it was again broken the following year.) We also decided to join gymnastics in high school when school started in September.

We would ride to the public pool, to the park, to Elephant Hill that was close to my house, and go hiking there. Elephant Hill was not a pretty place. It had sporadic trees and mostly dry, grassy areas. It was about five hundred feet high. But, it was a good place to get away from the local stuff that was going on. We would hike to the top and sit under a tree and just talk. We could see the local cemetery way down below us. At that time, in Pomona, there wasn't much to see. Now, there are three freeways and four malls and the rest of big doings that come from a place that is central to all areas. When I lived in Pomona, it was top notch. Now, it is pretty run down.

Dad finally had his Cobalt treatments at Kaiser Permanente Hospital in Fontana. He was down and out for a while. The donations from friends kept coming in. I kept working at the Texaco Station only many more hours now that it was summer time. Maybe sixty or more a week! In the day I spent most of the time with Gene and in the nights with Bill and Roger when I wasn't working. The days were, as I said, with Gene and fairly normal, but the nights were a little different. Bill, Roger and I would walk through the whole tract and check out cars. We would see if they were locked and most weren't. We would open the shotgun door (right side) and open the glove box and see what was in it. We would find money, gloves, sun glasses and all kinds of stuff. Bill found condoms once. He was elated. I didn't even know what the hell they were. So, we made a few bucks at night. Most went to cigarettes and the rest went to my house. We sold the stuff we didn't want in the next few days or so when we would go to town, to the kids we knew from around school. Life was great.

One night Bill, Roger and I were sitting around on the curb, in front of my house, trying to decide who to rob, kill or set fire to. Roger lights up a Kool. That's a cigarette he stole from his dad. He says, "Let's steal that car over there." He points to it, and it has a boat attached to it. "We can drive it over the driveways with one wheel on and one wheel off the curb throughout the tract. That will make the car and the boat go up and down and make us feel that we are in the water. (Very sick minds!) I'll drive and you two get in the boat." Hmmmmmm! "Good idea," Bill says! Chuck says, "What if we get caught?" "Yea, so what" someone mutters. "Let's go!" Bill got in the driver's seat and hotwired the car. You would have thought he had the key he did it so fast. In thirty seconds we are in the water. It was fun! We drove around the tract about three times or for about fifteen minutes. Up and down the driveways going around the cars that were parked on the street and jumping stuff that was in the boat, up and down as we went. We put the car and the boat back where we got it from, and ran like hell. This had to be about midnight or so. You guys are great! How did you get the car started? Can you teach me that? What fun!

One night we (Roger, Bill and I) were bored and decided to strip naked and run across the highway when cars came by. We would stand behind a bush, in the field, across from the Texaco station where I worked. When a car came by the highway, we would run across to the Texaco station and hide behind the gas pumps. Then, when a car came from the other way, we would run back and hide behind the bush. We actually had our underpants on. Cars would swerve and slam on the brakes and screech their tires. I would have Loved to have been a fly on the wall when some of them got home and tried to tell what they had just seen. Summer held a lot of fun stuff.

One day I was standing outside of my house, and a guy rode by on his bike. I yelled, "Hey, aren't you Brian?" He stopped and turned around and said "Yes. You're Chuck, right?" "Yea"! "You live near by"? "Yes, across the highway, in the other tract". We had homeroom together but were not really friends. He seemed like a nice guy. He said "Do you play poker?" I said "What"? "Poker, you know like cards." I said "No." He said, "Do you want to learn?" I said, "Sure, where and when?" He said, "Tonight at my house about seven 'o clock and bring five bucks." "Five bucks!" "For what?" "You need it to play poker." "Ok, I'll be there." He gave me his address.

Wow, now I had met a new friend, and he is going to teach me something brand new. Now, I can teach Bill and Roger something after I learned. Now where in the hell can I get five bucks? Five bucks was a lot of money then and I didn't have shit! I went to my boss, Fletcher, at the Texaco station and asked him for an advance. You would have thought I had asked him to cut off his balls or something. Christ, what an argument for thirty minutes and finally, he came up with the geedes. (Geedes. (Gee-dis) Slang for money.) I went home, did a few chores around the yard, mowed, watered, trimmed and all of that kind of bull shit, teased Mark, ate dinner, and left for the poker game. I walked up to the front door and knocked. Brian's mother said that they were in the garage and to go through the side to the back door in to the garage. I walked through the door and guess who I saw? Right! Bill. Brian said, "Hi," and Bill flipped me off (flipped me off, in this case, is an international term for Hi buddy!) There were a couple of other guys there as well. So, we started with the lessons and the obvious losses. It cost me my five bucks and took three hours to learn the game, but I did get the hang of it. Great, just f—g great! Now, I not only steal, and not just magazines but cars now, smoke, drink and am learning to cuss at a rapid pace, and now I am into gambling as well. (The bank job has to be close!) The poker game was held once a week, every week. I soon started to make a few bucks. Now, Brian, who affectionately became known as Knuckle Head Smith, had a sister. Her name was Alma. I have never heard a name like that before and never have since. At first I did not even notice her as she was a girl. She would come and go and talk to us during the games week in and week out. Just like one of the boys, kind of. Now, Brian was not like Bill and Roger. He didn't do dishonest things. However, he did have a hang up or two. One night, when we were having our poker game, a cat came into the garage. It was a hot evening. The large overhead door was open so this cat just lollygagged in. Brian had a dart board in the garage that we played until all the guys came to play our game of poker. Brian saw the cat, walked over to the dart board, took a dart and threw it at the cat. Nails it right in the head, and the cat starts twisting its head and runs out of the garage. We all looked at Brian; he looked at us and said, "WHAT? The cat should not have been in my garage, and I bet it will not come back." I ran out to look for the cat, but it was nowhere to be seen. From then on Brian became Knuckle Head! So, I am getting an education from every angle, sex, guys, thieves and mental cases. What next? (The bank job is only days away!)It seems that the only one I am not learning from is Gene. Unknowingly, the only good and normal thing in my life!

 I am still doing a lot of bike riding in my housing tract and am starting to meet others as I ride around. Some were girls, some boys, younger, older and the same age as me. At least I am starting to meet people after two plus years. I met these two guys. They were brothers and their names were Bob and his younger brother, by a year or so, Jimmy. Bob was my age and had attended Ganesha High school as a tenth grader all already. I knew them for the next ten years or so. We would ride bikes, hike Elephant Hill, and do many things together over the next seven years. Not super close but turned out to be good friends. Here is the kicker.

As you know by now, I can't meet anyone normal. These two guys would always fight with each other. Always! It didn't matter about what it was. "That's my shirt." Punches flew. I am showering first. Punches flew. "I got an "A" and you didn't," punches flew. "You did a bad job mowing the grass." Punches flew. It didn't have to be over anything important, and either one would start it anywhere at anytime or any place. They would fight at least once a day and sometimes it was really bad. Blood, a broken arm or a busted nose was not uncommon. Their mom had them go to a shrink more then once. When they were not fighting, they were good friends. We would try to do stuff with only one of them at a time, but they would fight over that. One would accuse the other that he was liked more, so he was the one who got to do something with us. Just like three year olds only much worse. Once in a while Bill, I, Roger or Knuckle Head would step in and try to break up the fight. They would start waling on us. It got to a point that we would be in a fight in which no one wanted to be. We would get angry and start to fight back. Eventually, we left them alone to kill themselves. Jimmy, some twenty years later, I heard, shot and killed Bobby and is still doing time. What I didn't realize was that I was learning something new, how to fight. Little did I know that the experience would come in handy.

Then there was Primm. She was a very nice girl but very over weight. She had a pretty face, really bright red long hair and was probably the nicest of all my female friends in that time zone. High school! She had very nice parents. If there was something going on that wasn't happening at my house, it was at hers.

Across from Primm lived Cynthia. She was the heart throb of all the guys. Even me, but I wasn't sure at that time why I was throbbing. (Still fifteen and a half and didn't know shit)! She was tall, blond, with long hourly brushed hair, tight clothes, and always very short shorts with a pretty face.

Not far down the street from Cynthia was Jane. Jane was much different than Cynthia. Jane was a really nice person, kind of like the girl next door, and seemed to share herself with most of us guys. Don't know how far she went with others, but I do know how far with me. She had half of her big toe missing. Maybe that was why she was so friendly to all. There seemed to be a competition between both of them.

Cynthia was beautiful, and Jane was super friendly. Neither one would put out, at least not for me. I would have not known what to do anyway.

On the street that was way in back of our tract and at the bottom of Elephant Hill, I met a guy. His name was Bob. He had a little sister named Diane who was maybe ten or eleven. Just about every guy found a way to go out of their way to try and to see her. Knowing that she was very young didn't matter. She was built like a brick shit house, in spades. She had a great face, but her body was unbelievable. She made the Playboy magazine women look like the witch from Hansel and Gretel. It was at this point that I stopped stealing Playboys and just closed my eyes and dreamed. Between Diane, Jane Cynthia I was slowly becoming a real man, not the thirteen year old one.

With the discovery of women in my life, I started asking questions to my friends. Bill, Bill and sometimes Bill! Who knows? Soon, I might have facial hair and may be elsewhere as well!

If you remember way back when our house was being built and we were coming out all the time to watch it grow, I mentioned the walnut trees. Well, walnut trees are pretty fun trees. They don't grow straight. They kind of grow up and out like out-stretched arms. This made it easy to climb. Boys will be boys. I used to climb up about twenty feet high and Mark up about ten feet. I am, today, still the more adventurous one. Mark and I were brain storming one day. (If you are reading this book, you know that is impossible for me.) We thought of building a tree house. It would be easy because of the way the wide, thick branches were growing. The process starts. Mark, his friends, and my friends and I found wood all over the place and brought it home. The neighbors, I am sure, thought that Dad was making a spare room for me when I was bad, or I was making a coffin for him because he didn't make it. There was a new housing project a few blocks away. The nails and some better wood that was needed for certain parts of the house were copped at the "night store." Being so close it was easy to get! I actually did most of the work, and in a couple of weeks, it was done. It was not only a thing of beauty but three stories. Yep, three stories. The top story was enclosed so when it rained we wouldn't get wet. How do you like that kind of thinking from a guy who's having a problem keeping his pecker in his pants and doesn't even know why it wants out! Tree house rich we were. Later in years, my family added a Dough Boy swimming pool on the back patio of the house. I hung a rope from the tree where our tree house was built. We would swing down from the tree house on the rope over the pool, let go and drop into the pool. What fun! *Mark was happier than seeing cows!*

The summer continued on. I spent day time with Gene, working, and the night time with the boys and now, sometimes, with girls. We even had a party or two and I enjoyed dancing with them. It was great. Fast dancing was ok. When the slow dances came on, everyone went for Cynthia and Diane. We would hold them real close, and you could feel their chests pushing against ours. I don't think Diane knew what was going on, and, anyway, her big brother was always at the parties to protect her. Cynthia sure knew. Man, did she know! You couldn't have gotten a hair between me and her at any place on our bodies when we danced. She did that with all the guys. We all tried to touch her chest, but she wouldn't let anyone do it. Not even Bill. Nobody would mess with Diane, mainly because she was too young. But, man, was she something to look at!

I was up to five or six cigarettes a day by now. One night, Roger said, "I copped some of my dad's Kools. Do you want one?" "Hey, free cigs are free cigs." That was the first time I had ever smoked a menthol cigarette. For some reason I got sicker than shit. I was puken like a champ. I was with Roger and Bill at the time. They said, "Let's go over here, in the darker area away from the street light, so that you can get your shit together." We walked about a block and sat down. I thought I was going to die. Man, was I sick!

While I was sitting there, a Mexican kid walked up to us and said, "What's going on?" Bill or Roger, not sure which one, told him. He started laughing and called me a weak chicken shit and a few other names and then started pushing me around. He was a pretty big Mexican. Not necessarily tall but large. Now, if there are three guys who you don't want to push around it's Bill, Roger and me. Not because we are so tough but the opposite. I'm a Jew, and we don't fight. We sell stuff! Bill, as I have mentioned, is a midget, and Roger is a skinny geek. Beating us up is no big mitzvah. This one Mexican dude starts pushing us around, and Bill and Rog take off. I am too sick to run. As they are running, they yell back that they are going to get help. Help! Who the hell are they going to get? There are only the three of us. I'm dead! This

Mexican starts to hit me and knock me around for no reason. I tried to protect myself (smack) and yell at the (punch) same time, "Why are (kick) you doing this to (slam to the ground) me? I didn't do anything to (punch) you." About this time, I figure I am talking to the wrong person. God! That's who I need. God! I started yelling for help at the top of my lungs. We were in front of a few houses, and maybe God lives in one of them. "Help, Help, Help! I yelled!" Finally, a door opens and someone yells, "What's going on there?" The Mexican guy ran off. "Are you all right?" I hear. Crying like a mother F—r, I whimper out, "Yes, I am fine. Thanks." The door shuts, and I continue crying. Unlike the thirteen year old fat Jew that just cries for no reason, I know why I am crying. Believe me, I know why.

About three minutes later, guess who shows up? Right, my two buddies. Where's the help you were going to bring?" "We saw him run away so we figured you were ok and didn't need any. If I could stand and I wasn't a Jew, I would have killed both of them! But as I said, Jews don't fight. They just stand there and get the crap kicked out of them as you may have noticed.

Now, I am bleeding at every place on my body. My clothes are torn to shreds. If I thought I was sick twenty minutes ago, well! So, if you had asked Bill what was the lesson that we learned that night, he probably would have said, "Don't wear good clothes when smoking Kools." Me, I am thinking I have to dump these two guys or learn how to defend myself! I figured I needed friends! "How do I get home, guys, I can't go home looking like this?" My mom, alone, will match the bruises if she sees me like this. So we went to Roger's house. He got some paper towels and wet them. I wiped myself wherever I saw blood and did the best to stop the bleeding. Rog got a few bandages and that helped. Man, did I ache and did I look like shit! I really didn't want to go home. I figured that when I went home and got to the door and opened it, Roger would go in front and Bill would walk on the side of me until we reached my bedroom. They would stay a minute or two and then leave by themselves. Man, I am glad this was summer and wasn't a school night. There is no way I could have ever gotten up to go to school. I was in pain and was very fortunate. Besides a very small cut that had already stopped bleeding, there were no bruises where mom and dad could see on my face. They were all on my body so Mom and Dad never knew. Most people wait years to die from smoking but no not me. It almost happened in three or four months. For some reason I never liked Mexicans from then on. Kools either! I didn't do much of anything for a week or two except go to work, and that was a major chore.

Summer was quickly coming to a close. I was going to be a sophomore, a tenth grader, low man on the totem pole! But the good thing was that the Los Angels County Fair was near, and I was closer to getting my driver's license.

I had taken auto shop and metal shop as my two electives. That was cool. Auto shop so that I would be able to work on my own car and not have to ask dad for money if I needed repairs. I was pretty sure I was not going to get a brand new Cadillac. Actually, I wasn't even sure that I was going to get a car. We, Dad and I, never really talked about it. I just assumed. The metal shop was for making a knife so when I met that Mexican again, I could kill the asshole. English was a given, but Mrs. Tacamori had retired so that was a break. So, I thought . . . . There was gym, history, math and choir.

Chapter Seven

High School! Pomona High School to be exact! Now, there was a beauty. It had burnt down about three or four years before I went there (don't look at me that way). There were temporary trailers that we used for classrooms. September, no air conditioners, no fans, and the windows were very small and did not open very wide. Hot, shit, Hot! It was a thirty-five minute school bus ride one way to Pomona High. I pretty much took the bus most of the time. Gene did once in a while, but his dad drove him most of the time. Roger's big brother drove Roger some of the time, but I never knew when. I could not chance going with him and not making it to school on time. Can't remember what Bill did, but he didn't go to school as much as the rest of us. Roger and Gene had auto shop with me, and Gene had choir with me, of course. I met a new guy named Owen. He lived near Gene so he was kind of far away, but somehow he knew Bill. (What a surprise) Bill, Gene and I had gym together. We were all kind of intermingled with our classes.

Nothing seemed to change as far as friends went. Gene and I stayed pretty tight in the day time with gymnastics and choir. At night, living closer to Bill and Roger, I spent most of that time with them. The new kid, Owen, would ride his bike over our way sometimes to join in the poker games. I must have been born in a cave. Everybody seemed to know everything about everything except me. I often wondered if all Jews were isolated from the human race at birth and put into a room with only a book about sales, attorneys, doctors and, maybe, an abacus.

Now that I am starting to understand women (probably the most ridicules statement I have ever made in my life), I kinda liked Alma, Knuckle Head's sister. At the poker game (at Knuckle Head's house) I started to make my move. Not even knowing what my move was! I asked her if she would like to go to the movie on Saturday, hoping that she would say no for two reasons. First, I don't know what to do on a date and second, I work on Saturday and have no money to take her to the movie even if I didn't have to work. She said she could not because she had way too many chores that she had to do this weekend. If I would like to come over for dinner, that would be nice. Man, did I luck out! I said, "Yes, what time?" Now that I think about it, that may have been one of the only times that I asked a female a question and I didn't get a question back. (There is just no accounting for youth.)

So, Thursday and Friday went as planned with school except for this Mexican guy who is on the bus with me. He keeps looking at me almost all the way home. Nothing ever happened, and Saturday comes along. I go to work with the thought of selling twenty cans of oil and a fan belt or two. In those days you pumped the gas, checked the oil and water, washed the windows, checked the air in the tires, and kissed the customer's ass if he asked you to do so. All this time, hoping that some big-breasted woman would call me over and ask me a question, like, "Was the air in the tires ok?" So that I could put my head in the window and look down her blouse as I answered her question. This was a normal thing to do in the late fifty's. (Not the looking stuff, the checking for free stuff). I know you youngsters (forty and below) reading this book can't believe what you are reading, but it is true. And to cap it off and to make it more unbelievable, the gas was twenty cents a gallon for regular. Ethel was two cents more. **Who?** Don't ask! So, let me tell you something. I am a quick learner. At the beginning, when I started to work in the gas station business, I was selling maybe one or two quarts of oil a day. After meeting the boys, I am now top salesman at twenty to thirty a day. I even seem to find a nail, in a tire or two, once a week while checking the tires for the proper pressure. Tires were a real good commission.

Well, my Saturday day job was over, and my Saturday night job starts soon. Alma! I jumped on my Schwin and pedaled home as fast as I could. It was only three or four blocks from work. If it was today and I know what I know now, I would have taken a shower, but being naive at this dating stuff, I changed my oil-soaked pants and shirt, only because I thought it would be tacky to go to dinner in a Texaco uniform. I combed the oil clumps out of my hair and zoomed over to my new Love's house for a free meal. As I am going out the door, my mom says, "Where are you going? I have dinner ready." I yelled back, "I have a date and won't need to eat, see ya later Mom." A DATE! A DATE! I was sure there would be a conference between Dad and Mom by the time I got back. Their good little Jewish boy only fifteen (fifteen and a half) already dating. Way too soon! Next, you know there will be grand-children! I know the way my parents think. I'm dead!

So, now I am at Alma's door knocking. Knuckle Head answers (I guess I should call him Brian tonight because his parents will be here.) Brian opens the door, and I walk in. Hair combed, clean shirt and pants, and smelling, I am sure, like an oil freighter. Alma is nowhere to be found. So, I sat on the couch with Brian and his dad and mom watching TV. I had met their mom before but not their dad. We sat around talking for a bit and then Alma comes in. After awhile, we all went to the dining room to eat. The whole evening was very nice. I forgot I was on a kind of date and was pretty comfortable. After we were done eating, Alma said, "Do you want to go to the garage and watch some TV?" Their garage was set up like a family room. (That is where we played cards on Wednesday's and targeted an occasional cat or two). Carpet, TV, couch, poker table and of course a dart board! So, we went into the garage and watched TV.

Alma sat very close to me and held my hand. It was kind of cool. I put my arm around her shoulders and leaned over to kiss her. She let me! Wow, that was something else! It was a long kiss, maybe two or three seconds. That was the first time I had ever kissed a girl except for the fat Jewish chick at my bar mitzvah party that nailed me in the closet two and half years ago. This was nice! No open mouth stuff. No tongue stuff. Just our two lips touching, holding a hand, and my arm around her! Nice! I didn't even look at the TV. Alma was a little older than me, probably a year or so. She probably had a little more experience than me. (Anyone could have, that was my first kiss.)We sat and talked and kissed for a while that night until Knuckle; I mean, Brian, came in and said, "Mom said it was time to call it a night." Let me tell you, that was the last thing I wanted to hear. But, I packed up my dripping little dead solider, gave her a hug, and went home. Boy, did I have a bunch to tell Bill!

School was fun, kind of. Not like I used to like it; it was different now, but still OK. I had metal shop. We had to make a ball-peen hammered ash tray. This, I found out, was what everyone in the world made for their first project. For a professional metal worker, it would take about twenty minutes. In shop, it took two weeks! We had to learn the properties of the copper we used, the technique of hammering the copper we used, the tempering of the copper we used before we hammered the ashtray and then how to mold the f—g thing so it would hold a cigarette. Thank God, at least now I smoked! What a waste if no one in our family had smoked! And so, the metal projects went on and on.

Towards the end of the year, I had made a bow as well as an ashtray. A bow? Yea, like a bow and arrow bow! I really can't remember how strong it was, but I think it was forty pounds. I did get an "A" on it. The only reason I even mention the ash tray and the bow is that they will both play a part of my life a little later on. So, remember them. That was metal shop!

Auto shop will play a big factor a little later on, as well. I got a great education from it and good grades, too. I remember the teacher was Mr. Rupert. Funny that he turned up in my life forty years later when I lived in Morro Bay!

English sucked! The best part of it was that Tacamori was not there. However, a new pain in the ass showed her ugly face, named Mrs. Clark. She was just as bad as Tacamori, only different. Sometimes, I think it may have been me! Naw! But years later I was diagnosed with A.D.D. in spelling, reading and comprehension! Now, I'm writing a—--—book! Geeeesch!

Math ah, now there was a subject. I could do nothing wrong. Everything came easy and I aced the class without studying. Maybe there was something to the possibility of that abacus at birth as I mentioned before!

Gym, short for gymnastics, I think? Gene and I both had the same class because we chose to specialize in gymnastics. Anyone who had gymnastics had it as the last class. The teacher could keep you there for a hundred hours after class and not get in trouble because you had asked for it. When everyone in the regular gym class went outside to play baseball, football, basketball or track, like normal people, Gene, I and a few others stayed inside and made a great attempt at killing ourselves by hanging on bars, jumping off of the rings that were way up in the air, and turning flips on the ground with no foam rubber under us and with no sense of direction as to what was up or what was down. They expected us to land on our feet! Maybe this was not for a nice Jewish boy like me. Maybe I should go back to the math class where I belong!

Little did I know, at that time, that the gym class and the chances that I was taking in gym class would be part of my wanderlust, go for it, do things different than others and want to be out there life style that I will follow full time, as my life goes on. But speaking of doing things upside down and a little different, I'll get right back to the gym shit in a moment.

One evening while Gene and I were sitting in a Denny's restaurant (please don't tell anyone we were at Denny's), we were asked, "What time is it?" by some good looking chick in the adjoining booth. I told her and that was that! After she left with a couple of girls, I said to Gene, "If I had told her a lie, I might have been able to start a conversation with her." He said, "A lie is no good." I said, "So, if I just showed her my watch and it read the wrong time, would that work?" Gene said, "I guess so, but why would you set your watch so that you don't know what the time really is?" I looked at my watch. I wore it with the face inside so there was less of a chance scratching the clear plastic face. (Notice, I didn't say crystal? There is a reason for that.) I noticed that I had to twist my arm and shoulder inward more to really see what time it was. I also noticed that if I just lifted my arm to look at my watch, it was easier to see but the time was a little harder to read. So, I reset my watch so that the re-setting knob was in the twelve o' clock position and not where the number twelve should be. Actually, there weren't any numbers on my watch anyway, just lines to designate numbers. So, that way, at a glance I could see where the little hand and the big hand were as well. The next time someone asks me the time, I can just glance at my watch and say, "It is five to five," and as I show the watch to whomever, I can say five to five and the person, will say, "That's not what your watch says. It says ten after eight," and the conversation starts. Hard to believe that after some fifty plus years, I still set my watch that way. The only difference today is that the people who ask me, "What time is it," at our age now, can't see shit any way. Now, where was I?

It didn't take long to find out what our long suits were. We had to compete in five events in order to be on the team and represent our school. I had very weak wrists so that eliminated the side horse. However, I would have made a great faygalah. (Yiddish slang for gay or lesbian). Gene was real long and lanky so he was out of free ex and tumbling. We both took high bar, parallel bars, rings and long horse. I took free ex and tumbling (six events). Gene took side horse for his fifth event. I was probably about 5'8" as I entered the tenth grade and about one hundred and eighty pounds and a muscle or two. (Svelte, compared to a few years ago. Hardly look Jewish now and don't cry much either, except when a Mexican beats the shit out of me!) I will take a guess that my measurements were about thirty-eight, thirty-four and forty. But, when you are fifteen/sixteen those aren't too bad. The Jewish baby fat is gone, and there is just regular fat! You should see me now at sixty-seven! Oi Vay! (Oi Vay is a yiddish term, meaning Oi Vay). But, not to precede myself, when I got out of college, I weighed one hundred sixty-five pounds and had a forty-two inch chest, a twenty-eight inch waist, and even today don't have a clue how big my ass was. But, the women always said I had a cute one!

Gymnastics was grueling. Between the gaining muscle and the losing of weight, as time went on and when a girl said, "Are you on a team?" I could say, "Yes." It felt good! The bad thing about that was that the girls had no clue what gymnastics was. The girls only had interest in football, baseball and basketball. Actually, it was not a problem. I was so into myself about gymnastics that I didn't care. Remember, I had set a school record in the fifty yard dash in junior high school. I actually never thought that was possible, and it felt great. Why couldn't I excel in this sport? Most of us guys actually showed off for the other guys who were in the other schools. They all knew how tough it was and how much work was put into it. It was a competition! Not a one handed catch, one time to be a hero or a fifty yard run to get laid. We walked away with bloody hands on a regular basis from the rings and the high bar. We were knocked out when our hands lost the grip on the high bar or the rings. We went flying off into space upside down and hit the floor. We pulled shoulders out of joint and had to come back in two days and try the same trick again. We didn't have three guys behind us to fill in the spot when we got hurt. We got up, got back on, and did the trick again until we had it right. To this day, I watch the Olympics and especially the gymnastics. I watch with envy as I see those heroes in my eyes, doing tricks that were not even heard of in my day. We thought doing a double back flip was the toughest trick in the world. I, even to this day, have a blood spot about six inches around on a training mat at Ganesha High School from trying it. I was out for ten minutes. That may have been what kept me from being great! Today, a double back flip is mandatory. But after all I have seen and all I know in the gymnastics world, I have to take my hat off to the girls who do the balance beam. To me, it is the most amazing thing of courage, skill, agility and dedication I have ever seen. Can you imagine me doing the beam and missing? Maybe they all started out as men and missed once? Could be!

Then, there was choir. About a month into choir, Gene, three girls, and I who had been singing together for a few years in choir, were asked to be a madrigal. "WHAT? What the hell is a Madrigal?" I asked the boss, (instructor) Mr. Frank Cummings, the director of choir, and he said it is a special group of ten or twelve guys and girls, equal numbers, that go places and sing for other schools, business organizations, men's clubs, and so on and so forth. They do not do things like the choir does. They don't stand still. They don't have to look straight ahead and watch the director. They don't have to practice like the choir and for the most part, they do what feels good to them, as they feel it, while performing. What is required is that you know your stuff so you don't embarrass your school and your director. It seems to me that had happened, in the past, only in reverse. (Remember the choir incident?) So, Madrigals it is!

Now, I am going to high school and am taking the bus everyday with this Mexican guy looking at me on the way home almost every day. I hated English and the teacher but loving gym, madrigals, auto and metal shop. Math was so so! Maybe just too easy!

As I remember it, the fair started about five days or so after school started and we got off half day to go to it with our free ticket. One of the girls in Madrigals (Judy, a cute, pudgy, happy face little blonde) asked me and Gene if we wanted to go with her to the fair. Her father was going to pick her up on Friday, after the half day at school, and drop her off at the fair. We both said "Ok, that's great!" I told Gene that I could not come up with a lot of money so I may have to hang back a little if you guys do stuff. He said he would bring enough for both of us, and when I get flush, I could pay him back. To this day, I still remember that kind of kindness and try to return the favor to others. So, comes Friday and Gene, Judy, Val, also from the madrigals and I went to the fair. (This might have been a date, and I didn't even know it!) This time it was a little different than the last when that I went to the fair a year ago. I paid to get in! We went on rides, ate cotton candy, saw displays, drank coke and lemonade, feasted on hot dogs on a stick, (well not the girls, nothing changes), went to the petting zoo, and even saw horses run in a circle for money. We thought about betting on them but no one knew how and we thought we might get caught (under age) and go to jail. I thought about calling Bill to see how to do that kind of stuff, but cell phones were not yet invented and a dime was still hard to come by. (Isn't that how much a text message costs today?) One thing led to another and soon it was eleven o' clock. Pick up time! I think we must have spent ten hours at the fair, and I don't think I knew anything more about either of the girls than I did before we entered the gates. But other romantic female interests, at that time, were not even on my mind. I was with (my woman) Alma! We had kissed, and she was the one.

School went on as usual for the next ten days but just about every night I found an excuse (to tell mom and dad) to leave the house and to go to the fair. I had a free ticket to get in. The hole in the fence! I just had to watch out for the Mexicans. The second night I was not very lucky, but Bill, Roger and Owen were with me when we met head on with you know who? The Mexicans! Now, if you remember, these guys told me not to tell anyone about the ticket free entrance, and here I have a plethora of dudes walking through like we owned the place. Now, we four are not exactly Coxe's army. Me, the chicken shit Jew, that just got beat to within an inch of his life from one Mexican. Roger, if he got hit in the face, it would explode twenty zits, and he'd die from lack of inner water and tissue. Owen I know nothing about, but as I look at him, he is hiding behind Roger and Bill. Bill is a f—g midget! Great, just great! We are doomed! The (I think) leader of the ten or twelve Mexicans is a smaller one. Not that they are all tall, because they are not. In fact, I think the tallest one was five eight or so, but they all weighed no less than two hundred pounds, and some of them had hair on their face. The leader, walked over to me and looked up at me, as he is only five four or so, and said, "I thought I told you not to tell anyone about this secret way in." (I didn't think he knew what the word entrance meant.) I said, "They were cops and forced me to tell them." All of the short fat guys started to laugh. The leader said to me, "Do you think that is funny?" I said, "No, but your hombres did." Where in the hell I ever came up with the word hombres I'll never know, but it just came out of my mouth. Believe it or not, my mouth has been getting me into trouble ever since. He, the boss, looked at the rest of his merry men and then looked back at me and said, "We will meet under the arch some day, and I will kill you." We all went in through the secret pass way. (At no charge, I might add.)

When we got in and went our separate ways, white to the right and brown to the left, I asked Bill what the heck did he mean about the arch way and he will kill me? Bill said, "He's bluffing and to not worry about it". Great, just f—g great! He's going to kill me, and Bill says not to worry. "What is the arch way?? Come on, Bill, you know everything, tell me." "OK," Bill said. "Follow me." So, we walked to the entrance of the fun zone. Bill pointed at the top of the entrance. There is a great big arch, not unlike McDonalds arch, but much bigger as to encompass the whole entrance way into the fun zone. It was a large, bright yellow arch with stars and stripes, and different fun designs on it. It was bright and fun looking as to represent the entrance to a fun zone. As I am facing it, in back of me was the horse race track and on my left was a lot of the housed exhibits. The entrance was lit very well, I am sure, to create a happy atmosphere as you entered the fun zone. So, what did he mean about killing me here? Bill was a little vague on this subject, but he said he thought that this was where the Mexicans, whites and the blacks met to fight. Fight! What fight? Jesus Christ, I'm going to get the shit beat out of me again! I'm starting to run out of excuses of why I leave home at night and why I don't come back until Mom and Dad are in bed. They are going to think I am a criminal. WHAT? Shit! Stealing magazines, stealing cars for joy rides, glove box thieves and now gang fights! One year ago my biggest problem was how not to take my little brother with me when I went somewhere. What next, assassinate the president? Anyway, we spent the rest of the night having fun in the fun zone although I did spend a lot of time looking over my shoulder.

School went on as usual, and I had a great time in Madrigals. It truly was a feel-free singing group. We dressed differently, and we could intermingle with not only each other as we sang but with the audience, as well. We sang songs from musicals and acted out the parts like, "We ain't got dames" from South Pacific. We got so good at singing that Gene, Judy and I thought we'd start a trio and try to perform and get paid for it. Her last name was Button so we called ourselves "Button and

Beaus." One of the guys from the madrigals (much later on we found out that he was a little light in the loafers) was Freddie. He was Ok as a singer but was a gifted pianist. We got him to play for us. I would have used the words "play with us," but you need to read the words, a few lines back, in the parenthesis. We never, as I recall, got paid for our talent, but we did get a lot of gigs for free and Loved all of them.

I had noticed some guys around school wearing black jackets with white leather stripes around the upper arm area. They were called letterman jackets. I noticed that some of them had a design on the back. I particularly was entranced with the ones that had a hobo with a stick over his shoulder and a bag on the end of the stick and a small dog on his right walking beside him. There was a name above the hobo. It read "Drifters." The design was multi-colored and very attractive. One day, I saw a guy who was in gymnastics with me wearing one of them. I called him over and asked him, "What's the deal with the logo jacket?" He said it was a club. "Want to join?" I asked what kind of a club? He said a very special one. I said, "WOOO! Are you going to tell me or am I going to have to guess?" (I would have said "kick your ass," but he knew me and that would have been a waste of words). He said, "You know Roger, right?" "Ask his big brother." This is getting to be super secret over a freaking jacket.

Well, I did see Roger's brother not too long after and asked him about the mystery club. He said they call themselves the Drifters and what they basically do is fight with the niggers and the Mexicans. These guys must be really tough. I know how tough the Mexicans are first-hand, and these guys beat up both colors? Roger's brother said, "Not at the same time, dummy. The leaders of each gang, aka club, meet with each other somewhere and pick a time when and where to meet. Then, they rumble. If you want to see first-hand what's happening, hang out at the fun zone. When you see two gangs there, follow them but stay way behind or you will be killed." (Didn't I hear that somewhere before?) Now, I am not much of a fighter but have had a little experience lately with the brothers, Bob and Jimmy. What I wanted to do was to get even with that asshole Mexican who beat the shit out of me for no reason. Just to do it! So, not knowing what I was in for, I joined the CLUB. I went to a couple of meetings and found out that all they do is call blacks and Mexicans lots of nasty names and make plans to kill them. I told the guys in the club that I don't know how to fight with anyone much less kill someone. They all laughed. I didn't see what was so funny. They said they would teach me. I always left the meeting feeling that I may have bitten off way more that I could chew. Hell, I am only a 10th grader and only want to get even with the one Mexican who whipped my butt. Not annihilate the race!

Although it seems I am on the threshold of murder, I still have my relationship with Gene. I just don't tell him what the heck is going on. Anyone with a sister named Neenepoo, I really didn't think he'd suspect.

Gymnastics went on as usual. The Madrigals went on as usual and the trio "Button and Beaus" plus one went on as usual. School went on as usual with everyday getting closer to owning my weapon of mass destruction. A car!

The fair was finally over, and I never got to fight anyone. However, I noticed that this Mexican kid in school always kept looking at me.

One night I was over Knuckle Head's for a poker game. Alma, his sister, said, "While you are waiting for the other guys, let's go for a walk." It was in late October or maybe November and already dark. I said, "Ok," and we went about a hundred yards. She stopped me and asked me to kiss her. I said, "Ok." Today, I would never have said anything but just have done it. With my luck, (with the time I took) between the O and the K, she could have changed her mind by then. We kissed for a half hour, and I was really getting aroused. I wasn't really sure what was happening, but I sure liked it. She put my hand on her chest. I was ready to go home and to burn my magazines. I had the real stuff now. Then, while I was rubbing her chest and really not knowing what to do (not unlike today!), she dropped her hand between my legs and started to rub, also. I don't know if she really knew what she was doing, but I had no knowledge one way or the other. I just knew it was as good as Barney and maybe better. I could feel myself getting wet. Kind of an ooze or drip! Just about then, she said, "We better go back. The guys are probably there by now."

This was my first experience with the term "prick teaser," only I didn't know it then and am not sure if she did either. Obviously, I didn't know very much at all. We all have to start somewhere. I went to the game and felt that all the guys knew what went on and were looking at my wet spot.

Now, in the next three or four weeks or so, Alma and I had gone for many walks. Things got wetter and better. Alma had the use of her dad's car so we went for a drive once in a while. We went to the cemetery and would park and make out for an hour or so. By this time I was feeling all of her parts and she mine. In fact, I got my first oral sex there in the car in the cemetery and trust me, the only thing that was dead there were the bodies that were six feet under. This shit was really great. It had been about two months now, and I thought we were falling in Love. Well, at least me. Although we still had not had intercourse, everything else we did and many times!

At this part of my life, I thought I could have taught John Holmes a thing or two. (Once again, for you younger guys and gals, John Holmes was vice president of the Soviet Union in the late fifties and defected to Iran, and part of him became the leader of that country.) I even started to shower after work and put on clean clothes before I saw Alma. I am pushing fifteen and three quarters and now bring on that bar mitzvah man shit!

One day, Alma said her cousin and boy friend were coming over the following Saturday. They wanted to go to the mountains to play in the snow. Would I like to go with them? Anything to be with Alma! Sure, it sounds like fun. We lived very close to Mt. Baldy. It was a very tall mountain but had only limited skiing resources. There were plenty of places to hike and sled. Saturday came along and so did Alma's cousin with her beau in tow. They showed up in his pick-up truck. This was in the fifties, so there were no back seats. Alma and I bundled up with heavy coats and a blanket or two and then jumped into the truck bed. The cuz and beau were in the WARM front seat, and we headed off to Mt. Baldy. The drive was only about twenty minutes or so to the base of the mountain.

It was still pretty warm as we got to the base. Fifty-five maybe! Then, we started up the hill. We finally got to a spot where we could stop and hike a little. We must have been about seven or eight thousand feet high. It was pretty cold, but we had our Loves to keep us warm. Or, so I thought. It had not snowed up there for a week or so. There was plenty of snow but also some bare areas where the snow had melted.

We got out of the pick up and stood around for a while and yakked. Then, Alma said to her cousin's date (I really can't remember either's name), "Let's go up here and see what is over the rise past the trees." He said, "Ok," and they started to walk away from the remaining two. I wasn't sure what to make of it as I really didn't know either the cousin or her friend. It even crossed my mind that maybe they were going to kill me. Then I realized they had nothing to get from me so that was out. Alma's cousin said, "If they are going to go that way, we will fix them and go this way."

Now, I am walking with a girl I met maybe two hours ago and my Love has gone AWOL. What the heck is going on? I am obviously the novice here. (The John Holmes shit is out!) She takes my hand and starts to walk up a grade and over a small rise. By this time, I could not see Alma anymore. I asked what's her name, what was going on, and she replied, "Nothing. We just have a little different interest right now." I said, "What are you talking about?" She said, "Alma said, that you kiss much better than my boyfriend does, and she wants me to make a comparison." I didn't even think why Alma was kissing this babe's boyfriend. I just said, "She said that?" "Yes, so I am to find out the truth. Ready?" Before I could say yes or no, she had a lip lock on me. She kissed pretty well! So, one kiss led to another and to another and to another. Then, she said, "I am really cold." She was in the warm truck on the way up here and only had a sweater on when we started to do our little walk. I said, "Stand real close, and I will keep you warm." (I could have offered her my heavy jacket that I was wearing, but didn't. Chivalry is dead at these cold temperatures.) She said, "Let's lie down over there and keep close for a while." (I was starting to feel like the lamb that was being lead to slaughter.)There was a dry spot where the snow had melted. We meandered over, and I did as she suggested. (I have been taking orders from women ever since.) We started kissing again and pretty soon we had our hands under each other's clothing (I think originally to keep warm but that reason halted abruptly) and were feeling each other up. This went on for about a half hour. Then, she pulled her skirt all the way up and took off her panties. I undid my belt and slid my pants down and we made Love. It was obviously the first time for me, and I thought it was great. I just wish I could remember her name! I do remember her getting up and going over to a pool of water where some snow had melted to wash herself off. I was still laying there in a trance. (Nothing changes) Just watching her! When I was finally able to move, I got up and thought about washing myself off also, but I could not imagine putting that probably thirty-four degree water on my privates. They didn't deserve that as well as they did today. So, I pulled up my pants, buttoned and belted up, and said that was great to her as I gave her a warm hug! She just looked at me and smiled. We started to walk back down the grade towards the truck, and I, assume, Alma.

I was just a little in back of what's her name when I noticed a big wet spot on her skirt right where there shouldn't be one. When we would return and her boyfriend would see it, we would be in big trouble. I told her it was there. She said, "Let's go back to where we made Love." We walked back, and she laid in the pool so her whole skirt got wet. When we got back to the truck, Alma and he were there. My new Love said that she had slipped and had fallen in a pool of melted snow, and they went for it. I never saw my new date ever again. It was hard to ask Alma about her walk.

Alma and I never went out again but stayed friends for a while. She finally met someone, got married, and moved out. To this day, I don't remember who broke my cherry or what really went on that day. But, I really do think that the girls had a plan. Maybe the cousin had a fixation to do a cherry or something like that. But how could Alma agree to that? I guess I'll never know. But, I can tell you this. She started a hell of a chain reaction that has lasted a very long time.

I am not sure if Alma broke my heart or I just lost interest in females, but my Love life came to a screeching halt for a while. My major interest turned to cars. Oh yeah, and a magazine once in a while!

Now, speaking of cars, one night Bill, Roger, Owen and I were really bored. "Let's go steal a car." Not sure who said it, but by now it could have been me. "OK, but not around here." We were kind of hot because of the glove box thing that was still on going and the car/ boat thing and a few other one nighters that I can't remember right now but similar to the naked running on the highway stuff. The four of us started walking toward the fair grounds. We walked about a mile or so up over the viaduct that went over the freeway. This area was the older and well-established area, but the viaduct was still dirt. We decided that this was a nice place to rip off a car, because the inhabitants in the area were older and probably already asleep. As we walked and turned with the road, we saw a really nice car, fairly new and not real close to the house. It was almost as if there had been another car in front of it that was put into the garage. Bill said, "This is going to be a snap!" First, he got into the car. The door was unlocked. He yanked the dome light out. He took off the emergency brake and let the car roll out onto the street and down the grade a little bit. At that point, we all jumped in as Bill was working on the ignition. Not more than thirty seconds, the engine was running. We drove off and went to the back road that was behind the tract of homes where we lived and extended about five blocks further until it came to a dead end. We had named this road "Magazine Road", because one day a truck flipped over that was full of magazines. They were all over the road for weeks. Unfortunately, not Playboys! We all took turns driving. The only thing that Roger did worse than playing guitar was driving. This was one scary guy behind the wheel! But, of course, not only did he think of himself as the second coming of Elvis but Mario Andretti, also. On one side of the road was the railroad track that separated the homes from the bottom of Elephant Hill. On the other side was a hay field that had recently burned down! In fact, this road was where my dad took me to learn how to drive while nearly beating me to death. After a while we got bored and decided to roll the car. A little extra excitement can't hurt. But where? This road was too close to home and might cause suspicion. Why not on the dirt viaduct close to where we borrowed the car? Great! That's it, and it will be easier to roll on dirt anyway. We drove up to the especially reserved area just for us and got ready. Someone said to Bill, "Have you done this before?" Bill replied, "No, but I have seen it on TV so many times it will be like second nature." "OK, let's go for it." Do you think any of us gave even a little inkling as to any harm that might incur to the passengers, or maybe that the car could explode? Or even how bad the owner would feel? Nope! Not a thought! Now, we were about two blocks from this car's original parking space, and we will have to get out of there pronto. We made our getaway plans as we were all going to go in different directions. Bill said, "Are you ready?" We said, "Go for it," and held on to the handles on the inside of the roof (sometimes known as leg stirrups), as Bill hit the gas. Not sure how fast we were actually going, but I suspect not more than twenty or so. Bill hit the brakes and turned the wheel to the left. We flipped the car over but only to its side. We were expecting it to roll over and over like in the movies. Bill's side was the exit side so he opened the door with the help of Roger and proceeded to climb out. Roger followed, then, Owen, then me. We looked at the car and then at each other and laughed and then ran like hell in the direction of our escape routes. We went directly home so not to be found together in case the cops were riding around and spotted us. Now, this was a lot of fun. I don't remember doing it at any other time, but what I do remember was the headlines in the newspaper the next day. It read: Police chief's car stolen and rolled!

Now, as I get closer to my driving days, I am still in gymnastics and Madrigals. I am still losing a little weight and gaining a little muscle and am getting friendly with the girls in Madrigals. Nothing romantic but I'm not afraid to talk to them and go places with them when I was invited. Gene, on the other hand, was more social than I. The coach in gymnastics, Mr. Vern Evans, was real happy with me and the same with Mr. Frank Cummings, the director of the Madrigals. In fact, Coach Evans was really happy I went out for the team, and Mr. Cummings wanted me to do a solo when we performed. The team was great, but I didn't have enough confidence to do the solo so I turned it down and Gene got the part.

Chapter Eight

It is birthday time and the number sixteen really didn't mean a thing to me although Mom and Dad had thrown me a little birthday party with some of my friends. What it did represent was

A driver's license!

My dad took me to the DMV. I stood in line for what seemed like six years. Finally, I got to the desk. They did a mug shot of me. My dad signed for me, and I was given my temporary license and was told that the real license would come in the mail in about four to six weeks. Shit! I got it! I got it! Just like James Bond, (007) I have a license to kill! I can't tell you how happy I was. I really have a driver's license! Now Mom and Dad can go get their own shit. I don't need them to be with me when I go somewhere. I got it! I got! My driver's license!

Now, I needed a car. I guess I could steal one! I knew how to do it. I needed to get realistic here. On a few occasions I had stolen my dad's forty-eight Buick and went joy riding. I would get the keys that were usually on the table. When Mom and Dad went to sleep, I would sneak outside and drive it. I never got caught or at least they never said anything. Driving Dad's car would be perfect for me. I knew how to drive it. Now, I don't remember what day it was, but it was a school day. The first day of my driving career! I asked Dad if I could take the Buick to school that day. Kind of like a birthday present. Dad said he didn't need it so it would be fine. He slapped me on the back of my head (zetz) wished me good luck, and gave me the keys. Mom was not at all for it and looked worried. I gave her a hug and told her that I would be careful. She smiled with a major lack of confidence, and I was gone.

At that point and for some reason, I thought of my cousin Arnold in Philadelphia. I wanted to call him and tell him about getting my driver's license. I remembered that he was a year younger. The last time that I saw him, he was pushing a Good Humor cart with a bicycle attached selling ice cream to make money for college. That was dumb, I thought. College! What fun is more school! Today, he owns three pharmacies, has four kids and seven grandkids, a wife of forty-four years and travels all around the world on a regular basis. How boring is that! Stealing cars, that's where it is!

I had already told Bill and Roger that there was a chance that I might be able to pick them up and drive them to school with me. I made the calls and picked them up. Man, was I stylin!

We left about a half hour early so that I could cruise around the school and show off. The guys and chicks would spot me and think that I was cool now that I was driving and had my own car. Most of the kids were driven to school by their parents even if they had their license. The kids would drive, but the parent would switch seats when they got to school and really drop off the kid. The parent would drive home and pick them up after school, and the kid would drive home. Not me, I am MAN! Thirteen plus! I have my own car, or at least it seemed that way to the other kids. Now, the whole morning as we went from class to class, my thirty-eight inch chest was about a fifty now. The lunch bell rang. This time, instead of going to the cafeteria for lunch, we met in the school parking area and all packed into my car. I drove to the "A & W" for food. There was Bill, Roger, Owen, Gene and two girls Bill invited (picked up) and me. There were seven of us in a six-seat vehicle. The Buick had a straight front seat so there were three of us in front and four in the back seat. We had an hour for lunch so we cruised around first to show off again. It might have been for the two chicks Bill had picked up. I was really cool. The "A & W" was about two blocks from school. We used to walk it in four minutes. This time with the car it took about twenty minutes. We got our food, ate, and now it was time to cruise a little before I needed to park and make class. So, I cruised around the school a couple of times at about ten miles per hour. As the last circle came before I was going to park, I was stopped at the corner of the school and had to make a right turn to get on to the main street to get to the parking lot. Just before I made the right turn, I saw a couple of chicks standing right on the corner. Bill said to punch it as we turned so that the tires will screech and smoke as we burned rubber around the corner. ("Punch it" means to put the gas pedal all the way to the floor. American slang and had nothing to do with my cousin Arnold or a Mexican.) I thought it would be cool for the girls in back of the car and the ones standing on the corner. They would look at me and think it was so cool, also. Being cool in those days was the ginchiest. Ginchiest means cool. (Surf slang.) So, Joe Cool, me, hit the gas pedal as the car turned. As we turned, the tires burnt rubber and screeched for at least forty or fifty feet. Smoke going everywhere! How cool was that! We are all laughing and having a great time until I looked in the rear view mirror and saw a cop with his lights on. I pulled over. He got out of his black and white, walked over to me, and asked to see my driver's license. At this point I am not a happy camper. There was no laughing any more by anyone. Hell, Bill was probably sweating it more than I. He could have had his picture on the post office wall for all I know. The cop took my license and walked back to his car for what seemed a day and a half. We are all speculating as to what is going to happen. A ticket? A warning? Does it affect us all or just the driver? No one is even thinking that we are all late for class. The cop finally comes back and says, "I see that your birthday was yesterday. Happy Birthday!" I said, "Thanks. What is going to happen officer" He said "I am issuing you a citation for excessive speed on the take off." (I remember those exact words today.) He said that because I was a minor, that a parent and I would have to appear before the judge who will determine the course of action. You will receive a notice in the mail as to the day and time of your appearance. He also said to please drive more safely. He handed me the ticket and left.

Not a word was said in the car. I drove to the parking lot, parked, and we went to class. The school day ended. I met the guys at my car. We talked for a while. Well, I did most of the talking. It sounded almost like crying, but I was more than thirteen years of age and not so fat anymore so it had to be something else. My dad was going to shit when he finds out I have a ticket. First day with my license and I screw up. I waited for sixteen years and now I could lose it. Bill said, "Don't tell him and when it comes in the mail, cop it. We will get someone to pose as your dad when you have to go to court." What a friend! Bill, you're the ginchiest! That was the plan. Gene thought it was a bad idea.

Some days I would have the car and some days, not. The days that I did not, I would have the bus driver drop me off about a couple of blocks before the school and walk the rest of the way. Didn't want to be seen getting off a bus. Not cool!

For the next month or so I talked to dad about him getting another car so that I could have the Buick. Eventually, he got a nineteen fifty-four Cadillac, but we shared the Buick for the rest of the year.

Gene and I still stayed close because of Madrigals and gymnastics. We didn't go to many schools to perform, but we did practice a lot in and out of school. We had an edge over the other Madrigals. We had Freddy, the gay pianist. He would take the sheet music home at night and sometimes Gene, Judy, Valerie and I and sometimes a few others in Madrigals, would practice into the late night at someone's house. This not only helped me learn the songs better but also kept me away from the bad guys. When I was singing I didn't think of the bad boys. When I was stealing, I didn't think of singing. When I was doing gymnastics with Gene, I was getting a better body and I really liked that. By the end of the year, neither one of us made the gymnastics team, but we were starting to look pretty good. I was losing weight and Gene was putting it on. Both of us were gaining muscle.

All through the school year I was in contact with the Drifters Club. They were obviously a gang as I watched more closely. I was not really a fighter, as you might have noticed by now, but I still remember that beating I took at the hands of a Mexican.

Speaking of Mexicans, that same one who kept looking at me on the bus and all through the whole school year finally approached me, and called me over. He said, "Hey Dogface, get your ass over here or I will kick the shit out of you." I had no idea what was going on except that it was like déjà vu with the other Mexican awhile back. I walked over to him, kind of scared. He was near the edge of the school boundary just on the grass. I said, "What do you want? My name is not Dogface." He said, "You are a dog face to me, you Jew bastard." I turned and started to walk away, but he grabbed me and said, "Don't you walk away from me until I tell you to," and slapped me in the face. I said, "What do you want? I haven't done anything to you so leave me alone!" He said, "I don't want to see you in school again, do you understand?" He walked away. I didn't know what to think. I had to go to school! I did see him a couple of times more through the school year, but he didn't say anything to me.

In the last couple of weeks of school, I saw him again. We were walking off campus at about the same time. He came over to me and said, "Follow me you dogface Jew" I said, "No I need to go home." He came over to me and started to fight with me. I couldn't run. He had me by the throat and started punching me and kept on punching me. I started to cry. I remembered it hurt. Then, I started to punch back, more out of fear then defense or offense. The more I punched back, the harder it seemed he hit me. He finally left. Once again, I got the shit beat out of me by a Mexican and don't know why. I found out later that his name was Montoya. I didn't think fighting was fun, but Montoya awakened a sleeping giant. Or so it seemed.

One day I walked into the house, and my dad told me to sit down. I said, "What's going on?" He said, "I received a call from the police department about you not appearing in court for a traffic ticket." Shit! I did not want to hear that. (I had gotten the ticket when it came in the mail and threw it away. I figured if I didn't show up, it would just go away. If this happened, I could just say I didn't see any mail for me that was a ticket.) "What ticket, Dad?" That was definitely the wrong thing to say. "You will not leave the house until we go to court with the exception of school. Do you understand?" "What about work? We need the money." "Not that much" he said. "Our court date is so and so and until then, your ass is grass and I am the lawn mower. Understand?" I was screwed. No car, no play, no work. In retrospect, I probably got off easy as Dad was too weak to beat the shit out of me which, when healthy, he had no problem doing in the past. Had this happened a little earlier, I would have figured that he would hire Montoya to do his dirty work!

We went to court, and I got a restricted license. I could only drive to and from school, work, and any errands that I was asked to do by my father and mother for a six month period. There was a dollar amount I had to pay as well. Dad took care of it, and we went home. Six months! This was going to be hell! I am out of school in a couple of months. The summer will be here, and no car for six months. Six Months! Shit! I can't tell you all the plans I had for the summer, and now, I am screwed. Just screwed! I waited for so long to be able to drive to the beach in the summer and now no car or license. I thought my bar mitzvah was to correct all of this kind of shit. Thirteen, I am Man!

No, I am grounded! This adulthood sucks. Dumb rules! Damn cops! I learned early to blame stuff on females whether it was their fault or not. Now, I have someone new to blame, cops. Through the next fifty years I averaged two tickets a year. All of them were speeding tickets except for the very first one. It was written as excessive speed on the take off. The last one, hopefully, was an illegal right turn in 2007. That one was ok, because I was hurrying into the Orleans Casino in Las Vegas. They all have something in common. The tickets were all the cops' fault, not mine. Had they not seen me do anything wrong, they wouldn't have given me the tickets.

Graduation and then summer as a sixteen and a half year old without a car. I'm doomed. Gene's father got him a car, actually a truck, a pick up truck. Gene had a couple of chromed spluie tubes put on (large exhaust pipes) that ran up the back side of the cab doors like big eighteen wheelers have. They sounded great. He named his truck, "Caldonia".

Now that Gene has a truck, and I have a bike again, I started to ride a lot more. The summer was here, and bikes were in vogue. I did a lot of riding around my tract that year and started talking to some of the kids I had met a while back. Primm, Cynthia, Jane, Bob and Jimmy and a few new ones. I met a new guy named Bob Smith. He was about three or four years older than I and was out of school. Unbeknownst to me, he had been out of school for years, maybe since ninth grade! He was having an end-of-school party and asked me if I wanted to go. I said, "Yes." He had invited a couple of the guys I knew and some chicks, also. I asked him why it was an end-of-school party if he didn't go to school. He said, "It was really his sister's party, Darlene." "Oh, that's cool."

The party was fun. I met Darlene and was fascinated with her. She looked very pretty to me but very aloof. Now, as fascinated with her as I was, I was more intrigued with Bob. He was studying to be a stunt man for Disney Studios. We would walk around, and he'd say, "Watch me." He would climb up on a house roof and have me pretend to shoot him. He would fall off and instead of landing on his feet; he would land on his back and roll. This guy was nuts! (Like I'm not)! I knew right from the start that we would be friends. As time went by, he would run in front of one of us who were driving and jump on the front of the car, hit it head on, and roll over the hood. He did it a few times to my dad when Dad was driving and scared the shit out of him. Bob and I became good friends; however, later on I became more interested in his sister, Darlene.

The not driving was a killer, but the stay at home thing was workable. At night when Mom and Dad would go to bed, I snuck out of my bedroom window and met with the guys.

I talked my dad into letting me continue to work at the Texaco Station. The need for money, I am sure, had something to do with it. One day, while I was working there, the boss said that he wanted to sell his Forty-nine Ford. I asked how much he wanted and he told me. Don't really remember the dollar amount, but I thought it was a deal. I asked him if he would take payments, and he said he would. Now, there was only one thing standing in the way of me and my new weapon. Dad! So, the next three or four days of conversation went something like this. "Please?" "NO!" "Please?" "NO!" "Please?" "NO!" And so on and so on. Well, after a week or so, I saw a little weakness starting in my dad's voice. I asked my boss if he would mind if I took the Ford to Tijuana and get it "Tuck and Rolled." I said it looked promising for the purchase, and I would pay for the "Tuck and Roll" job even if Dad would not let me buy it.

In those days they were the coolest seat covers, and all the guys with cool cars had it done. Tuck and Roll! My dad called it Tuck and Schmuck. (Schmuck, Yiddish, for a large penis) It cost hundreds of dollars here in the states but a fraction of that in Mexico. The boss said, "OK." Now, how to do this while I am on restrictions? Hmmm. I know . . . , I will tell Dad that the boss wants me to go and get it done so it will make the car more valuable so that he can get a higher price for it. It worked. Dad fell for it. I made the necessary arrangements and headed to Tijuana with Bill, of course. This was sometime in April or March, I think. We left on a Friday night right after school. It was a four or five hour drive from Pomona, to Tijuana and about the same to have the work done. Hell, I'd be back in time to go to work at the Texaco Station by eight or nine in the morning. Bill and I jumped into the short and tullied down to the Mexican boarder. I was glad I had someone with me. *You know how Mexicans and I get along.* Although now that I think about it, Bill wasn't much help last time!

We got there about eight-thirty or so. Friday night and Tijuana was rockin. There were Mexicans all over the place and almost as many sailors. The Mexicans all seemed to be looking at me. (Not too paranoid)! We drove around looking for the place for which I was told used cloth instead of paper for the Tuck and Roll. It seemed that every corner had a Tuck and Roll shop. We finally found the one that I was told about, pulled in, and immediately ten Mexicans were at the car. (I immediately got into a crouch position.) I could only think that this would be one hell of a beating I will never forget. However, they all seemed very cool. I asked for the boss, and he was standing right next to me. He said, "What can I do for you senor?" I said, "I was told about your shop and that you do the best Tuck and Schmuck, I mean Roll, and are very competitive, price wise." He said he was, and quoted me a price and a five hour job time. I told him that a friend of mine said that he had it done here and that it was much less than that. He came down in price. (I am sure that under his breath he called me a dog-faced Jew.) I paid him in advance. He said, "Come back in about five hours, and it will be done. It will be the best job that I will have ever seen. It will be even better than my friend's job. I said, "Great," and handed him the keys after that, Bill and I left.

Well, what do we do in Tijuana? Bill said, "Drink!" So, we walked down-town which was a couple of blocks from the Tuck and Roll shop. I had never seen anything like this. Every bar had a couple of guys trying to pull us in to their bar and a couple of girls hanging around that looked like they were fourteen or younger. They all advertised "All nude dancers." Bar after bar and block after block. Bill said, "Let's try this one." We walked in. It was called "The Blue Fox." Now, if you have been reading this book, you may have heard me say that I really can't remember this, or I think it was about this time or something to that effect more then once. Did I hesitate on the name of this bar? No! Why? Remember, I was sixteen, fifty plus years ago, and I still remember what went on in there. Even Bill was surprised. We sat down at the bar, and the bartender asked if we were eighteen. Before I could think of what to say, Bill said, "Nineteen and just enlisted." The bartender said, "What do you want?" I ordered a Seven and Seven, and Bill ordered a beer. Now, I turned towards the dance floor as I waited for my drink that, by the way, cost thirty-five cents. I saw a nice looking girl dancing with no top on. Hey, this is great, I thought. As I am watching the show, a chick sits next to me and starts rubbing my leg, rather high up, and says "Hello," in broken English. I wasn't sure what to do as there were a lot of Mexicans around. (I even gave thought that that could be Montoya in drag.) "Hi," I said back, and she smiled. Then one sat next to Bill. Not sure what she said, but Bill smiled.

The drinks came, and the show got better as the bottoms came off. I wasn't sure what to watch. The girls were whores, and they wanted me to pay them for sex. What was that all about? I wanted to check with Bill as what to do and how I should act and not to get the shit kicked out of me again while doing so. Bill seamed to be all tied up himself. I politely said, "No, thanks, maybe later." (It was like being in a clothing store, and being bugged by a pesky clerk. Almost!) I really didn't want later. I wanted now as her hands found the perfect spot, and I was getting excited. I immediately thought of Barney. May be this is how he learned what to do. I was not sure of anything right then, and she walked away. I started to watch the show as I had never seen a girl completely naked and dancing around like it was natural. I guess for her it was. One drink turned into another and pretty soon we were smashed. (Smashed, an American term for drunk.) I looked at my watch, and we still had three hours to go before the Ford was finished. Bill said, "Let's go bet at Jai Alai." What? "Jai Alai! We can make a few bucks and that way the Mexicans will be paying for our drinks." "Let's go." the Jewish drunk says!

So, we stumbled about a block or two and found the Jai Alai games. We bet about two or so games. Now, we had a lot less money than when we started. I don't even know what the hell I did and why. I said, "Let's go back to see the nude chicks again." We went back to the Blue Fox. This time there were no girls dancing around anywhere. We ordered our drinks and asked the bartender when the girls would return. He said, "Not for an hour or so but there is another show starting." If the girls were not coming back for an hour, what was the new show? I didn't think it could have been better than all the nude chicks dancing.

The lights got a little low, and some music started just like when the girls were dancing. As I was intensely watching the stage, I felt a hand on my leg again. It was another girl, just as pretty if not prettier than the first one, or I was a little more drunk by now. Anyway, she introduced herself. Then, this tall Mexican chick walks out onto the stage, and a drum beat starts. She starts banging her hips to the beat and starts to dance around. So far, I do not see anything different. Now, there were about fifty Mexicans and maybe half that many whites in this bar. Almost all of them were clapping and yelling something that sounded like "Donkey, Donkey, Donkey." The music got louder, and the clapping got louder. About three or four minutes into the dance, a small Mexican man walks out, and he's pulling a donkey on a rope. The music changes from a big drum beat to a slow, sexy tempo with a lot of saxophone in it. The lights got a little lower, and everyone seemed to get a little closer to the stage. I don't think there was a closed eye in the place. Even a passed out guy came awake. Bill and I looked at each other and with a gleam in our eyes, we smiled. I said "NO." Bill said, "MAYBE." The girl put her arms around the donkey's neck and then straddled her feet and legs around the donkeys butt just in front of his hind legs. She was upside down, hanging from the donkey, and then the donkey started to penetrate her. She wiggled around as to help him. Now, I don't know if you have ever seen an erection on a donkey, but it is huge. Even bigger than me! (Thought I'd put a little humor in as it is getting intense.) The music started to get louder. The saxophones were traded for a drum beat again. The girl started to scream. I was not sure what the donkey was saying, but in about five minutes or so, she quit and the show was over. However, did I get an education! What was even better, Bill didn't have it over me. We both saw it together. So, we both ordered a double and sat back with not much to say. It still was an hour until my car would be ready. Hmmmm, what to do? For one thing, we were both drunk so we said we can't drive home anyway. Let's just drink for a while. We sat there and talked about what we had just seen. More liked slurred about it. Maybe it was done with mirrors!

About that time two other girls came over and started playing with me, one on each side. Bill had the same treatment. Now, there were two girls, or maybe I was just seeing double. With being this inebriated and two girls, one on each side of me, had this happened today, I probably would have just passed out. But at this youthful age, all parts still worked. By this time, I didn't know who was pretty or who was not and could care less. The girls kept asking me if I thought they were pretty and which one I wanted, over and over. I finally made the mistake and asked how much. They said five dollars American. I was really not interested but for five bucks, I might be! Remember, I have only broken my cherry and that was awhile ago. Maybe I can use the experience. I might have forgotten how to do it. Hell, I don't know if I really knew what I was doing in the first place. So, being of the Jewish background that I am, I said, "FIVE BUCKS! Forget it!" One of them said how about two dollars for just one of us? (I think I missed a deal and didn't even know it!) I almost fell off the chair. I said, "Where do we go, I hope not right here." "No, over there" she said. She pointed to a little room about twenty feet away with a curtain for a door. I reached into my pocket and fumbled for the two bucks and gave it to her. She walked me to the room. Room! More like a closet with a short bench, maybe four feet long, and a Mexican blanket on it. Not giving any thought to how many other guys have been on this beautiful bench in the last five hours, she started to undo my belt. This was cool, I thought. I don't have to even undress myself. So, pants half-way down, and a guy stumbles through the door (curtain) with a chick and he says, "NO WAY!" The chick yanks on him. I guess they found another room as beautiful as mine. So, in about two minutes, I was pulling up my pants up and asking for a towel. I might as well been asking for my money back. I got zero, ziltch, nada, nothing. I got shown the way to the bar. Bill was still there with the same two chicks from when I left. He had a grin as big as the Grand Canyon. "Well, how was it?" I said, "I am not sure." He said, "Did you try to kiss her?" I said, "Yes, but she kept turning her head and wouldn't let me." He said, "Good." and started laughing his ass off. I couldn't figure out why. A month or so later, it finally came to me.

Now, it is about three in the morning and time to pick up the car. We took about an hour to go the two blocks or so but finally found the shop. The owner had put the car out on the street for us. We all went over and looked at the car. It was truly beautiful. What a great job they had done. We thanked him and started to get in the car and realized that we were way too drunk to drive. Bill and I agreed that we should get some coffee and maybe a morsel of food. We walked about another two blocks and found a cafeteria. We walked in and remembered that we were not to drink the water. Bill said, "You have had a ton of water in your Seven and Sevens. What do you think the ice cubes are made from?" "Right," I said, so that eliminated any worries about eating and drinking at this fine establishment. A really fat Mexican came over and gave us our food laden menus. We didn't need to order. We could have filled up from what was stuck to the menus. There was more food on the menu than the USA medi-vaced to Somalia. We were starving and ordered anyway. We had some food and about sixty five cups of coffee. Now, it's five o'clock ish, and I have to be at work at nine. Impossible! So, I will need to drive real fast. When it becomes light, about seven ish, I will call Chet (my boss) and beg off until eleven or so.

Under a panic we paid the bill and went to get the car. We were still pretty drunk but better. We walked about two or three blocks and could not see the car. We had been drinking so it was no shock. We walked around the block three times and no car. I said, "Maybe we are in the wrong block." "I am kind of lost," I said, "Let's find the shop and then we will find the car." We walked for an hour looking for the car and or the Tuck and Roll shop. Just about everything looked the same. Finally, we saw the Tuck and Roll shop. Now the car should be right over there. Nope, it's not. Well, maybe over there. Nope, it's not. Where the hell is it? Let's get rational here. We paid the guy right over there, and we walked out after it was done, right over there, right? Right! So, it has to be right there. It's not right there. Shit, it's gone! It can't be! It was there just an hour ago. It's gone. It's gone? What do you mean it's gone? Stolen! STOLEN? Can't be! Can be!

It's now seven o'clock, and a major panic sets in. We sobered up quick. Let's go to the police department and report it stolen. You never know. Maybe they already know where it is. We walked about five blocks and found the police department. They didn't speak as good of English as the whores did. We finally got the point across, filled out the paperwork, took their phone number, and started to hoof it home. All I could think about is the beating I was going to get from my dad, the firing I was going to get from my boss, and I would be working for the rest of my life to pay back my boss for the car. What I didn't know until the next day was that my boss had about a thousand dollars in tools in the trunk, and they were gone, also. How much crap can happen in a twenty-four hour period to one person? My whole life (all sixteen years) shot before my eyes in a second or so, I knew it was the end for me. Bill and I started to hitch hike from San Diego. We walked out of Tijuana, thumbs up, and our lives in wretched shape. I looked at Bill and said with a vengeance, "I hate Mexicans!"

It took about a half hour until we got a ride to Del Mar. Then, I had to face the music. It was about ten o'clock, and had I to make the calls. First, I called Chet, my boss, and told him what happened. He blew! He yelled that I would be working for the rest of my life to pay it back. (It seemed to me that I heard that somewhere.) He kept yelling and screaming. I could hear his father in the background yelling, "What the hell happened?" Finally, after I told him I would be back as soon as I could, we hung up. He never mentioned anything about me losing my job.

Now, the even larger phone call looms. Should I tell my dad the truth or make up some lie that coincides with the story I originally gave him? The truth seems to be in order. Take it like a man. (The thirteen year old, the Bar Mitzvah boy, the Man, SHIT!) I made the call. I told Mom, who answered the phone that I was robbed and that the car was stolen at gun point by five Mexicans. I have been in the police station for hours filling out papers and looking at mug shots. I have made a report with the Mexican authorities and should be home in about five or six hours. She could only say, "How are you? Are you all right? Did they hurt you? My son, Oi vay, my son Oi vay." So, I got the news to Mom, and she will break it to Dad. At least the news is broken, and he will have plenty of time to think about what he has to do and then maybe the anger will subside a little. No matter what I say or he thinks, I will get a beating.

Bill and I didn't have a lot of luck getting a ride home. (No luck, how can that be?) It was about eight o'clock at night when I finally arrived home. Bill went home with no problem. But me, that was a different situation. I thought about putting some leaves in my underpants before I walked in, but I am sixteen. Take it like a man. I opened the door, and my mom threw her arms around me and gave me a big hug and said, "Are you ok? Are you hurt?" "Are you hungry?" I figured this was the lull before the storm. I could not see my dad anywhere, so I figured he went to get the belt. I told Mom I was starving and hadn't eaten since five o'clock this morning. About the only truth I uttered in hours. She sat me down and put out a spread fit for a king. Mom was never the greatest cook although she had a few meals that were from the gods. As

I gorged myself, I asked where Dad was. Mom said he was lying down in the bedroom. "He was so worried about you; I think he must have fallen asleep. I will go wake him." I said, "No, don't. He can probably use the rest. Thanks for the food. I really needed it." "You are my son and anything for you my son. I Love you," said Mom. Mark came in and asked if he could have some of my food. Mom said, "Only when Chuck is done. He has had a very bad day." I could see the look in my brother's eyes and they said, "What did he do or destroy this time?" (I Loved being the number one son!) Dad never really said anything about the ordeal. Just a few questions and it was all over. What a relief that was. Like Bill said later, "I told you, lying is good." You gotta Love that guy!

Now, I am not only carless, restricted, and no potential in the near future of getting a car and I owe my boss the national debt. As I have said before, "I am screwed." Isn't it funny how we always notice the bad stuff and not the blessings? I did not lose my job. I didn't get the beating of my life. I got fed like a king, and Mom said that she Loves me. Something I never heard or saw in print from my dad until he was near death. Just his way, I guess.

I noticed in the paper (yes I can read) of a company named SCOA in West Covina that was advertising for help. Ah, the mind is working again. If I can get the job, I would need a car to get there. SCOA was about twenty miles from home. (I drive again)! SCOA was a big box store and probably the first or at least close to the first discount house ever. I asked Dad if I could apply and he said, "Ok, as long as it did not interfere with school."

I took his car and drove to West Covina. I was familiar with West Covina because gas in Pomona was usually about twenty-five cents a gallon and West Covina would have a gas war every two months or so. It would be five gallons for a dollar. I would drive there and fill up in West Covina. Hard to believe in today's market that a nickel a gallon would make a difference, especially driving twenty miles to save it. I applied for the job, and a few days later, I got a call to report on the job. I had worked it out so I worked at nights after school, something like four to nine. I kept my job at the Texaco station. Like I had a choice! SCOA started me at ninety-three cents an hour and said that after two months I would get a raise. I worked in the warehouse. This is as bad as my dad scraping pigs for Armour and Sons. A Jew in a warehouse, feh!

Now, I am going to school and working after school and on weekends. What a life for a sixteen year old. I would have off some week nights and every once in a while, a Saturday or a Sunday. That gave me time to go to town and to steal stuff with Bill and Roger and maybe have a date. Now that I have been laid twice, I need more women. Even though I don't know the name of the first girl with whom I was with, and paid two dollars for the second no name-lady of the night with whom I was with, I should have recognized that women were starting to cost me money. About a buck a piece! (Pardon the pun). Did I have more to learn!!!

My SCOA job in the warehouse lasted about three weeks, and then I was transferred to the Domestics Department. The manager was Max White, a nice little old Jewish man. He couldn't have stood more then five foot three. He may have been one of the nicest people I had ever met. He had spotted me in the warehouse and had me transferred. How he knew I was Jewish I don't know, but he said to me, in a whisper, that a nice Jewish boy should not be in a warehouse. (I didn't think it was that bad. I could only think of my dad's job scraping the hairs off pigs!) I could not have agreed more. I moved up to the Domestics Department and with it came a four cent an hour raise. Dad was proud. I was happy, too, ninety-seven cents an hour! That was what I was making at the Texaco station after working there a year. Now, I am wearing a suit when I go to work. Everyone had to wear a tie who worked at SCOA. Max taught me a lot about linters and pickers and threads per square inch and percale as opposed to muslin. (Finally, I knew more about something than Bill!) I became so good at this stuff that Max promoted me to Assistant Manager. (I guess being Jewish didn't hurt either.) I had been there only three months and I am now an Assistant Manager. WOW! Guess what? I am now making three figures. One dollar and two cents per hour! I can't even tell you how much money that was and how happy Dad and I were. To this day, I thank Max for taking me in and helping me get a real job. He was a mench! (Mench. A Yiddish word meaning a real man!) (Not a thirteen year old real man.) Thank you Max!

The school year is coming to a close. Gene, Judy, Val and I became a little closer. We spent a lot of time together being in Madrigals, practicing singing in our own trio, and going a place or two together. By the time graduation was here, Gene and Val were an item. I was still holding off for Darlene or Diane (the other Bob's little sister) to grow up.

Graduation came. I was out of school (sixteen and a half) and could work a little more. Soon to get my license back and now looking for a car. About this time Dad was back to work at Bond's Clothing Store in West Covina. Dad's cancer was cured, and everything seemed to be ok with him. He just had a little problem talking. (This, for a salesman, was not good!)

Just before school was out, I had made friends with another guy in the Drifters Club. He asked me if I would like to learn how to defend myself and if so, to come to the meetings and he would help me. In my spare time I would go there. He definitely would work with me. However, it was not all defense! We started to use baseball bats for offense and knives and occasionally had a lesson or two on how to use a gun. (I told him that I was very well versed in killing rabbits, birds and lizards with a gun, but he was not too impressed.) I was not really ready for all this, but I kept flashing back to the two beatings I took at the hands of the Mexicans, the loss of the car in Mexico, and the financial crises that went along with it. I continued to learn how to defend myself and how to engage in offense as well.

Summer was great! I spent a lot of time with Gene at the pool and bike riding. I also spent a lot of time with Bill, Roger, and, occasionally, Owen getting into trouble. I spent time with the Drifters, learning to fight and to defend myself. I wasn't really sure why we did this, but I was just happy to learn how to protect myself. You never know when a Mexican could be lurking behind a tree.

We (my family and I) spent a lot of time in the back yard barbecuing and having parties. Dad, eventually, had to have a tracheotomy because he was issued too much cobalt radiation when he had his cancer surgery. Although the cancer was cured, the radiation destroyed the muscles around his larynx. He had to have the tracheotomy surgery. (A tracheotomy is a breathing hole surgically put into a person's throat. To talk, one would have to temporally put a finger over the hole to let the air go back through the mouth.)

Not remembering that he couldn't talk without holding his finger over the hole in his throat, one day while barbecuing, he shot some lighter fluid from the can into the barbecue to help keep the fire going as it was dying. The fluid somehow dripped on his sock that he was wearing. The flame went from the barbecue back to his sock. His sock started to burn and was on fire. He started to yell and jump around screaming. However, no one could hear him because he was in such a panic that he didn't think to hold his finger over the hole in his throat. I can't tell you how funny it looked. My dad was in his tee shirt, a pair of shorts and black socks, no shoes, yelling at the top of his lungs, jumping all around, and his foot was on fire! No sound came out of his mouth although he was screaming at the top of his lungs. My brother and I saw it at the same time and couldn't stop laughing. We talked about it for years to come and still do when we go tent camping and are sitting around the fire at night. We talk about it and laugh our asses off.

Now, every once in a while, a hamburger joint in the area would have a special, twelve hamburgers for a dollar. We would bring them in instead of barbecuing. It saved some money and a few pair of socks!

My dad let me use the car whenever I wanted to as long as it was available. I remember I would take all of my daytime friends, Gene, Mark, my little brother, and all of his friends to the beach, at Huntington. I had gotten a surf board and was learning to surf. We would drive there bare-backed with only our swim trunks on. This exposed my shoulders and the top of my back to the kids in the back seat (my brother's friends, Bill Deaver, Rudy Lopez, (really happy about that one, "Lopez"!) Tom Valenzuela (this guy was white and I couldn't figure it out) Philip Daoussis, and Larry Hiensen.) Around that time I had a bad case of acne. A really bad case! My zits were the size of dimes, and they didn't miss covering a spot on my back and shoulders. Now, my brother's friends were a bunch of goody, goodies, just likes my little brother. But for the most part, they were all pretty quick and bright kids. All of them got straight A's in school. (B.F.D.! So did I at that age. Now look!) We would play the radio very loud as we drove to the beach, and all would sing along with it. There was one song that was played a lot. "My Boyfriend's Back" was the title. The songs words were actually "My boyfriend's Back and you're gonna get in trouble." However, when it was played on the radio with my brothers friends in the car, they sang it like this. "My boyfriend's back and it's really, really ugly." Especially when I had Judy in the car! I didn't really know if the reason Gene and Val were an item and Judy and I weren't yet was because I had bad acne or because I had to take my little brother and his friends along. The acne went on for the next two years until I could afford to get them evaporated off. The doctor would lay me on a table and take an electric needle with, I think fifty thousand volts, put it on the zit, and turn on the juice. The water and whatever else was in there would evaporate instantly. Not fun but effective. Gene, Val, Judy, and I would go to the beach without you know who sometimes. I did a little surfing, but, for the most part, we would lay on a towel, Judy and I, Gene and Val and just talk. We would feel each others bodies. It felt nice to touch a female's back, leg and hair and think about what else I might get lucky with sometime and feel.

Dad was now working and bringing home some money. One day, he came home with a nineteen fifty-four Cadillac. Green! Four door! It looked pretty nice for an old man's car. Dad said he got a pretty good deal on it and would I like to have the Buick? "Like to have the Buick, I said, Shit, yes!!! How much and can I make payments?" Dad said, "It's yours, free?" Free? Oh man, and it's still summer. Not a lot left, but summer.

When it came to buying and selling stuff, all of my family was never any different than that. (Well, maybe with the exception of my daughter.) We never sold stuff to anyone in the family. (Even until this day, if a family member would ask me for something, if it was real expensive, I would just ask for my cost back, and if it was real cheap, I would never ask anything for it.) Now, I could drive to SCOA and not worry about how I was going to get there. Maybe even get a few more hours on the clock.

It didn't take me long to realize cars were almost as expensive as women. The Buick needed tires. It was probably from someone burning rubber all the time when taking off. Who cared? It was Dad's car. He would buy the tires. So, I figured that he should buy them this time. "Dad, the Buick needs tires!" "Then buy them and it won't need them anymore." Guess that was a bad idea. I didn't have any money to spare, but I did remember seeing a sale on tires in West Covina. I looked it up, and the sale was still on. I went over to the tire store a little before I had to go to work at SCOA and asked how much it would be for four tires installed on my Buick. I don't remember how much it was, but it was way more then I had or could dig up. The salesman said, if I have good credit, I could charge them and pay it off a little at a time. We carry our own financing. Good credit. That was the bump in the road. I didn't have *any* credit. I told the salesman that and he asked me for a co-signer. Nope! I don't have one of those either. I said, "You know, I am making payments to my boss. Will that do?" Maybe! Let's call him. In one hour my car was wearing a brand new pair of shoes. No money out of pocket. It was like I didn't need money, so why not? As I drove out, the smoke from my new tires smelled great. Now, this is the American way. Credit! That was in nineteen fifty-eight. Man, what an escalation to date!

Chapter Nine

School started and as much as I used to like it, now it stunk! Homework, teachers, half-hour food breaks, smog, car gas that could be used for having fun!

The coach of the football team was hurting for players. So, Gene and I applied. (Gymnastics wasn't until the middle of the year.) It was just for back ups, as the regular players had been practicing for a month. Instead of gym class we had football practice. Gene and I never really got to play, but we were part of the team.

One day, the big deals on the team, the quarterback, an end or two, and a couple of the other guys who had clout with the team, suggested that the whole team have our heads shaved. I figure these guys have taken way too many shots to the head. What the heck would we do that for, a few of us who seemed normal, asked. "I think that it would show unity and solidarity and would be a psychological help when we meet the other teams," the quarterback said. I figure this guy needs a shrink! So, all of us (twenty-nine) went to as many barber shops in the area, as possible, to lose all of our hair after school. What was I thinking! I am Jewish and am supposed to be smarter than that. Obviously not! I am on a football team. Mom and Dad said, "No," but I was way too smart for them this time. I looked at myself after the buzz and almost shit a brick. Man, was I one ugly kid. A buzz! What the hell was I thinking! I couldn't get the phrase out of my mind. What was I thinking! What the hell was I thinking! Butt ugly! Hell, before that I had so much hair I made Elvis Presley look like he was thinning. I drove home, embarrassed to even walk through the door. So, I didn't. I knocked. Figured I would make light of it. Kind of a joke on Mom! My mom answered the door and said, "Chuck is not home from school yet." She did not know that it was me, her own son, the one who kicked the shit out of her ribs so that my little brother wouldn't grow. Me, Chuck! I said, "It's me mom, Chuck, your son." She looked at me with eyes as big as saucers and said, "Chuck?" "Yea. It's me." "Oh my God, what did you do to yourself?" (I remember it like it was yesterday.) "I shaved my head." "I can see that but why?" "All the kids on the football team did it. All of them!" "See, your father was right. You would get hurt if you played football. You damaged your brain." About that time she yelled, "Mike! Mike! Come quick!" Dad came running from my mother's screeching. It must have been some kind of a secret call for help that they devised at a younger time in their life. Dad, as he was running, was yelling, "Are you OK?" Very difficult to hear as he had the tracheotomy, but I could still hear him. He got to the door in one and a half seconds and took one look at me and said, "Football, right! You have lost your mind, right? Lost it!" I said, "How did you know it had to do with football?" He said, "I told you, you would get hurt, either physically or mentally. Pain is pain!" He turned to Mom and said, "The kid has lost his mind!" They just looked at each other, shook their heads, and walked away. Nothing more was said. It didn't have to be! Every time I looked in a mirror, I wanted to puke. I was the guy that every time I stopped at a traffic signal, I would run a comb through my hair. The original, "Cookie Cookie, lend me your comb!" Now, it's all gone. I felt like I was Samson and that Delilah was the quarterback. The next couple of days I wore a hat to school. I was too embarrassed to be seen. (I kinda felt like if I had a little more weight on and was thirteen again, I could cry and it would be ok.) But that turned out to be a problem. The school rules were that no hats were to be worn in class. So, I had to take the hat off while in the classroom. As I took it off, I felt like everyone was looking at me and as it came off, they were laughing. Whether they were or not, it didn't matter. That was the way I felt. A couple of days more went by. I took some mascara from my mom and painted on some side burns, long side burns, and kinda ran the mascara over the top of my head as to shade my bald scalp a little. I had thought I helped the situation, but as an after thought, I must have looked like a freak. (I still actually have pictures of my head.) The only good thing that came from it was that my hair finally grew back. Other then practice, I never played on the team. I never got any recognition as a stud, and I never got anything but humiliation. I couldn't wait for gymnastics.

About a week went by and the fair started. As I have said before, everyone in school waited for it to start. I got my free pass from the school and couldn't wait to go. I wondered if my free entrance was still there, but for now, I already have free admission, compliments of the school. The school I now attended was Ganesha High. A brand new school, almost. The first graduating class was the year before. When it opened, I would have been there, but I was a half year behind because of the moving from the East as I have said before. So, Gene and I, Val and Judy made plans to go the fair the first day it opened after our half day at school. My friend from the Drifters Club said they were all going to the fair on the fourth day, and asked if I wanted to go with them. He said if so, I need to show up at the club house two hours in advance. I wasn't sure why we had to be there so early, but I said, "Yes, I'd like to go with you guys." So, that was set. It was so cool that I could pick up Judy at her house and drive her to the fair. I had asked Gene if he'd like me to pick him and Val up, but he said no, that they would meet us there.

Now, all the time that I had spent with Judy, I had never kissed her. It just hadn't been that way for me, and I never asked her about it. We had a great time at the fair, as always. I didn't know if it was just the fair or the company, but it was fun either way. We went on the scary rides that turned you upside down and sideways, threw darts at a balloon, threw rings on a duck's neck, and threw balls at bottles. I won a large teddy bear, not the real big one, but a pretty big one and gave it to Judy. She Loved it. That may have started a new reaction of which I was not aware. The night, unfortunately, came to an end. Judy's mother was a school teacher, and their family was pretty strict about most things, especially Judy being with me. Now that I think about it, her parents must have known something that I didn't.

The next couple of days went ok as long as I didn't look into a mirror. Bill, Roger, Owen, Knuckle Head, and I went to the fair two days later and guess what? The free admission entrance was open. We all snuck in and ravaged the fair. Not to mention, not one Mexican around the entrance. Hooray! The fair was over at one o'clock on weekends, and we left at two-thirty. You might say we got way more then our money's worth. The next day was the day that the club members, the Drifters, were going to the fair. So, I showed up at the club house at the proper time. There were a lot of guys there whom I had never met or even seen before. I was introduced around and then the sergeant-at—arms said, "We need to talk." He was talking to me. I asked, "Ok what's going on?" He motioned to me to follow him. We went into the back room and sat down on a couple of chairs. He turned his chair backwards and sat. He said, "Do you have any clue as to what is going on here?" I said, "Not really." He said the club has been watching me, and they know that I am not a little goody two shoes. But they were not sure if I was the right material for the job. I said, "What is the job?" He said, "Beating up Mexicans and Niggers." I said, "Why do you want to do that?" (Secretly, I was already fifty percent on his side.) He said, "Because they are eating up our territory and need to be stopped." "Can't you just ask them to leave? And why do we have a territory and what do we need a territory for?" I asked. He said, "We have to have the ruling edge, so the Whites can be in charge." "In charge of what" I asked? He told me that I asked too many questions and if I am with the club next year, all would be explained. So, now I had to make a decision! "How do we do what you want me to do?" I asked. "You want to stop them and drive them away, right?" "We fight them and kill them if need be." "What, I asked. Kill them?" "Yes," he said, "kill them." I didn't think I could kill anyone. Not even my cousin, Arnold, for coloring in the lines all the time. (In fact, I had been remorseful about the lizards, rabbits and birds that my brother and I had knocked off in Hesperia a while back.) He said, "What?" I said, "Never mind." What did I get myself into here?

I asked for some time to think about it. He said, "Fine, but we leave here in about an hour to fight the Mexicans." I could understand fighting the Mexicans, but why the colored people? ("Afro Americans" had not been invented yet.) The way I saw it, it was the colored people (called by the gentiles) and schvartzas (called by the Jews) on the east coast and Niggers (called by the gentiles and the Jews) on the west coast were ok people. Hell, as I said before, in my kindergarten picture, there were three white spots (me and two other white kids) and the rest were black heads. I grew up with the colored people and had nothing against them. Why should I fight with them? Now, the Mexicans, that was a different story. I thought maybe the two assholes who beat me up would be there, and I could just get a little revenge. I would have plenty of help there. Really a tough decision! (If I had a brain it wouldn't be so tough. I would have said to myself, "Hit the road, Jack"). The good part was that we were going to fight the Mexicans first. Jesus Christ, I thought. What am I doing? I barely know how to defend myself in a controlled environment when I had practiced with the club. How do I do this in a gang fight thing? I went out and asked to speak to the sergeant-of-arms.

We went into the back room again. I asked him to explain exactly what and how this all happens. He told me the plan, and it seemed to be well thought out. This was a great plan on how to be killed! They have guns, knives, and baseball bats, also. They didn't tell me that part. Shit! What to do? He said, "All of the guys will be watching out for you a little more as this is your first time." That was comforting! All I could do was think of the beating I took at the hands of the two Mexicans. I said, 'I'm in." He said, "Good. I thought you would be!" Out of fear, I asked him if I should go home and get a tie to wear. He just smiled.

We got into five cars and drove to the fair. There were about twenty of us. We parked and walked towards the chain link fence. This was starting to look familiar. We made our way to a hole in the fence. My hole! I mean mine and the Mexicans' hole. I thought I had an exclusive on it! We made our way to the front of the fun zone under the bright yellow arches. Boy, was this starting to sound familiar. We waited for about ten or fifteen minutes, and then a bunch of Mexicans showed up. Two of our guys and two of their guys had a pow-wow for about three minutes or so like they were friends. Then, the Mexicans walked off towards the parking lot, away from the fun zone. I looked for my two Mexican friends but didn't see them. We all hung around for ten minutes or so and then started to go the same way. We must have looked funny to some people because most of us were wearing big coats and heavy jackets. It was about eighty degrees outside. The jacket was to hide the bats, sticks, knives and, I am sure, a gun or two. The sergeant-of-arms had given me a chain about three feet long and told me to double it up for quickness and strength. He also gave me a small knife. Maybe a four-inch blade! The only thing I could think about was how my life has escalated since I met the Catholic Barney. Twelve to sixteen! Four years and I went from a straight "A" student to a possible mass murderer.

I started to think of alternatives. Maybe it was the fat chick in the closet or maybe Knuckle Head throwing the dart at the cat or the cop that gave me the ticket. None of those worked. I was just a criminal, plain and simple! We walked about two hundred yards into the parking lot where there were very few cars. I think it may have been a restricted area. Great, now we are trespassing! Like that mattered at this point. The Mexicans were standing in a semi-circle and before I could think about anything, they started running at us and came at us with knives, chains, baseball bats and you know, just about what we had been given. I panicked. I didn't know what to do. All of a sudden, I didn't have to decide. I was hit with something, not sure what, but it hurt. I could only think of the beatings that I had taken at the hands of the Mexicans so I hit someone with the chain. Hell, it could have been one of my own guys. A white guy! Then, I got tackled and was on my back, a really bad place to be. Someone from behind me put his arms under my shoulder pits and lifted me up. That, for some reason, helped my confidence or maybe my stupidity. Maybe I felt that they were watching out for me. I saw a Mexican and went after him and hit him as hard as I could with my chain. He didn't fall. In fact, he came after me. We rolled around for what seemed like a life time. I was holding my own. All of a sudden, the fighting stopped. The Mexicans went to the right, and we went to the left. Both of us were heading to a different exit of the parking lot. *What the hell happened, I thought?*

A couple of the guys asked me how I was and if I could make it to the club house tomorrow at eight P.M.? I looked around and tried to count how many were dead. But, I couldn't remember with how many we started. I checked myself, and I wasn't even bleeding. I did hurt in a few places and figured I would be sore tomorrow. I walked home because I didn't know and wasn't told where the cars were and if I was supposed to go to them after the rumble. So, that was my first time in a gang fight, and I don't think I got beat. The fight seemed to take about a half hour. As I looked at my watch and remembered when we got there and how long it took to meet the Mexicans and then to walk to the fight area, the whole fight couldn't have taken a total of ten minutes.

As I walked home, I tried to figure out what we had accomplished and why it was all supposed to make sense. Beating people up for what? Territory! Am I protecting my house, parents and my little brother? Guess I will have to wait until next year when we do this again. If I do this again! Although I wasn't sure I was doing the right thing, I was getting to be a person without fear and would not be a patsy if confronted by the Mexicans again. I think!

I was anxious to tell Bill as he thought I was going to die. He knew how I had fought the Mexicans in the past. I awoke the next morning and couldn't get out of bed. Fortunately, it was Sunday. I was sore, really sore. So sore I checked for broken stuff, but I appeared to be intact. I stayed in bed most of the day and told Mom that I had been burning the candle at both ends between work and work and school and just wanted to stay in bed for awhile. Mom was always a pushover and bought it. So about five o'clock I got up and had a little food and then went out to find Bill and to give him a report on the night before. I found him with Roger at Roger's house. Roger's big brother was there and asked me how the fun zone was. He was the one who knew where we were to meet and what we were supposed to do. How he knew all of this I never found out but he was aware, somehow. Maybe he was an ex member?

I told Roger, Bill and Roger's brother what happened. I was proud telling them what happened and they were all ears. I also told them that I had a meeting in about an hour at the club. They wanted to know why and I said, "I didn't know." I was just told to be there at eight. I arrived at the meeting place, and everyone wanted to shake my hand. "You are awesome!" they said. "What a fighter!" they said. "I bet you can't wait to jump in there again and kick some more asses!" they said! (By this time, if I had known Cassius Clay, I would have taken him on.) The sergeant-at-arms walked over to me and said, "You should thank me." I said, "For what?" He said, "For picking you up off the floor before you got knifed." I said, "Thanks," and everyone started to laugh. One guy yelled out, "Are you Jewish?" I asked, "Why do you want to know?" He said, "Because you fight like one." I said, "Is that good or bad?" He said, "Bad!" I said, "Thanks." "But, I said, my butt wasn't quite up against the wall yet." "Ok, mister Six Day War," he said, you'll do."

The meeting started, and it was to get together all who wanted to fight the Niggers on Friday. I had a lot of reservations about that. I wanted to fight the Mexicans but not the colored people. I had nothing against them. In fact, I grew up with them and never had a problem with them. (My grandfather even talked to them, as I have previously mentioned.) The selling point was that we needed to keep up our fighting ability so we could whip the Mexicans when the fair ended. I asked, "So, we are going to fight the Mexicans again?" They said, "One more time and it would probably be on the last day of the fair." "I guess I am in. Same kinda thing?" "Yep, nothing changes except the color."

I am sixteen and a half and will be starting my eleventh year of school in nineteen fifty-eight and wonder if I will ever make it to age seventeen, alive.

Summer was over, and I was running short of money. I had been away from the stealing stuff for awhile. Not a lot of time to steal in the summer. Way too many other things to do! So, I went downtown and started to steal records from the music store again. I had started to do this towards the end of school last year and was doing ok for a small time thief. After I had stolen them, I would take them to school and sell them for fifty cents. Most of what I stole were forty-fives. They were small records (records, an American term for very old CD's and has nothing to do with holding your breath longer than your friend with a lung full of marijuana) and could be slipped under a jacket easily. They cost a dollar plus tax at the store, so at fifty cents a pop, I could sell all that I could steal as they were in demand. I was doing well. I could sell everything that I could get my hands on. (Pardon the pun.)

About two weeks into the stealing season, I was at a Miller's Surplus Store (now I think they are called "Outpost") in Pomona. I was starting to look pretty good as far as my body went. I thought I would steal a "muscular" tee shirt. I cased the joint and when the opportunity was right, I slipped it into my jacket. It was a purple one. I walked out the door and in a hot New York minute, there was a security guard's hand on my shoulder. I tried to run but he had a good grip on me. He put two hands on me, walked me back into the store to the back room of the store, sat me down, took the shirt and said, "What do you think you are doing?" I sat there like a bump on a log, kinda scared. This is the first time I had been caught. I was hoping Bill would still talk to me when I got home. Little did I know I was not heading that way. The security guard said that the cops were on their way, and I was to just wait here until they got here. There was only one way in and out of that room so I was dead meat. Ten minutes or so went by and the cops walked in. They asked me why I did it. I told them I couldn't afford to by it so I just took it. I needed some clothes. They asked me for some identification. I didn't have any with me. I had left my driver's license in the car. I told them my first name and that was all. They said if I didn't tell them who I was, they would have to take me to jail. I thought that they were bluffing. I was only sixteen and told them so. Sixteen year old guys don't go to jail, do they? They kept on badgering me about where I lived and who my parents were and stuff like that. I gave them nothing. I was tough. A Drifter! After about all they could handle of me, they put me in a squad car and took me to the Pomona jail house. I was starting to shake a little. I thought that they were going to warn me and try to scare me a lot and then let me go on the promise that I would never do it again. I was wrong. They took me in to the holding tank and started to fill out the arrest papers. All the time, asking me who and where my parents were. About the last thing I wanted to tell the cops is who my parents were. My dad would kill me if he knew what I have just done. Kill me! I was in the holding tank for an hour or so. A cop came in and asked me one more time. He said, "I have to put you in the jail if you don't tell me who you are and how to get hold of your parents. This is the last chance you have." All I could think of is the beating I was to get if my dad found out. I was really scared and almost in tears but said, "I guess you will have to take me." The cop said to put my arms in back of me, and he put a pair of cuffs on me. Shit, I am only sixteen! Now I am starting to shake. Up until now I kind of thought they were hoping I would break and tell them what they wanted to know. He started to walk me to the back of the room and through a door. As I walked through the door, I saw the cells through a little window in the next door that he started to walk me through. We walked through the second door, and there they were, the cells. The first one we passed by had a few guys in it, and they were lying down on their cots. The next one we got to had an open door, and he started to walk me in to it. I looked at the filthy toilet with no seat on it and no privacy anywhere. No bed, just a cot that was dirty and a roll of toilet paper on the floor and graffiti all over the walls. It was just too much for me. I had just passed the gate of the jail and said with a mouth full of tears, "Ok, Ok, Ok. I will tell you where my dad is. Just get me out of here." I am sure it was because of my mother that I broke. I couldn't take the sight and stench of the jail cell. She, like most Jewish mothers, had nothing to do all her life but to feed me, my little brother and dad, and to keep a major clean house. A major clean house! Sheets were changed weekly; dishes washed after each and every meal; house vacuumed daily, etc. etc. etc. How was I to live in this hell hole! I may be a potential killer, but I am a Jewish potential killer and need to kill cleanly. I knew the moment that I broke; I was going to get the beating of my life. The cuffs came off and the call was made.

In twenty-five minutes Dad walked through the police station's door. We, (my dad I, and the cop) sat down, and the cop told Dad exactly what had transpired and then looked at me and asked me if I had anything else to add, I said, "No, everything you said was correct." He told me and Dad that he was going to release me into the custody of my father and if this happens again before I was eighteen, there would be a huge fine and that I would be sent to a boy's camp until I was eighteen. Dad and I left and got into the Cadillac and drove home. Not much was said on the drive there. A few comments of how stupid I was for doing it. That was about all. We got home, and Dad said to go to my room. I did. I figured he wanted to tell Mom what had happened in private. About ten minutes went by and my bedroom door opened. Dad came in with a belt in his hand. He threw me onto the bed and started to whip me thoroughly and then hit me with his fists. Blow after blow and a few kicks as well. He'd yank me off the bed and onto the floor and kick me again. Fist after fist, kick after kick. After what seemed to be a life time, he finally left. I was crying and really beat up. Beat up bad. I felt like both Mexicans had gotten to me at the same time, only Dad's beating was worse than theirs were, easily. I was hurt!

I never made it to the fair to beat up the colored guys that week. I could hardly walk for the next three days. Between my lack of hair, my new limp, and black and blue marks over most of my body, most of my friends stayed away for a while. Especially the girls!

Now for what it is worth, I never stole a thing again, up to and including this writing. Well, maybe a lady's heart or two!

I went to the fair again with Judy. We were having fun together. I asked her to go to the show with me, and she said, "I'd like that." So, we seemed to be starting a romantic relationship. There was only one day left for the fair, and I had to go to it alone that night. It was kick Mexican ass night. I met the boys at the clubhouse, and we headed out for one last rumble with the Mexs. A couple of the guys said to me, "If I see anyone that looks like your dad, run like hell, because we aren't going to protect you. We were told he is one bad Mother F—r." Guess the beating I got got around somehow.

We met just like the other day and pretty much the same thing happened. We met, they pow-wowed, and we went to the parking lot, only a different location this time. We started to rumble again. I was more into it this time for some reason. It was like I was practicing for my own fight when I finally got to get back at the two Mexicans who got me. I had a small knife just like the one I had the last time, and a foot and a half long two-inch round wooden dowel. I was fighting with a pretty tough guy. He was getting the best of me. (Hell, I was still a little sore from a beating I had gotten a week or so before from an old Jew. Hmmm, maybe I am not as tough as I think I am.) For some reason he turned away from me, and I stabbed him in the back. He went down. I started to hit another guy and about four or five of us wound up on the ground brawling. Not sure how many were on my side, but I remembered that I shouldn't be down here on the ground. I fought my way back to a standing position. When I got up, there were a lot of guys on the deck. This was obviously a much more intense battle than two weeks ago. Another few minutes or so went by and as if someone were timing the whole event, everyone started to leave. There were three guys being dragged off by the Mexicans and one of our guys being dragged off as well. I was ok again. I had hoped the Drifters didn't think I was hiding during battle, because I wasn't. The guy that we dragged off had lost a bunch of blood. He wound up ok, but he did have about twenty stitches in his side. I can't imagine what my mom and dad would have said if it had been me. I probably would have needed another twenty stitches just from my dad alone! To this day I don't know what happened to the three Mexicans that were dragged off. I hope they all wound up ok. But I did stab one of them, and he could have died for all I know. I guess I will never know. That would make me a killer! I wasn't real proud then and certainly not now!

The fair was over, and things got back to normal. That is, about as normal as my life goes. Gene and I were really getting into the Madrigals whenever we could, also spending after-hours at the gym working on our routines for gymnastics.

One day one of the guys said, "Let's go to the hidden swimming hole tonight. It's still warm at night but won't be for long." Why am I always, always, always the one who doesn't know anything, I ask myself? "What the hell are you guys talking about now?" I asked. "What hidden swimming hole?" "You have never been there?" someone says. "No," I said. "Where and what is it?" "It's in the Claremont hills just before you start going up to Baldy." (Baldy is what we called Mt. Baldy, the mountain nearby where I broke my cherry and Roger broke his leg. But that is in a later chapter.) Does everyone keep things from me for a reason? "So, when and where do we meet? Is there a place to change to our suits and who is going?" "Suits, you don't need no stinken suits! We skinny dip!" "Skinny dip? What the heck are you talking about?" "No suits, dummy, no clothes. We go naked, bare ass and the girls do, too." "What!? What girls?" I am always in the dark! "What girls?" "We know a few who like to go skinny dippen." I said that I was not sure about this. I had never done this before. What if we get caught? Especially with girls! "We have never had a problem before. Why do you think we would have one now?" I said, "OK," and agreed to pick up some of the guys. We picked a time, about nine-thirty that night.

Now I am a nudist, and a trespassing nudist at that! Just add one more thing to my list of criminal activities! But, at this stage of the game, who's counting! So, I picked up Owen and Bill. Roger and Knuckel Head went with a couple of other guys. There was an area to park, so I parked. Then, we started to walk towards a brushy area and down a little grade. After about ten minutes we were there. It was pretty cool. Trees all around that you could climb. You could hang off a limb and drop into the water. The actual pool area was about thirty-five feet across and kind of circular. We started to undress. I was the last one to get naked. This was not really my bag. (I couldn't even do this with my Uncle Izzy at a men's club. Now, I am doing it with a bunch of naked women I don't even know.) I finally did and got into the water. The three of us were horsing around and then we heard voices. It was Rog and Knucle Head and a few other guys and two girls. I barely knew the guys but never met the girls. They all came over and said, "Hi." The guys introduced the girls to me, Owen and Bill. Bill immediately got out of the water and started shaking the girls' hands. I waved hi. The girls and the other guys undressed and jumped in. I couldn't take my eyes off the girls undressing. It was so cool. They just did it. Just did it! About a half hour went by and we all heard voices again. About five more girls and three other guys entered the sex pool. None of us knew each other, but everybody got undressed and jumped in. We were there for at least an hour having fun. This was the first time that I was feeling girls naked with wet bodies touching and sliding against me and an occasional feel of each other. The feels seemed to be by accident by the girls but not by me. I tried to make it seem like an accident, but I think the girls knew better. Sometimes it was impossible to pass by me without some kind of touching as there was an object sticking out that I couldn't control and they kept hitting it. But I am sure I was not the only one copping a feel. This was really nice, I thought. To this day, as I remember it, it still feels pretty good, wet bodies touching. Very sensual!

Some time went by and the two girls that came with Knuckle Head and Roger got out, toweled off and the four of them who came together left. It was about eleven-thirty or so and a booming voice yells out, "Everybody out of the pool and you are under arrest." Nobody moved as we thought it was Roger and Knuckle Head playing a joke until we all saw a cop come in sight. We are all dead! Disgraced, humiliated and just plain screwed. The cop said that this was private property. "You are all trespassing and if you are all naked like I think you are, the offense will be lewd in public as well." He had us all get out of the pool and get dressed. Now, I don't think any of us were eighteen yet, so we probably won't go to jail. (But I had thought that once before.) I had seen enough of jails anyway, and, as far as I was concerned, it was more of my dad, again. I don't think my body had recovered from the last beating enough to handle another one.

We all walked back to the car scared shitless. At least I was. He got a legal pad and had all of us write our name, address and phone numbers on it. He said, "I am going to give you all a chance and not report this, this time. But if I ever see you here again, you will definitely see the judge. Do you understand?" We all said yes. Some said thank you, but all made for the cars in case he had a change of mind. I can't tell you how relieved I was. Man, no beating. Safe! I'm out of here. *I thought!* As I was about to get into my short (Short, Mexican slang for car.), shit, those guys are starting to rub off on me. I'm starting to talk like them. Shit!), the cop said, "Charles, come here." What! What did I do now I thought? Bill and Knuckle Head got into the Buick, and I went towards the cop. He said to me, "Do you know who I am?" I said, "No. Why?" He said that he was my neighbor. I said, "You are?" He said, "I live three doors down from your family." I said, "Ok. Now I know. You have all the pretty roses in front, right?" (I was familiar with the roses as most of us were. When we had a date, we would steal them and give them to our dates. I would even give some to my mom on occasion.) He said, "Yes." He told me that the only reason that he let us go is because he didn't want me to get in trouble again with my dad. He said, "I heard about the whipping you got recently. It was pretty bad, huh!" I said, "Thanks. I really appreciate it." What did I do, make National T. V.? (Now, this cop was a real jerk. Nobody liked him, not even the adults. He would never associate with anyone and if a dog walked on his lawn, he would blow his top. He was just a real grouch!) He told me to hit the road and never to do it again. He also said, "Try and get Bill on the right path if you can. He's heading for big trouble in the future." Like I was a mister goody two shoes myself and had any control over Bill. I said, "Ok" and got into the Buick and left. Gee, I thought. Dad is getting a heck of a reputation. Then I thought more about how I felt in the water with the girls for a very long time.

Now, as I said before, gas money was starting to get tight. I was never going to steal again, so I needed an edge besides working to get some extra cash. Now, working at the Texaco gas station, I remembered there were empty coke bottles on the side of the Coke machine. Let me explain for the new kids on the block. In days of old when nights were bold, there were these really tall red machines. If you put a dime in it and opened the door in front, you could pull out a bottle of Coca Cola. They were glass bottles at this stage of the Jurassic period. When you were done drinking the coke, there was a metal rack attached to the side of this big red machine so that you could put in the empty bottles. Some time through the week, the coke man would pick them up when he filled the big red machine with cokes again. One day, when I was working at the Texaco station and not peeping through the peep hole that went from the back room into the ladies room, the coke man came to fill the machines. I asked him if they destroyed the bottles or refilled them. I was just making conversation with him. I also asked him when he usually picked up and refilled the machines. It was always in the daytime and on Tuesdays for us at the station. He volunteered that his route was every weekday, eight to five for all of Pomona. Big red machine after big red machine! AH HA! Light bulb goes on!

I rounded up the boys, Roger and Bill, and proposed a question to them. What do you think about taking (I didn't want to use the word "stealing" because I do not do that anymore.) empty coke bottles from all over Pomona and turning them in to the liquor stores for the two cent deposit? They looked at me like I had the plague. Cop bottles for two cents. "That's nuts," they said. "What do you think we will make, a quarter a week?" Laugh, laugh. "You've lost it!" "Ok," I said, but I have a plan." "Go ahead," they said. "We'll listen." "Here's the deal. We pull the back seat out of the Buick, and one of you guys stay in the back and one sits up front with me, shotgun. I swing right up to the big red machine, and the guy in front opens the door and starts empting the coke bottles as fast as he can by throwing them to the guy in the back seat so they don't break. We hit and run, hit and run. I bet we can fill up the empty back seat in a night. That's a lot of two cents. Well, are you in?" Bill says, "Hey Rog, what do you think?" Rog says, "I'm doing nothing this week. Let's give it a try." They say in unison, "We're in."

The first night we got about a hundred bottles. One hundred bottles at two cents is two bucks. That's almost a full tank of gas (Eat your hearts out, you young kids.) And that is just the beginning. We started to do this almost every night when we had nothing to do. I worked a lot of nights until nine o'clock in West Covina so we had to do it late sometimes. But, as we got good at it, we were reaping anywhere from three to five bucks a night. One time, when we took the bottles to a liquor store, we watched where the clerk put them. He would stack the wood containers with the empty bottles in them outside, right up against his back fence. When the store was closed, we would back the Buick right up against the fence, stand on the back bumper, reach over the fence, and grab four or five full cases of empty bottles at a time and scram out of there. The next night, we would take the bottles that we had *borrowed* the night before right back to the same liquor store where we got them from the night before and get money again for the same bottles. Somehow, it didn't seem like stealing at two cents a bottle. It was just a fun job to make a few bucks.

It was getting into winter, and snow was starting to fall on Mt. Baldy. Mt. Baldy, as I have said before, was the highest mountain in the area and about twenty-five miles to the base from my house. One day, the boys and I decided to take a drive to the snow level. We made it there. It was beautiful, all covered with snow. (Not to mention a few fond memories.) We sat around in the car smoking and wishing we had a sled. All of a sudden someone said, "I know. Let's use the hood of your car." "What!" I yelled. "What the hell are you talking about?" Owen says, "On your car the hood does not open like a normal car, right?" I said, "You are correct." On my forty-eight Buick the hood opened from the side and not the front like conventional hoods opened. You could open it from one side or the other side so that you could work on the engine from either side. Why it was designed like that I didn't know. It just was. However, I think I know now! If you opened the latches on both sides at the same time, the whole hood would just lift off. Now, I don't know if you can remember what a forty-eight Buick looked like, but the hood was kind of like an upside-down canoe cut in half at the middle. It was a little wider, proportionally, especially at the back area where it fitted onto the frame of the car under the windshield. We pulled the hood off and carried it up to the top of the hill. There were five of us so it wasn't real heavy with all of us carrying it. When we got to the top of the hill, we turned it upside down. I got in the front where the kind of point was, Roger and Knuckle Head right behind me on either side, and then there was Bill and Owen in the back. Bill and Owen kind of laid down on it with their feet and legs hanging off the back of the hood and in the snow. We figured that as we were going down the hill, one of the back guys could steer us by dragging his feet in the snow, causing the hood to turn. Dragging the right leg would make us turn to the right and so on and so forth. So, here we are with this man-made family-size sled and pushing with our hands to get us started down the hill. It worked! We started to descend the hill. Owen would drag his leg, and we would turn. Then Bill would do the same. This was great! What fun! We started to get a little speed up and when the trees started to whiz by at a thousand miles per hour, we realized there was no way to stop this thing. No brakes! We were in deep doodoo. We started yelling to Bill and Owen, "Drag your feet! Drag your feet! Drag your feet!" They kept yelling back, "We are! We are! We are!" However, we were not slowing down. We were going too fast, and the small amount of drag wasn't helping much. Now, as I looked up, there was a tree right in front of us, maybe fifty feet or so. I am in front and in real trouble. I yelled, "TREE! Jump!" I bailed. Knuckle Head bailed. Bill and Owen just let go and slid off the back, but Roger, who wasn't real agile, was only half off as the sled hit the tree. Roger went flying off at a fairly fast rate of speed. We all start laughing. That was cool! That was fun. Let's do it again. Hey, Rog, how you doing? Rog, where are you? We couldn't see him as he was flung around the tree and down the hill a little. No sound from Roger. Nothing! Not a peep. "We better go see if he is still alive," Owen said in a joking manner. We got up and started to look for Roger. As we just got to the part where the hill starts to slope, we saw Roger crawling up towards us. He didn't look real good. He said, "I broke my leg. My leg is broken." Are you sure? How do you know? Maybe you just twisted it." As we got a little closer, we could see that his leg was going the wrong way. It was broken all right, really broken! We managed to get him and my car hood off the hill and started to drive back to civilization. Roger was obviously in pain. We stretched him out in the back seat, and Bill sat on the floor with him. The rest of us were in the front. Roger said to take him to the hospital and not to say anything to his parents yet. We need to make up a story that wasn't too lame. He said, "My dad wouldn't ever believe the truth." Not to mention that he would say that I was much smarter than to do something like that.

We drove him to the hospital and left him there, and then drove to his house to tell his folks what really happened. We made up the story that we were horsing around in the field that had burnt down a while back, (We all know which one that was.) Roger tripped, fell and broke his leg. They went for it! I guess I need not tell you that we never went sledding again using the hood of my car for a sled. Roger was on crutches for a month and then limped for the next year. But with his Elvis Presley suave and looks, no one noticed!

In the next couple of months, things were a little slow. It was a cold and rainy time of year, and that restricted a lot of fun stuff. School took over, and Madrigals and Gymnastics were on the top of my list. I was still getting "A"s in math and "D"s in English. Auto shop was fun, and I was learning a lot about engines, transmissions, and cars in general. I now had wood shop. It was ok, also.

Christmas came and went. I spent a lot of time with Judy, especially at that time of the year. January came and with it, my seventeenth birthday at the end of the month. It was warm in January, for some reason, unlike the previous December. (Global warming was not invented yet so it couldn't have been that.) Mom said, "Why not have a birthday party in the back yard? It seems like it will be nice out." I thought that sounded great. I invited a bunch of kids. I invited Bill, Roger, Owen, Knuckle Head, Bob and Jimmy (the fighter brothers), Bob Smith, the fall off the roof of the house and jump in front of a car guy, and, of course, his sister, Darlene whom I still liked, and Diane, the young chick with a great rack and body. Oh wait, the word "rack" has not been invented yet. She was stacked, really stacked. Although a little younger, it did give us something to look at. And, of course, her brother, what's his name, to protect her. There was Primm, Cynthia, Jane, and Jimmy Smith, no relation to the other Smiths, but his parents looked a lot like my Uncle Izzy and Aunt Molly and were friends of my parents. There were Gene and Val, Judy, and a few others from Madrigals whom I invited. Others were invited as well as my little brother and some of his friends. All in all, it was a pretty large group. Parties were second nature to the Gerson family. From birthdays to the New Year's party and many in-between, we were pros at them.

One day before the party, I was with Bob Smith, the jump off the roof of the house guy, with his sister, Darlene, whom I liked. (Did I mention that?) He recently had an interview with the Disney Studios about a job. He was very high on his ability to do stupid stunt stuff because of the recent interview. So, in the recent glory of his own mind, he said, "Why don't we do a stunt at your birthday party?" "Say, that would be great! What do you think we should do?" I queried. I'll think of something. Give me a day or two.

A day or two went by, and Bob came over to my house and said, "I've got it!" "Ok, hit me with it." "You are kind of going with Judy, right?" "Yea!" "Most of your friends know that you kind of like my sister, Darlene, right?" "Yea!" "So here's the deal. Sometime in the middle of the party, I give you a hard time about my sister. Judy is there, of course, and she hears me say to stay away from my sister. You get pissed at me, and we start fighting. (Right here, I may have a problem as he is not a Mexican.) You grab me from behind around my neck and pull out a knife and stab me in the back. (Should be easy, I have had practice!) I fall down with the knife sticking out of my back, and you run to the back of the yard, jump the cinder block wall, and disappear. While I lay there bleeding, every one is grouped around me. As I lay there dying, you come from the other side of the house and yell, "Surprise!" I get up, and we all start laughing. What do you think?" "It's great, but how do I stab you with the knife and then have it sticking out of you?" "Not a problem, I have it all worked out. But we will need to practice it a few times." Done deal! The party is in three days so when do we practice this stunt?" "Tomorrow, right here in your back yard." "Ok, be there or be square."

Tomorrow comes, and Bob shows up with a roll of tape and asks me if I have that ash tray I made in metal shop and some cardboard. (I knew some day that that ashtray would come in handy.) I went and got the ashtray. We went over to the garage and found a small cardboard box. Bob said, "Watch." He cut the cardboard box in about four small pieces about three or four inches square and taped them to the inside of the ashtray. He then put the ashtray between his back and the belt on his pants. "There," he said, "Do you have a knife, you know like a pen knife?" I went and got my little brothers Boy Scout knife. (Note that little brother is a Boy Scout, and big brother is literally stabbing his friend in the back. Did I ever mention that my brother and I were different?) Bob turned away from me and said, "Stab me in the ashtray." I pushed the knife through the cardboard until it hit the back of the metal ashtray. He said, "Let go." The knife stayed in. If you hadn't seen the cardboard and the ashtray, you would have thought that I stabbed him in the back. Bob said, "The trick is to know where the ashtray is at all times." He said, "Take the knife out and try it again." This time he pulled his shirt down and said to do it. I was pretty sure where the ashtray was and gently stuck him again. Dead center! He said, "You have to do it hard or it won't look real. Remember you are supposed to be mad at me." I grabbed him by the neck and rammed the knife into the ashtray and said, "How do you like that, asshole?" He said, "That was great". Then he gave me a small rubber bladder, like a thing from a toy or something. When you squeezed it, air would come out of a tiny opening in the front. When you let go, it would open back up and refill with air again. I said, "What's that for?" He said, "The blood." (This guy had everything worked out.) "The blood?" I asked. "Yea, get me some ketchup and a small bowl." I brought the supplies to him. He squeezed some ketchup into the bowl and then squeezed the air out of the little bladder and put the open end in the ketchup and let go. As the bladder opened back up, it sucked the ketchup in it instead of air. Now, he said, "Hold this in your hand and when you stab me this time, squeeze the bladder at the same time. There will be blood where you stabbed me." Is this guy great or what! We practiced it several times over and over. Argue, grab neck from the back, pull the knife, stab and squeeze, look around and then run and hop the wall. Just like it had been drawn up. This will definitely be the highlight of my party. "I'm loving it!" (Sorry, Mac Donald's. I said it first.)

Now it is party time, and everyone shows up. I had hooked the record player from the house to some speakers we had out side, turned the volume up, and we were dancing the night away. Dad bought a ton of food and chips. Mom made the tables look like they were set for a king. The kids kept pouring in, and the music never stopped. We had plenty of soft drinks. A few of the guys brought a little harder stuff to help liven things up a little.

I don't remember exactly what song it was, but it was one that had a real sexy beat to it. One that when you danced to it, you really didn't dance. You kind of banged your hips forward and backward to it. Just a bump and grind kinda song. So, Bill (Mister Sex Bomb) started dancing to it with some chick and about a half a minute into it, she quits, embarrassed, and turns and sits down. Bill was really getting close and banging all the way. My mom got up and starts banging with Bill to the song. After a half a minute later, Bill quits with a huge red face, really embarrassed. Mom out-sexed him. We all looked at Bill and pointed to him. He got up and went into the house. But on his way in, you could hear him mumble, "She's way too much for me." That's my mom! She was always hot. I always wondered if Dad knew. I didn't ever have a friend that didn't like my parents. Ever!

I started to open gifts so the party noise dropped a little. Right after the gift opening is when I was supposed to make a remark about Darlene and then the fight and stabbing with Bob was to take place. I finished opening the gifts and as it came to the end, just before the music got loud again, Mom came out with a cake all full of glowing candles. Eighteen of them! The first seventeen candles were for my age and one extra for good luck. (That was a waste of a candle.) I cut the first slice of cake, again for good luck, and we all started stuffing our faces. Just about when everyone was done eating, I exited to the bathroom. What I really did was to get the knife and the "full of ketchup" bladder and then come back. The music hadn't been turned up yet, so I made the remark to Bob very loud about Darlene. He yelled back at me. You could hear a pin drop. All eyes were on us. Then, we started to push each other and wrestle around on the ground for a bit. We both stood up. Then, I pulled the knife and bladder from my pocket, screamed something at Bob, turned him around, grabbed him by the neck, just like practice, and stabbed him with the knife. This time, for some reason, maybe because it seemed so real, when the knife went in, I twisted it. (Or, I guess it could have been the Drifters training.) Anyway, for some reason, it didn't feel the same as practice. The knife seemed to go in a little easier this time. Not as solid. I looked around. All eyes were still on us. (This was so kewl!) I ran to the end of the yard, and hopped the wall just like planned. (This was really cool. It almost felt real!) We had everyone fooled. What a great idea Bob had. It was just really great!

Now, as I came around from the other side of the house, everyone was looking over Bob. Hell, he had been stabbed by his buddy and is laying there dying. I walked up and yelled, "Surprise!" Everyone stopped and looked at me with wonder. I said, "It is all a fake. Made up! Bob and I put it on for you. Wasn't it great? We really got you, didn't we?" Some of the guys started to smile and some did not. The girls didn't smile. "Hey, Bob, you can get up now. Bob?" Bob didn't get up. I walked over to him lying on the ground and bent down. I heard him say, "You missed the ashtray!" "Oh shit! Are you sure?" He just looked at me. Now, Mom knew what we were planning and had advised against it. There was no way I could let her know what just happened. The girls backed away. Bill and Owen, (Roger was on crutches for some reason) helped lift Bob up and walked him to the back bathroom. We lifted his shirt up, and he was bleeding a lot! (Kinda looked a little like ketchup!) I opened up the medicine cabinet and looked for some hydrogen peroxide to clean the wound and some bandages. Both were there because Dad used all that kind of stuff to clean his tracheotomy tube. We cleaned him up and bandaged him as well as we could. The bleeding was now at a much lesser flow. You could see he was in pain. He only spoke once the whole time we were all in the bathroom getting him bandaged and what he said was, "Why did you twist the knife?"

He stayed in the bathroom for awhile. Mom had asked about him because some one said Bob was in the bathroom not doing so well. I told Mom that he had a little too much to drink, and we were nursing him along. She bought it! She always bought it! Bob was twenty-one already, and Mom knew it so it was really no big deal. Darlene and I didn't see much of each other after that. Why, I don't know. Maybe because I tried to kill her brother! Bob didn't hang around much either anymore. Although every once in a while he would see me in my car and would jump in front of it. Guess he healed ok. He did start working for the studios not long after, and I never really saw him anymore. For all I know, he is still jumping off buildings in some of the movies I go to see.

Now, one of the crazy things that I had picked up as I was rolling my humble way through life, was the need for multi-speakers in as many places as possible. In my room, my car, and even outside for the parties we had. I had hooked up at least four speakers outside, on the patio, from our stereo in the living room. Wires, we had wires! You practically had to literally fly outside to keep from tripping on them as you went out. My car had four speakers. The two that came with the car and the two I put in the back package tray. Awesome sound, just awesome! My bedroom had six speakers hooked up to the stereo. Four of the speakers were standing in the corners about a foot and a half high and two were hanging from the ceiling. It was so cool to just turn it up and blast the sound. (I wonder why I wear hearing aids now!) Well, if you really knew me then, I was never happy with what I had. I always wanted a little more. So, I figured it would be great if my T.V. was hooked up to the speakers. (I had my own T.V. in my bedroom.) WOW! Would that be a super sound or what! I sat down with my back up against my lower window. There was a large window divided into four sections. Each section was about two and a half feet wide and maybe three and a half feet high, extending from the floor almost to the ceiling. I turned the T. V. around a little bit so I could work on it. The back of the T. V. was now in front of me and my back against the window sitting on the floor. If you are now like I was then not knowledgeable about currents, and if you had an active imagination like I had, you could visualize the major sound that will exude from the T. V. as soon as I hook up this wire to that wire. WALLA! Great sound, right! As I went for the hook up, I just barely grazed the back of the picture tube with my wrist. I kind of touched a little silver band that was wrapped around the back end of the picture tube. Now, I need to tell you that the back of the picture tube has a little different current than the speaker wires. About fifty thousand volts difference! You think that Viagra is something great. Wait until you get hit with fifty thousand volts. Everything I owned stood up straight and hard! It was like in the movies. My hair looked like I had on a fright wig. The major difference was that not only did my hair stand up on end, but I got shot right through the window I was leaning against and about six or seven feet further into the back yard. I am sure that I gave out a blood curdling yell as I shot through the window. My mother must have heard me and came running into my room, yelling, "What happened? "Are you all right?" Then she yelled, "Where are you?" I was nowhere to be found in the room. Today, if there is a speaker problem at home, I jump in there and try to fix it. But to follow suit, as my dad did with the taxis and my little brother did with the cows, I never will try to open the back or try to fix a television again!

We, as kids then, and as kids still do now, have a week off at Easter time. It's called "summer spring break," "Easter week," "hell week" and I am sure a plethora of other terms of which I am not aware. Now that I was a driver, I was invited to many other events by many other people. There was always room for another car. During spring break I was asked to go to Balboa for the week. I am sure that my parents are going to be really happy about this. For those of you that are from the east coast, Balboa is a small island on the west coast near Newport Beach and Huntington Beach. It was mainly for rich people who wanted to live by the water and spend way too much money for a house payment. I personally had trouble believing what some people paid for housing there. The houses were very small and the prices were very high. I was never then, or am I now, rich enough to understand why people do things like that. I am still having trouble paying big monthly payments for my little car and this is years later. Surprisingly, Bill and Roger did not go with me for some reason. Maybe no car! It was a friend of Owens who invited me. I was looking forward to it. There would be nothing but sun and beautiful scantily clad bodies lying around, getting tan. The nights were promised to be full of drinking, dancing, and getting laid. I could dance and I could drink, but I was a novice at the getting laid part. Remember, only twice so far. Once with someone I didn't even know and once with someone I couldn't even see. Not a good track record! But I was young and game for almost anything.

It turned out that we had a five bedroom house for five days. Not a standard run of the mill house. In fact, it was more like a rental and probably was. Like I would have known the difference then! I don't know if it was free, but no one ever asked me for rent money. However, there was a daily donation for booze money. (I think it would have been cheaper to have paid rent.) We started out with about six or seven guys and maybe three girls. I knew only Owen. But that would change shortly. I was happy that I had lost all that weight and started to look like a jock. Thank God for gymnastics. I couldn't wait to put on a swim suit and let the chicks eat their hearts out. (Eat their heart out is an expression that my mom would use often. Later, I found out that everyone used it. I just didn't know what the hell it meant). The days passed fast. We were doing everything from swimming and boating to laying out getting a great tan. Most of the time there were females with us guys just hanging out. They all had great bodies and long hair and flat tummies. Surfer types, California girls, and everyone knows that they are the most beautiful chicks in the world. They would have their hair up and sometimes down and sometimes in tight braids and pony tails, blondes, brunettes and redheads. It all worked for me. Large jugs and small ones and I never saw a one-piece bathing suit, ever! Night time went as promised. Dancing, drinking and it seemed that every bedroom was not available for sleeping the last three nights. By the third night there were at least ten chicks and another guy or so in our house. Why not? The chicks had a place to flop with or without a guy and no strings and never had to pay for a drink, food, rent or anything. All was provided! Now, it seemed that most of the guys kind of hooked up with a chick the first day or so and stuck with them unless something went haywire. Then, they would just find another, either here or elsewhere and bring them home, so to speak. No one really gave a dam. Just like being married today, huh!! Right!

Anyway, I was kinda playing the field but had a couple of chicks in mind. I am not sure if I was waiting for the right moment or if I was just chicken to get laid. I started to get friendly with this one chick who had really long blonde hair. She was, in my mind, beautiful. Great face and shape and her hair went to the middle of her back. Her hair was very thick and soft. It just gleamed, even just out of the ocean. We started to hang out a lot. I can't remember where she was from or how she got to where we were, but I was starting to fall in Love, at least for the weekend. The second to the last night we did it. I think it was great. But most of all, I remember running my hands through her hair and Loving it. All through the next day she was all around me. Rubbing my back, stroking my hair and rubbing me where I liked to be rubbed. It was ok and enjoyable but I wanted to do other stuff. The week was coming to a close and there were still things to do. Surfing, swimming, drinking and a lot more looking! Like the other chick I had my eye on earlier. I started to talk with that other chick that I liked, and the Blonde with the thick hair was not happy with that. To make a very long story shorter (I am sure that every one of you men have been through it), the thick-haired blonde got really pissed off at me and started to hit me and yell and call me dirty names. She actually scratched me and made me bleed in a few places. I didn't understand what was going on, but I took a beating both physically and verbally. She was anger personified! The rest of the day and night I spent most of the time with the new chick. We did spend a lot of time together, but we never got around to doing it. Why, I can't remember. We just didn't.

One thing I do remember very well. I had to leave early in the morning. A couple of the guys had asked me to take them home, and it was going to take most of the day between them and getting home myself. So, before I left, I made my way into the sleeping area where the thick-haired blonde chick was sleeping. She got really blitzed drinking all day. Really drunk! I think she even puked. She had put her hair into two braided pony tails (I guess to keep them out of the vomit) that were about eighteen inches long. I got a scissor and made my way towards her. She was out! I proceeded to cut off her pony tails. She never awakened during the surgical procedure. I loaded up the guys, said my farewells to the few who were awake and left. To this day, I am sure she would like to kill me. I am just not sure for what. The ponytails I took or the piece of tail that I took. Probably both!

Now, a funny thing seemed to happen after that. Believe it or not, I started collecting ponytails and hanging them from the ceiling of my bedroom. Most of them were given to me, just for my asking. Some donated when a chick decided to cut hers off herself, and maybe one or two more to which I helped myself. Now, most of the guys I knew had model airplanes hanging from the ceiling in their rooms. But that's just another reason why you are reading this book.

Easter break came and went way too fast. It was starting to get towards gymnastic time and that was cool. One of the guys in gymnastics was named Steinwitz. That was his last name and he wasn't Jewish. I never could understand that. It just seemed to me that he should be. His first name was Jeff and he was a senior. I kind of looked up to him. He was very good looking, had a great smile, soft spoken, lots of muscles, and was a really nice guy. He and I would horse around when time permitted. We would do tricks like you would see on T.V. or in a circus. He would lie on his back with his elbows on the mat and hands up, and I would put my hands in his and do a handstand on his hands. Then, he would push me up in the air by shear strength, and I had to balance and not fall. Not sure who had the hardest part. Those were the things we did just goofing around. Sometimes I would hang out with him. Was I his best buddy? No, not by a long shot, but it was always cool to hang with a senior. He was on the gymnastics team for the last two years and was a shoe-in for this year as well. Gene and I were on the team last year but did not compete against the other schools. Sort of second string but that would all change this year. However, we did receive our letter, jackets and all. The funny thing was that the jackets were exactly the same as the Drifter jackets (black with a white stripe); only these had a huge "G" in front instead of the Drifter logo on the back. Proud, you bet!

Summer was not all that far away, and my female life was really not that important to me right then. I was seeing Judy casually and dating others when I had the time. Although I was having fun with a few other girls and getting laid on occasions, there was no one really special in my life. There was one girl that everyone wanted to bed. Her name was Ann. She was very pretty but wasn't a knockout beauty wise but had that sexy look. She would date, but you had to play God to even get a kiss. No one had ever been to bed with her, at least that we knew. She must have been saving herself, for what we all asked. I promptly said, "Probably for me." I had asked her out on an occasion or two, but she always had an excuse. She always told me to keep trying because she liked me. (Unlike today, they say no and have no reason. "Just bug off asshole!)

One day Gene said he and Val were going to the movie and wanted to know if I wanted to double with him. Gene had really been spending a lot of time with Val lately. In fact, so much time that I was getting a little jealous. I asked him what she had that I didn't. He told me, and I said, "OH THAT!" Anyway, I asked Ann to go to the movie with me. She said, "Great!" Gene, Val, Ann and I all went to the movie. The drive-in movie! Those days you didn't go to a walk-in movie. In a walk-in movie you have to watch the picture. In a drive-in movie you can watch your date unless, of course, a bunch of guys went. If a bunch of guys went, you could and did smuggle about three of them in, in the trunk, and that way it was a lot cheaper. And by the way, if any of you think that that is an old wives' tale, you are very much mistaken, not to mention the booze that went with us. Gene drove and Ann and I sat in the back seat. A plan, for sure! Don't remember what movie was playing and probably didn't care, but as time went on, Ann and I got hot and heavy in the back seat. I was touching her and she was touching me. She would only let me touch her on top and not below. I tried and tried but it wasn't going to happen. However, I did change tactics and slid my hand down the back of her skirt. It went far enough to touch something that was foreign to me. It felt like a round hairy thing. It was about the size of a quarter and stuck up about an eighth of an inch. I politely asked her what was it, and she said a birth mark. I immediately thought of Ann back east. "A birth mark?" I said. I have never seen one that stuck out that far. "Yea," she said, "I know." It is different. She also asked me not to tell anyone about it. I said, "No problem" and continued to make out. She was a really good kisser and very warm and affectionate but had a very strong constitution and would only go so far. We were both really hot but it went nowhere. I could hear Gene and Val in the front seat giggling softly. The movie was over and we went home.

The next day I had bragging rights. No one had ever gotten as far as I had, no one. None of my friends believed what I told them, that I had my hands on her tits (not her brassier), the real things, flesh in hands, and hands down the back of her skirt, also. I never lied about what happened. I had to prove that I was the man! It really did happen!

I told my buddies that they could not say a thing about this. They all swore that mum was the word. I told them about the mole. The mole that I had sworn to Ann about, which I would not say anything. That mole! I figured that they would believe me because no one had ever said anything about it and that I was the only one who actually felt it and told about it.

By lunch time Ann was all over me like a cheap suit. "Why did you tell, why? No one had to know. You promised me you would not say anything. I knew I should never have gone out with you, Asshole!" I think she was mad. Needless to say, we did not date again, but my friends knew that I was telling the truth, as no one would have gotten that mad over a lie. No one!

Now, a lot of us used to go to the El Monte Legion Stadium for dances on the weekend. It was very cool and a lot of chicks and guys went there. I can't remember there being less than two hundred or more at a time. If memory serves me correctly, it was on Friday nights and started about eight and was over about one. Five hours of women and fighting. What, fighting? Yes, fighting. El Monte was a town with the majority being Mexicans. OH NO, NOT AGAIN!! Actually, I never went with the thought of getting into a fight because I was there for the chicks. But on an occasion or so, we did mingle a little. This was not anything like the fair grounds. When there was a fight, it wasn't Mexicans against the Whites. It was just a guy or two or three getting into it over some chick or something else, but mostly over a chick or two.

At my school, there was one Mexican I really could kick the shit out of. His name was Sonny Knight. He doesn't sound Mexican to me, but he was a Mexican. The reason I said I could kick the shit out of him was because he was blind. Blind, like I can't see. But for some reason I had made friends with him. (Maybe because he couldn't kick the shit out of me) Were we great buddies? No, but we would have lunch together sometimes in school. I would help him step over something that was in his way and just simple things like that. He was kind of heavy, maybe five feet seven inches like most Mexicans I knew, and a senior, obviously a grade ahead of me. What I didn't know about this guy was that he played piano and sang. He was not in choir or Madrigals or any place that I would have seen him or known about him. Another thing that I didn't know about him was that he had written a song.

One time when I was at the El Monte Legion Stadium for the dance and not the fighting, Sonny was there. They stopped the music and made an announcement that Sonny was going to play and sing a song that he wrote. A lot of people figured it was a good time to go to the bathroom or have a smoke or a drink of booze that they had hidden in the bathroom or somewhere on the grounds before they had gotten in to the dance and before the security guards were there. I was not one of them. They rolled out a piano from against the wall and the piano bench. Sonny walked over to the piano and tons of kids huddled around him. I was one of them. I was hanging on the back of the piano and all went silent as the piano began. Sonny started to sing. No one was dancing, no one. Not a sound was heard except from Sonny's throat and his fingers. I couldn't believe how great it was. Remember, I am in Madrigals and had a trio that sang for others and had a little knowledge about music. I figured I was a good critic. It was a very slow song and so romantic. The song was finally over, and he got a standing ovation. Not that anyone was sitting and got up and clapped because we were already standing. The clapping went on for what seemed like twenty minutes. Sonny stood up and said, "Thank you," to everyone and he played the song again. This time I can't tell you how many kids danced to it. All of them were very close and a lot of kissing began on the dance floor. Finally, he was done. This time there was not as much clapping, as most of the kids on the dance floor had each other's tongues in their partner's mouth. I guarantee you that there was a whole bunch of babies made to that song as there was to Johnny Mathis' songs. The dance was over and we all went home.

A couple of days went by. I saw Sonny at lunch and had asked him about the song. He told me that he not only wrote both the notes and the lyrics but that he had submitted it to a record company who was considering it for a single. Sonny also told me that he told them that if they were to use it, he would not consider anyone else to sing it except himself. I thought this is one tough blind Mexican. (Maybe I can't kick his ass!) Telling a record company how to run their business! I told him to let me know what happened with it.

About a month or so later he told me that they said OK and that he was to record in a week or two. I was really happy for him and for me because I knew him. But, in all actuality, the chances of being a song that I would hear on the radio would be probably null and void. I wished him the best and left. In about a month or so, I did hear it on the radio. Not once every two weeks or even once a week but over and over on a daily basis. To my knowledge Sonny never had another hit record, but he did hit the top of the charts with this one and was number one for a couple of weeks. He is now classed as one of those one hit wonders. I have the song on tape and have it on a CD. You can still buy it if you purchase the right Oldie but Goodie CD. I do listen to it on a regular basis and sometimes cry and wish I was with someone to dance. I often wonder if Sonny is with us today. I suppose you would like to know the name of the song. It is "Confidential" by Sonny Knight! Somewhere around the late fifties!

The summer was approaching at a rapid pace. Graduation! Whoopee! I hated English and would be done with it soon, but there was someone who made my being in English class tolerable. Her name was Gail. Gail was a very pretty girl, fairly short red hair, about five feet six inches tall and freckles. The kind of freckles that were very attractive and she had a body to die for. At my young and tender age, the only female that could hold a candle to Gail was young Diane. Diane, now, was only about fourteen if she was that. Gail was stacked like a . . . . I don't know what! If she was in this time zone today, you would say she had a rack that made a full-grown moose look like a doe, a tiny waist, and full rounded hips. Playboy material for sure! One day she never came back to English class. Shit! Or any class for that matter. I had to study English now and look at the English teacher. We, Gail and I, used to talk a little, but she was a very quiet girl. I never knew anyone whom she dated or even was close to. Not even a female. She was the same age as me and had the same classes as me, but I didn't disappear like she did. She never finished school here. She disappeared with only a month and a half to go to eleventh grade graduation. A lot of us had noticed her. The guys especially! Not too many girls were friendly with her. But rumor had it that she got a chance to do a Playboy centerfold shoot and did it. Then the school found out about it and expelled her. I never did see her in Playboy, although I did see someone who could have been her. The way they touch up people for that kind of stuff may have made it a little harder to visualize her. However, the name was different, also.

That could have been normal as well. One good thing that did come from it was that I had another reason to read the Playboy magazine!

It is really getting close to graduation. My friend, Jeff, the almost Jewish guy from gymnastics, asked me if I was doing anything for the senior all-night party. OK, once again, I will explain something to you. You guys and gals my age know what the hell I am talking about and tonight when you go to bed, I am sure will have a wet dream in remembrance. For the younger guys and gals, I will explain. The senior all-night party is exactly what I just said. The graduating seniors, after the graduation ceremonies and after the dinner with the folks and after all the hoopla, get to go to a place of their choice and spend the whole night with whomever they choose. Most of the grads went to the beach with a whole bunch of their graduating friends and had a big bon fire and took their sleeping bags and about a gallon of booze each, a chick, a condom or two, and spent the night in glory. They then woke up at the break of dawn and had been so drunk that they didn't know if they had gotten laid or not. Because of their hangovers, they really didn't give a shit. Now that you young'ens are up to speed, I can continue.

I said to Jeff that I was only a junior and he said that he knew that. Jeff said, "I have a friend who needs a date to the senior dance and overnight party. Would you be interested?" This is a major deal. A male junior going to a senior all-night party is unheard of. It happens, but it's very rare. The first thing I said is, "How bad is she?" He said, "Would I steer you wrong?" I said, "Don't answer like a female and answer the question with an answer, not with a question." He said, "She is extremely nice." I said, "So what's the deal?" Extremely nice and she can't get a date and wants me, a junior! Does she even know me? Has she even seen me? Does she know that I am a broke kind of guy? What's the deal?" "Whoa, big fellow," Jeff said. "Yes to all of the above. She broke up with her boy friend not too long ago and really needs to be with a nice guy for a change. You are not going to get laid, but I guarantee you that you will have a nice time. She already has the dance and dinner tickets. All you will have to bring is the booze and drive to the beach. I told her about you. She has seen you, and it is just fine with her." She just wants to finish out her senior year with her friends with whom she graduated and have a great time in her last days at school." I said, "Ok, fine, but if she is a dog, I will never talk to you again." Now that I think about it, in all of these years, I have never changed my way. I am still a gentleman no matter what I think on the first date. A commitment is a commitment, and you keep your word all the time.

On the last day of school for seniors, I went to pick Naomi up at her house. Naomi is a really great name. The more I thought about it though, the more I knew that I was headed for tragedy. Jeff would never point her out to me or tell me her name. He just said that I wouldn't be disappointed. Great, just fuckin great! Ok here comes the moment of truth. I have my suit and tie on for the dance and dinner and my towel and swim suit packed for the overnight at the beach. I knocked and the door opens. A very tall, beautiful-dark haired lady answers the door and says, "Hi Chuck." I immediately thought that could not be her, but before I said, "Are you Naomi?" She said, "I am Naomi and I hope you are not disappointed." I almost shit my pants. This chick was beautiful. Great body, beautiful face, long, dark hair draped over one of her eyes and then down her back. (I immediately visualized her hair hanging from my ceiling) tall but not too tall, and a smile that could kill. She wore a long black dress that was almost to the floor and very tight to the body. (And what a body) I knew I had been in an accident on the way over here and had gotten killed and was in heaven. Then I came to the realization that I was never destined for heaven, so I guess I was just the luckiest guy in the world and owed Jeff big time. While all of this was happening, I was looking over my back to see if this was a set up for some reason. I said, "Are you ready?" She said, "Ok." We got into my auto and sped away. I can't remember where the dinner-dance was or even if we danced. If I had my way, we wouldn't spend much time there and would be the first to leave and head to the beach. This chick in a swim-suit has just got to be a knockout, and I can't wait to see her.

I remember driving to the beach. There were already a bunch of cars there. No one was supposed to meet there, but it just was a popular spot to gather, park, and watch the sun set. Some of us made a circle, kinda like the covered wagons of old yesteryear. We got a huge bon fire going right in the middle and broke out the beer and booze. Some of the guys brought the wood and some the beer. There were about three or four guys there that I kinda knew from school. Just about everyone there were seniors except for me. I was ready for some teasing but it never occurred. Car radios blasted. Blankets broke out, and we all took turns changing in the back seat of the cars from the Semi-formal attire to the swimming apparel. In my case, I went first. It didn't take long. Then, Naomi went and did take a little while. I am sure she had to get out off a bunch of stuff that I didn't. While she was changing I started to think of how the night would go. I know what I had in mind and not so different than most of the other guys around here had in mind with their honeys. But I am a little different than most of them. Most of them brought their girl friends and or at least someone they had dated once or twice. Me, that was not the case! We did communicate well and had a lot in common because of the people we knew. Conversation is a whole lot different than making Love, especially for the first time with someone you just met and actually knew her name. Not to mention, I was probably a novice compared to her. She was a year older and just broke up with her boy friend. I am sure that they were having sex. So she, I am sure, was much more experienced than I. I was sitting on our blanket as she exited the car. I was so much into my night dreaming that I didn't even notice her get out of the car until she sat down next to me. Now, I am pissed at myself as I really wanted to see her standing with her swimsuit on. However, she made up for it. She sat down, and I mean right down very close to me and gave me a very nice kiss. No tongue or a major embrace but a really nice and warm kiss. I was dumb founded. Like the idiot I am, instead of saying thank you or giving her a big smile or even a little kiss back, I said, "What was that for?" She said (just like a female and answered the question with a question), "Didn't you like it?" I said, "Like it? I had been dreaming about that since you opened the door and I saw what you looked like." She smiled and kissed me again, and this one was even better. The only thing that was going through my mind right then was where we were going to do it, on the blanket, in the back seat of the car, or a little ways down the beach in the sand and, hopefully, on a blanket. She broke my thinking process with a request. "Would you get me a beer?" I got up and as I did, I caught her eye looking at me standing. I thought "Is she looking at me for the same reason I wanted to look at her when she got out of the car with her swimsuit on or was she looking at something else?" Either way, I made sure I held in my stomach in, stuck out my chest, and proceeded to get the beer. Now Arnold Schwarzenegger I was not, but I was starting to have a pretty good body. (Note the picture on the next page.) Not bad for a used to be fat guy.

Certainly nothing to be ashamed of and I think she knew it. We both had a few beers and after a while she said, "Let's go for a walk." Ah Ha, I thought, this is it. I said, "Do you think we should take a blanket?" She said, "No, it's not that cold." Not the answer I was looking for. We walked for quite a while. We stopped and kissed and looked at the moon often. I never touched her intimately and the same went for her. But I can tell you that she had a great body.

I couldn't keep my hands off of her. I kept touching her hair, running my hands up and down her body, especially her bare belly and back and almost all the time making sure that my hands slid from her suit to her bare legs and behind her butt. It was really nice. By the time we made it back to the cars, I was ready to take my problem in hand myself. Where was Barney when you needed him! We sat down, had another beer, and made the decision to just sleep outside on the blanket under the stars. I was thinking that this may be the toughest night I will ever have in my life. However, I did think that when she finally goes to sleep, maybe I could cop a little feel. She did have a great bust. Now that I think about it, I have always been a bust man. I wonder if she had anything to do with it! I am not really sure what time we had fallen asleep, but somewhere between then and wake up time, there was a hand on me where it shouldn't have been. It was not mine or Barney's. We made Love for most of the rest of the night.

The morning came around and a lot of us went to breakfast at, I think, it was Sambo's. OK for you youngsters. Once again I will teach you something. Sambo's was a very successful restaurant chain very similar to a cross between Lenny's and I HOP, except for a few things. Sambo's specialized in pancakes like I HOP. They also had waitresses who knew what the word service was, not like Lenny's. (My philosophy on Lenny's waitresses is, that they are trained for two weeks. Then they work at a given restaurant until they are let go for whatever reason. Then they apply to a different chain of restaurants, and give such bad service that the customers of that restaurant start going to Lenny's. It is a full circle with Lenny's winning by constantly increasing customers.)

Sambo's was really a great restaurant but a bunch of people of color took exception to their logo. At least that's the way I heard it. It was a small black kid and a tiger chasing his tail. These people (in my opinion) basically put Sambo's out of business. In fact, to my knowledge, the only one still existing is in Santa Barbara, California. I also think that there was a book called "Little Black Sambo" that they were against. Now where was I?

Oh yea, breakfast. After a GREAT breakfast I drove Naomi home. Needless to tell you, there wasn't a kid that night who got a good night's sleep, whether they got laid, drunk or both. I am sure, just like me, that we all took a long nap that day. I hope they all had dreams like I did. I never dated Naomi again. I did make a few calls but reaped no harvest; (You don't think it was my lack of sexual knowledge and performance, do ya?), however, I did think about her often. Not to mention I had some great bragging rights. A junior invited to a senior all-night party by a senior girl, who was awesome!

That was about the conclusion of the eleventh grade and what a conclusion it was. I would have figured that I would get beat up by a Mexican and spend much of the summer in a hospital. Instead this! Eleventh grade is done. I am seventeen and a half and the summer is here! Next year a senior and as I have said before, I will be CHAI COCKED (high cocked)! A real BFD!

Chapter Ten

Well, just about the first thing I did to get the summer going was to buy a Nineteen Fifty-Five Chevrolet Bel Aire two door stick shift, two-tone Blue. This car probably occupied eighty percent of my time in the summer. I don't remember what I did with the Forty-Eight Buick (probably sold it to a ski supply store), but a Fifty-Five Chevy was the car of the day! I must have gone through six thousand dollars in car wax alone. Every chance I had, I would take it to Ganesha Park, put it under a tree, and spend thirty hours each day waxing it. Ganesha Park was in Pomona and not far from where Judy lived, so I would invite her to help me wax it. She seemed to look at things a little different than I did! She wasn't much help!

There was a drive-through restaurant called "Henry's" on the corner of Foothill Boulevard and Garey Avenue in Pomona. It had a regular restaurant on one side and an attached covered open-air part built in a horseshoe shape on the other side. You could pull in and order some food and usually a great looking chick would serve you. Anyone who was someone cruised through Henry's for hours every time they would have the chance, especially at night so your highly-waxed auto would glisten under the overhead lighting. No matter what time of day or night or in fact no matter what day it was, you would always see someone you knew. It was really popular. Round and round and round we would drive at about one mile per hour, so all could see the great cars we had. If anybody ever wanted to tell the guys who were cruising around how great their cars were, they couldn't. One of the unwritten rules to cruising at Henry's was that you had to have your radio so loud so that everyone *inside* the restaurant knew you were there. The amount of gas that was wasted cruising around Henry's probably helped start Texaco's rise to fame and fortune, along with my oil sales and with the help of Sid Caeser, of course. ("We're the men of Texaco; we work from Maine to Mexico; there's nothing like this Texaco of ours!" etc. etc.) (Forget it, you young ones I'm not going to explain. Ask your Granddad.) Now, even with all the wax I put on my new short (Short. Mexican slang for car. Mexicans just keep showing up in every aspect of my life.), it still lacked the shine that I really needed to be noticed as I cruised Henry's. So, a paint job was in order. Walla! Midnight Blue! Earl Scheibs' best. I think it set me back about thirty bucks, but I could not wax it for a month. Oh no, my summer was ruined! I did get a brand new set of three-prong chrome spinners. Man, were they beautiful. The lights would hit them at Henry's, and they would just sparkle.

After the chrome wheels I started to do other things to my fifty-five. I put a plan together so this Chevy would be like no other Chevy in the country. This was the first car that I really picked myself. No one was going to top it. No one! The newest rage was four on the floor. For you who know little or nothing about automobiles, four on the floor was where the manual shifting lever was on the floor instead of on the steering column. It had four gears instead of the normal three: first, second, third, and fourth or low, medium, high and OH SHIT, that's fast! It wasn't easy to do this conversion because my Chevy originally only had three gears like most cars normally had. Thanks to a lot of training in the two years of auto shop, I had gained a lot of knowledge. Metal shop helped, also, as I had to do some welding around the hole that I had to make in the floor to put the gear shifter through. It took about a week of fooling around with it but I got the job done. Now, I can race! I had to set the rest of my plans in motion.

I went to the junk yard and bought a pair of Nash Rambler front seats. (Yes, you youngsters, there was a car called a Nash Rambler. In fact, there is a song about one that outraces a Cadillac.) I don't know why Nash made these, and I am sure it was not for the same reason that I wanted them, but they reclined. They reclined all the way back in the Rambler. Once again, I had some trouble installing them because of size. When I was finished, they did not fit exactly flush when the back seat was all the way back, but they did do the job. What job, you ask? You will have to use your imagination for that one. Actually, what I had in mind when I thought about putting them in was, to sit in the back seat and be able to stretch out when at the drive-in movie. Me, her, and a blanket in the winter, could be fun! They did prove effective! Now, I had the new Midnight Blue paint, bitchen chrome wheels with three-prong flippers, four on the floor, and my new reclining seats.

What's next? Well, I'll tell you what's next. What good are reclining seats if you are not real cozy in them, right? I needed some mood inspiring decor. I put contrasting blue, short soft-haired carpet throughout the whole inside of the car. On the side of the doors, on the front part of the dash board, and on the back package tray was all carpet. On the top of the dash I put very long white-hair Angora carpet. It was very soft and the chicks Loved to touch it. (I am talking about the carpet.) It was the kind that you would find in a very expensive home on the bathroom floor. (Is that an oxymoron?) The whole thing didn't take that long to do, maybe a couple of weeks or so. All this work on my car had been done throughout the summer and not back to back, but I want to construct my Chevy so you know what I actually wound up with and how cool it was.

Carpet installed, I felt something was still missing. Lighting, that's the ticket. Lights! You all know how good I am with T. V. wiring right? Now, I can transfer my expertise in that area to an automobile. I completely wired the car's dash and side panels with small red lights and had them concealed by the overhanging fibers of the carpet. I installed a toggle switch on the dash board so that when I flipped it on, the red lights would go on. By being partially concealed by the carpet, a red hazy glow was created and not a bright light. Light blue carpet, red lights and roll back seats. Sexy? You bet! Now I have this whore house on wheels ready to roll.

One day as I was talking to Bill, he said, "This car is for catching women, except for the four on the floor, right?" (The four on the floor was for running from the ugly ones.) Right! "Why not add a little something for the guys?" Bill asked. Although I had been hanging out a little less lately with him, he was still a good friend. "You do plan on still hanging out with us guys, don't ya?" he said. "Yes, of course," I retorted." "So what's the plan, and how much trouble am I going to get into this time?" He laughed and said, "This is cool. You know how the windshield wiper water thing works, right? You push the little button on the dash, and water squirts out onto the windshield of your car so that your wipers can clean the windshield. We convert it from water to alcohol!" "What?" "It's easy! Look. You replace the large plastic container under the hood with two smaller glass ones. Then, instead of the two hoses that run to each side of the windshield, we run them through the fire wall into your dashboard. Add an extra button on the dash so each hose has its own button. Then, fill one glass container with vodka and the other one with bourbon. Pull out the hose of your choice from the dash into a glass, push the button and we can drink and drive and never have to stop except to pee." I'm thinking this guy is nuts! Well it took two days, and we were drinking and driving! If I could just figure out a way to install a toilet! I thought about Tuck and Roll or Tuck and Schmuck, as my dad called it, for my seats. I had such a bad taste in my mouth from my last experience that I decided not to take the chance. It seemed that Mexicans and I just don't mix.

One of the hottest things at that time was to lower the front of your car, unless you were a Mexican, then you lowered it all around. I gave it a lot of thought and decided not to do it. I figured that if I lowered the front, someone might think I was half Mexican and that just wouldn't set right with me. Let's see, Gerson the Mexican, just like Stienwitz the Jew. I don't think so! The way I saw it, right then and there, the only good Mexican was a blind one.

When I had time, Gene, Val, Judy and I spent a lot of it going to the beach, Knots Berry Farm, and of course, now open, Disney Land. I had quit the Texaco Station and was doing full time plus at Scoa in the domestics department. It just seemed, in general, I was straightening out a little and not doing the wrong things as much. I didn't find myself at home much either. Every once in a while Dad would ask me to take Mom to the doctor, the store or somewhere, and Mom wouldn't go in the rolling whore house so I would take my dad's Cadillac. As you probably remember, my dad had cancer and used to smoke three packs of Lucky Strike cigarettes every day. When he found out that he had cancer, he quit smoking right then and there and never touched a cigarette again. He had an extremely strong constitution. However, he did replace cigarettes with gum. Stick gum. You know Wrigley's, Black Jack, Doublemint and the like. There are twenty cigarettes in a pack and times that by three packs, that's sixty cigarettes per day. That meant he'd chew at least sixty sticks of gum each and every day. My father had no idea what a trash bag was. When I got into his car, I couldn't believe it! There were no less than three to four inches high of gum wrappers on the floor of the whole car. I almost couldn't find the gas pedal. I started to laugh so hard that I started to cry. My mother, on the other hand, who drove with him on a regular basis, could not see what I was laughing at. I said, "The wrappers." She said, "The what?" I said, "The wrappers. See all of the wrappers on the floor?" She said, "So." When I got home, I asked Dad why he didn't throw the wrappers out or into a bag or something. He said, "What wrappers?" I said, "What wrappers, the gum wrappers that are on the floor of your car." He said, "So." It's kinda like "Who's on first?" Again, you younger ones ask your granddad about the "Who's on first shtick."

One afternoon, in the dead of summer, I remember being with Gene and Owen. I think Roger was there as well. We were going to have a watermelon throwing deal at Henry's Drive In. I am sure this was not sanctioned by the restaurant. I remember picking up four or five watermelons and asking the produce guy to cut them into fourths. I even remember the price of them. One penny a pound, now hard to believe! We pulled into Henry's and parked. Right across from us was another car. I could see that they were eating watermelon. Before we could order a coke and fries, the two back doors opened and two guys heaved watermelon at us. We opened our doors and retaliated. Did you ever see watermelon splatter on a car's windshield? It really makes a mess. Just as I was going to throw another piece, I got hit with some from a car that had just pulled in that I hadn't noticed. Now there were three cars and watermelon flying in all directions. The girls who worked there as waitresses didn't know what to do as they were trying to serve other cars that were not participants in this great sport. I think the best they could do was to stay out of the way. There were a few other cars there with kids just having lunch or something. You could see the kids in the cars trying to get out and get the free watermelon that was lying on the ground. But Dads and Moms kept the doors closed tight. I am sure they thought that at any time there could be a display of guns. This went on for two minutes or so but it seemed like a half hour. Out of ammunition as you will, we pulled out and left. Just as we were pulling out, the police were pulling in. Why they didn't stop us is a mystery because I had watermelon all over my car. Possibly who ever called them might not have said what exactly was going on. I don't think I could have handled another jail thing and beating thing by Dad.

Every once in a while I would stop into the Drifters club house just to see what was going on and to see if they had killed anyone lately. They always treated me nicely. I guess it was because I was a member. Although not the best fighter, I did go with them. Summer was almost gone, and the fair would start soon. You know what that means . . . . the fights!

Occasionally, sometimes Bill, Roger, and I would climb Elephant Hill. It was right behind our tract where we lived. Elephant Hill was only five hundred feet high, had very little green grass, and just a few trees near the top. It was a kind of getaway from humans. Not many people or even kids would hike up it because it was so desolate. We would hike to the top and lay under one of the few trees and smoke ourselves silly. Roger kept smoking his dad's brand, Kools, because he could steal most of them. I smoked Viceroys at the time. I never smoked a mentholated cigarette again after the stolen one I got from Roger, when I almost puked myself to death, and then got beat up by the Mexican. In fact, I can remember one day, I was broke and had no cigarettes. I took a newspaper with me up the hill, and rolled some of the dead grass in it, and smoked it. Although I could not talk for the next two days from the pain of inhaling, it was better than a beating. Can't remember what Bill smoked.

One day I was doing a lot of thinking. The fair was close and I would have to fight. I will be a senior this year, and what would I do after I graduate? Where is my relationship with Judy going? How's Dad's health and just thinking about a bunch of stuff like that. I decided to climb Elephant Hill and spend some time in solitude, under a tree, thinking. I did exactly that. I found a small, almost grassy area amongst the very dry stuff under a small tree and pulled out a frajo (Spanish for cigarette), lit it up, and began to contemplate my life. Not really sure how long I spent up there, but I went through many cigarettes. In fact, it was starting to get close to dusk. I started to walk down the hill and about four or five minutes into my retreat I smelled smoke. I turned around and the whole f—g hill was on fire. I thought, Jesus Christ, I did it again. I started running down the hill because I didn't want to get caught up there. I never even gave a thought to being burned to death. I ran like hell and finally got to the bottom looking for the police and/ or the fire department. Not to help out but to hide from them. I made it down all the way in safety and never saw anyone or heard any sirens until I got to my house a good seven blocks away. I was terrified this time because I saw the flames and the whole hill on fire heading towards the houses at the bottom of the hill. Believe it or not, not a single home went up in flames, but I am sure the last row of houses in the tract was scared to death. Thank God they didn't go up in flames.

That was where little (big if you get my drift) Diane lived. We certainly don't want to lose her.

It was probably about midsummer, and my family decided to throw a big barbecue party. All were invited. Dad was to barbecue hamburgers and hot dogs, being very careful of where he shot the barbecue fluid this time and, of course, was not wearing any socks. There were at least fifty people. We were having a good time, laughing, eating and just kicking back. Somewhere in the midst of all the fun, I must have pissed off my dad. I can't remember just what I said or did, but he got real mad. He started slapping me around. I got embarrassed with so many people there that I started to bad mouth him back. Not the norm for me. The more I said the more he got pissed. He started to come at me again so I just ran to the back of the yard and leaped the five-foot cinder block wall to get away from him. (I knew that gymnastics would someday come in handy.) As I got my first leg over the wall, a spear shot passed me about four or five inches on the right. My dad had picked up the aluminum bow that I had made in metal shop (it was lying on the ground by the garage un-strung) and tossed it at me out of his uncontrollable madness. (He did have a tendency to throw the closest thing at hand at me more than once.) I am not sure but, if it had been a few inches more to the left, I probably would have been dead. When I got over the fence, I stopped to look back because I couldn't believe that he had done that. I saw Mom giving Dad about all the hell he could handle. Although I did not go back home until night fall, I did have a smile on my face for most of the day.

We lived near an old graveyard maybe three or four miles away from our house on Barjud. It wasn't far from a home for the mentally retarded (The word "challenged" was not yet invented), and ill. Just about everyone knew about both places because to leave the Pomona area, north bound, you had to pass them both. Sometime we guys would go to the cemetery and park with our dates and make out. There was a fairly long drive to get to the grave area, after you would pass the entrance, and we would park in the drive and not the cemetery. There were a lot of trees around that provided darkness from the night moon so that no one could see into other cars if there was more than one car parked there.

One day Gene and I were talking about double dating to the drive in. I am not sure which one of us thought about it but said, "Why don't we set up a scare show at the cemetery and scare the hell out of anyone who goes there? We can find out who might be going there on a Saturday night to make out and be ready for them." This sounded really cool. Gene and I spent the biggest part of the day putting up ropes attached to trees so when we would pull on them from a distance, the tree limbs would shake or drop down. We spotted flashlights around so we could shine them from behind a tree and make a dim shine on a tree or two. We even got a werewolf mask so when a car pulled in; one of us could run across the road. The car head lights would shine on us as we ran across. We set the whole thing up just great. I even got a child's small play horn so that we could make a strange sound. I am sure we included a few other things that slip my mind after so many years. Gene already had a date with Val for the Saturday night that we decided to do this spook stuff. Actually, as I had mentioned, we had been talking about a double date. Gene was having a mind problem with canceling his (already made) date with Val to do this spook stuff. So, we decided to have Gene and Val be the victims, and I would scare the poop out of Val.

After the show at the drive in, Gene and Val pulled into the cemetery where I was waiting and was completely ready for them. As their car pulled far into the drive just before the cemetery area, I ran in front of the car wearing the werewolf head gear about thirty feet away. Val said to Gene, "Did you see that?" Gene said, "What?" "Something ran across the road. Gene said, "It was probably a rabbit." "No, Val said, it was huge." "Huge? Gene asked, I didn't see a thing, and I was looking that way because I was looking for a place to park." "I am telling you, I saw something," Val said. Gene parked the car. (At a later time he said to me that it was all he could do to keep from laughing and to keep a straight face.) They parked and Val was a little edgy. They started to make out. I pulled one of the ropes, and a tree limb fell over the car's front windshield. Then, I let go, and it returned to its original resting place. (Pardon the pun.) Gene, of course, made sure that Val was looking that way and he was not. She jumped up and said, "Look, a tree fell on the car." Of course, Gene turned and there was nothing. He said, "What's going on? Do you want to go home?" Val said, "No, but please lock the doors." Gene did. A few minutes later I flashed a flashlight and sounded the horn. Val saw and heard both. She said to

Gene, "Ok let's go, I'm scared." Gene said, "Scared of what? I don't see anything." "Did you hear that sound?" Gene said, "It was probably just the trees rustling from the wind." Val said, "I don't think so." I gave them a three or four minute break. Then, I ran in front of the car again about fifteen feet away with a flashlight behind me as to show me but not real good. Obviously, Val at this time couldn't keep her eyes off the cemetery and wasn't doing much kissing. She said, "I have to go." Just about then I pulled another rope and hit the top of the car with a tree branch. It made a loud noise, and Gene said, "I heard that, did you?" She said, "Let's go. Get out of here." Gene said, "It was just a tree branch hitting the car from the wind. I'll get out and check." "NO! NO!" Val said. Please don't get out and let's just leave." Gene said, "Relax. This isn't a scary movie or something. I'll check it out." Gene got out of the car, and Val locked the doors after him. Gene walked around a bit, picked up another prop we had hidden, and then he ran back to the car yelling, "Let's go let's go." But the doors were locked. As Val reached over to unlock the doors, Gene had set a bloody hand and partial arm we had made on the hood of the car. Gene got in and Val said, "What did you see? What did you see?" Gene yelled, "Nothing" and started the car, put it in reverse and as he started to back out, he said to Val, "What's that on the hood?" Val looked and then let out a blood curdling scream at the top of her lungs. "GO! GO!" Gene hit the gas, and they were gone. I am not sure what exactly went on for the next hour or so, but Val didn't talk to me for about a month and as for Gene, I don't think he ever got laid again by Val. The next day Gene told me that he, himself, was starting to get a little scared, even knowing what was actually going on. Guess I missed my calling, but I don't think there is much of a demand for a cemetery scare guy!

 Judy and I started to spend a lot of time together towards the end of summer. In fact, Gene and Val made up, and the four of us spent a lot of time together. Judy and I got very close. She was different, nice, caring, soft and warm. She wasn't the most beautiful girl I had slept with in all my worldly experiences; (although very pretty) there was something very different about her. I think you would call it being in Love. It was nice to spend time being intimate with someone and knowing the girl's name. Once again, we spent a lot of time going to the beach, Disneyland, Knots Berry Farm, and just hanging out.

Chapter Eleven

Summer ended. I am seventeen and a half, and school is starting. A senior and to be the second graduating class from this new school, Ganesha High School, in Pomona! It seems like a long journey from a man at thirteen to a big shit on campus at seventeen. I thought about a recap of what has transpired from birth to date, but I would have to add a whole new chapter. This book is already too long.

The first few days at school were easy because I had to look forward to the fair. My classes were math, gym, Madrigals, history, (another pain in the ass class), auto shop, and of course, home room.

The fourth day after class (about one o'clock because it was a half day at school so that we could go to the fair with our free ticket), a guy walked up to me and said, "Are you still in?" I looked at him and I said, "Are you Ted?" He said "Yes." You look a little different from a few months ago." He said, "A couple of niggers altered my face a little bit not long after school was out." "Shit, are you all right?" "Yea, I'll live. I can't wait to get back at them in the next couple of weeks." He obviously was a Drifter. I said, "When is the first meeting?" He said, "Tomorrow night at eight." I said, "I will be there." Not really sure I wanted to be there, but it was kind of a natural reaction answer.

I picked up Judy, and we went to the fair. Gene and Val met us there. We spent the rest of the day and well into the night just having a great time. Cotton candy, fun zone rides, throwing darts and looking at the special art work exhibits, bird displays, petting zoo, and so on.

The next day, after dinner, I made my way to the club house for the Drifters' meeting. Like the year before, I was still sitting on the fence. I didn't mind mixing it up with the Mexicans but had my reservations about the blacks. The first rumble was set for Saturday night. I told them I had to work at Scoa Saturday night until nine o'clock and probably wouldn't even get out of there until nine thirty. By the time I would get to the fair, it would be ten o'clock or so. They were supposed to meet at nine thirty under the Golden Arches, and it had already been set. I volunteered to help pick up the wounded and got a laugh from the guys. "Ok, killer, the Sergeant at Arms said, next time." I got lucky again. The first rumble was with blacks, and I would miss it.

Now, about this time in my life, I started to realize that my little brother and I are the exact opposites. I will start pointing this out occasionally and, as to this date, nothing has changed. We are still opposites. About the only thing we have in common is that we both like vanilla ice cream and Laughlin better than Las Vegas. He wasn't even too crazy about our mom, and I thought she was just great. Just to give you an idea about what I am talking, as I am readying myself to kill or be killed, my little brother, Mark is a boy scout and trying to learn how to save people with artificial respiration, gauze and a band-aid. In fact, I like cows and he doesn't. Go figure!

The first couple of weeks at school were going just fine with Judy, the fair, and spending a lot of time outside school practicing with the Madrigals, not to mention gymnastics. The Madrigals had a lot of performances scheduled, and that was always cool because we got out of school for most of them. The gymnastic away schedule was full, also, but that was usually after school.

Not far away from where I lived was Bracket Field and Puddingstone Dam. Bracket Field was a small airport that will come into play much later in years. Puddingstone Dam was a NOW event. That was where I learned about snipe hunts and the submarine races. One day, Bill asked me if I had ever been to a snipe hunt. I said "Hell, I don't even know what a snipe is." He said, "Me, Owen, Roger and another guy, whom I didn't know, were going Friday night and asked me if I would like to go?" I said, "Sure." 'What do I do?" Bill said, "You need a date and a large paper bag, like a shopping bag." I said, "I'll ask Judy if she will go with me. I'm in!" Judy said, "OK." I told Bill and he said, "Meet me at the cement parking area at the bottom of Puddingstone at nine-thirty and make sure you bring the bag." I said "I will be there or be square, but what is a snipe?" Bill said, "You will see when you catch one."

So at nine thirty sharp we met Bill, Rog, Owen, and a guy named Fred and their dates. Bill told us all what we were to do. He said, "Spread out with about a hundred yards or so in between us, and don't be within eye shot and or hearing range. We need our own space and quiet area so that the snipes don't get scared because of other sounds." He told us that when we are set in our own area, that we are to stay bent down low or even to lay down and to flick the bag with our fingers that we had set on the ground beneath us. The flicking sound will attract the snipes. They will go into the paper bag, and then we are to shut the bag real fast to trap them. When we have one, come back to the car area and wait for the others to arrive with their catch as well. So, Judy and I headed off to a remote area all by ourselves as did the others. What we didn't know is that there are no such things as a snipe. We were the only ones who didn't know it. About midnight or so when we were tired and our fingers were sore from flicking, we started to walk back to the cars. When we got there, there was a note on my car. The note read in real big letters, SUCKER!

The next day I took Judy right back there to watch the submarine races. That is when you park in a real dark place high up on the dam's ridge and wait for the submarines to surface and race against one another. While we are waiting for them to appear, you make out with the one you are with until you get tired and then go home. You then tell the girl that we will have to try again another time and hope that she does not understand what's going on. Judy was a blonde!

For the next few days at school, they were having "vocation day." That is when you fill out a questionnaire and special counselors tell you what you are best suited for when you graduate. So that Daddy won't have to support you anymore and that you can go to work yourself. (Hate when that happens.) You spend a full day listening to talks about different types of jobs. Then, you fill out the questionnaire about yourself and wait a month or so for the results. Mine came back and I thought it would have included an application for a gun license. But as luck would have it, it read the best area for you dip shit, (I added the "dip shit" myself) is in the aircraft industry. It also read that the aircraft industry was hiring right now and included all areas of aviation. The list of openings included pilots, runway personal, mechanics, administration, etc. etc. Hmmmm, I thought, mechanics but dismissed it because it involved work! But keep that thought in mind.

I got the report that all went well at the fair involving the Drifters and the blacks. Not a death they said, but we did kick a lot of black ass. (I am sure that the blacks said the same thing about us white asses.)

The next week we got a short schedule for our performances with the Madrigals. We were all stoked. It included about four or five schools in a four week period, starting in a week or so. We Madrigals had started learning the music and words from the musicals "South Pacific" and "Oklahoma" last year and had continued with it so far this year. Even though it was only a couple of weeks into the new school year, we pretty much had the songs down pat. We were given the choice of three songs from "South Pacific" and four from "Oklahoma." We chose "There is Nothin' Like a Dame" where only the guys sang and the girls would make faces or do something silly. I was asked to do the solo lead in "Some Enchanted Evening" but, as usual, didn't have the guts for a solo, and no one else wanted it. It was a powerful song, and the guys just didn't have the lungs I did. We also did "Bali Ha'i" which was a great song to do. There were a lot of antics that were available to do. From "Oklahoma" we did "Oklahoma", of course, which is a powerful song in itself. Val asked to do "I'm Just a Girl Who Can't Say No" because she was the lead solo in practice. It is not only a great song, but we all wished it had been true, (lucky Gene) so we all agreed to it. We did "Oh What a Beautiful Morning" with the lead by Butch Abarvitz (Another guy who had a Jewish name but wasn't Jewish) and "Kansas City". All in all, we had about a three quarter of an hour show. That worked perfect as the kids had an hour to get from their class, view the show and then go back to their next class.

Now that we all were elated about the songs and the schedule, we thought we'd do something nice for our illustrious leader, Mr. Cummings. (I am sure you all thought we were heading somewhere with all this boring music stuff, right?) Mr. Cummings drove a VW bug. So, the next day, we guys in Madrigals decided to put his Volkswagen in the hallway blocking the door in front of his classroom while he was in his class. When he tries to open the door (which opens out) after class, he won't be able to. Now, a VW, although small, is still a little too heavy for one person to move about thirty or forty feet from the parking area to the classroom door. We decided that we all would have to go to the bathroom at eleven o'clock. We all got out of our respective classrooms and met in front of the VW in the parking lot. Ten of us picked it up and put it, not only in front of the door, but put its nose to the door. Normally, that would not matter, but there was a wall directly across from the door, about twenty feet or less from the classroom door. If he found some way to get out of the classroom, he could not drive it away.

There was no room to do so. (Are we having fun yet?) We did all of this in about five minutes or less and then found our way back to our respective classes.

I, nor any of my cronies, were aware of how he got his car out and in a drivable condition, but the next day, there was a flier on every one's desk in the school telling about it. It said, if they find out who did it, or if it ever happens again, the culprits would be expelled from school for sure. They never found out!

Now, like I said before, my little brother, Mark, was real different from me. Opposites to an extreme! While I was painting houses for punishment, he was collecting rabbits and guinea pigs to play with. When Dad was getting me out of jail, he was taking Mark to Boy Scout camp. When I was stealing and rolling cars, he was helping Mom clean the house. Totally different! (I don't *think* my mom played around! We couldn't be brothers. Could we?) The reason I bring this up, again, is that by coincidence, I was standing at the edge of the school yard after gym, waiting for the bell to ring so I could go home. My little brother was doing the exact same thing at his school, at the same time I was, also waiting for the bell to ring so he could go home. I was driving my own car, and he was to take the bus. We both got out at the same time. I went straight home and so did he. I will give you the end first! He got there an hour before I did. Soooo, what happened? He got on the bus just like a little goody, goody does and probably studied on the way home as well.

On the other hand, it was about thirty seconds before the bell was about to ring, and I couldn't wait for it. I left early and, low and behold, the assistant principal saw me and dragged me back to the coach's office. Gym was my last class. She asked the coach if I was given permission to leave early, and the coach said, "No." The assistant principal picked up the phone from the coach's desk, asked me for my home phone number, and then called my mom. She told Mom what had happened and asked permission to crack me with a board three times. I didn't actually hear the answer, but I got the crap spanked out of me. The coach got the honors and used a board with holes in it. Three cracks and I was in a lot of pain. The coach and the principal said, "We will see you tomorrow." I left. My ass hurt so bad that it took me a half hour to be able to sit on my car seat. It just amazes me how two brothers can start out doing the exact same thing and end up with such a different outcome.

It was time to meet with the Drifters tonight and to see who we were suppose to kill, maim, dismantle, kick, smack, stab or just, in general, destroy and where. I headed to the meeting and all the boys were there. We all stood by as the sergeant-at—Arms told us what and where. Tomorrow night, the same place under the Golden Arches, and the Mexicans. That would be Friday. If I don't get killed, I would have two more nights left to go back and enjoy the fair. Of course, I always gave thought that I could go back one day looking a lot like Quasimodo.

School was over for the day, and I raced to SCOA for a short four-hour night at work and then bolted to the fair. I could make it to the fair by eight thirty in time to grab a hot dog on a stick and a lemonade. I got there as planned, washed the dog down with the lemonade and found my way to the Golden Arches by nine o'clock. It was a really warm night, maybe ninety out. Some of the guys looked pretty stupid with a long coat on. The leaders, as usual, met and pow wowed for a minute or so. While they were yakking, I was thinking how much I was going to miss this shit next year. Yea, right! The talking was done, and the Mexicans headed towards the parking lot as usual. Then, about five or six minutes later, the whities headed in the same direction. I had nothing to use at that time as I was running late. When we got through the parking lot entrance, one of the guys handed me a sap and some brass knuckles. Jesus, I thought, can't they give me the same killing equipment all the time? I'll never get used to this stuff. Sticks, knives, clubs, chains and now this shit! Even cops get the same stuff! I didn't like this stuff. You have to be real close to someone to use it. With a stick or a club you can hit and run. With this crap you can hit and get knifed before you have a chance to run. Not a happy camper. Had my boss at SCOA been a female, I could have blamed her for scheduling me the day of a rumble. Had I been there early I could have picked my weapon of choice. But Max was too nice of a guy to blame, so I have these little shitty things to use. Who knows, maybe it's my time to play frog.

We all walked towards the far end where there was NO light. None at all! It was a very dark area. Before I knew what hit me, something hit me. The game was on. As I said, I was forced to get in close and bang away. And bang away I did. I could only think about the beatings I had taken for no reason at the hands of those two Mexicans. And the more I thought the angrier I got and the closer I got in the mix of things. There was blood flying everywhere and a lot more groaning that was noticeable. I don't know if it was because I was closer to the middle of it all, or because it was the last day of the meet. I could feel that there was much more intensity than ever before. I was suddenly on the ground! A group of us all hit the asphalt at the same time, the good guys and the bad guys. How many of us fell was not clear but maybe six or eight. I was getting hit hard and started bleeding from the mouth and somewhere from my leg. I fought my way back to a standing position and started to help a couple of guys stand up also. Then I got cracked across the head with something hard enough to cause me to pass out for a second or two. (I should have left those assholes on the ground and ran.) Groggy, but I was up again and trying to protect myself. I noticed that I was playing defense and not offense and that was not good for me or my fellow Drifters. I found the closest Mex and popped him with my sap. Somewhere in this mess I had lost my brass knuckles, probably when I hit the ground and passed out. Why I still had the sap was a mystery to me unless I had been thinking of Barney for some reason. All of a sudden, as usual, it all stopped as fast as it all started. There were a lot of injuries on both sides. We all tucked our tails between our legs and limped home.

    I looked like shit. I went back to the clubhouse to assess the damages. I didn't want to go home looking like this. I went inside the clubhouse, took off my shirt and looked into the mirror. I was bleeding from my head, mouth, my side, and my leg. The good thing was that I didn't feel as bad as I looked. I spent an hour cleaning myself up. Guys came in and left as I was attending to myself. Talking shit! Some of them asked me if I would be back next year. I only said that I had to live through this day first. They laughed. I didn't! I never went back.

    However, I did see some of the members from time to time as we did live in the same area. But the fair, I am sure, will never be the same to me. I often wonder if I was to go to the fair and hang out by the Golden Arches if I'd see a bunch of guys wearing long trench coats in a hundred degree heat! Eventually, maybe five or six years after my time with the Drifters, the cops, I think, made a movie about them. I am not sure why they did it, but it was shown to driving school classes and in home rooms in high schools for a few years that I know. You may have seen it yourself. It was titled "Gang Boy," and it started with a black Ford convertible driving by with a few hoods in it. One of them throws a Molotov Cocktail into a palm tree, blowing all the fronds off it in a fiery blast. Probably the closest to a movie star that I will ever get. However, I did buy a new jacket similar to the Drifters jacket and had a new inscription put on the back of it. It read, "Bring on my cousin, Arnold now."

You know, things just seem to happen to me for some reason. I am sure it's not me. I'm just a victim of circumstances. We, the Madrigals, had one of our first performances at a school about a week or so after my last encounter with the Mexicans. My face was cleared up and fortunately my singing ability had not been impaired by a couple of blows to the throat. The school where we had to perform was about twenty miles away. We arrived a little ahead of schedule to make sure that we were not late. We didn't want the kid's assembly to be held up for any reason. It still was a school day. As luck would have it, the assembly was late to organize for some reason. We had about three quarters of an hour to kill. Some of us went to the cafeteria and grabbed a coke or a sandwich. Some of us just milled around the front of the school, where the bus had dropped us off, and I was one of them with a couple of others. With all of this time to kill, a few of us slipped off to have a cigarette. A no-no of course! We were on school grounds. We just hid around the side of the bus where we could not be seen and lit up. There were about four of us. Individually there probably wouldn't have been a problem, but with four of us, there seemed to be a bunch of smoke coming from the bus. Mr. Cummings saw smoke and came over to the bus and saw us all smoking. Shit, we're dead! What lousy luck. He told us to put them out and get into the bus and wait for our time to perform. He also said that he had no alternative but to turn us into the principal. We did our performance (beautifully I might add) and headed back to school to finish the day. At the beginning of my last class, I received a note to see the principal after school. As I walked into the principal's office, all my cronies were there. Smoker number one, number two, and smoker number three and of course, now me. We were given a pink slip that read, "You may not come to class for the next five school days." The principal said, "Your parents will be called shortly so they are aware of what transpired and why." I went home. My dad had not come home from work yet, but my mom was already on the war path. She was yelling and screaming (she did that really well) that I will never graduate if I keep this kind of stuff up. You will be punished for this she said. It's a disgrace! A nice Jewish boy like you, a disgrace! Wait until your father comes home. You'll see. That's what I was afraid of, my dad. Mom was a first class screamer, but Dad usually had other plans. It had been a long time since I had gotten a beating, so I guess I was due. Just wish he was a Mexican so I could hit back.

Dad came home, and Mom asked to be alone with him. There was a very perplexed look on Dad's face and a not so happy look on mine. I exited! About three months went by or so it seemed. Then I heard a call to me for an audience. Dad and Mom were much too quiet and way past normal for a situation like this. Not good, I told myself, not good. By now I should be crying like I am thirteen and much fatter. They sat me down and told me that my punishment is that I had to paint the inside of the house. "Paint the house?" I said. I don't know anything about painting houses. Nothing! I can't even stay in between the lines in a coloring book! I can't even imagine what the trim will wind up looking like." They said "You will learn, and it has to be done in time to go back to school in five days." Ok, I thought. It can't be any worse than a beating.

We all went to Sears the next day. Mom picked out a few colors for different rooms and bought the paint, brushes, rollers and a metal pan for the paint roller and plastic tarps to keep the paint off the rugs. I was all set to paint. Now, as I said, I was not a pro at this by any stretch of the imagination. In fact, the closest I had ever come to painting was coloring with my cousin, Arnold, and you know how that turned out, as I have just mentioned. I got up early and painted until dark day after day after day. This was not fun. I had paint on every part of my body. I don't even know how paint got to some parts; it just did. Turpentine was the drink of the hour. Paint all over and so was the turpentine. On me, the rugs and the walls that were to be painted. After three days I couldn't even eat. There was such a bad smell in my nose and taste in my mouth that nothing was good. I would normally eat a loaf of bread a day. Half would go to baloney sandwiches and the other half would go for toast with my coffee (I learned to say coffee correctly by the time

I was fifteen), in the morning. I was eating so much less that mom started to get worried. But Dad said, "Paint!" Dad was always the boss. That's the way it was in those days. Men ruled. Actually, men seem to have the last words nowadays as well. The bad part is the last words are "Yes, dear."

Finally, the last of the painting was done. I hadn't seen a car, a girl, a friend, or as a matter of fact, light, for seven days. This may have been the only time in my life since the turning point when I met Barney that I couldn't wait to go back to school. I think it was mid-week when I opened the door to my house, no wait, my newly painted house, and saw the sky, smelled the air, and cried a little when I saw my car. I got in it, turned the key and before I hit the gas, I promised myself that I would never paint anything again, ever. I really hated to paint! There wasn't any part that I liked. Not even staying home from school.

The fair was over, and the Drifters were done for now. Now, I had a little time to kick back and enjoy life a little. My classes were not that hard except that I had to make up a week's worth of work that I had missed while I was enjoying my new career, painting. My life as a Madrigal was really fun and now it was getting close to the time gymnastics was beginning to start. The real time was after Christmas, but a lot of hard work was starting now. About two weeks after my imitation of Rembrandt, we had another school for which to perform. In fact, it was John Marshall Junior High where my "Highly acclaimed" little brother went. The school was so jammed with kids that we had to give two assemblies. We, at Ganesha High, were only a couple of miles from that school, so we were asked to car pool and to drive our own cars. I am sure the school saved money that way. We got there on time and almost immediately went to our first performance. Butch and Gene both had solos. We did the same show that we had done a couple of weeks ago at the pre-painting school. The first show went just great. We all exited and went to our cars for a forty-five minute break. Why it was set up that way I have no idea; it just was. Some of us got in our cars and drove around. Some went and bought a coke, drank a little water or like me, had a cigarette. I had learned my lesson and now smoked cigarettes only off campus.

I got into Butch's car and while we were driving he said, "Do you want a drink?" I said, "Of what?" He said, "Bourbon." "Bourbon! Are you nuts?" "They'll never know," Butch said. We can buy some mints at the liquor store and load up with them before we go into the assembly hall. "Ok, let's do it." We pulled around the back of a liquor store, parked, took a couple of hits off his bottle, put it under the seat, and walked into the store to buy the mints. All was going just fine. Mints in tow, back into his car, found the bottle again, another couple of hits, and we were off. We drove to the school and saw that the rest of the Madrigals were still just standing around. We drove up to them and asked, "What is going on?" One of them said, "It's about a half hour yet." Butch said, "Do you want a hit off my bottle?" He said, "Yea" and jumped in with both feet. He called another couple of guys over, and they took part in the drinking frenzy. There were about five or six of us who helped kill the bottle. Hmmm, we killed a full bottle of bourbon in less than an hour. Butch hid the empty bottle under the seat. We all got out and headed towards the others who were standing around waiting for the nod to get ready. But, as of right then, nothing! We decided to do the mint thing now so they would start working. The problem, now, that was that there were six mint users and only enough mints for two of them. Butch, who was feeling no pain, as he had much more to drink than I, started to get pissed off at the other guys pulling on his pockets trying to get at the mints. Finally, the little white pills fell out and were up for grabs. We all seemed to get some and all was ok.

We finally got the nod to get ready to go in and perform. But now we had a real problem. Butch was shit faced. He was having a problem standing. I was a little woozy as well but nothing compared to Butch. We, as Madrigals, had a lot of room to do as we wanted when we are on stage singing. We might have been able to keep him erect and out of eye shot with everyone in Madrigals helping, but Butch had a solo and that was a big problem. Sing, hell he couldn't stand. He was to sing "Some Enchanted Evening" and that's a powerful song and takes all that you've got. He's dead! Fucken dead!! We all lined up and were leaning on Butch as to keep him up. We are all horsing around and all seemed to be going ok, considering. Gene nailed his solo, (of course, he was not hitting the sauce with us), and we, as a group, nailed the songs like we were pros. The kids were laughing and singing along with us, and all is well with the world.

Second to the last song is Butch's solo. It is time. Butch doesn't even know it's his turn. We slightly nudge him to the front and the music started. Butch starts. Butch is still standing. (Hard to believe) Let me explain something to you. I have karaoked for years, some good, and some bad and, of course, I have sung in a few groups as well as Madrigals, but for a guy who knew his stuff like Butch did, and was never off key, he sounded like the proverbial alley cat. No wait, worse. Not only was he never on key, he sang verse where there was no verse. He wobbled, staggered and then, to add insult to injury, he talked about stuff, while on stage, that had nothing to do with anything. At first we all felt really bad for him because we all knew what it was like to be off key and screw up when singing. But our inner pain turned to giant laughter, and we just couldn't stop. He was so fucked up that it was funny, no, hilarious. Really hilarious! I really don't think he knew he screwed up. In fact, I don't really think he knew he was on stage.

The performance was over. As we all went through the exit door, there was a booming voice that yelled, "No one goes anywhere. Walk over to the grass and stop." It was Mr. Cummings and the principal of the school. We all had to go through a breathalyzer test. Not like the one we go through now if we get stopped by a cop. We had to breathe into both Mr. Cummings nose and the principal's nose as well. In less than fifteen minutes there were six of us who were not going home. Well, not right away, anyway. If you are wondering why I put this in my book about drinking at school (many kids have been caught drinking at school before), it is because this one gives a new meaning to the term expelled. One fourth of the dirty two dozen were transported back to our school, Ganesha, and we were sitting in the principal's office as our parents were called up, one by one. Then, hearing that little Johnny is expelled for a week, please pick him up, one by one. We were picked up by our parents, one by one.

Now, if you recall, I was just expelled from school just three weeks ago and escaped a major beating by my dad. I had thought he'd kill me. He opted for me to paint the house instead. That may have been more painful to me in the long run. But the house looks brand new inside. However, soon it will be covered with a blood red color about the time I walk through the door. I can feel it already.

I was picked up from school in a couple of hours after all the others had already gone. My dad never said anything, just like last time, which was still very fresh in my mind. I walked through the door in front of Dad and was ready for a zetz on the back of my head with a two by four, but nothing. Again nothing! This was starting to get scary. I walked into the living room and saw my brother Mark, with a snicker about his lips. Does he know something I don't know? I thought. My dad and Mom sat down with me and said, "You just won't learn, will you? Are we bad parents? Do we treat you poorly?" Not waiting for an answer, "Do you hate us? Why? Why?" About this time I am really feeling like shit! Whale shit! You can't get any lower than whale shit. I probably have the best parents anyone could ever have, and I just cause them crap all the time. "I need to change," I thought. "I need to change." Dad said, "You are getting too old for me to whip anymore, and I am tired of it. So, before I picked you up from school, your mother and I, (I just happen to gaze over at my brother, and he was smiling again.) decided that you are to paint the outside of the house this time and scrape it as well. We will pick up the materials tomorrow at Sears, and you can start right away." In less than a second, all the remorse just drained from my heart. I looked at Mark, and he was doing all he could to keep the laughter back. I could see tears in his eyes, and they were not from pain. I looked at Mom and Dad and begged, "Please no! I hate painting, I hate it." My cries fell on deaf ears much like Moses' cries fell on the Pharaoh's when he cried, "Let my people go." Where can I find a staff? I knew I was to be punished, but this? Not fair, not fair!

This time there were pluses and minuses. The minuses, however, were many and the pluses were few. One of the pluses was that I was to be outside and not have to inhale the paint fumes and could smoke while painting. I did not have to lay plastic and be careful about dripping paint. The negatives were many: much harder work with all the scraping. I would be fighting the elements outside with the wind blowing, and I would have to be painting, shit! Just shit! Well the week went by in a month or two and I was ready to go back to school. I could just feel my parents eyes digging into the back of my head as I drove off thinking, "How soon is it going to be when they get the call again?" This time I promised myself that I was not going to let them down any more. Not because of them, but I can't stand to see my brother having so much fun! *Just kidding*!

It was starting to get cold out, as Halloween passed, and we headed towards November and December. It was hard to believe that I am still in Madrigals and haven't been kicked off the gymnastics team, either. In fact, Gene and I had started a duet as well as the trio we had with Judy and (the gay guy Freddie), the pianist. Gene and I sang acappella. (No gay guys for us.) Actually, Freddie was very close to all of us. Gene and I talked Mr. Cummings into letting us do a duet while performing with the Madrigals. We sang "Silhouettes" originally done by the Rays. I got to do the high part. Gene was a base and I, a baritone. There were pretty high notes to hit, so when I had to hit them, I learned to pull hard on the front of my Jockey shorts.

Gene and I were thinking about our vocation results and if we should pursue them. As I mentioned, I was suited for the aircraft industry. Gene's results came back saying he was suited for police work. No shit! Hmmmm, how different than me! Whoda thunk! Wonder if he knew my brother!

After checking things out, he decided to go to L.A. Tech in Los Angeles. They specialized in Political Science majors. I said, "I will go with you and see what they have to offer, possibly something for me in the aircraft area." We made an appointment and went there on a Saturday. There wasn't much for me, but Gene got all charged up with what he heard. It was not cheap to go there, but Gene's parents had a few bucks. I am sure they would be glad to pay for his schooling. As it turned out, Gene did go to that school and became a cop in the town of Upland, California. He probably thought his first arrest would be me. Easy prey, as he kind of knew what I was involved in but kinda turned his head. Hopefully, our friendship would be more important. Then again, maybe not!

I signed up at Mount San Antonio Junior Collage aka. Mt. Sac. It was a two-year school that was free (except for books) because of the great county that we live in. *Just like today!* It was in the town of Walnut just ten miles from where I lived. Gene would have to move to L.A. when it was time for him to go to school and we were sad that we would be apart for so long. Although I had joined a junior college, my dad was stoked. A son of his going to college, what a mitzvah! Especially this son! (Dad never had that option.) That is, of course, if I lived long enough to go.

Christmas time was upon us. Gene, Val, Judy and I spent a lot of time window shopping. It seemed that Bill, Roger, Owen, and Knuckle Head were not as much in my life anymore. Whether it was me growing up a little and seeing the light or my life was just getting fuller with other things, there was not much time for them. But whatever it was, I had been getting into enough trouble all by myself without their influences. You know the painting things! However, one day Bill said that he had something he wanted me to see. I walked over to his house with him, only six or seven houses down and across the street from my house. (I may have mentioned that before.) We walked into his bedroom, and he slid the closet door open. I couldn't believe my eyes. There were three kittens that were hung to death with handcuffs. One end of the cuff was around the dowel that you put the hanger on when you hang your clothes up. The other end of the cuff was around the baby kitten's neck. It was so sad. I know that I am an idiot, sometimes, and have been the biggest jerk in the world as well, sometimes, but this, this is way beyond my scope of humanity. I said "Bill, why did you do this?" Bill said, "It was this way or flush them down the toilet. I didn't want to take the chance stuffing up the toilet." "No, Bill, I meant killing them. Why did you kill them?" "They were getting too big and were starting to roam around the house. My dad would have been mad at me if he knew I had them." "Your dad is hardly ever here. You could have put them in the garage, maybe." "No, he sometimes puts the car there. I had to do it this way." Now, in all the time I had known Bill and all that we had been through together, I only saw Bill's dad maybe three or four times and mostly it was a hi or a bye. I never asked Bill what his dad did for a living or why there was no mom or anything else for that matter. That really is none of my business. (In fact, I am still that way today. I figure if someone wants to tell me his business he will. It's not for me to pry.) But this time I had to say something. So I asked, "Is your dad that bad of a guy that you have to kill animals rather then tell your dad what is going on?" Bill said, "He gets real mad real easy." I said, (very much out of character) "What does he do for a living?" Bill said, (I wasn't really ready for this but) "He's a cop!" Right then and there neither of us was in a joking mood, so I just said in a small tone, "A cop!" "Yea, Bill said, A cop. I never told you that before?" "No, you never told me that before." Sadly, at this moment, the dead kittens were not at all on my mind as I was stunned. Stunned! "Is that how you know all about all the stuff you know about? Geeese, I can't believe it. Does Roger know and Owen? Knuckle Head!" "Yea, I think so, Bill said. I think so."

Once again, with all the knowledge I have gained in my life, both good and bad, in the last years, I still don't know what the fuck is going on in the world. I have been in la la land. Many years later in my life I dated a lady named Lynne. To this day, I don't know how she ever made it alive for so long. She walked in la la land all of her life. A multitude of car accidents (over fifteen), operations, and many things that I don't have time to get into right now, but there will probably be a portion of her in a much later chapter. I have to ask myself, "Am I still that way today, as she is?" Obviously, I was into my late teens and was not aware of anything. How long does this kind of a thing go on and why? Lynne's sixty! We took down the little dead kittens and took them to a small creek not far from where we lived. It was a place where we all went to smoke our cigarettes years before and buried them. I think that was a turning point with me and the boys. Not that I was any better than they were, because I probably wasn't, but I just think I had a bigger conscience.

Christmas came and went and the New Year was approaching. I was not into football much, but the New Year's Parade on New Year's Day in Pasadena, California was a real big deal then. I guess it is still today, but a little bit different, I assure you. Someone always had a New Year's Eve party somewhere. I stopped going to my dad's parties when I found out that girls were different from boys. So, why drink with Dad's cronies? Gene and I made up that we were going to go to the parade and would leave the party about two am. Gene didn't drink (DUH!) so he could drive to the parade. Our girls, Val and Judy, were not allowed to go with us. Their parents said it was too dangerous out there at this time of the year. There could be hundreds of cars and drunks all going to the parade. (I knew one of them.) Gene borrowed his dad's new Ford Ranchero so we could have a nice dependable vehicle to drive. Pasadena was a long ways away and with all the traffic there would be, we would have good breaks and clear vision for the drive.

We left the party without incident or women. Feh! We got into the Ranchero and got to the parade site about three ish, may be four. Pulled into a close parking lot (unheard of today), took our blankets, wood and paper, walked to a site on the sidewalk, and sat down to wait for and watch the parade. (Unheard of today!) We had brought some wood and paper for a small bon fire to keep us warm. (Really unheard of today!) We had had no sleep and tried to catch a wink or two. There was so much noise and it was so cold even with the bon fire that sleeping was not an option. Not to mention a plethora of great looking chicks doing the same thing we were. There were some guys near us who offered us a swig of their booze. I of course, accepted. I believe Gene said he had to drive. (However, booze was not allowed there, and you know how these potential cops are.) The parade was great and when it was all over, it was a mess to get out and back on the freeway heading to home. After a half hour or so, we were doing about fifty, fifty-five in the right, slow lane. We shouldn't have had the heater on so high especially without any sleep. Gene was getting sleepy and started to nod off. I yelled, "Do you want me to drive?" He flinched and said his dad said no one drives his car but him, period. Of course, Gene, being the obedient child that he was, duh! I didn't get behind the wheel.

There was some road work on he shoulder of the freeway, and there was a bunch of white metal rods sticking up about three or four feet high to keep you off the shoulder. Gene dozed of again and by the time I grabbed the wheel, he hit at least ten of them. These were not real heavy metal rods, but they did make a mess on the right side of the car. The head light on that side was non-existent and the quarter panel was hanging on by a thread near the right-hand door. I thought, if this was my dad's car and it happened to me, I would have to paint the Taj Mahal! However, the Ranchero was drivable. We managed to pull off the right front quarter panel and put it in the bed of the Ranchero. Guess who drove home! So that concluded another year in my life. Even doing something that was not unusual, there was still something different in my life, and nothing will or has changed to date.

January first gone, and the New Year takes over with my birthday on the twenty-third. Now, in retrospect, many years later, it was about that time in my life that something quite unusual started to happen. Things seem to come to me. I really never picked anything anymore myself, whether it was good, bad or indifferent, whether it was a job, wife, friends or whatever. They just seem to come my way. It was like I never had a goal to shoot for. Nothing has changed as of this date. Things just seem to happen. Unlike my little brother, who had nothing but goals in his life and worked hard and hit all of them.

I thought about having a birthday party but couldn't think of anyone who wanted to be stabbed in the back. So that was out. Eighteen! That was a great number, eighteen. So, now I am eighteen and absolutely nothing to tell you that happened that was funny, sick, unusual or interesting. Figure that out. Maybe I am growing up. I was sad, but my parents were elated. No principals or cops! No dumb hair dos, bruises or friends over that they didn't care for. Just a couple of months of normalcy!

Late January was the start of gymnastics competition with other schools in our district. We figured we had a chance to be number one because we had almost the same team as we did last year. There were a lot of the juniors coming back, like Gene and myself that had experience in competition. In general, we thought we could kick ass. There was only one exception. I am not sure if it was Azusa or El Monte High. They had one kid named Munger. Not sure if I ever knew his first name, but his last name was a household word in the world of gymnastics. We had competed against him for the last two years. He always got an incredible score. Tens abounded with him. He competed in all strength events. Rings, parallel bars, side horse and high bar! No one could beat him. No one! He had a big advantage. There was a reason he had an advantage that no one else had nor did they want to have. He had something wrong with his legs. Whether it had been polio or something else, no one really ever knew, but his legs were no bigger around then maybe ten inches. I can't imagine one of them weighing more than two pounds or so. However, his chest had to be at least fifty plus. At this time in my life, I was approaching a forty-two plus chest. I thought I looked pretty good and was very strong, but this guy was enormous. All muscle from the waist up. We all but conceded a second place to him in those events. Unfortunately, I had three of them and Gene had four. However, there was always a chance that our team, as a whole, could beat his team even though Munger wins all of his events. We just have to win the rest of them. If we win this current meet with Mungers school we are a shoe-in to take the school division championship. But Gene and I are not going to shine individually against Munger. Hopefully, we can take second against him individually and help with the team points. We felt pretty good as we beat all the other schools in our division, with only one left to beat. If we beat all but Munger's school, (as long as we are not disgraced) we should win the district championship easily. With that thought in mind, the whole team really started putting in extra effort. You could see it in our eyes. Quote from a Rocky movie, we had "The eye of the tiger."

Between gymnastics, Madrigals, auto shop and occasionally getting laid, I was really enjoying school. What's not to enjoy. It seemed like since the Bill, kitten thing; I was kind of keeping straight and narrow. Gene, Val, Judy and I were spending a lot a time together just hanging out, practicing and performing, but as I mentioned recently, things just seem to find me.

One day, Bill came to me and asked if I wanted to make some big money. (The image of me machine gunning down the big cats at the San Diego Zoo came immediately to mind.) "How big and what do I have to do?" I reluctantly asked. He said, "You are going to like this. A friend of mine is looking for a few guys to fuck older women. He's willing to split the money fifty/fifty." "Are you nuts? Why would I want to do that? That's what a girl friend is for," I retorted. Yea, but she won't give you two hundred and fifty bucks for doing it, will she? "How much? Two hundred and fifty samolians just for doing some old woman?" "Yep, that's right." "That's good, no not good, that's great money, but I don't think I can do an old lady, and besides, why me?" "My friend is starting up an escort business in this area and needs good looking studs as well as women. You know, like you with a great body and looks and a little smarts. In fact, if you know anyone else who may be interested, let me know. I will talk to them." I immediately thought of Gene. You know, the cop! Yea, that'll work. Right!

I told Bill I would think it over and let him know soon. I really had no intention of doing it. The idea of me in bed with some old lady wasn't an image I really wanted to look at. Hell, I was dating a pretty lady my own age. Why an old women? I'm thinking sixty ish or so. You know, someone that I would Love to have right now, today! (How time changes our thinking, huh!) Two or three days later Bill came to me and said, "Come here. I want to show you something." We walked about a block, and Bill pointed out a lady about thirty-five or so and said to me, "What do you think of her?" "Pretty nice," I said. "Why?" "She's your first trick if you choose to play ball for my buddy." "Trick, what is a trick?" I asked? (Once again, I am about to become a fucken hooker and I don't even know what the hell anyone is talking about that is in the business in which I am about to embark.) Bill told me that is someone who is your victim. "Oh great. So how does this work? I just walk up to her and ask her if she wants to fuck. Then put my hand out, and she will cross my palm with two hundred and fifty bucks?" "No, not exactly! You will be given a time and a place to pick her up. You will dress nice and take her to dinner at a nice place. Then take her home and screw her for a couple of hours. You can do that, can't you? Then you leave. The next day you see me. I will give you your two fifty, less the dinner cost. So, it would be smart to take her to Mac Donald's. It's cheaper. I am just joking," Bill said. "I will give you your two five oh and bring me the dinner receipt. I will cover that as well. But remember, you can't do just this one. You have to commit for others as well. Some may be not as good looking as this one, in fact, maybe, not so good looking at all. What do you think?" Jesus Christ, I guess, just add this to an already long list of crime and corruption. I'm starting to make Al Capone look bad! How do you pass up two hundred and fifty dollars and a nice dinner and get laid as well with a nice looking chick? "You don't!" said Bill. "When and where?"

    I had given thought to how Judy would perceive this as well as Gene when I told them that I kind of have a new part-time job. Then I thought better of it. I just treated it, in my mind, as a job and nothing else. A good job! A very good job that no one has to know about! No one! Heck, what are a few hours here and there out of my life at this young and tender age. Especially at that rate of pay, tax free. I am not going to spend a lot of time giving you the dirty and intimate details that went on with every lady I met with for about six months, but I can tell you this. I not only learned many things about having and giving sex from my boss, like what to do and how to do it, but how to abstain from climaxing as well, for hours and hours and how to get started again after just thirty minutes or so after a climax. It is amazing how women Love to have sex for a couple of hours or so, climax and then again in the next few minutes. Ahh, to be young again! Hell, I'd settle to find a woman that just wants to do it once at my age now! Oh yea, with me! What a turn around. Fifty years ago I GOT two hundred and fifty bucks to do it. Now, I have to go to Las Vegas and GIVE two hundred and fifty bucks to get it. And the word, "twice" is now foreign! With the exception of a couple of canceled dates with Judy and a few dates that I had that I would have wanted to be with Judy instead, I made a lot of tax-free money. I never recommended any one else for the job as I wanted it to be my secret. The business folded up in about six months or so. I think the cops were getting a little close to the boss. Being a smart guy and having made a lot of money, not just with me but with all whom he had working for him, both men, oops, I mean boys and girls, and I guess women and men as well, he scrammed. I never knew who he really was, and never ran into anyone else who worked for him. Maybe it's a good lesson in business! Keep all employees away from each other and don't get greedy. When it's time to go, its time to go! That may be where the expression came from "Take the money and run!" In fact, Gene, Judy and Val could have been working for him, and I would have never known.

I have always heard that if you have sex before a sporting event, it zaps your strength. Well, I did not find it to be so with me. With all the extra curricular activity I was having, I excelled in gymnastics. My events, with few exceptions, went great. It was about late April and we had beaten all schools like we thought. Individually, Gene and I were number one in our respective events and were assured of a letter. The locking up of a letter may have caused some guys to back off a little, but not Gene and I. We both wanted Munger! Only two schools left and the next one was Munger's school. We got to the school about seven o'clock P. M. and started to warm up. The meet was at eight! Some of us guys came in our gym suits and some had to change. Gene and I had to change. We were at Munger's school (like they needed an advantage) and asked where the locker rooms were. Some lady, I don't know who she was, probably a mother of one of the competing kids or a teacher watching that we don't steal the bleachers or something, said, "Over there" and pointed. Gene and I walked to the back to change. There was a bunch of guys changing and among them was guess who? Munger! We had only looked at each other momentarily a year ago.

This time Gene went over to him and said, "Hi, my name is Gene, and that's Chuck over there. We kind of met face to face last year when you took us apart but never really introduced ourselves." He looked up and said, "Can't wait for the repeat this year," then looked down. Gene kind of stood there for a few seconds, looked at me, looked around and saw a lot of snickers from "not our team mates" and walked back to where I was. We just looked at each other and finished dressing. Back out in to the gym, we did some stretching, rolling, jumping and twisting. On the high bars it was flailing around, pulling ourselves up on the rings, the parallel bars and trying to kill ourselves on the hardwood floor. It was time! The coaches called us together, and we all stood facing each other in the middle of the gym. We were waiting for Roseanne to sing the National Anthem, but she must have missed the bus. The coaches gave us a good well wish, and we all shook hands, even Munger. We went to our respective benches and started the games.

We at Ganesha High were all charged up. We all knew whom we had to beat. It was like our whole team was against one person. Even though Gene and I were tops in our events, on our team, there were others who did the same event. If one of us did not score high, another guy had a chance do so. I would like to tell you that, in the end, like so many movies, when the underdog beats the villain and wins the girl, was our fate. But in reality, Munger was just too strong. In fact, I screwed up in one event, badly. But so did Munger in that same event. He went before me and that is probably why I screwed up. I tried too hard knowing that I really had a chance to beat him. However, that one was the event that Gene won for himself and for the team. It was a moral victory for Gene and really helped the team. Yes! But the overall score went in the direction of Munger's school. Not a lot, but enough.

Now, we went home with a little pride knowing "The Munger" was beat by Gene. Of course, had Munger not screwed up as did I, Gene probably would have been beaten as well. No matter. We still knew that we were going to win the championship by beating the next school. They were a weak team and there was going to be no problem with them. The championship was ours. However, Mr. Evens, our coach, would not let us celebrate until we actually beat them in the next week or so. Adults, don't you just Love them!

April goes, and the next week, just as we predicted, we whip that school's butt! We are the champs! The next day when we went to school I had girls kissing me whom I didn't even know. This was our first team championship in anything. Remember that we are only the second graduating class the school has ever had. We never won anything last year and no football title this year, no swimming title, no nothing, just us. The champs! The first school title in history for this school! Not only is my blood on the training mat in the gym but my name is in the school records forever. From a thirteen year old fat cry baby to an eighteen year old (so many things I could put in here and none very good) stud. A kissable stud, I may add.

The month of May once carried a special day at school. It was called senior ditch day. It was a day that was designated for seniors to cut school without penalty. You didn't have to ditch but if you didn't want to go to school, you didn't have to. Unfortunately, my year was the year that the school board cancelled it. Last year's seniors got to ditch, but this year's seniors did not. Is that a bad wrap or what? What crap! Last year it was sometime at the end of May, the twentieth, I think. It was not fair. We even won the championship. Doesn't that count? Bill and I were talking about how nice and warm the day was for the end of May. We were sitting on the curb across from school as there were ten minutes or so before the bell rang to go to class. Roger joined us, and he lit up a ciggy. Owen must have seen us and mozzied on over, also. I looked at them, and they looked at me. We all thought of the same thing. All we need is Knuckle Head and we're out of here. We are not gong to let them steal our designated day from us, are we? Where is Knuckle Head? We saw his car pull in the parking lot. Roger ran over and called to him to come join us. The five of us decided that we were not to be cheated from our day. We all jumped into Owens' car and were gone before the school bell rang. Talk about fast decisions!

We pulled out onto Valley Boulevard and turned right, pulled into the parking lot of Denny's restaurant and parked. Well, here we go again. "Trouble, just trouble," I said. "Don't worry, we won't get caught. I'll have a friend write a note for us from a doctor, and you can take it to school tomorrow." "Ok let's do it." "Where are we going to go?" "It's getting hot, right?" "Yea, so?" "How about swimming at Puddingstone Dam?" "Yea, right, like who brought his trunks?" "Trunks, we don't need no stinken trunks. Let's do it!" A fifteen minute drive and we were there. What a life. From a thought to swimming in eight seconds flat!

Puddingstone had a very steep cement grade from the road at the top to the bottom of the top of the dam where the water was. You can lay your towels out (that is if you thought about bringing a towel) and get a tan, oh yea, and watch the chicks. However, this day there probably won't be any chicks. But who needs chicks when you are with your best friends. (Notice that Gene is not here. Not, that he isn't my best friend, but I am sure this would not be his cup of tea.) So we parked and walked down as far as we could on the cement, stripped down to our undies, and jumped in. We probably hit the water about nine-thirty or so. We splashed around joking about how the other seniors were busting their asses at school and letting the system beat them out of their day. But we, we were not to be denied! Roger was one of those guys who was as white as a ghost. When we noticed him starting to get a little red, we said our canary is warning us that it's about time to get out. Not that we were so worried about getting burnt, but that would certainly be a tip off that maybe we were not at school. I believe it was Owen who said, "Are you worried that if we get caught, you will have to paint your neighbor's house?" Everyone seemed to think that was very funny. Well, not everyone! We walked uphill to the car and by the time we got there, we were just about dry. We put on our clothes, started the engine, put the car in gear and asked, "Where to?" We all looked at each other with a question mark in our eyes. Roger said, "If one of you guys were a girl, I'd stay here and wait for the submarine races or get a bag for a snipe hunt." We all laughed and then Bill said, "If you had a bag, you should use it for the chick you would be with. I've seen a few of them." A lot of laughter started and from that rag another started and then another.

After a half an hour of slamming each other, someone said, "Hamburgers anyone?" We drove back to Pomona and hit the local hamburger joint, Henry's. Filled our bellies, cruised around Henry's about seven hundred times and were off to a local French fry house. It was a place where a lot of our school chums met after school and loaded up with fries and a cherry or vanilla coke or the like. What made this place different was that you could get an overflowing shoe box full of fries for twenty-five cents, as long as you purchased a coke at a normal price. Knowingly, we had already eaten, but as teenagers, in a few minutes, I am sure we would be hungry again. We would probably see some of our friends here. It was about two-ish now, and school was about to get out. In ten minutes this place would be packed.

While we were hanging around, Bill made a call to some chick who worked for a doctor. He gave her the correct spelling of our names and made arrangements to pick up the doctor excuses that night at her home. She asked if we would like her to make a couple of calls in the morning but we said no. Bill thanked her for all of us and then we ordered the fries. We made a time to meet the next morning to get the excuses from Bill so we could stagger in at different times with them. All fired up and approaching dinner time, we all headed to our respective homes.

As soon as I walked in the house, my mother asked why I did not go to school today. My mouth dropped open as wide as it could. What makes you think I didn't go? (I looked over my arms to try and detect a sun burn area that was red.) I just know. I can't believe you just can't stay out of trouble! I don't know what to do with you! I am sure your dad will have something to say about it. "Mom, how did you find out? Please tell me," I asked. "The school called to see if you were sick." I said, "Sick? Why do you ask?" "Charles did not show up for his first two classes." Shit! I'm dead! I started thinking about painting the neighbor's house as we joked about earlier. There was no way, no way! I promised myself I would never paint anything ever again, and I'm not going to! Dad walked in and before I could say a word, he yelled, "You made me proud going to college, but you can't even go to high school. I'll give you classes!" Right about that time, I knew that house painting was not the order of the day. I was sitting on the sofa. I started to get up but got knocked right back down with an open hand smack. Then, I was hit with a bunch of punches and blows from a very mad and irate father. I finally fell to the floor from the punches, and he started kicking me. After a while I started feeling no pain. I was just doubled up and could only feel and hear thuds. In fact, I started to think that this was a release from all that happened from all of the other things when he made me paint the house instead of a beating. I was numb all over from the blows. I looked up and saw my forty-pound test, aluminum bow that I had made in metal shop (you know, the one that he threw at me and just missed by inches of spearing me in the back a year before) in his hands. He started hitting me with it. Where it came from I have no clue but he definitely had it. He was out of control. Rage had taken over, and there was no stopping him. I was bleeding from every part of my body. Face, hands, back, stomach, legs and feet. Not an inch was missed by him, not an inch. I really don't know how long this went on, but finally Mom stepped in and Dad stopped. Mom said, "Go to your room." I couldn't. I couldn't stand much less walk. It took me a long time to crawl to my bedroom. I could not go to school the next two days. I heard Mom answer the phone both days and heard her saying, "Yes, he's here but not feeling well." Now this beating at age eighteen was the last beating I have ever gotten from my dad or anyone else for that matter of fact. Even the Mexicans! I cried like a baby from the beating, but it was not the last time I cried.

However, there is a lesson or two and a moral to this beating. The lesson is; if you remember, at the very beginning of this book, where I said that I beat my son with a belt (actually, I started by throwing a television at him which he blocked with his strong arms) and to this day, it still haunts me! I can still see him lying on the bed, in his room. He turned his head (after I don't know how long into the strapping I was), and looked at me and then just turned away, like the pain just went away as the numbness set in. I can relate to both beatings as I have been on both sides of them. Did my dad regret that beating he gave me as I did my son's beating? Of course, so, he had to. I know that my dad Loved me as much as any father could. I know I Love my son as much as any father can. To give beatings like that is not anger but only rage that had been pent up for a long a time from past deeds I am sure. Was I the biggest jerk son to my parents? Yes! Was my oldest son the biggest pain in the butt to his parents? Yes! Was a reprimand deserved? Absolutely! Like the one my son and I were given? No. My dad, I am sure, took it to his grave, as I will have to do some day. The beatings can't be taken back.

The second lesson I have learned is that history does repeat itself, and we, as parents, should always be aware of it. If it happened to, with, or for a parent, there is a good chance it could happen in some form to their offspring. Don't let things build up inside you. It makes anger turn to rage, and that is not good! Had I let it go a long time ago, or had it never happened, I may have prolonged my heart attack.

Thirdly, the moral of the story was, that from that day on, I never cut a class all through college, where it is permissible, or called in a day sick from work, ever! Not to mention that that was the last time my dad ever laid a hand on me. Regret or guilt, I will never know. Now, in retrospect, as I am writing today, May two thousand and nine (In fact, it is Memorial Day, talk about fighting.), the pain I felt from the beatings that I took from Dad and the Mexicans, I think, was because of fear. Now, with Dad, of course, I never even thought of hitting back. One of the Ten Commandants (possibly the only one) that I followed was to "Respect Thy Mother and Father." On the other hand, fighting with the Drifters and a few other incidents taught me that you will feel much less pain if you don't have time to think about the fear. Fear is why there is the pain. So, if you keep focused on what you are doing and not what can happen *to you*, there will be less pain. From this time on, I really feared no one or no thing. (Accepting the inevitable and moving on as far as physical fighting generally goes in life.) Always keeping in mind that retreating is much less painful than fighting. As most Jews will tell you, we really need to have our backs to the wall with no way out before we explode. The bad thing, in a way, is that you have to be the aggressor and throw the first punch. Not really what I am all about. However, with some fights that I will have in the future, I seem to fare much better because of my new philosophy.

Finally, graduation day is here. It is about one hundred and ninety outside. There were caps, gowns everywhere, and tassels hanging in front of our eyes so that we couldn't see where we had to walk. Our graduation took place at the fair ground where I have spent many moons and had many memories, a lot of good and a lot bad. We all walked from the parking lot to a plethora of folding chairs on the grass in front of the podium in an organized A to Z fashion. I was about three or four students in front of Gene, and I got to graduate before him. I never let him forget it. I always said, "The brighter kids got to graduate first." Of course, he retorted, "You got out first because the principal tried to get the bad ones off the grounds as quickly as possible."

The whole ceremony took about two hours. By then we all had melted from the heat. Hats flew in the air. We all hugged each other and went to the grandstands where our parents, relatives and friends (I would have used significant others, but I don't think there was such a term back then.), were and did the same. I said, "See ya" to Mom, Dad and my little pain in the butt brother, grabbed Judy, Gene had Val in tow, and we headed for our cars. We had reservations for dinner at the Old Hickory Inn in Azusa. It was a very classy restaurant with valet parking. Gene got there first. (Not because he drove faster than I, but I didn't have both of my hands on the wheel as I drove). He valet parked. When I got there, I parked myself. Judy, I am sure, would have Loved to valet, but nobody, and I mean nobody, drives my car. However, when I walked to the restaurant from the parking lot with Judy on my arm, I still remember what she wore and how she looked. She was so beautiful. She had on a purple taffeta dress with purple chiffon netting over it. I couldn't wait to make Love with her. She looked so beautiful to me. We went in, our table was ready and as soon as the waiter came over, I ordered a seven and seven. No luck! How about a coke? That worked. The dinner was super, and I picked up the check for both of us. Dad had given me the money as part of my graduation gift and told me to pay for Gene and Val. How kewl (Kewl, the new spelling of cool I picked up from my granddaughter Heidi. I know I had used it earlier in my writing. I wanted you to think I was illiterate and was trying to write a book. Did I fool ya?), was that. Check paid, bellies full, and as we walked to the door, I asked Gene if he was going to the beach for the all night party. He said, "No." I didn't ask. Knowing him, he could have been headed to church. However, that may not have been too far off. Gene and Val had gotten very close.

Judy and I jetted to the beach as fast as we could. I had a bottle of vodka and seven up. Judy drank the seven up. We spread out a blanket, changed into our swim suits, pulled out the chips and dip, and a portable radio. There were a lot of others all around us. There were two high schools that graduated on this night, Ganesha and Pomona High. Very much rivals! We spent the night, and I won't tell you what really happened that night. I don't want to embarrass Judy if her children or her husband ever happens to read this book. As a matter of fact, there have been a few episodes I have already left out for the same reason.

Chapter Twelve

Summer! I am eighteen and a half and a hundred years of wisdom under my belt, so I thought. Schools out and summer is here. The first thing that I did (and this may have been the start of my life style for years to come), was to take a road trip with Gene to San Francisco! His sister and husband had moved there from San Diego not long ago. We would have a place to stay. We wanted to see the Kingston Trio. (Once again, for you under the age of maybe, fifty, "The Kingston Trio" were three Jamaicans who played for the San Francisco 49ers in the nineteen seventies. They were; a quarter back, wide receiver and a running back. They were all world renowned.) However, when we were there we never got to see them. We had planned a two-week trip but for some reason I don't remember much of it. However, I do remember two things for sure. I don't remember who, why, or what for, but at one time we had a chick in the back seat as we were driving somewhere. She would giggle and continually rub her hands together. This went on for a long time. Almost like a horror movie. It was obvious that she liked me (sure, I get all the nutty ones, now and then), but I was spoken for and anyway, she was definitely a loon. I can't remember if she was hitch hiking and we had picked her up or was a friend of Gene's sister that needed a ride somewhere. I just don't remember, but it has always stuck out in my mind.

The other thing that stuck out in my mind from that trip was when Gene said he saw a lion. A black lion! Now Gene wasn't given to lying or hallucinations, but he almost came unglued. It was late at night, maybe midnight or so, and I had the wheel (how unusual) and Gene was sitting shotgun. We were driving south on Highway One somewhere just below Big Sur. Even with my driving attitude, I was still going fairly slowly because of the narrow and very winding road. Gene yelled, "I saw a lion." "Yea, right," I laughed. "No, really I did. It was black and just off the side of the road with a huge head and yellow eyes." I asked him what a lion would be doing here. He said, "I don't know but I saw it. Stop, go back, and I will show you." Not even thinking that a lion could be near,

I did a turn about and headed back towards the "out-door zoo." Gene said, "Go slow. I think this is where I saw it." We drove around for ten minutes pointing the head lights in every direction possible but never saw anything. Nothing! For years we talked about it, him with his lion and me with the chick in the back seat. I am sure it probably shouldn't even be in this book, but it is dear to me. I guess you had to be there!

Mom and Dad were heading to Las Vegas one day and we, Mark and I, went with them. We stayed at the Hacienda which was the first hotel on the strip in those days. The Mandalay Bay stands there now. It was a place of wonder, Las Vegas. You couldn't tell night from day . . .

or day from night. Twenty-four-seven action and not much has changed today, in that respect. There were no electronic slot machines. You had to put in REAL coins and pull the handle to make the wheels spin. If fact, on some of the slot machines, there were four wheels and not three that spun around so you could win. One of the only things that have not changed since then is that you still have to be twenty-one to gamble. Whether it be slots, Black Jack, or whatever. Twenty-one years of age or jail!

So, of course, I wanted to play the slots. They looked like so much fun. I knew nothing about the other gambling games. But slots, what's to know? Put in a nickel and pull the handle and win! We were walking through the Hacienda looking for a place to eat. Dad said, "Stay here on this side of the casino and wait. *I'll be back.*" (Wonder if he knew Arnold Schwarzenegger?) He and Mom walked away. I said to Mark, "Let's put in a nickel and spin the wheels." Mark went in to a white out and full-blown panic. "No," he said. "You're going to go to jail. You'll be caught. Don't include me. Dad said no!" And on and on and on! "I'm going to do it," I said. I looked around and didn't see any cops or security guards. I reached into my pocket and found three nickels. I put in one and pulled the handle. Nothing happened. I did it again, and I hit one Cherry and three nickels came out. WOW! Now, that's the way to make a living. (How little did I know?) I put in the three nickels at once, the maximum, and pulled the handle. Voila, I hit four Cherries. The bells went off and whistles blew and a bunch of people came over running to see what I hit. Four Cherries paid out fifty bucks. I got fifty bucks for only three nickels. Wow! But, as I looked down, nothing was coming out of the machine like it did the last time when I hit and the three nickels fell out. Nothing! Nothing! I asked the lady who was standing next to me why I heard no sound of falling nickels and why I saw none either. She said, "Because you hit a jackpot. They physically come over to you and will pay you the fifty dollars in cash. That way they hope you will give them a tip." "They come over to me?" I said. I was coming close to shitting my pants. "Who brings it over?" I asked. The lady said, "A slot attendant and a security guard." "Security guard! I'm going to jail! Why didn't I listen to my little brother? I'm dead!" I can't even tell you how many times I have said that in the short amount of years that I have been alive. "I'm dead! I'm fucken dead!" I won fifty bucks and I bet they won't let me have the money to take with me to jail, either. I can't wait until Mom and Dad come to bail me out. I can hear it all again. You're a miserable son! Why can't you be like your little brother? It's never a dull moment with you, is it? And so on and so on. What the hell am I going to have to paint this time? The casino! Shit! But when you are hot you are hot as I have learned later in life. I was hot enough to win the fifty dollars on the third spin and so the luck stayed with me as Mom and Dad came back before the security guard did with the attendant. I told Dad to stay here. They were going to give him some money. The attendant walked up and laid fifty somolians in my dads palm and walked away. I went from a goat to a hero in thirty seconds and no jail time. Dad was all hugs and smiles. Mom was doing some serious kissing and as it turned out, dinner was on me and a bunch of bucks to spare. My brother just shrugged his head and walked behind me as we went to the restaurant.

    Now, that was a fun thing but as it turned out, that may have been the root of all evil. I wound up with a gambling problem some years later that started with a separate event that was very similar to this one and may have led to that easy-money feeling. The few days left of our vacation consisted of swimming in the pool and going to Las Vegas-style shows with all the feathers and semi-clad beautiful ladies. Of course, we all shared in the great food as well. However, I did manage to stay away from all slot machines.

    During the summer Gene and I made a few trips to L. A. Tech. in Los Angeles so that he could get oriented with the area. The smog was so bad there that sometimes I couldn't see the smoke at the end of my cigarette. I figured he'd be back in Pomona in no time. Once again, I was wrong.

Judy's mom and dad were never real excited about our relationship. I think they tolerated it because of us singing together in Madrigals or as a trio. As soon as school was over, I think Judy had some pressure to end it. Not that I was such a bad guy, but Judy's family were pretty Christian and me being a Jew, I don't think they were too excited about that. So, as life would have it, by the end of the summer, we were just friends and not an item anymore. It's funny that I was sad about it because I really liked Judy. In comparison to some other break ups I would have, in the future, this was a pretty easy one. In fact, somewhere near the end of summer, I think it was Primm, the heavy set girl friend, who was part of our little group where I lived, had a friend up from Arizona for a week or two. Not sure if their parents were friends or what, but I fell in Love with her fast. She had the most beautiful blue eyes I had ever seen in my life and yellow, long hair and a beautiful body to match. It is hard to believe that I can't remember her name. There was a song out about that time named "Pretty Blue Eyes." It really fit the bill. She was only here for a little while and really didn't have much to do with me. We did kiss a few times but that was it. I really think she was the reason that I didn't cry over the loss of Judy. I also think I learned a big lesson. It's so much easier to get over someone if you can replace her with someone else right away. Even if the replacement isn't forever, it just works. Now that I think about it, I might have bedded her. After all, I can't remember her name!

Maybe that summer was one of transitions for many, with the end of school and many going to college or out there trying to find a job. Gene seemed to fall into that category as well. Transition! Right at the end of summer, Gene announced that he and Carolyn were to get married. CAROLYN! Who the hell is Carolyn? What happened to Val? Carolyn? Now, we all knew who Carolyn was because she had been in Madrigals with us for most of the three years and was a very good singer. How the hell did she fit into the equation sure puzzled everyone. Where the heck did Val go? I was as close to Gene as anyone was or closer. I had absolutely no idea that there was a break up and a new union of these two. Then, you put on top of it, MARRRIGE. The only thing to expect is that a baby is in the works, which in those days, came as no surprise to anyone. In fact, a common joke for a marriage proposal was, "You're what?" Now, everyone always has their own opinion of people. Although Carolyn was a nice person, I never saw the comparison between Val and Carolyn. If I were to rate them, I would put Carolyn at a five and Val at a nine. But that's me and my opinion. As it turned out, Carolyn was not pregnant and they didn't have children for the first four years of their marriage. To this day, I never asked and I never knew why Gene did what he did and or why. Their marriage lasted about ten years and then they divorced. It was nasty. The last time I saw Carolyn, she was about three hundred pounds with a very bad attitude and a far cry from that very thin lady in school with a smile on her face.

Chapter Thirteen

Summer flew by, and college started for both Gene and me. Gene was in Los Angeles, and me, in the little town of Walnut, not far from Pomona where I lived. I always had a problem with reading, comprehension, and spelling and always thought that it was because I did not like them. Not until I was about fifty-eight or so and dating a special ed teacher, Lynne, did she tell me that I had Attention Deficit Disorder. (A. D. D.) Here is a kid in college who cannot read well, comprehend well, and certainly does not know how to spell, trying to get through college. Not an easy task. (Now, I am writing a book. Go figure!) My major was aeronautics. Of course! That's what they told me to do in high school so I did it. I had three hours of lecture and three hours of classroom lab on Monday, Wednesday and Friday. Not to get ahead of myself, but I had to buy books about airplanes and engines that cost well over a hundred dollars and all through school I never cracked them. Well, except for one. Thank God for the lectures and my enjoying them. My other classes were algebra, a piece of cake I thought; marketing, a natural for a Jew: and business law, another one for a good little Jewish boy. My parents couldn't have been happier.

The first week of school I seemed to be missing something. I was happy and school looked to be a great challenge. I wasn't sure what it was, but I figured it was just the feeling of being in college and not high school. Gene came home for the first weekend. We got together for a long breakfast on Saturday. We talked for hours and then he said, "How about the fair just for old times!" (Like it had been years, right)! Right then, I knew what had been different the first week in college. It wasn't college. It was the anticipation of going to the fair that had me all screwed up. Kind of withdrawals, I guess. No fighting with the blacks and the Mexicans. No Judy or Val and Gene. Just college! Gene and I agreed to meet at the big clock around six o'clock that night, Saturday, just the two of us. I asked, "What about Carolyn. Where is she?" He said, "She's at her mother's house in Pomona and wanted to stay and chat. I guess work on the colors or invitations for the wedding or something like that."

The day went fast and before I knew it, we were at the clock. The first thing that we did was to scarf down two dogs on a stick and a lemonade. I am sure I have told you that the best dogs on a stick and lemonade were at the fair. They were to die for. (Now that I think about it, I almost did a couple of times waiting to meet the Drifters.) We started to walk around the exhibits. We started with the bird house, small animal displays, house wares, gardening area, motorcycle sales area, and many, many more to kill some time before we went to the fun zone about nine-ish. The fun zone was always more fun after dark. Well, I guess that depends on who you go with. As we were walking around, we saw a trampoline and kids jumping on it. Gene and I had plenty of trampoline time logged in high school, and we both were pretty good at it. It was not a competition event at school or we both would have done it with the team. We walked over to it and guess who was running it, Yep, our old high school gym coach, Mr. Evans. We walked over to him, shook hands, and exchanged amenities. He said, "Why don't you jump a little bit and show these yea who's what a little class is?" Most of the kids who were there were under fifteen and with their parents. Jumping was free and the line was long. I never knew a kid who wouldn't like to jump on a trampoline. There were plenty of spectators, young and old. Gene smiled at me, stuck his hand out and his arm out, then tucked it back to his stomach as he bent half way over as to let me go first. I smiled back, slipped off my shoes, did a handstand on the outside rail then tucked myself over, and rolled on. I jumped for about five minutes or so. As I got off, you could hear the applause and yelling. Gene was not quite as flamboyant as I, but he also did about five minutes and received a loud applause. We talked for a minute or so and walked away feeling pretty good about ourselves. I can't tell you how many times I did well in gym and got booed from the other team. It is nice when someone appreciates you.

We did our fun zone stuff and about eleven o'clock we headed for Henry's drive through for some vinegar-soaked French fries and a vanilla coke, talked for a bit, and then we both headed on home. I didn't see Gene for awhile after that. It was back to school and try to get good grades to make my parents happy. If it wasn't for them I am not so sure I would be in college. I was having trouble with my schedule and full-time work at SCOA so I applied for a job at Shopping Bag (a grocery store with a separate department for non-foods, clothes, paper goods, tools, and so on.) They were eventually bought out by Von's Grocery Company. I got the job, and they were willing to work around my college schedule. In fact, they were very interested in all who applied who were going to college. I was sad not to work for Max at SCOA anymore but he understood as I knew he would. In years to come, as I eventually got into business for myself, I tried to pattern myself after him. I'll always remember him. Thanks, Max. May you rest in peace!

I had a choice to work in the grocery department or the dry goods section. I knew nothing about lemons, meat or cereal other then you eat them (With exception of watermelons. They were to throw as well.), but Max taught me about linters and pickers and threads per square inch and things like that. I chose the dry goods department. I was assigned to the store in Sierra Madras near Pasadena, about thirty minutes from home and school. I was not having much trouble with any of my classes except for one. Believe it or not, algebra! Me the guy who was a genius in math and never got anything but A's in high school and now having a major problem with algebra. It got so bad that I even had to open the algebra book and ask for some tutoring from a chick who was in the class. It did no good. From kindergarten to college I never failed anything. Guess what, algebra! To this day, I still can't believe it. Awe well!

One day I was in the lecture part at my aeronautics class and my teacher was, believe it or not, Mr. Looney. He had been a World War Two pilot in a B Fifty-Two bomber. Through the three years that I had him as a teacher, he told many stories about the war and his plights. I won't bore you with them all, but there is one that I think you can laugh at as well as visualize.

One day, he and his crew were delivering two hundred dozen eggs; five hundred pounds of chocolates, and of course, many dozens of nylons to the troops somewhere near Germany in his B Fifty-Two. All of a sudden, they were attacked by Japanese Migs. Now, I know you can't see his face as I could when he told the story, but I hope you can visualize the plane in your mind. They were in a dog fight for ten minutes. I really don't know if they won the fight or the Migs just left for whatever reason, but when it was over, Mr. Looney described the inside of the plane as one huge omelet, from turning upside down fifteen times and the plane going from side to side and on its side. The eggs were flung all over the inside and getting in everything. He almost couldn't see through the cockpit windows. It must have been a horrific mess. He said it was bad enough that the dog faces (This time it had nothing to do with me.), didn't get their eggs, chocolates and nylons, but it took them a week to clean up the inside of the plane so it was safe for take off. In fact, Mr. Looney said he was finding chocolate bars under things in the plane for months.

In my aeronautics class there were many guys and one girl. She was spoken for so we really didn't pay much attention to her. Well, at least I didn't. Now, remembering that I was spending six hours a day with these guys, three in lecture and three in shop, it wasn't hard to get close to some of them. Although they were far from Jews, they wound up with more names then they started with. First there was Ed Spell. He was from Lone Pine, California. Lone Pine is near Mammoth ski resort, a very active volcano, as we speak, not far from South Shore Lake Tahoe, Nevada. Ed was an Indian, Cherokee as I remember. We appropriately called him "Cherokee." He had a Love affair with alcohol, beer, in fact. (Hmmm, an Indian that likes alcohol? How unusual!) He Loved it so much that when "the boys" would go out drinking and driving some nights, he would sit in the back seat of my car, hook the open quart of his beer in his lower lip, rest the bottle against the side of the car, and let go. It was like an I V drip. He would never touch the bottle until it was empty. In a night he would go through at least four quarts and never talk and never pee. I looked for a girl like that for years and never found one.

Then there was Terry Whitenow. Now, here is a case! I never had the guts to even talk to him until he finally spoke to me one day and then I was terrified, especially to shake his hand. Terry had a problem, no wait, he had many problems. The biggest and most obvious one was that he walked with a limp. He was built a lot like Munger whom we competed against in gymnastics. He had a huge chest and small waist, kind of like he worked out in a gym on a regular basis. As time passed, I found out that he was missing a leg and had a wooden one practically all the way up to his hip that he screwed on and off. All of his strength that should have gone to his leg went to other parts of his body and he was very strong. He never smiled and was never friendly to anyone. I had him in another class, as well.

One day, he got a girls attention and said, "Watch." He put a thumb tack, you know, the kind you put into a cork board, into his leg and the girl screamed. He once sat in class and lit his Argyle socks on fire and watched them burn around all the way up to his calf. This guy was a couple fries short of a Happy Meal! I did not want to shake his hand after I saw him one time walk up to a stranger, introduce himself, and then shook the new guy's hand so hard, that three fingers actually split wide open and blood started gushing out. This was for, as far as I knew, no reason, just to do it. As years passed I saw him do it several times. However, for whatever reason, he took a shine to me and became one of the guys. Thank God! It's nice to know he was on my side. He was nicknamed "Mad Dog" the rest of the time that I knew him.

There was another guy with whom I became good friends. I have racked my brain trying to think of his name, and I can't remember it. (I hope we didn't make Love!)The four of us pretty much palled around together. Now that I think about it, probably a replacement for Bill, Roger and Owen.

Speaking of them and because they will not be in anymore of my book or at least I think that way now, let me tell you what happened to them. As far as I know, Roger married a lady from Fontana who had five children, and they were living happily ever after. Owen, I totally lost tract of. Bill, as it were, I had bumped into him, maybe fifteen years later, and he had been in the armed services. What branch I can't remember, but he was six foot three and I hardly recognized him. We talked for awhile and went our separate ways. Many years later, maybe in the mid-nineties, I was having financial problems because I spent all my money courting a chick named Bonnie (later chapter for her.) There were many collection agencies after me. Call after call month after month. At one point a guy named Bill called me from a collection agency and asked if I was the Charles Gerson who went to Ganesha High. I thought it was just another tactic to get me to pay an old bill or credit card debt. I said, "Yes, why?" He said that he was to collect a debt for about six thousand dollars but wasn't sure if I was the same Charles Gerson. I said, "That's me." He said, "It's Bill, Bill from school." "Hey Bill, how ya doing?" I said. He said, "How did you get into this much trouble?" At that point I almost died laughing. Bill, asking me about getting into trouble! Hell, he was the cause of ninety percent of what I had been into for years. I heard on the other end of the phone, "You stupid shit!" He hung up, and I have never heard from him or the collection company since. Now, where was I?

With a couple of months of college under my belt, there was a Halloween dance (sock hop) in the school gymnasium. I and my new found friends, Cherokee, Mad Dog, and, what's his name, decided to go. (Damn, I only palled around with him for three years, how I could not remember his name!) Anyway, we met at the school parking lot about eight o'clock and were not in Halloween attire. I was game but Terry, I mean Mad Dog, probably would have come as a baseball player with his leg over his shoulder as a baseball bat. Not a pretty sight. We met and went into the gym and in about an hour or so we were bored. Let's go and get some beer, someone said. I can't imagine it being Cherokee! We got into my car and headed towards Pomona to a liquor store. The drive was about ten miles or so. We hadn't been driving more then two minutes or so when a car pulled up alongside of us. Someone started yelling something. I could not make out what they were saying, but it may have been that I had a low tire or even a flat. I told Cherokee to roll down the window and to see if he could understand what all the yelling was about. As he rolled open the window, I noticed that there were four Mexicans in the car. Right then and there, I knew what was going on. Mexicans, I just can't live without them. Cherokee opened the window and as he did, a full beer bottle was tossed through it. (Obviously not Jewish Mexicans or the bottle would have been empty.) There was beer all over. I am sure Cherokee was pissed because of the waste. Then, another one was thrown at my car. I am sure it had made a dent. Now, I was pissed! I tried to outrun them, but I was not going to run a stop sign or light just to get away from them. I didn't need a ticket. I was trying to get away. Mad Dog kept saying, "Stop so I can kill those bastards." Now, I am not sure what he was talking about, remembering he only had one leg that worked, but I kept driving. Another bottle hit my car, and the yelling kept on for another five minutes. We were hanging out of the car, and yelling back, and making finger jesters but had nothing to throw at them. Anyway, if we had, Cherokee probably would not let us toss them anyway. The yelling got to a fever pitch. There was no doubt that they wanted to rumble. There were five of them as I later found out. Only four of us and one only had one leg. Mad Dog, sitting down at an arm wrestling match, I am sure, could kill anyone, but outside in a brawl on the street, I was not sure he would be of much help. As it turned out, both cars came to a major five-way light intersection at the same time. This was the largest intersection in Pomona. Two of the roads led on to two major freeways. Another two led to the major streets to downtown Pomona. The fifth was to the airport, Bracket Field. Not only were these streets, two and three lanes wide, but they had a plethora of street lights. Being a major intersection, there was a bezillion kilowatt of power lighting the whole area. I was not sure how long the signal light had been red or how long it would be before it would turn green, but as I looked out my window, I saw that it didn't matter. A split decision had to be made, run the red light or get out of the car and fight. They were getting out of their car and were on their way over to my car.

As it turned out, I didn't have to make that decision. Mad Dog, Cherokee, and what's his name were already out of the car and heading to meet them halfway. Jesus Christ, I'm thinking. We're in the middle of the major intersection, and there were fifty cars in the other lanes (four of them) all looking at us with their headlights on. It was like we were the main event at the boxing matches. I had a tire iron under the front seat and grabbed for it. As I reached it and was coming up, I got smashed in the face with someone's fist. Lucky, I guess. It could have been a beer bottle. Then, whoever it was that hit me, was thrown to the ground by Cherokee. I was able to get out of the car and jump into the mix. Now, from being from the same camp as Mohammed Ali, Michael Spinks, Rocky, (not necessarily Marciano), and the Drifters, I had no problems fighting. The only thing I lacked was Num Chuks. I had been previously searching for Bruce Lee for instruction. The only thing I could think of was that they were Mexicans and had no problem waling on them.

Soon, I looked over and couldn't believe my eyes. Mad Dog had his leg in his hands and was killing some guy with it! Just beating the crap out of him! I didn't even see him take it off. He must have done it a long time ago while in the car in anticipation. I didn't know whether I should laugh or keep on hitting someone. I am telling you, it looked very funny. We all started to hit anything that moved, as long as it was brown and they kept hitting anything that was white. Rolling around on the ground, standing up or whatever, it was a war. You could already see blood and bruises forming. It was just like the fairgrounds all over again. I am not sure how many times the light turned to green from red and back again, or if it did at all, but it seemed like a life-time before we all heard the sirens and saw the lights.

Shit, the cops! We immediately stopped fighting and got back into our respective cars. We tried to brush our hair back and looked at each other and blotted the blood from our faces. I am sure the Mexicans were doing the same. The cops knew exactly where to stop. We didn't think they could see us fighting from so far away but somehow they knew. Fucken cops! Parents have eyes in the back of their heads, but cops have them everywhere. They are like flies. They, with their Christmas tree lights going full blast, and now turned off sirens, all six cops from three cars got out and half came to our car and the other half went to the Mex's car. They shined their flashlights in the car and on all of us, not saying anything except, "May I see your driver's license?" Just shining and looking and looking and shining. I finally said, "What's the problem officer?" He looked at me like I was from Alpha Centura (the next solar system from ours) and said, "Do you think I am stupid?" In any other situation, I, and I am sure the others in my vehicle, would have Loved to answer what we had on the tip of our tongues, but considering what actually was going on, I said, "No!" He asked where we were coming from and I said, "From the dance at Mt. Sac." He looked at all of us in the car and said that we looked like shit and asked us if we had been fighting? In unison there came a response, "No sir." He said, "Are you sure?" Yes sir, officer, we are just heading in to town to pick up some chicks. I was scared to death of what Mad Dog might have said, but all was cool. (or kwel, your preference) I just met these guys and have not really figured them out yet, especially Mad Dog. I have seen what he can do just for his amusement and not out of anger. The cop said, "Go home and clean up. The way you look right now, you couldn't pick up a dog." I am not sure what the cops said to the Mexicans, but I figure the same thing. The cops got into their cars, all of them, and sped off. A sigh of relief came from all of us, and we could hear the exhaling from the Mexicans' car as well. We looked at each other and then at the Mexicans car. We told them to follow us and we can finish this. They said, "OK" and followed us as we took off very slowly. We drove about a mile towards the Mexican area of town. There were not a lot of places to start whipping on each other that was dark and isolated. But the Mexican area, (not us White guy's first choice) had a bunch of vacant dirt lots and not many street lights because the Mexicans had shot them out. We pulled off the main street and down about a couple of blocks, stopped the car and got out. Right behind us were the Mexicans. They pulled over right behind us and got out. Not sure who said it, but I heard, "Ready assholes?" I said, "With or without weapons, dick heads?" They said we can beat your asses with our bare hands. I said, "To do that you would need Munger on your side." (Jokingly, I was referring to the Munger that was against us in gymnastics!) Both sides looked at me like I was nuts. Then I heard someone say, "Munger, heh! What do you know about Munger?" one of the Mexicans asked. I said, "Why?" He said, "That's my name, asshole, my name." I said I knew a guy in gymnastics with that name and he was a M—r F—r. He said, "That's my brother, asshole." I said, "No way, asshole." He said, "He beat your ass, didn't he?" I said, "You bet he did." If it wasn't for him, our team would have gone undefeated. He said, "Did you know him?" I said, "I tried to get friendly with him once, but he wouldn't have it. He's an asshole just like you." "Fuck you, asshole," he said. I can go on and on, but you may be getting the drift. Obscenities flew for ten minutes but not a punch. After all the crap talking was done and over, we white boys took the Mexicans for hamburgers and cokes. We sat in some dive hamburger joint and bullshitted for an hour or so, shook hands, and we all walked out together. To this day, I can't believe that we fought at that intersection! It was like being on T. V.

Well, it's heading towards Christmas time and the cold weather. Gene announced his and Carolyn's wedding date. It was in December when he would be home from school for the holidays. Carolyn had gotten a job after graduation working for a stock brokerage firm in Pomona. Gene asked me to be his best man. Carolyn had asked one of her best friends to be her maid of honor. The date was set, and all was coming together nicely considering school, work and all. Gene and I were spending a lot of time together when he was home. More than with Carolyn it seemed. About ten days before the wedding day, Carolyn said that she wanted me to meet one of her co-workers form the stock firm. Her name was Heather and was a very nice lady. I said, "Not a problem." Carolyn said, "She will be at the wedding, and I will introduce her to you." "Fine," I said and went on my merry way.

The wedding day came and all went great. Gene was very handsome and, of course, I was, also. Tuxedos and spiffy, highly-shined shoes, awesome! The ladies were all beautiful as well. After the service we all got to eat for free. Gene had a very nice dinner planed. Just before we sat down, Carolyn came up to me and said, "Guess what?" I said, "What?" She said, "Heather, the one who I was going to introduce you to, came over to me and asked who you were." I said, "Great, but who is she?" Carolyn pointed her out and said, "There. She's the tall one." Tall she was, about my size. However, very pretty from where I was standing. But, we all know that, that can be deceptive. I sat down to eat and didn't meet her until later. The dancing began, and Carolyn was all over me, like ugly on an ape, to ask Heather to dance. (To this day I still have a problem with asking anyone to dance.) So, I so coolly sashayed over and asked her to dance. She said, "Ok." I walked her to the dance floor and started to dance amongst all the others who were out there. This was a problem. I felt very uncomfortable. She was so tall and not exactly built frail. Certainty not fat by any means but an all-around larger chick than I had been used to. However, there was one extremely large and redeeming benefit in being with her. Tits! She had a pretty good set of knockers. With me, that had always been an equalizer for things that I had not been too crazy about with a chick. We danced about three or four dances together and talked while we danced. I told her that I had to leave because I was the one that had to short sheet the bed and put sand in it before Gene and Carolyn left the wedding hall. Now, I hate to admit this, but I really think both of them were virgins. Gene was nineteen and Carolyn eighteen. It's a disgrace! What was this world is coming to? I left and did my dirty deed and got back in about an hour. You would think that their honeymoon was at Gene's house. No doubt, with them it could have been. However, they were going to spend the night at a local hotel and then fly to Hawaii for a week. Gene's dad and mom gave them that for their wedding gift. How cool was that. I couldn't wait for them to get back so they could tell me all about Hawaii. I only read about it and saw the great pictures in magazines. I never thought it was a real place! I spent a little more time with Heather and got her phone number. I told her that I'd call her soon. The wedding was over, and everyone went home.

I called Heather soon after and asked her if she would like to go window shopping. It was Christmas time and very cold out. Window shopping was, in my eyes, a fun thing to do this time of the year. She said, "Fine" and I picked her up at her house in La Verne. She introduced me to her mom, we left. That night we spent four or five hours together talking. She had a lot of baggage for a seventeen year old soon to be eighteen in February. (I went Christmas shopping and am Jewish. So who's to talk?) I was to be nineteen in January. There was about a year and a month difference. If you are into things like this, I am an Aquarius and she, a Pisces. Today, I know that when you are dating, there are some things that you don't divulge until at least the third to the sixth date. Those days I guess you let it all hang out. She talked so much that night I didn't have time to tell her about my life story. Had I, I am sure that we would have not have had a second date. She told me that she had a year and a half old daughter from a guy named Bob. After his graduation they had moved to North Carolina to have the baby. Although Heather graduated with honors, she never did graduate with her classmates in the school ceremony. It was a shame for many reasons. She not only was a straight 'A" student with honors and was liked by all, but, she was elected as the homecoming queen and never got to sit on her court because she was so pregnant. (School policy, as I remember.) When they moved to North Carolina, they had no money and shot squirrels for food. I had to think back when my family had groceries laid on our front door so we could eat. I knew how bad it could be. Their relationship lasted about six months. Heather came back with her baby, Holly Diana, and moved in with her mother and father back in La Verne. Learning all of this in a few hours while Christmas window shopping. Shit, I am glad I am Jewish. I don't think I could handle this had I been Christian. I knew that her not being Jewish, I did not have to worry about marrying her and inhaling all of her baggage. Just keep my mind on her large breasts and may be getting laid. Yea, that's the ticket!

Gene and Carolyn got back from Hawaii, and I spent hours with them. I think I had a better time listening to them and what they did and saw than they had being there. I told them I had seen Heather once and that I thought she was an nice girl but a little too much for me, with a baby and all that other crap she had to endure. She lived in La Verne. It was on the way to my new job at Shopping Bag in Sierra

Madre so I would stop in on the way and say hi to Holly and Heather's mother, Vena. I kept on stopping by for weeks just to say hi. Heather and I went out a few other times. The more that I stopped over their house on the way to work, the more I saw Heather, I started to like Heather's daughter a lot. The more I dated her, the more I kept finding out about her that was not good. Not Heather personally but the family in general. Like, her father was an alcoholic and would beat her mother up on a regular basis. In fact, Heather told me that when she and her little brother, Richard, were small and would watch T. V. on Saturday morning, the beating Heather's mother would get and the yelling was so loud that they had to move closer to the T. V. to hear. Their necks would hurt the next day from looking up. Amongst all of this, there were good things, as well. When Heather was an eleventh grader, she was the queen of the Blue Angles based in San Diego at that time. Was she a good looker or what! I'll say! The romance went on for a while and the longer it went on, the more I was falling in Love with Holly, the daughter, and not Heather. I even liked Heather's mother. (Now I know there will never be a marriage. How can you like a mother-in-law?) In fact, I liked her a lot. I am sure that even up to this day, no one in the family believes it. I seemed to see Vena more than Heather every time I stopped over on the way to work to see Holly. Most of the time when I stopped by in the mornings, Heather was working. Vena and I would talk. She would go out of her way to make me coffee, especially in the early morning on Saturdays. I would hold Holly and play with her. One night, when Heather and I were on a date, Heather told me that her mom wanted her to break off our relationship because I was a Jew. Heather's family was very strict Baptists. You know no drinking, smoking and so forth. Heathers response, as she told it to me was, "I am just dating him, Mom. I'm not marrying him!" Famous last words!

January, my birthday, came and went. February, Heather's birthday, came and went. We were dating pretty seriously by this time, as time permitted. But I was involved with school and the new job and did not have a ton of time to spend on romance. But with summer on its way, things would lighten up a little.

About this time, in March or April I think, I was asked to be the manager of the dry goods department for the Shopping Bag Store where I was working. That meant two things to me, well maybe three. First, more money! Second, my parents would be so happy, especially my dad having a manager in the family. (That would be as close to a doctor as he was going to get, at least from me anyway.) Third, I would have Sundays off and could spend time with Heather and Holly. Kind of like a family thing. I accepted the position and because of it, practically started a new life.

Many things changed just because of the hours and the money. This job, like the one I had at SCOA, required a suit and a tie. So, from a very young age, maybe sixteen or seventeen, I wore a tie and for many years thereafter. So much so, that until age fifty-five or so, from early morning, I never took my suit and tie off until I went to bed. It just became a part of me.

School was becoming fun as I spent a lot of time with the boys. Hmmm, that term again. We ate just about every lunch together and in between classes when we had a break, we seemed to find each other. In the first year, I saw Mad Dog split two more guys' fingers with a hand shake. Why, I'll never know, but no one ever reported him. I started to learn all about airplanes and how they work. Just to give you an example, we all know that we put oil in our automobiles and go on our merry way and don't give it a second thought. But, think about this. An airplane uses oil, also. You put it in the same way as a car, basically. But why, when you fly upside down, doesn't the oil spill out or stop lubricating? Just thought I'd give you something to think about. There are so many differences in cars and airplanes that it really kept up my interest. I was getting good at it. The really bad thing about school was that I just could not understand algebra. Things went from bad to worse. Business Law was really interesting. I Loved it because most of it was discussion. Discussion from the book, but I grasped it well without it. A lot of it was common sense and logic. Although I am not Mr. Spock, I was intrigued with it. Marketing, I started thinking that it should have been my major and not a minor. It was just about all discussion and about prices and displays of product and what people want and why they want it. It was a really fun course. I will tell you one thing that I disagreed with them and, to this day, still do, and that is that, I was told that the most important thing why people stay in business is for customer satisfaction and the second is for profit. I firmly believe the reverse. A Jewish thing maybe! I don't know!

Chapter Fourteen

School is out and the summer begins. I was working forty-four hours a week as a manager and now, no school. Great! Time to spend with Heather and Holly and, for some reason, my little brother and his friends seem to be around a lot more. That would make them all about fourteen. Adolescence, boredom, needing advice, who knows, but they all seem to be around a lot more. One day, Mark asked me if I would drive him and a few of his friends to the top of Elephant Hill, you know the one that had a fire recently. Hmmm. You could drive to the top from the opposite side of where we would hike. At the top was a police gun practice range. If it was not in use by the police, anyone could use it. You had to be eighteen or with someone who was eighteen. So, I loaded up about four or five little guys and their B B guns (Red Riders, of course), and I grabbed my twenty-two rifle. We were off. We went to the gun store and bought ammo and then headed up the hill. Now, I know you are waiting for some kind of a sick ending, like someone got shot or whatever, but I will have to disappoint you. All went well, but it is a real good segue to the next round. There is a place called, "The Salton Sea" not far from San Diego. Or was it Palm Springs? It was all desert around this very shallow, extremely salty body of water. The kids, Mark's friends, asked me to take them there so they could shoot their B B guns at something other than a target in a gun range. I had nothing to do that weekend, nor had I ever been there before so I said, "OK." In a week or so later, I loaded up the small boys and guns and we were off. It was kind of nice to be looked up to by Mark's friends. It kind of made me feel like a guru of some sorts. Not to mention, I got to spend some fun time with my little brother. There were five years between us so we kind of did our own things. We finally got to the Salton Sea, and it was hot. I mean hot. Over a hundred, I am sure. Probably one ten if a degree. I parked the car, and we all got out looking like General Patton's troops searching for the Borsch. We grabbed our guns and started to look for some lizards, snakes, birds, fish, and elephants, anything at which we could take aim. But after a half hour we saw nada. Not a thing was moving, nothing. It was just too damn hot for a mammal and too salty for fish. So, here we are all sweating like pigs, guns loaded, and the only thing we can see is each other. Right! Hmmmm, just us! OK, guys, let's choose up sides and shoot at each other. We all think we are marksmen, right, so let's prove it. I am not real sure, but this may have been the determining factor that turned my little brother into an extremely conservative person for the rest of his life. Now that I think back on it, at this young age, he did get with the program. So, here's what we did. We chose up sides, and we were to shoot at the other team. We would hide in the shrubs, behind the few trees that were there, but mostly behind sand hills and a few large rocks that were scattered around. It was kind of an adult game of hide and go seek. Instead of tagging you when you were found, you were shot at. Fun, heh! Now, the rules were as follows: you were not to shoot at anyone because we are not doing this to kill anybody. We are to shoot near the person. If we are great shots like we think we are, this should be no problem. You are killed if you are hit with flying sand. Did you ever get hit with flying sand that was kicked up at you by a bullet traveling at about a bazillion miles an hour? Fortunately, the kids had only B B guns, but the king, me, had a twenty-two. These guys were in trouble, and they knew it. Here we are in the middle of nowhere and are just about ready to start shooting at each other, sweat dripping into our eyes, the sun glaring with blinding rays, tempers are on edge from the heat, and just about the time that someone was going to yell, "Hide," I said, "Wait a minute. This is nuts. It's too hot to do it this way. Let's take our clothes off." We might as well get a sun tan. YEA everyone said. We put down our assault weapons for a minute or two, stripped to our skivvies, and then picked up the surrounding arsenal once more and ran for cover. I am not sure if anyone ever saw us that day, but it had to be pretty comical and scary at the same time, seeing a bunch of nuts running around pretty much naked and shooting at each other. As I recall, there were three on each team. The kids were having a great time. I am not so sure whom they were trying to shoot real close to the other kids (maybe they were afraid of shooting someone's eye out), but it was like playing real cowboys and Indians. Then there was me. I was then and, still am to this day, (that's why I am writing this book), a little more reckless than most. I was trying to get as close as possible. I mean inches. The kids were hopping from bush to rock and playing their game of cowboys. I would wait until one would put his head out or a foot and take aim and shoot. I know a time or two I almost shot off a toe. I could hear them saying, "Did you hear that bullet? It almost hit my head." After all was said and done, no one got hurt, and we all had a great bunch of fun. However, I did hear one of my brother's friends say to him, "I think your brother was shooting at me a lot more than anyone else." Hmmm, I don't know why he would think that. His name was Rudy LOPEZ! We had so much fun at the Salton Sea that we went back a few times and repeated the same ole stuff. For some reason, Rudy LOPEZ never went with us again. In fact, it is good that he didn't. Had he gotten shot, he would not be the big honcho he is today. He owns a company in the Bay area that produces a hot-shot soft drink called "Pump" and is doing very well. Not to mention, he is on his fifth or sixth white wife and all were blondes. (Maybe he was not too crazy about Mexicans either!)

    I told some of my friends about the Salton Sea, and they tried it with me. The big guys! But this time we all had twenty-two rifles. In fact, one of the guys had a thirty-thirty and one had thirty-ott six. Now were talkin! Pretty much the same thing happened. We all had a blast, and no one got blown away. However, there was a lot more blood this time. No direct hits but a lot of near misses that ended up in rock chips flying up and hitting us, and sand doing the same thing. We older guys, like me and the kids, did it about three times and then it became too far to drive in relationship to the fun.

    The Fourth of July came along. My dad had a barbecue party. This was no big deal as my dad's parties go, but there was one incident that was, at the time, very funny and timely. It was later in the evening, and we had shot off all the illegal fireworks that we had. Just about everyone was in the house drinking. My dad and I were taking movie camera pictures of all the drunks that were in attendance for future viewing and blackmail. It just so happened that I was doing the taking at this particular moment. The music was playing loud, and it was kind of a Hawaiian song. My dad started to do the hula. He saw that I had the camera on so he walked up about six or seven feet in front of me, still doing the hula, turned his back to me, bent over and dropped his shorts to the floor. Normally, this would have been a classic for all eternity in our family archives, but as freaky luck would have it, a little girl about four-ish just happened to walk in between me and my dad at exactly the same time he dropped his shorts. I relatively shot nothing but the back of her head. To add insult to injury, wondering what I was doing, she (the little girl) turned and looked at my dad just as his shorts hit the floor. I got everything on camera except for dad's bare ass and balls hanging down. However, little Michele, to the day my dad passed away, could never look into his face again. By the way, little Michele is the little sister to Rudy Lopez, the millionaire Bump drink guy, in the Bay area. You know, the Mexican that took a lot more rounds from my twenty-two than my entire brother's other friends, at the Salton Sea. It seemed that I did a lot more with my brother recently as I may have said. In fact, we did some camping all over. One of the places we camped was at Big Bear Lake in the San Bernardino Mountains. An area named "Burnt Flats". (Sure sounds like a place I should be.) We, of course, would take our B B guns and twenty-two's just in case there were woolly mammoths and dinosaurs to deal with. I remember one time a friend of mine went, named Ed, and also a chick named Patty D. (Last name withheld because of future content.) The young kids (my brother's friends, maybe twelve or thirteen this time), were kind of getting used to being shot at, whether from me (mostly) or from the other kids that went with us. But this time, we were all sitting around, had not yet lit the fire pit, and were laughing and having fun. Ed said he had to take a shit. Probably more then we needed to know at the time. We all were young in those days, and we didn't need, "no stinken toilets or showers." Ed headed over to the designated crap and pee area behind a few bushes. My mind started to work overtime. I got all of the kids and me to quietly sneak over and just about the time he started to do his business, we all jumped towards him and yelled. I think that may have been the way the term started, "He shit a brick." This guy was so scared and startled that he pooped all over his own feet and shoes. What fun! Well, for us anyway. Now, the fun doesn't stop here. Billy Weaver, one of my brother's closest friends then and still is today, had to do the same thing that Ed did. However, it was the next day. We were all sitting around just like the day before. Bill headed for the bushes. Knowing that he would be alert for some of the same tricks as the day before, I yelled, "Don't be scared back there." We all laughed. As soon as Bill was out of sight, I told my brother to hurry and get the video camera. He said, "Why?" I said, "Just hurry." He ran one way, and I ran the other and got my twenty-two rifle. I told my bro to start shooting now, and I will do the same. Camera rolling, I started shooting as fast as I could into the bushes. Out came Billy yelling and screaming obscenities with his pants half way down holding them with one hand and making finger gestures with the other. All caught on camera. I still have the footage just in case he ever runs for a public office.

Now, I had mentioned a chick named Patty that was with us. I had dated her for awhile. She was a pretty religious girl and not Jewish but Catholic. Although I had never gone to bed with her (not because I had not tried a bazillion times), but because of her religious beliefs but, I had gotten to first base and maybe second a few times. She had very large breasts and being only eighteen and five-feet two, they were very noticeable. I had had my hands full with her if you get my drift. She was different from any other girl I had been with before. By now, I had become a pretty good stud and seen a lot. (I would like to have said a really big stud but why lie.) She had inverted breasts. For you less knowledgeable people out there, inverted breasts are when the nipples are recessed instead of protruding outwardly. I had told my brother and his friends about them. Not that they knew what the hell I was talking about or even cared. (Except Larry Winezin. He was much like my old friends Bill and Barney.) I said if you guys want to see them, I will get her to go into the back seat of my car and start making out with her. Keep walking by and when you see that you can't see me any more, that's when I will have her laying down on the seat and will have them out for you all to see. I'll keep my mouth on hers so she can't see and won't be able to see you guys looking in. All went as planned, except for the "she won't be able to see you all looking in" part. As we were making out, she wanted to get on top so they would hang in my face. As she tried to move on top, she saw them all looking in and drooling on the windows. Needless to say, she never talked to me the balance of the camping trip. She just walked around looking at the ground. I told her it was all in the name of knowledge. I just don't understand you women! Sometimes you wonder how you get started in different things. Here is one that I do remember. As I may have mentioned, my mom and dad were famous for having parties. This one hot summer day, we, my family and I, were over a good friend of mom and dad's, Mitzy and

Jock's house, swimming in their pool. Jewish, yes! Where the name Jock came from is beyond me. (Maybe he had two names like my aunts and uncles, and no one could pronounce it.) Now, Jock was a retired sheriff at a very young age. He developed a limp when he walked from carrying his gun in his back pocket. Some use to say that the reason he retired was not retirement at all but that he shot his dick off one day when the gun discharged all by itself, and he got off for disability reasons. Most of us who knew him, knew he would never get off again! After the swimming was over, the adults decided to go over to my house for a barbecue at the famous sock and foot burning area in my backyard. All went as planned and normal. No foot fires either. Everyone was getting plastered and dancing and eating and having just about as much fun as anyone can. Night time started to fall. The adults went into the house, and the kids dispersed to wherever. It was approaching maybe eleven o' clock, and I went home to go to bed. The door was locked. Hmmm, that's funny. Maybe all the adults went somewhere (I thought), and I am locked out until they come home. I decided to look in through the upper window where I could see into the living room. I had to get the ladder from the garage. I climbed it and looked in. Shit, was this kwel. (Kwel, granddaughter spelling again) Everyone was there, and they were watching triple x rated adult movies. I had never seen anything like this before. No one ever told me there was such a thing. Where the hell are Barney and Bill when you need them? I didn't know how long I could watch them before someone would see me in the window, but I stuck it out for a long time. I am telling you I saw some awesome stuff. I had wished I had seen this a long time ago. It would have helped me when I had to be with those older women. In fact, I think I remember one or two of them asking if I would do "this or that," and I thought they were nuts. I wasn't getting paid enough for that sort of thing. (Now *I pay* for that sort of thing!) I never got caught, and I never mentioned it to my dad. But from that day on, I have always had an x rated video or two in the house. Next!

These next few things aren't really anything about me directly, but they are so unusual Mom and Dad wise, that I thought I'd throw a few of them in.

My mother was known for her legs, different hair dos and colors. She was not afraid to mix it up with any and all of the men in her life.

She was always the life of the party whether Dad was there or not! Whether it was mine or Mark's friends or the bunch that Dad ran around with. Although she was a very classy lady, when it was time to do so, she could cuss, drink and party hardy with the best of them. Maybe my Bubba was right and she was a shiksa. But the main thing she was known for, that all others would comment on, was her hair color or colors as it may be. I am not exaggerating. My mom changed hair color at least two times a month for ever! For ever! For ever! She would go from blonde to dirty blonde to brown to red to reddish blonde to dark brown to light brown to platinum blonde to very dark brown to %^&*()_and on and on and on. You get it? I and everyone else who knew her would not even comment anymore. It finally became a standing joke. When her friends would greet her, it would not be "Hi Lil." It came to be "Brown today, huh!" Until the day she passed away, she had all her hair, thick, and all there. I definitely didn't get my roots (pardon the pun), from my mom. However, I often wonder if I may have had something to do with it when I shaved my head a few years back. Now, my dad was a different case. The word "case" doesn't even begin to describe him. Like the time I had to paint the outside of the house when I got expelled. It was a nice neighborhood at that time, and all the houses seemed to be nicely blended in. Well, until I had to paint. He wanted purple. Not pale lavender or a soft beige but purple. So, he was the boss and, "So it is written and so it will be done." Purple it was!

Dad had to wear a small bib over the hole in his neck (tracheotomy tube) to keep from shooting phlegm out if he coughed. After awhile and getting comfortable with himself, he did not want to take the trouble to put it on sometimes. So, for the rest of his life, he usually could not see out of the car window from coughing while driving. At dinner time we all had to be aware of a cough. We had a signal to warn the others at the table if he was to cough. It would give us time to duck.

My dad smoked three packs of cigarettes a day. When he found out about the cancer, he quit cold turkey and never looked back. I believe I have mentioned that before.

My dad got diabetes, probably from all of the gum he started chewing when he quit smoking, and he also had been using five packs of sugar in his coffee at least five or six times a day. When he found out about the diabetes, he again quit cold turkey and started to use saccharin. It was still five packs per cup. However, now there were hundreds of small pink papers all over the house. Just like the car with gum wrappers. (Thank God he wasn't a Canadian white rat!)

Dad would like to have been thought of as "the great outdoors man," especially when he was involved with the boy scouts. My brother, instead of robbing, cheating, stealing, hooking and playing cards and all of the other things that I did to get this world-wide education and knowledge, was a boy scout. You know, mister goody goody. Save the world stuff. When the scouts went on over—nighters, Dad would be the first one to volunteer to drive them there and be a figure head for all who went. What many never knew was that when all went to bed, Dad would hop in his car, drive all the way home, sleep in his own bed, and then get up as early as it took to drive back so he would be up and about for the scouts in time for them to start breakfast on the stoves or Barbecues with or without socks on fire.

Dad had two very unique talents when it came to taking movie pictures with his home video camera. He actually took a lot of them because, as a family, we were always going some place different and would have lasting memories that way. But two things happened in just about every video. It would have been a little bit different then if your dad had taken them. First, Dad had no patience, just like my little brother. But in Dad's case, he would start taking pictures and would never stay in one place for very long. It was like standing ten feet away from a train that was whizzing by at a hundred miles an hour and looking straight at it as it passes. All you really see is a blur. That's the way we saw the pictures after they were developed. (Ok, for you kids, look up the word develop in your Funk and Wagnall. Ok, for you kids, a Funk and Wagnall is a dictionary. Hmmmm, I don't know if they know what a dictionary is, to be honest with you.)Well let's move on. Just about all the pictures my dad took were really tough to figure out at what we were looking. Truly, that tough! That is number one. Number two is really kind of funny. On cameras, in those days, there was a small window with a counter that when you looked into it, you could see how much film you had left or have already used. The standard roll was fifty feet. My dad, for some unknown reason, could not figure it out. He never knew when he was out of film. He would guess and then stop taking pictures. But instead of just opening up the camera and taking out the used roll of film, he would turn the camera towards him, look at the counter, and then push the take button until the film ran completely out and the little box read "out." So, although this is not a really big deal, it did have a very funny ending. Remember, I said it was very difficult to see what was on the film after it was developed. There was one image that was unbelievably distinct at the end: the hair in my dad's nose for at least twenty seconds! On every fifty—foot roll!

While I am on the subject of the camera, we made such a production of Dad being such a slob that he made me film him suctioning (cleaning) out his tracheotomy tube to prove to the world that his family was wrong about him. The real story is that Mom used to do it for him and if she hadn't, he couldn't breathe. This may have been the only fifty-foot film that was ever taken and was seeable, and, really, who wanted to?

My brother, Dad and I would go golfing every once in a while. However, it was almost impossible to concentrate, not to mention embarrassing. Dad, like Rodney Dangerfield in the picture "Cady Shack," would dress just like him. Fortunately, we were a threesome, and no one would catch up to us so we avoided a lot of stupid looks and, I am sure, comments. Well, except for the starter!

Mom had been asking Dad to get us a very nice cabinet for the dining room for her best dishes and flatware. One day, Dad came home from work and told Mom that he had gotten it and that it would be delivered tomorrow afternoon. Now, Dad was the kind of guy who was always willing to help others, no matter who they were. Sometimes to a fault! I can't think of anyone so far, in my lifetime, who had a bigger heart than Dad. I just don't think they make them that way anymore. The delivery truck came, and from the house to the truck, it looked beautiful. But when we got it into the dining room, there was just something that wasn't right. It seemed to be a little crooked in some places and off center in others. Not real sturdy and what should have been more to the right to match the other side was not. One of the shelves seemed to be lower on one side than the other. You would have thought it was made by a one-armed carpenter had you wanted to joke around a bit. Just about the time the delivery men left, in walked Dad with someone. That someone only had one arm!

School is starting again. It is September nineteen sixty-one, and I am nineteen and a half. All of my buddies are back in class with me, and things seem to be all right with the world. We even have a new President of the United States whom everyone seems to like. (One exception was Fidel Castro.) A guy named John Kennedy (JFK).

Later in the year, I was transferred to a Von's Shopping Bag in Upland, California. Von's Grocery Company was going to start closing some of the Shopping Bag stores that they had purchased for whatever reason. (They never seemed to confide in me about those types of things.) As much as I thought I was becoming a big wheel (manger) with Von's Grocery Co., they neglected to confirm that to me. I wound up working under a manager named Chuck Parker. I had been reduced to an assistant manager under Chuck, but I still retained my manager salary. Chuck had years with Von's. I was happy to have the chance to work and learn under his regime. We hit it off very well. Chuck was (on the side) seeking a little relief from work without anyone knowing it. So sometimes he would take off, and I would cover for him. We actually became friends of a sort. He was probably fifteen years older than I, but we were both on the same page. As I look at it now, I realize how important it was and how lucky I had been finding great people to work under to teach me about business. Max White, Chuck Parker, and even as far back as Fletcher at the Texaco Station, teaching me trust and physical labor is where it all starts. Did I see it then, no, nada, nothing, not a bit! I only saw bosses who wanted you to do their bidding for them. So, one day, Chuck and I decided to dig in and show the powers that be what great sales people we were. Kind of put our names on their lips. Not for money but for the glory. I think at this point there must have been a hundred stores or more. I am sure that our names will never reach their ears. The dry goods department, although we always had a much higher margin than the grocery department did, always had much much smaller sales than they. We devised a plan and needed to test it out first before we contacted the power. Chuck and I started taking items that were not selling very well and making big end displays with them. Remember, we are in the dry goods department and kind of segregated from the grocery part of the store and kind of independent from the food stuffs. We did have the walk-by traffic. We would make the huge-end displays where the customers had to walk by. We started to kick butt. We were selling more of the crap items than the other stores were selling the hot stuff. One day, when Chuck was off, I thought I'd do something really dumb. I took a bunch of stuff that sold for two dollars and sixty-nine cents, (there were three or four items that were selling at the same price) and made a huge end display with them where the traffic was. I marked the items three for ten dollars. Chuck came in the next day and jumped my butt big time. That was until I told him that I had sold at least twenty-five percent off the display before I left for home. From a goat to a hero in sixty seconds! Well, that was with Chuck, anyway. We did it for about three months, selling crap that we had been stuck with for years and, at the same time, breaking the past years profit records by a bunch. So much so that the power we wanted to hear about us heard about us. They came out one day and asked how we were doing so well all of a sudden. With huge smiles on our faces, we told them what we had done. They were not happy campers. We almost lost our jobs. We were badly written up and criticized mercilessly. They said we were cheating the public, and Von's could get sued for it if anyone complained. They asked whose idea it was, and I chimed out, "The janitors." (Joke) "It was mine," I said. They just shook their heads and walked away. At the time, it was not very funny. I could just see me going home and telling Mom and my proud dad that I went from being a manger to a vagrant out on the street. But, as time went by, I kind of thought I had the right idea as a thinking business man. I had asked my teachers in marketing and business law what they thought. I moved to the head of the class in marketing and to the back of the class in business law. What the hell fifty-fifty isn't that bad is it?

Now, speaking of Chuck (my new boss), one day he came to me with a land deal. He told me that a company would like to pick him up in the morning and take him to a land presentation in Lancaster, California. They would provide him with lunch and then bring him back, with no obligation to purchase anything. They did say it was the "deal of a life time." Chuck asked me if I would like to go as well. "When" I asked? He said "Thursday." I said, "I have to work that day." He said, "Helen is also scheduled, and she can handle it alone." I'm in! Free lunch and get paid while I am chauffeured to Lancaster in a limousine. That night I was really high, not only that Chuck asked me to go with him, but if I bought something I would be a chai cock (pronounced high cocked. I believed I have mentioned that before.), land owner. I wanted to tell some one. I called a friend and said let's go to dinner tonight. She said, "Ok." We met, had dinner and I bragged about me and the potential land deal. Then we went to an open field to make out. I was in a convertible, and we were in the back seat. She was lying down, and I was on the top head to head. We were just starting to remove our clothes when she said, "Is it raining?" I said, "No, why?" She said, "I am getting wet, I think." I looked up and got the shit scared out of me. A cow had her head right on top of us. When I looked up, her nose was touching mine, and she was drooling like a leaky shower. My yell scared the hell out of my date, and she yelled louder than I. I shriveled up and she certainly was out of the mood, so we sadly wiped ourselves off from the cow saliva with my shirt and drove away. What I should have done, but didn't think of it, was to call my brother. He would have Loved to see a real cow up close and personal.

Thursday came and we were picked up early and on the way. There were six others who went, two ladies and two married couples. There were eight of us heading for a free lunch and a talk. Now, I had never been to Lancaster and to be perfectly honest with you, I never even heard of it. When we got there, all I saw was desert and more desert. Not a tree, not a spring, not an animal, not another human being except for us ten. There were eight passengers, a salesman and the driver, who, incidentally, never came out of the limo. The only good thing I could say so far about Lancaster that day was that it wasn't one hundred and ten yet. It was only one oh four. The drive had taken about three hours as I recall. The salesperson was in the back with us and didn't shut up the whole way. He told us the size of the lots, the potential of the lots, the water situation with the lots, what would grow and what would not grow on the lots, how much cheaper it would be if we would buy ten lots, how far the lots were from people. You might say he told us lots about the lots. The bottom line was that you had to buy four one acre and a quarter lots, totaling one five acre parcel. Each lot was one hundred and twenty five dollars equaling a total of five hundred dollars for the whole parcel. Why they said the lot thing and not just the parcel thing I have no idea. It seemed to me it would have been so much simpler. Now, let's remember, I am talking nineteen sixty-one here. That's when five hundred dollars was five hundred dollars. I was still paying for a Ford I never owned and for the tools that were in the trunk, books for school that I basically never opened, and trying to voluntarily help pay back some money Dad had to borrow when he was ill. There was a lot of money going out and not much coming in, or as far as that goes nothing to see or touch for my out-going money. Just out go. Not to mention, I now have a girl friend and her little daughter whom I need to spend a buck or two on and you never know, that could be money out the window as well with no return. Five hundred was out of the question, even on payments. Chuck and I talked about it for the next day or so. We even thought about going half on one parcel. That way it would only be two hundred and fifty each. The bottom line was that we never took advantage of the so-called "deal of a life time." Well, I am sure that we have all had, at one time or another, the same type of deal offered to us and passed on it. I am sure that most of them were really not "the deal of a life time" and as a matter of fact, in most cases, you would have gotten stuck for a bunch. The land that we were so tight fisted on and past on six years later was bought and made into the Lancaster Airport. The non tight-fisted owners all made a ton.

I already had my twentieth birthday and was well into being an old man. Still living at home and attending school and working a lot of hours for Von's. I was getting really serious about Heather as we were spending more and more time together.

I really never gave it a lot of thought, but it seemed as quickly as my hoodlum days had jumped into my life starting with Barney and seemingly ending with Bill, that's how fast they seemed to dissipate. I was becoming a real man and not the thirteen year old one that Judaism brought on. Those six or seven years had brought me a hell of a lot of experience and knowledge in many many ways and people I obviously will never forget, whether for the good or the bad.

It is late in the year of nineteen sixty-two, I'm twenty years old plus. Dad started to have problems with his neck. Let me refresh you. Dad had cobalt treatments (radiation, a new form of cancer cure at that time) for the cancer in his larynx a few years ago and now has to breathe through a tracheotomy tube. The cancer was cured and all seemed to be just fine with the exception of him coughing and not covering up when he did, which was really our problem, I guess. We had to know when to bob, weave and duck.

Dad started to notice a very small fissure or two in his neck. He went to the doctor, and they gave him some stuff to rub on it, and said to keep track of it. If things do not improve, come back. (Like he would not keep track of the holes starting to form in his neck!) A few months went by. The holes were not only getting larger but more were forming. It was doctor time again. The doctors put him through a bunch of tests and said to come back in two weeks. By then we, as a family, were really concerned. We could see that if this kept up, you could see through his neck. If there were many more fissures to form, the potential of his head falling off because he would have no neck to support it could be possible if infection didn't get him first. This sounds a little funny but did seem possible. The tests came back, and none were of any help. More tests and more worry. Another month went by, and no decision about anything had been made. The only thing that was for sure was that Dad had thirty or forty holes in his neck, and we literally could see into his neck. There were big worries about infection as well as all the neck falling away. What apparently had happened was when they gave Dad the cobalt radiation they gave him way too much. It definitely killed the cancer but also destroyed all the living tissue and whatever else is in the neck. All was dying with no way to stop it. There is one thing that everyone who knew my dad would say: he had a constitution rival to none. No matter what, he always had a smile on his face, and all was right with the world. While our whole family and all of Dad's friends were planning for the worst, he is still going camping with the scouts, working as hard as he can, and still being the best kind of person he could possibly be. There was always a smile on his face and a joke in his heart. He would let nothing get to him. He had a saying that he used to say all the time in a joking way and it still echoes through my brother's mouth and mine on occasion. "If you die, you die." I am not one hundred percent sure what he really meant, but at this time of his life, it had a meaning to all of us.

Dad got a call from the doctor that was in charge of his problem. They wanted to see him. It seemed that someone had a brainstorm. Mom and Dad drove to the hospital, Huntington Memorial, in Pasadena, I believe, and met with a team of boneheads. They came up with a plan and Dad agreed to it. Like he had a choice! His fucken head was about to roll off his neck onto the floor. Just think if that had happened, then I would really have something to write about in this book. You may have a Cyclops or something like that in your family, but I'd have the headless horseman in mine. Mom and Dad came home and revealed the plan to all the family: me, Mark and Mitzi, our dog. Are you ready for this? Even if you are not, you are gonna hear it. They decided to take his chest off and put it on as a new neck. What the fuck are they thinking??? They take the skin off his legs and put it on his chest. I hate to tell you this, but as serious as this is, right now, as I am writing, I am laughing my ass off because I know the ending. His chest off and put it on his neck? What are they thinking! It is starting to remind me of that old joke when the guy has plastic surgery on his face. His skin is taken from his ass and put on his check. Every time his mother-in-law kissed him, he laughed like crazy.

So on with the surgery. Here was the plan. The doctor was going to cut a piece of his chest off, starting from the bottom of the right areola across to the bottom of the left areola, coming up about four inches and then back and down to the right areola but just stopping about an inch before he got to the place where he made the original cut. That would leave an inch or so still attached to Dad. Then, taking the slab of meat he had cut off and turning it upside down and putting it on the neck area and then sewing it in place around to the back of the neck as far as it would go. I can't even imagine a doctor telling me that this is what they are going to do to me. I would have had to eat a gun before I'd go through that. But, not Dad! He looked forward to it. The reason that they left an inch still attached to Dad at the areola was to keep fresh blood circulating and trying to keep the newly cut slab alive so it would adhere and start to grow onto the neck area. The operation took place, and Dad was in the hospital for ten days. They wanted to keep an eye on whether the slab of meat was still alive. Not to mention the graft from his legs to his chest. If the slab was to die, Dad would follow it not long after. A huge crap shoot! Well, let me tell you, it worked! Dad is, to this day, written up in the medical journals. Maybe this was meant to be his legacy in life for all to share and benefit from. I really don't know if anyone ever got helped because of Dad's ordeal, but I do know one thing for sure. The best guy I ever knew in my life was still alive and kicken.

I would like to end that story right then and there, but there is a part that grew from it. If you can recall, I told you that when my dad had the tracheotomy tube put in he sometimes would not use a bib over it. When he coughed, the phlegm sometimes would shoot out all over. Now, try to imagine this. (if you are squeamish, pass this page) A month or so after the operation, Dad would sit at the dinner table with no shirt on. He would sit back, and all we could see was this kind of monster. (He wasn't very pleasant looking in any sense of the word.) He had freshly sewed patches on his chest, a chest not where a chest is supposed to be, but it is now the neck. The hair on the neck is now growing up instead of down, and a silver hole in the throat, not to mention a huge twisted knot protruding out about an inch and a half on one side where his neck is still connected near the areola to where his chest used to be. He would sit like a king, proud and strong, shirt off whether it was just family or friends over. Not a pretty picture but that was our dad and we Loved him. Thank God it was Mom who had to sleep with him.

It's about Christmas time and the shopping starts. I'm home from school for a few weeks. Gene is back in town, and we spent a lot of hours together. He, get this, decided to become a cop. Me, best buddies with a cop. Will miracles never cease?

I remember spending a ton of time shopping for and buying stuff for Holly. It was almost like she was my daughter. Just two years old in October but smart as a whip and cute as any kid could be. I just Loved looking at her little face. Heather and I were really getting close, but I think was more in Love with Holly.

Chapter Fifteen

Today we hit a milestone. January twenty-third nineteen hundred and sixty-three, and the writer of this book becomes Black Jack. That's for all you gamblers. For you who are not so inclined, how about twenty-one and legal as can be.

I had big plans for this day. I and a few buddies from school headed to Las Vegas. I had been working on a gambling system for months and couldn't wait to try it out. We got there in track record time and checked into the first casino on the strip. The Hacienda! No sense wasting time driving any further. They are all the same, right? (The Hacienda is where I hit my fifty-dollar jack pot when I was not quite totally legal.) It was where my parents always went when they headed to Sin City. I was not sure back then, but they actually went to shows and saw guys like Frank Sinatra and big-time show productions with feathers and bare-breasted girls. I didn't get it. They could have been gambling all that time.

Now, I worked on this system for months, like I said, and always won, always. It was on the crap table. It was rather simple really, but you needed patience, a lot of patience. I was to bet the eleven and win. The bugaboo was that I did not bet the eleven until there was one hundred rolls of the dice without an eleven showing up. Then I would bet it. If no eleven would show that time, I would place the number again twice more and then double my bet only after each set of three rolls without an eleven coming up. Going only five sets and then stopping and starting the whole thing again while waiting for one hundred rolls without an eleven. That way I could only loose ninety-three dollars at a time. Always in practice, I would win within five to six rolls after I started my betting. I found a table, and bought one hundred dollars in chips, and brought out my pad and pencil and started to count. Finally, after seven or eight hundred rolls of the dice, two hours plus, and a lot of evil stares from the stick men because I was taking up space without placing one buck on the table, the dice went one hundred rolls without an eleven. Now, I was in action. Big time! I put one dollar on the eleven and immediately got applause from all who had been standing around the table for awhile. Even the stick men! (For you who do not gamble much, a stick man is someone who has lost so much money gambling that they can't afford to eat very much so they are very, very thin. For you who do gamble much, you know that I am lying.) By now they all knew my name and what I was waiting for. The roll came out, and it was not an eleven. I placed my dollar again and lost that bet also. But I had no fear as I know how to do this. I practiced it enough. I placed the next dollar and nothing. Now, I had to double up to two dollars the next three rolls. The first roll came out and it stunk also. I placed my next two dollars and hit. I was stuck seven dollars total so far, but just won, at fifteen to one odds, which returned me thirty dollars plus my two dollars back and that put me ahead twenty-five dollars. I think the monetary return was not halfway as fulfilling as the applause from most of the people around the table. Some of the newcomers did not understand what was happening. I was twenty-five dollars ahead and in only two and a half hours. That is about ten dollars an hour and tax free. I think I was on to something here. So, the next twenty-one and a half hours took about two weeks to pass. Well, it seemed that way. I had promised myself that I would only stay at the table twenty-four hours total, win or loose. For the most part, my buddies went to bed and I went through about thirty dealers. I stuck to my guns and only went to the bathroom after an eleven was thrown. I drank mostly Coca Cola and an occasional seven-seven. No food. I lost a couple of times and had to start over, but I also won a few times. When the twenty-four hours had come and gone, it was time to pack up and leave. I was ahead one hundred and forty-seven dollars! That is about six bucks and twelve cents an hour tax free. My system worked. Was it worth it? Not at a dollar starting bet. Multiply it by a one hundred dollar starting bet and you would have made fourteen thousand seven hundred dollars in that twenty-four hour period. Would it have been worth it? You figure it out. However, the cost of the space shoes I had to buy from standing in one spot for twenty-four hours did detract from the profit. Well, that's January wrapped up in a nutshell.

February had arrived with a bang. (Pardon the pun as you will shortly see.) Heather and I went to dinner at a place called the Brazila. It was a small hotel and dinner house not far from where I lived. Very up scale. Heather, in her whole life, never had a cup of coffee. With her alcoholic father, a cocktail was out of the question. I had been working on her for a year at this point. It is hard for me to see anyone I go out with a tea totaler. Especially, if for some reason, she wound up in the family at a later date. So, after dinner, we went down to the bar where there was a dance band. We shimmied up to it, and I ordered a seven-seven and for her, a screwdriver. She looked at me as if I had put a gun to her head. She leaned over and whispered in my ear, "What the *heck* are you doing?" (She didn't cuss either. How I got hooked up with this chick I will never know.) I'm only nineteen (to be twenty in a week or so), and you know how I feel about me drinking." I said, "Shhhh, try it, you'll like it." So, that night she did drink it. It took about three hours to finish it but she did it. That was just one of a million things Heather did for me in the next thirty years, whether she wanted to or not. She was in Love. The night was full with dinner, dancing and drinking. My kind of night! Later that month, she had her twentieth birthday. I really can't remember what I did for her, but I am sure it was nice. I was then, and am now, that kind of guy. I am pretty sure that night we also made Love. That was the twentieth of February nineteen hundred and sixty-three.

About five weeks or so later, at the end of March nineteen hundred and sixty-three, I proposed to Heather. I proposed with pretty much the run of the mill proposal of that day, and time, "YOU'RE WHAT??? Pregnant, shit! Pregnant, Shit!! Pregnant, Shit!!!! How'd that happen? Now what do I do? What the fuck do I do!! I am a nice Jewish boy and these things don't happen to us. Ask Mom! Ask Dad!! Not to Jews! (Can they still make me paint?) Mexicans, Mexicans it happens to. Blacks, it happens to them also. I am white and on top of it, Jewish! It doesn't happen to us. Shit!" I was very upset with her. "How could you let this happen to you?" I am screaming, and she is crying. At this point everything is flashing through my mind, abortion, murder; it's not my problem, and many more thoughts that had no meaning except for someone that was scared to death and has no clue as to what was really going on. Pregnant, geeeesch!

Well, after three hours of me yelling and her crying, it all started to settle in. I know, in my short life that had already passed, all twenty-one years of it, I had done and had been, a bad ass, dumb ass, and pretty non-caring ass at times, but this is different. This involves the rest of my life. I am Jewish, and I do not run from trouble like this. I am just so glad and thank God Heather was not a Mexican. So, as things calmed down, we started to talk about what to do. On her end, it was pretty one way, get married and have our baby. Me, although I really liked Heather, I was in Love with her daughter and not yet her. Not in the true sense of marring Love anyway. Not to mention, I was not ready to get married. I still had school to finish, cars to race, guy things to do, not to mention I have to tell Mom and Dad. OH SHIT, AGAIN! They're going to kill me. They *will* have me paint the whole town of Pomona! Me a father and a husband! Not good, not good!

I started to think about what the positives were. Heather was from a Baptist up bringing. Not good. Her father was an alcoholic. Not good. She wasn't even a U.S. citizen. Not good. She was a World War Two baby. Her father "Joe", who incidentally I liked a lot, knocked up her mother "Vena" when in Australia. When Heather was two, she and her mother came to the United States. That was one of the problems with that war. All the men were scared stiff and the women took advantage of it. (A little humor there!) I know there are some positives here somewhere. Oh yea, Heather was the class queen of La Verne High. She was also the queen of the Blue Angels based in San Diego, at that time. You know that famous flying group. (I may have mentioned it before.) No question she was a looker. Oh yea, her uncle Bob Baldish was one of the top ten golf course architects in the world. That's a good one except that I would not know whom to tell or brag to as I didn't play golf although I had stolen some clubs before! Another good one was that she was a second cousin to Lawrence of Arabia. Normally, that would be a good one, but again, who am I going to tell? My Jewish family that I am now related to an Arab! Not to mention, he was gay. Great, just great! Heather's family didn't have a dime between them so riches were out. Things are starting to look very grim. Oh yea, big tits. How could I forget them! To make a very long story short, we decided to set a wedding for May sixteenth and just play dumb. We figured that way when the baby comes, we will just tell everyone that it came early. That way no one would figure that she was pregnant on our wedding day. I am sure the very short notice would not have been a tip off. About a week later Heather and I were sitting on the couch with my mom and dad and I said, "Heather and I decided to get married on the sixteenth of May." A big smile came over my mother and out of her mouth came, "I am so glad. I really like you; Heather, and now we have a year to plan for this great celebration with my son, Chuck." I looked at Mom, (Dad hadn't said a thing as of this point) and said, "No Mom, this May." "Why so soon, why? What's the rush? There's no time to plan and invite and to do for, why?" "That is just the way Heather and I want it. This is her second marriage, and she doesn't want a big ordeal. Me, I don't care one way or another." (As I write this today, I can see how big of a fucking asshole I was. I was not only to Heather, but especially to my mom. I deprived her of her first wedding planning.) "It would be very nice if you just support us."

Now, asking a Jewish mother to be quiet and not say anything when her first born son is to get married for the first time is like putting a big juicy cow in front of a Tyrannosaurus Rex and saying, "Stay!" Christ, in just one day, she had Heather picking out the invitations and doing the colors. Dad never said much, but he did ask me the next day to sit down. He was going to prove to me how it was nuts because I/we couldn't afford it. This guy came up with a bzillion stories and scenarios that proved we would be on the streets in a month. Actually, I was doing pretty well with the new job. Heather was still working for the stock brokerage firm, and she was making a buck or two also. However, I had bought a nineteen hundred sixty-three Chevrolet convertible in February, and Dad really set his sights on my payments. (He said the same thing when I bought the car and there was no Heather or a wedding.) No matter how grim Dad made it sound, I was able to give him a good answer. This went on for two hours. It ended up with Dad saying I was nuts. Not unexpected! Mom was excited, and I think Heather was more at ease because of it. Nobody pointed a finger and accused her of being pregnant, but I am sure it was on a bunch of minds. I know that the female is supposed to pay for the wedding, but not only was her family moneyless and certainly not real crazy about Heather marrying a Jew, but they were very cheap as well. I have no idea how much the wedding cost, but Mom and Dad did it up great, right in their home. Heather wasn't born Jewish so we couldn't have a Rabbi marry us. Dad got a judge to do it. As it turned out, the judge lost the check I gave him for the ceremony. He asked me for it a couple of times, thereafter, but somehow I never came up with it. He played frog six or seven years later. Like a bookie friend of mine used to tell me, "Death cancels all debts!"

Let me tell you, a lot of stuff went down by the time May sixteenth came around. There were arguments between my side and her side, and arguments between Heather and I and not to mention my dad still on the war path about finances. All this time Heather was trying to wear tight pants and loose shirts so that no one would notice a little bulge starting. We must have had a hundred people at the wedding. We got some great gifts like an electric blanket that I just got rid of a year ago even though it was still working. G. E. I believe. There was a box with a draw string, and as you pulled it out, just about every four inches or so there was a silver dollar that was attached and came out. Well over a hundred of them. The list went on and on and on. Of course, the crème d' la crème was from my mom and dad. They bought us a house! A HOUSE! Yes, a house! Well, the down payment anyway, and it was only four blocks from them. It didn't matter to me, and, in fact, I never gave it a thought, but Heather seemed to have a problem with it. In fact, that was most of the conversation we had as we drove to and the days that we were on our honeymoon. We will get to that in a minute. The booze flowed like water, the food was non-stop, and the music and dancing were unbeatable. Dad had a friend take the pictures. He got so drunk that he dropped the camera and fell into the waterfall that Mom had in the living room. There were few pictures of the wedding and a very wet spot on the living room rug for a week to come. As you can see an event like this somehow just sticks in your mind, forever. You really don't need pictures to remember it. Heather looked so beautiful as she walked down the aisle. The ceremony was outside in the backyard. Holly was the flower girl, and Gene, of course, was my best man. Heather had a girl friend named Janis Tate as her maid of honor. (She had a nice set of knockers as well.) Heather's father gave her away. When it was all over and done, he handed my dad a five dollar bill and said that it was all he had but that he needed to contribute to his daughter's wedding. (Heather's mom never even offered to help with the wedding.) Dad said, "Thanks," smiled, and took it. The wedding went on through the night. My bride and I tried to get out by midnight but it was very hard. So many friends and so much fun! I remember it like it was yesterday.

Heather was nudging me to leave, and me, the proverbial party animal, not wanting to leave all the fun. It's not like I was going to get laid for the first time or something. What was the rush?

Now, the day before I was to get married, I decided to build a surf board rack for my new convertible. We were going to Santa Barbara for our honeymoon. I planned to do a little surfing while Heather got a little tan. My brother Mark said it would take days to build it so he would help. I said a couple of hours. Of course, I was right! Hell, it took a couple of hours just to get the parts and another eight hours to finish it. Mark was laughing all through the building process. The more he laughed, the more I got pissed off. By the time it was done, I couldn't stand up straight from bending over the trunk for so long.

So, after enough nudging, we got into the car, bags, wedding dress and surfboard on top of my brand new, self-made, surfboard rack and off we went. (Not unlike my dad twenty-five years before me) I am not sure what Heather was thinking at this time, maybe a new life for her and Holly, although it would be much different than the mundane existence she had lived for most of her life. Hopefully, it would be a better one. I, on the other hand, was wondering if I had made the right choice. A year ago I was a street brawler and a single college student and in two little words (you're what?), a husband and family man. What was I getting myself into? We made it to Santa Barbara in just a few hours and checked into our room. All seemed to be going just fine. We got in very late and got up the same way. It had to be noon ish. The hotel was decorated in a colonial motif. White pillars and very wide steps and close to the beach. We got up, had a very nice and leisurely breakfast in the hotel, and then got into the Chevy. The one with the brand new surfboard rack and headed to the beach. The sun was a lot hotter than it should have been for that time of the year. I was not really up on Santa Barbara's weather, so for all I knew, it was normal. Heather helped me get the nine foot five inch long, double Redwood stringer, fifty-five pound board off very carefully so not to damage my new precious rack. Within five minutes of hitting the beach, I was in the water. Heather, spread out a towel and proceeded to absorb the sun. Heather was as white as a ghost and extremely fair skinned. Not to mentioned soft and very smooth. I, because I surfed kind of regularly, was already tan. I must have been out in the water for two hours or more and finally came back in. I took one look at Heather and almost shit my pants. She had fallen asleep and was completely fried on her front. I mean fried! I woke her up and told her she needed to get out of the sun. I took her back to the hotel. She tried to take a shower, but it was too painful. She was done for a week. A lobster plus. That killed any sex. She couldn't even put on clothes. She was bedroom bound. Normally, I would have liked that, but not this time and this way. I spent the next three days surfing and Loving it. Seeing how the honeymoon part of Santa Barbara was over, I called up a buddy or two to surf with me but none could make it. The last day we were there, we checked out and went to have breakfast at a little restaurant nearby. It was kind of a funky little place (funky, for you younger people, means kind of neat), on the way home from the hotel. I parked and we went in. We sat down and ordered our food. Heather turned to me and said, "Don't look now, but at the next table, isn't that Peter, Paul and Mary?" I gave a quick glance, and I'll be damned. It was! What a nice way to end our honeymoon with a great topic to talk about when we get home. Once again, for you youngsters, Peter, Paul and Mary were a religious group that went all over, entertaining the troops of the Vietnam War with another person you probably don't know, Jane Fonda. For you people my age, smile!

It's time to head home to our new house. The one Dad and Mom got for us without mentioning it. You know the one that now adds big monthly payments to our already (not able to pay according to Dad) regular bills. Heather, for some reason that I never did understand, really didn't want to live there. (That was not the first time I didn't understand a woman.) Not because of the house but because of the close proximity to Mom and Dad. We moved in and started to un-wrap our gifts. The house was a four bedroom two bath house with a mortgage of somewhere in the area of thirty thousand dollars. We picked up Holly the next day after we got home from Mom and Dad's. The first night we wanted to break in the new house. Heather's sunburn was starting to get better so we could, you know what! We, of course, got the master bedroom, Holly had her choice, and we made one into a den and bar. The other was reserved for you know who.

The beginning of the week all was back to normal. Heather went back to work, and I went back to school and Von's. In the next couple of weeks or so, Heather and I decided to take a drive to Palm Springs and show Holly how the rich people live. It was probably mid-June or so. I put the top down, loaded the two beautiful chicks in, and off we went. It started to get very hot as we drove, Heather asked me to put the top up. I won't say that I have a stubborn streak, but, you probably will notice it as time goes on. I said, "No. That's why I bought a convertible so I can drive with the top down." It got hotter and hotter, and Heather said, "Holly was getting sick from the heat." Now, you have to remember that I am a novice at being a father with understanding and compassion in family affairs. So, I said, "No" again. Just about the time we hit Indio, another hell hole in my life, Holly puked all over the top of the chrome center divider that divides the driver seat from the passenger seat. I guess it could have been worse. I had just installed, right in front of the center divider, a brand new record player. In fact, it was an album player. Nobody had an album player, nobody. I would put on an album and listen for an hour before I had to change it. How kewl! Now back to the puked on divider. I don't know if you know what kind of a center divider my Chevy had, but it was long, from the front of the seat all the way to the back of the seat, maybe eighteen inches and had deep groves in it for design. I guess it was hotter than I thought because as the puke hit the chrome center divider you could hear it sizzling and got baked immediately. It smelled just great, also! The only thing that was more upsetting to me as the puke hit the divider and was being baked into it was the look I got from Heather. Guess I am starting to learn to be a father. Lesson number one was put the top up when in one hundred plus temperatures and with the kid. The lessons came in hordes, and I started to learn to be a dad. Holly was just two and soon to be three in October. I am not sure what she was thinking at that time. The good thing was that if she was giving me the same look that Heather was, it still had to be cute! However, I had that Chevy for three years after, and could never get the puke out from in between the grooves. Fortunately, the smell dissipated.

 The summer came and went. I finally graduated from a two-year school in three years. Dumb? I guess! Maybe I just had a lot on my plate. Between work, family, marriage and a bunch of other stuff, it just took its toll. But now I am an "A and E" mechanic. That is someone who can fix *airframes*, "A" and aircraft *engines*, "E". All I have to do is apply and get hired on somewhere and start making the big bucks. When I took the aptitude test in high school, they told me that everyone was hiring at that time. Aircraft was in real big demand. Well, I did not find it that way. Maybe if you were into spacecrafts and not the run of the mill airplanes. So Von's was my call to fame right then and there. Kind of a waste of three years of college, I guess. Later on, I figured it out that there was some merit to the three years, but it did take awhile. I thought of getting into the marketing end of things which was of great value later on and, of course, the fun class, business law. But business law meant you had to read stuff. So that was out.

Summer was almost over and the fair started. I couldn't wait. Thought I'd see some of my friends. But to my surprise, nada! No one that I knew was anywhere. Either they all got killed or put in jail or maybe found another place to play or maybe I just missed the proper night. I guess it was all for the good, as Heather really didn't know about the gang, OOPS, I mean the club stuff. There was no way that I was going to introduce Heather or Holly to my old friends. The fair was the fair. Holly Loved the petting zoo, and Heather Loved the garden stuff. I could hardly stay out of the fun zone. Not sure what the real attraction was, but I really Loved it there.

Not long after our marriage, Heather had asked me if I wanted her to convert to Judaism. I said it wasn't necessary but if she really wanted to, it was fine with me. The Jewish religion is a little different than most in that they really don't want any converts. She decided to do it anyway. After a series of meeting with the rabbi, she was on her way to becoming a lot better Jew than I ever was, and it was all her decision. I really wanted her to do it, but I never said it to her because I didn't want it to be my choice. It had to be hers and only hers to really want to become a Jew.

In the Jewish religion, after you have fulfilled all the requirements, you become reborn, so to speak. You are taken into a large special pool and completely dunked a few times, totally naked to purify you spiritually. When you come out of the last dunking, you are a newborn Jew. This is called a mikva. She will have a new name. She will not be married anymore and have no past life and whatever else goes on in those rituals. When Heather was finally ready to be Rachael Gerson, the Jew and not Heather anymore, it was late December, December sixteenth to be exact. The new wedding was set for three or four hours after the mikva. It would be terrible if she had the kid before we were married. Then the last seven and a half months would have been for naught. Heather was about nine months pregnant to me and only seven and a half to everyone else. (Yea, right)! So when the rebbitzen, the rabbi's wife, tried to dunk her three or four times that is required, Heather was so buoyant that the rebbitzen couldn't do it alone. She had to call for help.

When all was said and done, Heather now emerged as Rachel to all Jews but chose to remain Heather to all others which was fine with me. Heather dressed and went outside the mikva room where I was waiting for her. I started to give her a big kiss. Well, I tried to anyway. The rabbi stopped me and said that we were not married anymore so no kissing. When we go home to get ready for the wedding, we don't do anything. I got his drift! We went home. Heather took a shower and dressed as did I. Not together of course! She promised the rabbi. We made it to our second wedding in the afternoon, Sunday. There were some people there at the shul (another word for synagogue) as there was Sunday school, and some of the regular congregation was there for their children. Many there, if not all, with the exception of our Jewish friends who were invited, did not know us. This is really a legal wedding and has to be done and is given a wedding certificate.

Heather started to walk down the isle to be married by the rabbi and, of course, the traditional breaking of the glass after. (A Jewish tradition for luck) Picture this, remembering that the majority of people do not know us. Heather started walking down the isle with this huge stomach (and she was big), and her dress was continually flying out from the baby kicking like he wants out NOW. I am sure that there will be many people who are members of that synagogue but didn't know us months earlier that will never make friends with us. Even my own friends told me it looked very funny. Finally, the wedding was over and we all went home.

Well, about the thirtieth I found myself racing to the hospital in Fontana California. Kaiser, I believe. I had insurance from Von's Grocery Company and it covered everything. In fact, from the time Heather started going to the doctor to the time we left the hospital with our heavenly package (if we only knew), my whole total cash outlay was five dollars and ninety-five cents. That was because we bought a six pack of formula as we left the hospital. Try and find that kind of insurance today. Finally, Heather went into labor. Like I knew what that was. Heather had told me that the first time with Holly she was in labor for thirty-six hours. Well, this time she cut off thirty-three percent. It was only twenty-four hours. Not really knowing what was happening and not too crazy about hanging around the hospital anymore after fifteen hours or so, me and the guy (the girl's husband from the next bed over) left and went to celebrate at a bar. We told the girls that we'd be right back and hit it. I really didn't understand why the girls were so upset. Hell, we were back in three hours, plastered but in time for the happy occasions. Both gave birth within the same hour. Never a problem! I am sure Heather forgot about it soon after birth. (Yea, right!) After a day or so we took the little guy, twenty-two and a half inches, ten-plus pounder home. We let him drive! Now this guy had the brightest red hair I have ever seen in my life. Heather had auburn hair but nowhere in hell like this kid. I am trying to figure out if I went through all this marriage shit for naught. It must be the milkman's kid. Oh wait, we didn't have a milkman. When we got home, he gave me back the car keys, flipped me off and went to bed. That's when I knew we were in for a lot of trouble.

Now, I don't know if I have mentioned it, but I have always been a party animal. New Year's Eve was the night we got home with the new arrival. It was like he intended to be born on the thirtieth just so he could screw up the New Year's Eve party Heather and I were suppose to go to. I fixed his little ass. We got home, got dressed and took the little shit with us. He was the hit of the party. Heather was beat by kissing time so we had to leave early. Twelve-oh-five! I never got over being pissed at her for wanting to leave early. After all, it was New Years!

Now, it is January first nineteen hundred and sixty-four. I will soon be twenty-two.

This year was not a huge eventful year, but we did work on the house a little bit and got a swing set for Holly and David. David, for King David, was the name we came up with. David Brandon Gerson. Jews, as I have said before, are supposed to name our children after someone who died in the family. His Jewish name is Benjamin Duvid. Benjamin, for Betsy, my mom's mother. I fought hard to name him Barjud, the street we lived on, but Heather just wouldn't go for it. Women!

Later in the summer, while I was working for Von's, they sent me a bunch of pillows to make a huge display and I had to mark them down to try to get rid of them. The way Von's worked was, as each store started to sell out of a particular item, they would send the remaining meager inventory to other stores so those stores would have more inventory of that item. When those stores sold out most what they had, they would send their meager inventory to another store and keep doing it until the item was all sold out from all stores. When I got these pillows, I noticed that they were The Beatles pillows. They were about ten inches square with a blue border and a white face with a picture of the Beatles on it. I think it read, "It's a hard day's night" on it. Von's had been selling them for about three months and inventory was getting very low. They are starting to be passed around from store to store to "dump" them. Now I have them. I received about a hundred to a hundred and fifty of them. They originally sold for nineteen ninety-five each and were now marked down already to nine ninety-five. I have the last of them and will probably reduce them to six ninety-five or something like that.

I had noticed that the Beatles were giving a concert at the Hollywood Bowl in a week or so, sometime in August, I believe. Hmmmm, the ol' marketing from college and a little Jewish thinking started to kick in. If I could get that day off, I could buy the pillows myself and go out there and probably double my money selling them on the street. I checked the performance date and asked for the day off. Granted! Now, all I have to do is get them at the right price and it's like money in the bank. It just so happened, that Chuck, my direct boss, was off that day too. In fact, he took off two days which made this markdown stuff a piece of cake. I did have the authority to markdown items but if Chuck was here, I would have probably had to ask him. He's gone and I am acting manager. Kuel! Kewl! Cool! (You pick!) The day of the concert came. I had marked them down to ninety-nine cents each and bought them all. There were one hundred and twenty-seven of them to be exact. If Chuck had asked me why I marked them down so low, I was going to tell him that someone said they would buy them all if they could have them at a buck each. Chuck didn't like to have the marked down stuff in his store anyway and probably would have patted me on the back just because they were gone.

I got to the Hollywood Bowl at five or so and parked my car in a lot across the street near the entrance. I grabbed as many as I could in my arms and started to cross the street. Before I got thirty feet from my car I was asked how much for two of them. I said they were twenty-five each but if you take two of them, I'll let you have them for forty bucks. Sold! Hell, I got one third my money back and didn't cross the street yet. I went back and got a couple more and made it to the other side of the street. I sold the eight I had in ten minutes and went back for more. In about two hours I only had seven left. A cop stopped me and asked me if I had a permit to sell them. I said, "No, I didn't know I needed one." The cop told me to pack it up and hit it before he sighted me. I said, "Yes, sir, officer," and went to my car, got in and drove away. I drove past the entrance and then around the back yelling only two Beatle pillows left, only two. By the time I left the back side, I was on empty and I don't mean gas. Not one pillow left, not one! I cleared about twenty-five hundred on an investment of one hundred and twenty seven dollars and realized there was another world out there. Needless to say, the next night the bride, the kids, and I celebrated and had a great dinner at Mac's. The bank saw the rest.

Heather, now that she is a Jew, started going to the synagogue kind of regularly. Heather got friendly with a lady named Pam. Heather didn't need to work anymore as the two kids were a full-time job. I was doing just fine financially, especially with the extra money on the side every once in a while. Pam's husband was named Mike. The four of us got very friendly throughout the year. Mike worked for his dad in the electrical supply business in Los Angeles. Pam and Heather stayed home with their kids. One day Mike went to work and his dad, Sam, (aka Carload Sam) said to Mike, "See if you can find me a hunk of electronic cable with these dimensions in a junk yard." Sam sold electrical conduit and was so good at it that he got that name, "Carload Sam," because when every one was selling a roll at a time, he was selling, you guessed it, a carload at a time. A carload was a rail car, like on a train. Obviously very successful! Mike called around and found that piece of cable in a local junk yard for about fifty dollars. Mike told his dad that he found it. Carload Sam called his customer and asked how much he was willing to spend for it as Sam knew nothing about cable, only the conduit that it ran though. Sam was not going to charge his customer much as he was really doing it as a favor. This customer bought a ton of conduit regularly, and Sam was just trying to help him out. He told Sam not a penny over seven thousand dollars. Sam shit his pants. Mike and Sam talked for about an hour to make sure it was what the customer wanted. Sam finally said to Mike, "Go buy it and if it isn't the right stuff, we will just throw it away." Mike went and bought it. It was really heavy, and he had to have help getting it into his dad's pick up truck. Mike took it over to the customer and low and behold, it was the right stuff. Bought for fifty dollars and sold for seven thousand. To quote Sam, "That's what I call a business." "I need to be in the electronic and not the electrical business," he said, talking to himself.

To make a long story very much longer (and I will), Sam had Mike, father and son, open a division of the electrical business and called it "Telco." The cable that they sold had been a form of underwater telephone cable for a submarine that was in dry dock for repairs. "Telco" (Telephone Company) it was. This all came down somewhere around November of sixty-four. Mike was put in charge of starting Telco and getting it going. Mike was a year younger than I was and he was prematurely bald. He had just about as much hair then as I have now on the sides and trust me, it's not black! Mike mentioned to his wife Pam that he was looking for an outside sales person. Pam mentioned it to Heather, and she said something to me about it. Now, I am not sure if I had mentioned it before, but just about from here on out, and through the rest of my life, I very seldom picked anything for myself. It somehow finds me and picks me, no matter what it is, even starting with my wife. I never saw her, but she was pointed out to me and introduced to me without me asking about her or ever even seeing her. That was then and this is now.

Heather asked me to talk to Mike. Maybe there would be something good to come out of it. After all, we were all friends, and maybe I could get a break with Mike. I really didn't think that I was going to be in the grocery business forever. We invited them over for dinner one evening. Heather made a beautiful meal and, as usual, the table was fit for a king. We talked and talked and the bottom line was that he wanted me to work for him for two-fifty or three bucks an hour, or something like that. It's been a while. Drive in to Los Angles forty miles one way at the height of traffic both ways and sell electronic wire and cable. No insurance for the family and no assurance that I will even have a job in one month or two. He did tell me that if it went well and we were still in business in five years, he would give me five percent ownership in the company. So let's recount all the pros and cons. I am making four dollars per hour now with Von's. That's a buck more than Mike wants to pay me. I have insurance for the whole family through Von's, and they pay the premium. Mike has no insurance for me and my family and no plans to get any. Von's is only a fifteen minute drive from home. Mikes job will be forty miles one way through the most congested highway in the world to Los Angles. Von's, as I already have experienced, has opportunities for advancement. Mike will give me five percent ownership in five years "IF" we are still in business. "IF" we are still in business, we could be just hanging on by a thread and who would want the five percent? It's pretty easy to see where this is going! So, I gave Von's a three week notice and started for Mike in January of sixty-five. Sick? You can answer that one.

Chapter Sixteen

So, a brand new life begins. I thought this getting older was for the better. How quickly we learn.

Although I am working for Mike, we are working out of his dad's office. Now, this is one "old school Jew." Mikes dad! We not only had to have our hair cut every three weeks, but our nails had to be manicured along with our shoes shined. Christ, no one said anything about that. To me, it was kind of girly. As time went on, that may have been the only thing that Heather liked about the new job. Sam, Mike's dad, insisted that I start from the office every day. (So he could keep track of me, I guess.) After all, he was paying the bills. I thought it would have been better and more productive to just start hitting the accounts right from home, but for the first two years, I had to go into Los Angeles each and every day. One thing I didn't account for was the time to and from there, on the freeway. Although it was only forty miles each way, it was well over an hour in time, and things got worse as time went on.

It got to be ritual, Mike and I driving in to L.A. together and home again at the end of the day. We only lived about two miles from each other so it was no problem. This way, we could discuss business while driving. I don't know what was more taxing, the drive to and from or the manicure every three weeks. What the hell is going on here? A couple of years ago I was a criminal, and now I'm a pussy getting my nails and hair done. Oh, yea, let's not forget the shoe shine! One thing that was good was that whenever I was around for lunch, Sam would buy it for Mike and me. That was the good part. The bad part was that Sam would eat with us. By itself, that doesn't sound unusual. But here's the problem. After two weeks of eating with him, I could have ordered his food. It was always the same old shit day in and day out. Again, by itself, that doesn't sound that bad. Who cares if he eats the same thing each and every day? No skin off my nose. However, he was always on a diet and he also had gout. I am no doctor and really don't know if cottage cheese is one of the prescribed medications for either, but he never went a day without it. Again, that doesn't seem that bad all by itself. I don't know what gout is. I don't know if you have it in your hands, lips, mouth or wherever else you might get it, but when he ate the cottage cheese, it would shoot out all over the place. It would shoot on the table, on the floor, on the waitress if she happened to be walking by and, most importantly, on me. Every fuckin day I was sprayed with cottage cheese. Every day! Some days it was so bad I thought it was snowing in June. And then, of course, Mike and I couldn't even look at each other or we would break out laughing so hard that we would start shooting shit out of our own mouths ourselves. I don't know if Sam ever knew what was going on, but this went on for years. Years! Sometimes, when we would walk into any of the restaurants we frequented, the waitress would look at us and start breaking up before we even got to our table. No matter to which restaurant we went, in the garment district, they all knew Carload Sam and, unfortunately, us. I even remember one time, Mike and I met Sam at a restaurant for lunch. We had come from the barber shop and shoe shine guy. When I left, in less then an hour, I looked down at my newly shined shoes. They were loaded with cottage cheese. How the hell that happened I have no idea, but they were. I was just waiting for Sam to notice them and start bitchen at me for not having my shoes shined.

Mike worked the inside sales and I the outside. I would get to work, drop off Mike, and hit the road. I would try to get back about five at night and get on the road home so I could have dinner about six-thirty. The drive was a minimum of one hour and ten minutes. That was in the first year of work. As time went on, the drive got longer and longer both ways. After the first year I can actually remember sitting in one spot for ten minutes at a time. In later years it was at least one hour and thirty minutes each way. I actually can remember kind of falling asleep, like a twilight thing in a daze, while driving and awakening twenty minutes later ten miles further down the road and have no recollection of how I got there. I never hit anyone, never had to slam on the brakes, nothing. I was just there. That happened often, at least once each week. That was the deal in the morning going in to work. The return trip was a little different. No matter what time I would get back to the office and pick up Mike, if it was before six-thirty and then left, it would take at least an hour and forty-five minutes to get home. That would be eight-fifteen. If we left at seven-thirty, an hour later, we would get home at eight-twenty, five minutes later and save all that driving aggravation, stress, as well as gas.

Mike and I started to hit a bar or two before we headed home to kill a little time. There were many bars in the down town area as well as restaurants. The office was a half a block from Pico and San Pedro in downtown Los Angeles. (Aka, L. A.) Neither Mike nor I were big drinkers at that time, but it was something to do. While we were in the bars, we tried to sell tickets to see Sam eat the next day, but there were no takers. Our wives were not real crazy about it either. They couldn't eat until eight-thirty or so, and both Mike and I just about all the time missed eating with the kids.

I was learning that to get a head in this world, you had to sacrifice something. Just wish it were the bills and not missing dinner with the kids. In fact, sometimes Mike and I would just eat out and kill time that way. One time, when we decided to eat in L.A., Mike called Pam and told her that we were going to stay in L.A. and eat. She would, in turn, call Heather and let her know. Nothing unusual as this happened at least three times every couple of weeks. In fact, the girls liked it sometimes as they did not have to cook. They would meet with the kids at a Mac Donald's and have a little girl time together.

There was one time that was a little different. As Mike hung up from the call, he noticed a phone number on the wall in the phone booth. (A phone booth for you youngsters is what superman changed his clothes in when Lois Lane was to busy to do the wash.) It read, just like you see in the movies, "Call me for a good time." Mike looked at me and pointed, and I looked over and read it. We looked at each other and said, "Probably a hooker." We both agreed and headed to the restaurant for a meal, joking and laughing as we talked about the phone number. We got to the restaurant and there was a forty-five minute wait. Not good! Jokingly, I said, "Let's call the number and see if she will feed us instead of fucking us." We started to laugh again. But this time Mike started to walk towards the phone booth. At first I thought he was looking for superman. Not so. He was looking for the number. I said, "Are you nuts?" He said, "If she (and we are assuming it was a she and never gave a thought to anything else) would leave her number on a phone booth wall, she probably can use some money for feeding us."

He made the call. It went a little like this. "Hi, I am Mike and saw your number in a phone booth. Are you the one to whom it is referring?" She (and it was a she on the other end of the phone call) said, "Yes, what do you want?" Mike said, "My friend and I are hungry and just want to eat. Will you feed us?" Now, this chick has to think we are loonies and will probably have the cops there when we get there, but she says, "Come on over, I have food." Go figure! She gives us directions to her place, somewhere in Malibu Hills. Mikes dad, Cottage Cheese Sam, lives not real far from there so Mike is kind of familiar with the area. Me, I would have been lost in a hot New York minute. We get there in twenty minutes, and she greeted us at the door. Mike and I had made plans that if things did not seem to be what they were supposed to be, we would be out of there at Olympic track speed. However, she seemed very pleasant and about thirty-five or so. Pretty! She invited us in to sit and offered us some coffee. Our conversation went something like this. "What do you boys really want? I don't believe the food story for a minute." "You don't," I said. "Then why did you invite us over?" I asked. Mike was starving and said, "Right now, I don't care at this time what you are selling. Do you have any kind of food? We will be glad to pay you for it." She said, "You are telling the truth, aren't you?" Mike said, "Yes, I am hungry." Now, if Barney or Bill had been here, they could have turned over in their graves the way this was going down. "Mike," I said, "I think she is selling something else and not food." "No matter," she said, "I will bring you some food." Just a couple of minutes later, she came out with a few sandwiches and chips. She offered us tea but neither one of us was into tea. We got done eating. Now we can talk turkey. "So," I asked, "What are you really selling?" She said, "A toe job." I have been around the block once or twice as you have already read, and I know she has ten to fifteen years on us, but I have never heard of a toe job. I said, "Have you mispronounced anything?" She laughed and said, "No, your hearing is just fine." Mike chimes in and asked, "What the hell is a toe job?" She said that she takes off our shoes, washes our feet, and then sucks our toes for about twenty minutes. The whole thing takes about a half hour. "Want to try it?" Mike looks at me, and I look back at him and both of us shake our heads. Not sure who asked, but one of us said, "How much?" She said, "Forty dollars and I won't charge you for the food." I said, "First of all, I don't have forty bucks on me and if I did, I don't think I would pay forty dollars for a TOE JOB!" Mike said, "Why not? It sounds like fun." "Not for me, my friend, not for me." In fact, even until today, I feel funny about someone touching my feet that really don't belong there. Mike said to her, "How about two for fifty?" (How Jewish of him.) I looked at him. She looked at him. I shook my head in disgust, and she shook her head. "Yes." Mike looked at me and said, "You first. I'll buy." I said, "No way, Jose. I want to see you come out with all ten still wiggling, attached and able to walk." Mike looked at her and said, "I'm game. Let's go." I went into the kitchen, and scarfed around for a little more food, and tried to listen for blood curdling screams so I could rush in and save the day. But nada, nothing. All was quite on the home front. Not a peep. A half hour went by. I saw the bedroom door open, and Mike was walking out very slowly. Very slowly! In fact, he was only walking on his heels, one heel in front of the other heel and then again. I said, "Are you all right? "Are you OK?" He said, "I will never see toes in the same light as before. Never!" I asked him, "Why are you walking like that? Do they hurt?" He said, "Hurt? Are you nuts? I don't want to loose the feeling that I have by touching them on the ground." "Are you serious?" I asked. He said, "Just wait until you come out and see what you are walking on, your heels or your toes." "OK, let's go for it." Well, about a half an hour went by, I came out walking on my heels with a huge smile from ear to ear. I looked at Mike, and gave him a thumbs up, and made my way to the couch, slowly, very slowly. I said, "Pay the lady and let's get out of here." "Do you have an escalator" Mike said? We chatted for a minute or so and left. It was now ten-thirty. We still have an hour to go before we would be home. "Ok, let's get on the road. We can call and say we are stuck in traffic. There was an accident and have been stuck here for two hours." That sounds great except cell phones have not been invented yet, dummy! Shit! Now what do we do? "We could wreck the car and say we are just getting out of the hospital." "Yea right!" "How do we explain the car with no damage?" "I can fix that." "Don't you dare!" That's about the way the conversation went for twenty minutes as we were driving home. "We can't tell the truth, right?" "No shit, Sherlock! I don't think so." "Well?" "Ok, here is the only way to get out of this with very little pain. Let's get drunk." "Oh great, that's a real help." "Yea, we will forget about it, but what about the wives, dummy?" "No, listen. Let's go into one of the local bars, nail about three fast ones, and then call Pam." "No, you mean Heather." "No Pam." "Ok, we'll flip for it." "We will have her or they pick us up and just plead stupidity for not calling." Afterwards, it was too late. We were plastered and didn't think about it. "Deal! Let's get to the bar fast." So it is written and so it will be done! Even in a bar, drunk on our butts, the boss is the boss. I made the call. "Heather, can you come and pick us up and call Pam to let her know Mike is ok and on his way home? I'm sorry, honey!" "I'll honey you!!!" So, as usual, one thing led to another. Mike could not get up in the morning. Not sure if Pam beat him or if he was hung over. I drove to work alone and late myself! I stayed in the office and worked the inside making calls and such. Lunch time came. I thought I would beat Sam to the lunch thing. Hey, Sam, how about if I treat you to Ptomaine Tommy's for lunch? Ptomaine Tommy was a street vender who probably made about a million dollars selling hamburgers out of a push cart with a grill in it in the middle of the garment district in downtown L.A. There was always a twenty-person deep line from eleven o'clock to two-thirty. There was a reason for it. You couldn't beat the flavor or the price. Sam's retort was, "They don't have cottage cheese," but thanks for the thought. Actually, Sam would never talk like that. He was crude and really didn't care about whose toes he stepped on as long as things went his way. I told him I was in the mood for a burger. This time I escaped the white chunk shower. This was about the middle of the year of nineteen sixty-six.

One day Heather and I decided to go over and see her dad. It had been a while. He had moved out of the house on Sixth Street where Heather grew up with her mom, Dad and little (six foot-six but five years younger) brother, Richard. I guess Vena, Heather's mom, had enough with him. So Joe, Heather's dad, had moved to a small apartment and had been living alone for about six or seven months. He was a butcher for a local market and had been there for years. He may have had a drinking problem but he was a damn good meat cutter. And to be honest with you, I liked him. He was always good to me. We walked up the steps and knocked on the door. Again and again! No answer! I knocked on the neighbor's door and asked if they had seen Joe? They said they hadn't seen him for three or four days. We kind of got a little worried. I went down to the landlord's door, knocked and asked if he would let me in to see if Joe was there and was ok as he wasn't answering the door. The landlord said, "No problem," and the three of us proceeded up the stairs. The landlord opened the door. It didn't take a rocket scientist to figure out what the problem was as the smell almost knocked us all over. Joe was dead in his favorite chair in front of the T.V. which was still on. We called the police. They came over and then called the coroner. The police made a short report and told us where Joe would be and how to get in touch with the coroner. We immediately went over to Heather's mom and relayed the news. She could have cared less. We called all the relatives and they, for the most part, seemed to feel the same way. I took it upon myself to make and to pay for the arrangements and the burial. Four days later Joe was put into the ground and all who attended went back to Heathers mom's place for a small wake. The attendees were mostly the few drinkers in the family. All in all, there were about ten or so. I hardly new poor Joe! He wasn't around much when I was. It was kind of like the song from the play "Oklahoma." "Poor Jud is dead." So after Joe's death, not that there was a lot of interaction with his side of the family before, but now it was basically non-existent. I am not really sure how I dealt with my first death and burial, but I figured I was being groomed for something really big to come later, in my youthful age. I already knew how to stab people. Now I knew what to do with the body.

The rest of the year really had no major events, neither good nor not so good. I turned twenty-five but chose not to go to Las Vegas and to make a killing with my crap system. In a month Heather turned twenty-four and that was no tzores either.

I had a friend but can't remember his name off hand (this is happening too often) who had a partially constructed boat. It was a completed wooden frame with some of the plywood already on one side. He decided not to finish it and asked me if I wanted it. He already had all the materials. All I had to do was put it together, fiberglass it, paint it (this could be a problem), and then I could do the fishing thing. Let me regress a bit. If memory serves me right, somewhere earlier in this monstrosity I am writing, I had mentioned that Jewish men have only one major tool. The telephone! (Wait, there is one other tool but it doesn't work that well anyway.) That way they can call for any kind of help when something is broke or needed to be built. That Jewish tradition was handed down to me on a silver platter. My Jewish tool box consisted of a flat (butter) knife for undoing screws, a roll of tape for the wife's mouth when she starts screaming, "Can't you fix anything?" and a tube of glue. I don't know what the glue was for, but Dad had one in his tool box. Possibly to glue back together what he may have broken as he was fixen. So with all of this construction background, I said, "Sure, sounds like a plan."

In a week or two I walked outside the house and low and behold, blocking my car from driving out of the driveway was a boat frame, wood crap, side boards, a top, nails, glue, (hmmm) fiberglass, epoxy, cans of paint strung all over, and a very pissed-off wife. I failed to mention anything about the boat and its parts to her. David, my oldest son, and only son at that time couldn't wait to jump in the mess and throw shit all over. My daughter Holly, pushing six and dressed in the same attire as Heather, (matching pant outfits of red and white) just stood there and shook her head as well. You know, you just can't make everybody happy all of the time. David and I started to move the wood onto the grass as I started to explain to Heather why all this wood and part of a boat was here. Not easy! It was mid-summer. I was doing so good at work that I could afford to take a day or two off and work on the boat, and of course, weekends. The family was really crazy about that. My friend did leave me some instructions and with the help of some friendly gentile neighbors, I finished it. I actually found out what the glue in my Jewish tool box was for. It was to help keep the bandages on my new cuts. Frame, sideboards and top, nails, glue, fiberglass, epoxy and paint, it was finally done. I bought a thirty-five horse power Evenrude engine, hooked up the steering wheel to the rudders, added a couple of seats inside and with thumbs on my chest, it was finally done! However, after all was said and done, I realized I didn't like to fish! Great, just great! I guess we could use it for a ski boat. I am not sure how many of you bought this book or just found it under your Christmas tree because it was a cheap gift, know anything about boats, but this finished monstrosity (painted red and white by the way) was eighteen feet, eight inches long, eight feet four inches wide, and sat in the water fully loaded, about three inches. It won't tilt! Heather was happy about that. There was less chance of drowning that way. But what she didn't know was that it might sink the first time we put it in the water and got in it. I didn't tell her, either!

It is time to give it the big test. Where and when? I really didn't want to tow it with my sixty-three Chevy Impala convertible. I wasn't sure I wanted to be the one who tried it for the first time. Sinky, sinky! As it turned out, Dad just bought a Lincoln, sixty-eight, I think. "Hey Dad, how about I take the Lincoln for a long ride and check it out for you so if there is anything wrong you can nip it in the bud and take it back to the dealer so he can fix it?" After all, I did have all that auto shop experience. Dad said, "Where would you take it?" I answered, "I think Lake Tahoe would be good. That way I can see if it over-heats and or lugs down going up and down the little hills they have." (Little hills, Yea right!) I also did not mention that I was going to tow a boat. He said, "Sounds good. When do you want it?" I told him I would get back to him. Heather and I agreed upon a weekend and we were off. We could have left earlier, but Heather had to buy stupid stuff, just like a woman. Life preservers for the kids, an ice chest so the food won't rot, the food, and you know things like that.

We drove to Tahoe. I need not tell you how beautiful it is there. We found a launch ramp and backed the boat down. I stopped just short of the water. We transferred all the food, ice chest, the kids, about six tons of towels, sun block, lip gloss, and water bottles from the car to the boat. "Got everyone and everything in?" I yelled. "Affirmative," Heather screamed back. I carefully backed the boat into the water and told Heather to hang on to it as I parked the car. The kids were inside the boat, and Heather was outside the boat hanging on so it wouldn't float away. It took me about two minutes or so. When I got back I screamed, "OH SHIT, you're sinking." Heather didn't even notice it. (Sometime later she dyed her hair blonde!) Then she started to yell, "Get the kids. You need to save them! Forget about me. Get the kids." I was not exactly sure what was wrong with the boat and why it was sinking, but I did know it was in about two feet of water or less. I don't think anyone was going to drown at this point. I looked into the boat as I thought maybe I didn't seal something with my tape and glue. As I peered into the back of the boat, I saw that the drain plugs were not in. As a matter of fact, for the next four years or so that I had the boat, I did that more often then not. I told Heather to hang on to the boat and that the kids were not going to drown. If they did, I would buy her a dog. I went and got the car, pulled the boat out, let it drain fully, put in the plugs, and put the boat in the water for the second time, parked the car, got in the boat and floated out, away from the ramp. You could lean over the side and paddle with the oars that I had bought. So David, of course, decided to row while we were drifting. He rowed on the left and then pulled the oar out to go to the other side to row and when he did, he wacked Holly right in the face with the oar. She started to bleed. But never fear, amongst all the stuff that Heather had bought, there was a first aid kit. Gee, what a surprise. So, after another delay of about a half hour, I tried to start the used Evenrude engine I bought so we could get on our way. Guess what? Ah ha, I fooled you. You thought I was going to say it did not start, didn't you? It started just fine, and we were on our way. Lake Tahoe is approximately eleven miles wide and twenty-two miles long and about a thousand feet deep in its lowest abyss. We drove all over and many times we would stop and look down to see things creeping and swimming fifty to a hundred feet down. That's how clear the lake is. The kids Loved it. I was fascinated as well. Heather couldn't understand why we could see so far down and couldn't at home in the streams we had been in. (The blonde dye job has to be coming sooner than I thought.) We floated and drove for a few hours. The way the boat was made, it had about seven feet of shade from the steering wheel to the front, under the top of the boat. The kids could lay under that part and keep out of the sun. About three hours into the boat fun, the motor stopped. Just quit! I flipped the top of the casing on the motor up and checked it for fuel leaks and anything else I could see that may have gone wrong. I saw nothing. I leaned over the side of the boat to check the prop. Alas, the problem found. This was to my amazement. There was seaweed all wrapped up in the blade. Seaweed in Lake Tahoe! Who'd a thunk! Lake Tahoe at that time was ninety-nine point nine percent pure. (It is just ninety-nine point five percent today.) It was just my luck to find out what the point one percent was. So, I spent the next half hour untangling the seaweed. It was really wrapped up in the blade, tight. Tons of it! Finally, problem solved. After all that, it was time to get out of the boat and put on the feeding bag. We had a very nice time the rest of the weekend, got home, reported to Dad that he bought a great car, thanked him, and went home.

As I have said before, I was always asked to do things by my little brother who is not so little anymore. In fact, he is eighteen and just graduated high school where he also lettered in gymnastics. A comparison of the two of us, gymnastically speaking would be, I was more fluid looking but he was better at it. I had been known as "The Great Back Flip," and he was called "The Monkey." Anyway, one time he asked me to take him, his main squeeze, and some friends to Mexico camping. Well, you know how I feel about Mexico and Mexicans in general, but I really liked all of his buddies so I said OK. We actually took four cars, but Mark always kind of looked up to me for some leadership in these kinds of situations. I took the lead driving, and we made it to Rosaria Beach with which I was familiar. This particular camping trip would not be in this book except for one of Mark's best friends, then and still is today, Rudy Lopez. Lopez, heh! This guy just keeps popping up. (My life is constantly surrounded my Mexicans.) We set up camp and started to build a fire to cook dinner. There were maybe fifteen of us. Mark was dating Myra at that time and actually did wind up marring her. Myra was born in Scotland. (Maybe the only thing that Mark and I had in common, then and now, was that Heather my wife, was born in another country also.) Rudy Lopez was dating a chick named Sandy and eventually married her. This whole trip and story is about Sandy, Rudy's first blonde wife. Once again, you need to try to visualize the situation. Here we are in the middle of nowhere, one hundred degree's at five o'clock in the evening, and nothing but sand all around us. The guys are getting the fire started to cook hot dogs and hamburgers, and some corn on the cob. The rest of the chicks with us are pouring beers and making drinks for the guys who are now in a hundred and twenty degrees because of the heat from the fire rings where they are cooking. Sandy comes out from Rudy's car with what looks like a hat box. She asked in a bold voice, "Where is the electric plug?" Most of us who heard her said, "What?" She reiterated, "The electric socket so I can plug in my hair dryer." Hair dryer! Who the hell brings a hair dryer to the desert and what do you need a hair dryer for? She opened up the hat box she was holding and pulled out a huge blonde wig that was made up as to go to a formal wedding or something like that. "Are you nuts?" was yelled by someone. She said, "I want to look good for dinner, and I need to change the style a bit. It looked a little crushed. Rudy always likes me to look good for him." "Yea but this is the Mexican desert. "I am sure he will make an exception this time," was blurted out by someone. It was not me. I couldn't talk, I was laughing too hard. In fact, mostly every one of us was laughing. Sandy started to cry so Rudy took her back to the car and talked to her. All seemed fine in a few minutes or so. After we all stopped laughing, we went back to doing what we had been doing except the conversations had changed a little. All of a sudden, guess who was standing amongst us with another huge box? Yep, Sandy! (OH, by the way, Sandy is a blonde and she had a blonde wig. I guess that was because she was a blonde.) Knowing she was crying a bit ago, one of the guys said in a very gentle tone, probably Rudy, "What do we have this time?" Sandy said, "It's not another wig so don't worry, but I do need a large mirror. The one in Rudy's car is too small." I can't tell you how hard it was to keep from laughing even though she looked so sad and helpless. You could see everyone had this explosive look on their faces. Someone said, "What do you need a big mirror for?" She said, "You laughed at me because of the wig I brought so I won't wear it, but I still need to do my face." She opened up the new box. In it was about ten thousand dollars worth of make up. Christ, this chick is nuts! We all came unglued. We all started to laugh big time. Even the girls who tried to be sympathetic and consoling the first time with the wig deal came unglued. Sandy just looked at us like we just didn't understand. She said, "I told you I need to look good for Rudy, so why are you laughing?" The more she talked, the more we laughed. She finally went back to Rudy's car (I guess to cry or to plan an all-out attack at night to kill us all), and we never saw her again until it was time to eat. Now, you would think that it all would have ended with the two embarrassments. But this Sandy was cut from a different mold. The chicks started to hand out the paper plates and put beans, corn on the cob, hot dogs and hamburgers on them, cups of beer or soft drinks, and straighten out a blanket or some towels to sit on as we ate. A couple of the guys brought folding chairs, but most of us sat in the sand. Just about everyone was sitting and chowing down as Sandy exited from Rudy's car. All mouths opened wide. I actually saw food falling out of some of them. Sandy had on a long flowing gown, white, from ankle to neck. I thought I had seen Scarlet O' Hara from "Gone with the Wind." Nobody said anything at first. I think they didn't know what to say. No one laughed. I don't know if that shock was too much for them. She sashayed over and asked where the table was. That was it, the straw that broke the camels back. All I heard was yelling, screaming, farting and big-time laughing. It went on for ten minutes. Every time someone would look at her, they would start laughing again and again. Sandy never said anything. Rudy motioned to her to sit next to him and she did. She pulled her beautiful gown about half way to her stomach so she could bend her legs to sit down. She sat and began to eat. The laughter did not stop all night. It was sporadic but every time some one would look at the dress and the abundance of make up, it was hard not to envision her with the wig on as well. Like I said, they actually got married but it didn't last. Rudy was a hard worker, but I don't think he made enough for her to spend. I don't know if they ever had kids, but if I had to guess, probably not. It would have messed up her hair!

All of the time that Heather and I were married and before, Heather's ex-husband would come over every other weekend, pick up Holly, and take her for the day. When we were not married it was tolerable and understandable. Now, it was confusing for Holly as well as maddening and unsettling for Heather and me. We had devised a plan to obtain her adoption. We had already asked her ex every day that he picked up Holly to give her up. The answer was always an emphatic no! He had to pay Heather child support and we knew that he was having a hard time making the payments to her. Sometimes he would miss one. We would bring it up, and he eventually would get caught up. Heather and I decided to not say anything when he missed a payment. The more lenient we got, the more he missed the payments. We would ask him for a payment but not real vigorously. The payments started to come only once a month and sometimes nothing for two or three. By the end of a year or so, he owed a bunch. We called an attorney and had him ask for all the arrears to be paid in full or we would have to put him in jail for failing to pay Heather the child support she was entitled. The shit hit the fan. Big time! He could not come up with the money due so it was go to jail or sign the adoption papers. Now, Holly was mine forever. Ours forever! I never stopped Loving nor thinking of Holly in any other way but as if she was my natural born child. In fact, from time to time, I would (not thinking) answer someone's question about her with, "She gets it from me or my father or mother." Now I have two kids, Holly six and David three, and one in the oven. What the hell, I am making good money and soon to own a piece of Telco Wire and Cable because we are doing very well. Of course, I had a lot to do with its success. Holly was a tall kid, but David was as big as Holly and three years younger. Heather and I knew that we were not only headed for trouble with David because of his height, but because he was already beating the shit out of all his "little" friends as well as being very destructive in general. He would knock over lamps just to do it and kick the dog just to do it and a plethora of other things. Just too many to mention! It seemed that we were raising the devil. I was secretly waiting for the fires to begin.

Heather finally popped and now we had three. He was the only planned child out of the three. We figured that he would be the president of the United States, the ambassador of good will to the world and the Holy Grail of our family. There is always a lesson to learn with anyone and anything as time goes on. We'll get back to this in another chapter. So, as I have mentioned much earlier in these three hundred pages or so, the Jewish people name their children after the dead. My wife wanted to name this new born Aaron. I'm still working on the name Barjud. My parents (already causing problems) want us to name this kid Samuel for my father's dad, my grandfather. Heather is big time opposed to it. I am not real keen on it ether. We bought you a house! We let you use our new Lincoln! We put on a great wedding for you! We, We, We!!! The crap was hitting the fan faster than we could scrape it off. How do we get out of this gracefully? "Got it! Simca" I said, "Simca." "What the heck is a Simca," Heather asked? In Yiddish Simca is Samuel. We have to have a Yiddish name for the kid anyway. We will tell Mom and Dad that we are going to name him Simca, for my Zada, Samuel, and that, of course, is much more important than any American name. It's his real name. Not some drecky name like Bill, John or Joe. All is good with the plan except for one thing. The American name has to start with an "S" also to tie the names together. Back to the drawing board! Aaron was out! Barjud was out! I suggested Samson like in Samson and Delilah. He was kind of a king, right, Heather? We already have a David, like in King David, of the Jews. Let's cover all bases. Heather was not smiling. She said Samson was to close too Samuel. Let's see what name starts with an "S" that we can live with. Actually, we should not have to go through all of this just to name a child. Why doesn't someone change this rule? Like I have said before, even the Catholics can eat meat on Friday now. Why can't I name my own kid what I want? Barjud! Another bad look from you know who! So after much thought, and I really can't remember who came up with it, we now have a "Sean" (double oh seven style) in the family. Holly, David and Sean are all about three years apart. We sure planned that great, didn't we, Heather?

Not much happened at work for the next couple of years with the exception of a promotion and with the promotion came a little more money. Not a lot but a little more. (You know how those Jewish bosses are.) The funny thing is that with the promotion to National Sales Manager, there was no one to National Sales, Manage. There is just me in the sales department, so I hired some reps to sell for us. Out of state, of course! That way I can continue to keep my brand new status of "National Sales Manager." I hired one organization in Texas and one in Denver, Colorado. It was my job to kick them in the butt on a regular basis so that they would make sales. Now, this in itself is not a big deal. (I would have said no big tzores, but you probably have already forgotten your Hebrew lesson.) Because it is me, there is usually a goofy story that goes along with something that is normal. This is no exception. One weekend I decided to go to Texas, San Antonio to be exact, to kick the reps in the butt. I booked passage on an airplane and got a room for the weekend at the Hilton, I believe. It has been a while! Being the youngster that I was then, there was a river that ran very near the hotel. I believe it was called the San Antonio River. Today, it's called (internationally known as) The River Walk.

One evening, when I was done with the business at hand, I went to the bar in the hotel. Had probably twenty-three too many (everything was on the company now that I was the National Sales Manager) and started talking to this very pretty lady. Well as pretty as a woman gets after forty-five or so drinks. She was probably a ten and a half, on the way too much drinking, and then seeing, a female scale. We talked and drank and talked and drank and then just nodded and drank and then just drank until one of us suggested to take a walk and get some of that beautiful Texas night air. We went outside and walked over to the river. Talk led to kissing and kissing led to touching and before I knew it, we were naked in the river and doing it. We were standing at a part of the river that had a four or five foot drop, kind of like a little waterfall. I laid her (Pardon the pun.) against the bank of the waterfall area, her feet in the water up to her thigh (the river was not real deep,) and her head was over or about even with the top part of the slow flowing waterfall. As things started to happen, she started to really move and jump around. I thought I really found a live one. Man was she into it. Jumping and moaning and then screaming. It seemed like she was yelling stop, please stop. In fact, she was screaming stop. She jumped out of the water still yelling, and I am yelling back, "What did I do wrong?" She screamed back, "It's not you, it's them." "What them?" I asked. "Them, the bugs," she said. "Bugs" I said? Yea, look, they are all over me." I jumped out of the river and low and behold, she had at least ten crawdads stuck to her. Crawdads, what a trip! I helped peel them off of her and that was the end of that romance and a waste of the company's bar money. I sobered up real quick. Hell, I had a room and opted for the river. DUH! So that was one experience that this National Sales Manager had that I don't think many others have had, whether a National Sales Manager or not.

Now, let me tell you about just one other as there have been many. I flew into Denver to bust the balls of the other rep first thing Monday morning. I got to my motel room late Friday, maybe six o clock P.M. I thought I'd spend some time there until I had to work with them Monday. I had never been to Denver. It was still pretty warm so I thought I would take a dip in the pool first and then get dinner. I put on my swim suit and thought I'd do about two or three laps under water. Usually not a problem as I was still in pretty good shape from gymnastics. Not to mention I was a pretty good swimmer, just not good enough to make the swim team years ago. So, I dove in and got to the end of the pool, turned around all under water and when I got about to the middle of the pool, I lost it. Gasping for air and floundering, I came up and out of the water, thinking I was going to drown. Shit, what was wrong? That should have been a piece of cake. A lap and a half is kids' play. Maybe the flight here had something to do with it or maybe I was coming down with the flu. Man, I just didn't know, but I was a little scared. I pulled myself up and out and lay on my towel for a bit. Instead of going to my room first, I thought I would grab a toddy and take it to the room. I stopped at the front desk to ask them where the bar was. I started yakking with the desk clerk and in my rambling; I had mentioned that I almost drowned a few minutes ago. "Yea," he said, "a lot of them do." What is that all about I thought. He said, "You must be from L. A. or someplace like that, huh?" I said, "Yea, how did you know?" He said, "We are six thousand feet higher than you are used to, and the air is much thinner here than there. Your lungs don't work right for a week or so." I'm thinking shouldn't that be posted on my room's wall next to the check out time? Hell, I almost died. "Thanks," I said, "and where is the bar?" This job is great, drinking and eating for free, just great! I got my drink, went to my room, took a shower, making sure not to stay under the water too long. Dinner, what and where to go for dinner and a little something to do after I eat? After all, I had Saturday and Sunday to play in Denver. I asked my social director (same desk clerk) where to eat and where to go after. The first thing out of his mouth was, "Thought you'd be back and ask that." (This guy needs a life!) He said, "Are you looking for good food or women?" I said, "Do I need to choose or can I have both?" He said, "Try right next door. There's a restaurant and night club with topless dancers and good music. The food ain't bad either." I walked over and got a table, ordered some food and a cocktail. My buddy, Mr. Desk Clerk, was right. The food was just fine. I finished about nine and walked through a hallway to the bar. It was a good size bar, maybe twenty-five tables or so on a tiered floor. You could sit up high in a booth or lower close to the stage where the ladies danced. I sat down close. After a couple of cocktails and a bunch of winking at the dancers, one came over to my table, sat down and said, "Would you like to buy me a drink?" I'm thinking, "Oh boy would I." She was very attractive. I hadn't noticed any crawdads hanging off her, and I had seen her dance topless already. Right about now, I am trying to figure out if this is ok in Denver because in California it would be a no, no. "Sure, what's your pleasure?" I said. She ordered champagne, and I got another scotch. My drink cost three-fifty and hers was twelve dollars. What the hell, I wasn't paying for it, the company was. After three or more drinks each, I was feeling no pain. She asked for another one and, of course, I said, "OK." She was pretty friendly, if you get my drift, and could really handle her booze. She went to the bathroom and I, for some reason, took a sip of her drink. Seven Up! It was just Seven Up. I am getting screwed by her and not the way I was thinking. She came back and I said, "You're just drinking Seven Up." She was appalled that I had tried her drink and said, "Go to hell," got up and left. I told the manager and he could care less. It was like I had a huge sticker on my forehead that read "L. A. Sucker!" So now it is about eleven o'clock. I am stinken drunk and more than that, pissed off at myself for being taken by a tramp. That was the first and only time I got completely taken by a female. That I know of. It was a good lesson for me and kept me on my toes the rest of my life when involved with women, in that respect.

Well, except for one time in San Francisco when I picked up this absolutely gorgeous oriental (Asians were not invented yet) chick hitchhiking, got her to my room on her suggestion, laid her on the bed, put my hand up her dress, and got a hand full of balls. But that's another chapter. The bad thing about that is, she may have been the most beautiful woman I had ever seen. Kissed great also! Feh!! I paid my bill very reluctantly and started to walk out of the bar. It was a two-minute walk to my room. I was putting away my credit card as I walked out, not really looking where I was going and bumped right into a female walking in. Before I could say excuse me, she said, "Been drinking?" I believe my retort was, "Me, drinking?" We were face to face, maybe six inches away, and I just kissed her. She said, "Do we know each other?" I said, "Your lips seem familiar." She said, "Are you buying?" Instinctively I said, "No, but my company is." I did a one-eighty, and went back to my personal booth, and sat down. The first thing out of my mouth was, "Do you drink champagne?" She looked at me funny and said, "No, why?" Just wondered! We closed up the place about one-ish. Both made it to my room, well at least I think it was my room, and spent the night. If you gave me a million dollars I could not tell you her name. However, she was a free-lance writer for a couple of newspapers. Don't know if I slept any, but we did stay awake doing something pretty fun.

In the morning I panicked. The sheets where completely red, covered in blood. It looked like a bloody massacre. She, in the dark of night, started her period and by the look of it, never stopped for six hours. You would think a person would feel something like that! But I'll never know. I am man! We folded the sheets and covered them with the bed spread. So the maid (that I would have to face at some time I am sure and I just hope she does not tell the desk clerk what she found as I am sure he will have a very profound statement about it) would not see them as she walked into the room. My new found friend said she had to get home and clean up as she had to go to work. I asked if I could have her number but she refused. I think she thought I was going to make her pay for new sheets. But she said, "I want you to call this number" and wrote it on a business card along with the name of a chick. I asked, "Who's this?" She said, "A friend. You'll like her." My ex-new-found friend walked out the door and, just like the quick abrupt meeting of her, was about as a quick a loss of her and never to see or hear from her again. Bumped, drank, fucked, bled, walked and didn't have to pay for a thing. What a life!

About the time the door closed as she walked out, I was on the phone to this new name in my life. Not really sure what was going on, but I was starting to like Denver a lot. The phone rang and rang. I left a message explaining what happened and left my phone number and room number at the motel. I would have given her my cell, but they still have not been invented. I showered and dressed and went to breakfast. I got back about one o clock and thought I'd try to drown myself again. But when I got into the room, there was a message for me on the phone. It was the new chick. She had left a message to call her. I did and we met that night for dinner. She was prettier than the other one. The only thing these two had in common was that I can't remember either of their names. After dinner we went for a drive. She showed me a couple of places of interest and then we made it back to the room. This lady was very different from the first. We talked, laughed, and then fucked. But first I had asked her how her health was. She said she doesn't have a period anymore. Think she talked to the other one? She knew exactly what I was referring to. I must have impressed the first one, so she shared me with her best friend. How nice! This one left the next morning just like the first one did; only this one gave me her phone number. I called for a couple of months and we talked a bit. But, between work, wife and kids, I never seemed to make it up there. Ever since then, I have had a soft spot for Denver. I even root for the Broncos from time to time.

The kids were growing up. Heather was becoming the greatest mom there could ever be. (Just about as great as I was an asshole.) Not to mention, as I would walk in from work, there was always a scotch and soda waiting for me. Almost any time I'd walk in. It was turning out that my not so want to be married situation may have been not so bad after all.

It was in the middle of nineteen and sixty-nine, and the moon landing was about to get under-way. (For you youngsters who didn't make it through high school or you older guys that were doing way too many dubees at the time, the moon landing was the first time anyone dropped their pants, bent over and fell to the ground.) There was a guy named Buzz or something like that (Did you ever notice that whenever something great happens, it's always some guy with a really stupid name?) that spear-headed it. I really don't know how many people in the world were watching, but it had to be all of them that were privy to a T.V. and a few from outer space that didn't need one. (T. V. for you younger guys is a very large box that usually sits on a large stand. You can see and hear the same thing you can on your Blueberry, Blackberry or Dingleberry.) As the world watches Buzz, buzz off, me included, all were in aw. I am not sure if you can remember, but when they came back after all that first step shit, they left the Luner Excursion Modular (LEM) there to record more stuff, like will the flag keep on waving with no atmosphere and will the same wind that blows the flag around blow the rocks around so the face of the man in the moon will change and all kinds of stuff like that. (Personally, I really think they just forgot it because of the liquid celebration they were doing.) You are probably wondering what the hell I am putting this world record and unbelievable event in my book for, and how am I involved? Well, let me tell you. We already know that I am in the business of selling electronic wire and cable and have been for some years now. Correctomundo! Telco Wire and Cable had evolved over the past four and a half years because I had been most of the sales force and worked very hard to earn my five percent ownership which will be coming up in a very short time. My sales territory was everything but Texas and Colorado. (We didn't have any other sales people!) One market I called on was in the San Diego area of southern California. Among many other companies that were involved in the space race, like General Dynamics and Northrup, was a company called Ryan Aeronautics. They were a company that built altimeters for the aero space industry. An altimeter is a device that measures the distance from the bottom of the air craft to the surface that it intends to land on so that the pilots inside know how fast or slow to land and how far they are away from their landing surface. Well, I, the greatest salesperson on earth, or at least for Telco Wire and Cable, had sold this great company some silver-plated Teflon coated wire for their projects. Now, because their claim to fame was their altimeters, one would have to assume that my wire was put into their altimeter and was on that historic flight to the moon. Now you would think I have the right to brag, right? "My wire is on the moon, right?" Well kinda and kinda not! In fact, a few weeks later after all was said and done and our astronauts went through their parade and all the world was cheering, I decided to brag a little that it was my wire that was still on the moon as a apart of the LEM, and was still there because they had left it there to continue to send back images and data. What I should have done was brag to my friends and family. But noooo, I had to brag to anyone and all whom I knew, even my competition, you know, the other distributors of wire and cable that I talked to on occasion and didn't sell Ryan Aeronautics.

Being that I was a good salesperson, no, a great salesperson, and I am sure that at one time or another I had taken away a sale or two from the competition, they put out an all-points bulletin that Chuck, the sales person who works for Telco Wire and Cable, had sold Ryan Aeronautics in San Diego the wire for the altimeter for the moon landing, and that it was faulty wire. That's why NASA left it on the moon. They couldn't get it back. Great, just great! There's goes my reputation! Next!

As life would have it, I recently met a lady about a year ago or so, two thousand and eight. Her name was Karen. She wanted me to invest in a documentary about the lost tapes of NASA's flight to the moon, in July of nineteen-sixty-nine. You know the moon that has my "faulty" wire *still on it*. She got my interest! Maybe I can go there and visit my little wires that caused me so much embarrassment. You know, "that moon"! Apparently, the original NASA tapes were lost and then found forty years later with a few other tapes that had been bought by a guy in a NASA auction. He really didn't know that he had those tapes. However, no one had the right equipment anymore to view them. The guy who bought the tapes, sometime later, found a guy who had a machine that could do the job. As he viewed all of the tapes he realized what he had. My friend Karen, the lady who I had met, decided to make a movie about it. She has called it "July Moon". She recently told me it has had a limited screening in New York and a big premier is planned in Las Vegas, soon. She even said that I would be invited. I will let you know how it all turns out in my next book!

The last month of the year was upon us at Telco Wire and Cable. I asked my boss and friend, Mike, how were we doing business wise for the year? I have really put in a lot of work and hours to build up this company from scratch. I hope we are making this the best year of them all. Mike turned to me and said, "We are doing great, and you have a great bonus coming." I smiled and walked away. It was Christmas time, and we closed a couple weeks at this time of year for the holidays. Usually the last two weeks and re opened on the second of January. It's nice to be Jewish. We not only get our own holidays off but the Christian ones as well. Around the fifteenth of December I was given my bonus check. At that time I asked Mike when he would have the contract for me to sign for my five percent ownership of the company. His reply was, "What ownership?" I said, "Five years ago when I left a company that was paying me sixty percent more than you offered and a company that I had full and total insurance for me and my family and at no charge to me and I was only a few miles away from home not forty, you told me that in five years, if we were still in business, that I would have five percent of Telco Wire and Cable." Mike's reply was, "I don't remember any of that." I said, "I get Bupkus on Toast, right?" (Meaning nothing) He said, "You have a very good salary, don't you?" I said, "Yes, but I was not working for a salary. I was working for ownership." I said a very sarcastic, "See you tomorrow" and walked out. He knew I was really pissed. I am not sure, but all of this happened in the middle of the week, and there were just a couple of days before we broke for the holidays. I shut up, cashed my bonus check, and figured I would have time to cool off the next two weeks. I went home and broke the news to Heather. She took it very well although I knew she was hurt as much as I was. Not sure if it was not getting ownership in the company or because I was hurting. She was always on my side, no matter what. Needless to say, she never talked to Pam again. That night I could not sleep. Over and over I played Mike's promise to me. I knew I was not wrong. I just knew it.

I was in the office early the next morning because I couldn't sleep. This time of the year I was in the office a lot because many buyers were off or on vacation or took off early to shop for Christmas gifts or whatever. I went out mostly on appointments. Mike called about ten o'clock and said he was not going to be in today as he had shopping himself to do. I wondered if that was the truth or he just didn't want to face me. Anyway, I was all alone watching the store. A buyer from Hughes Aircraft called and asked me if I had a certain type of cable in stock. I said, "No." Then I asked him, "How fast do you need it?" He said, "Now!" I told him that I would do my best to find it and call him as soon as I know something. Realizing that he would be calling everyone in the world to get it, I hustled my butt to find it. When they say, "I need it now," it is usually for a submarine or some kind of a navy vessel that just came into dry dock for repairs and needs to be out in a very quick turn around time. At that time it is not how much the cable is but how fast can you get it here. I found it in New York, got the price, called the buyer back, added a bunch to my cost and said, "I can have it in your hands tomorrow by noon." He gave me a purchase order, and I bought the cable under my own name and had it shipped to Hughes Aircraft. I never gave a thought to cheating Mike out of the order as I felt it was partial payment for the screwing he gave me.

After I had completed all that had to do with the order, I sat down and thought that was so easy why don't I just go into business myself? Hell, I practically built this one. Why not another! I went through all the customer lists and marked down the ones that really liked me as their salesman and then a few others that were on the fence. All in all, I had about thirty or so customers. I went home that night and told Heather that I was quitting my job tomorrow, Friday, with Mike and was going to go into business for myself. Heather never ever cussed, but this time she said, "Are you fucken nuts? How will we eat or pay the rent or put clothes on the kids? Are you fucken nuts!" I said, "Calm down. You sound like my dad when he did his best to tell me we couldn't get married because I can't afford it. We made it then didn't we?" "Are you fucken nuts?" again came from Heather's mouth. You can yell, scream and pull your hair out of your head if you want to, but the bottom line is, I am quitting tomorrow and January second, I am the boss of a brand new wire and cable company. Why don't you just calm down and try to think of a name for our new company. She even made herself a cocktail. She very seldom drank, too. I went into work about noon and both Sam and Mike were already at work. Mainly wrapping gifts and munching on some food they had brought in for the help and us. I said, "Hi", sat down in a very quiet atmosphere and gulped down a plate full of goodies. Nailed a cocktail or two and said to the both of them with a smile on my face, "I am giving you a two-week notice and will not be in on January second." I thought that was pretty kewl, because I had the two weeks off anyway so I really didn't lose any work time. Paychecks had already been written and cashed for the holiday pay off time. I turned and walked out the door and never looked back. I could hear Sam saying, "Come back, Chuck" but I kept walking. I never heard a peep from my friend of six years and boss of five, Mike.

When I got home Heather said, "Pam (Mike's wife) called and wants to know if we would like to join them for a Christmas dinner and cocktails on them?" "I told her no we had other plans", Heather said. "I hope that was ok?" So, as a celebration, I said to "Big H," (my cutize name for Heather); Lets go to Vegas for the weekend before it gets crazy with New Years Eve." I could use the away time anyway as I will have to work endlessly when the new year comes and the new me and company start. We did exactly that. I think we checked into the Hilton. We were having a really great time and about five or six o'clock, someone from the casino just walked up to us and asked us if we would like to see the "ELVIS" show for free. Needless to say, I said, "He is in the army, I believe. So what's the joke?" "No joke", they said. Tomorrow is his first show since he was released from the Uncle Sam Show. Tonight is his dress rehearsal show, and we want it to be a full house for him. The show tomorrow is sold out but there are a lot of unfilled seats tonight. So after his arm twisting we accepted. (Yea, right!!!) I can't tell you how great the show was. We were close to the stage and could see his every expression and even the sweat rolling down his face. To this date, I have seen many shows in Sin City, and not very many have compared to "ELVIS".

The two weeks went by very fast. My dad had a fit with about the same intensity as Heather did, but it was all for naught. I did have to go through a three-hour lecture of how I could not afford to do it and how it takes a bunch of money and years of acquiring that special knowledge to start a new business. I spent the two weeks finding a warehouse, rounding up a small amount of equipment that I could get by with, paper supplies, phones set up, and everything that most people take five months to do because they took the time to plan it. But this was a forced move out of anger and resentment. I had never even given it any thought beforehand. I was all ready to receive my five percent ownership. I am sure that Mike thought I'd be back in a month or two begging for my job back, and that's probably why I made a success of it. Crawling had never been up my ally and still isn't, up to and including today. However, if you think I hadn't given it a bunch of second thoughts, you're wrong, but I was now committed. It was kind of like that line in a Clint Eastwood movie where he said, "Do you feel lucky, well, do ya punk?" The difference is that I took the shot like the kid did; only this time I won.

Now this is and was a major turning point in my life. As I hark back and think what my life would have been if I never took the job with Mike five years ago and stayed with Von's Grocery Company, I probably would have had a great life with a wife that loved me. I would still have children that would have Loved me and a gaggle of grandkids that would have Loved me. But that was faith and I am sure, divine destiny why I chose the course I did. Today, I am still not sure why because I am not the happy camper that I would have liked to be. But we all make our beds and have to lie in them. Not to mention, I would not be writing this book. And so the story continues.

Chapter Seventeen

I named the company Pacific Cable Corporation. Once, again, I did not really choose to go into business for myself; it was by chance like so many other things in my life were. Most people spend months and even years planning to be their own boss. Me, two weeks! I had a two thousand square foot building in Upland, California, almost on the corner of Mountain and Ninth Street. It was mostly warehouse with a small office and bathroom. Heather started as my secretary. Although as time went by and I went through a handful of secretaries, no one compared to her. Not even close!

I started to make calls by phone, and to get orders. How cool was this? This time, when I made a hundred bucks from an order, it went into my pocket. I made a profit the very first month and never looked back. After a year or so I was doing so well that we bought a home in Alta Loma.

As the business kept picking up, I hired a manufacturer's representative to help sell. I was starting to have a lot of inventory. I kind of focused on the type of wire that was used for sound and telephone installation. I never passed an opportunity to bid on some submarine cable. In fact, I made friends with one of the buyers who worked for Hughes Aircraft Company. We, he and his wife and Heather and I, spent a lot of time together in Balboa. He lived in Newport Beach. We were friends for a long time until he moved on to another job in another state. But for all the time we spent together, he never gave me a break with his ordering. I did do a lot of business with him by just having the chance to bid on everything that came across his desk. When he got married, I gave him a cruise to Hawaii for the both of them. Heather was not real crazy about that. We had never been to Hawaii and in fact, with the exception of Santa Barbara for our honeymoon, we had not been anywhere and that did not change for a long time. There are a few things that I need to mention about this time period with Lad (Ladisloss). That was the buyer's name (my friend) and his wife was Elaine, more commonly call "Laners." They had a friend whose name was Bob, and his wife whose name escapes me right now, but I think it was Susan. (Some time later, Susan had offered me her body, but I didn't even give it a thought, as Bob was my friend and, anyway, I was married.) Bob was a nut and fit right in with me. In fact, he put me to shame sometimes. Hard to believe! Good thing I didn't know him years ago. I just want to tell you about two times that he had total control of the floor. Once, all three couples were in line to buy tickets to the movie and the line just was not moving. We were about ten or twelve feet back from the ticket window. Five minutes before hand, we were ten or twelve feet back from the ticket window! Bob really had to pee badly. So badly, that he couldn't wait any more. It was a very cold night that night. His wife Susan was wearing a very heavy coat and boots. Right on the sidewalk where we all stood, he pulled it out and peed into his wife's boot. Those days six or seven inch high boots were in fashion. His wife was so shocked that she couldn't move. He finished, she went to the car, and we never talked about it ever. Lad looked at me. I looked at Lad. We then turned and looked at our wives, smiled, and both of us undid our zippers. However, neither one of us pulled it out and peed.

As I recall, the peeing event was better than the movie.

Another time we, Heather and I, and seven or eight other couples, including Lad and Bob went camping just south of Tijuana, Mexico. A place called Rosarita Beach. (Ring a bell? Sandy and her wig!) It was the dead of summer and very very hot. There were five or six cars, and we put them in a circle like covered wagons would have done a hundred and fifty years ago to protect themselves from attack by Indians. In our case, it was from the Mexicans. You know how I feel about them. Along with the six inch high boots at that time in winter, there was another fad going on in summer. Putt putts. Mini bikes! Motor scooters! Semantics! Pick one. All the same hasari! (Yiddish slang for same old crap, or thing!) I had brought one, Bob had bought one, and a few others had also. Now, try to picture this setting. We, the cars in a circle, are about thirty feet from a cliff maybe one hundred feet high. You have the water below the cliff and then, in order, the car circle about thirty feet from the cliff and then about another fifty feet or so further, were the porta potties. It was so hot there that no one wanted to walk to them. So we (all of us major considerate guys) would at any time the ladies asked, drive them over to the toilet, wait for them, and bring them back to the car circle where there was a little shade. We had strung together blankets between the cars, held up by the rolled up windows. It wasn't originally in the best interest of the females who were with us. It was also to keep the beer in the coolers out of the direct sunlight. I am sure that every one of us has visited one of these porta potties at least once in our life time. Hopefully it was in the United States where there is some kind of cleaning rules. In Mexico, that's a different story. The reason we made camp fifty feet away from them was because you could smell them from forty feet away. If you don't mind, I won't belabor the point. I am sure by now you get my drift. So, getting back to the story, Bob's wife, (the pee in your shoe girl) needed to go to the toilet. Bob put her on the back of the putt putt and off they went to the porta potty. I and a couple of others were standing there when Bob's wife asked him to take her. What she didn't know was, as she got on the putt putt, Bob turned to us and winked. We just stood there and waited. He got her there and nothing different happened. We were disappointed. Bob was usually pretty funny. We thought that he might try to scare her or do a wheelie or something like that. But nothing! Nada! But instead of waiting for her, he drove back to us. We looked at each other because we always waited for our wives. Not that we cared if they had to walk back, but they usually had a beer with them and you never know if a Mexican would try to steel it from her on the way back. Bob came back with this great big smile. Obviously, the shit was on. He turned the putt put around, revved up the motor and said, "Watch this!" Now we were, as I have mentioned, about fifty feet from the potty. Bob popped the clutch, did a wheelie, and headed straight for the potty at full throttle. He hit that son of a bitch straight on and knocked it completely over with his wife in it. He went down, the potty went down. He got up and all you could hear, over and above our laughing, was this female screaming at the top of her lungs, "Help!" I guess she thought there was an earthquake or something. She crawled out of the door and saw Bob standing there, laughing so hard that he couldn't move. Let me tell you, she beat the shit out of him. Eventually, he was on the run with her right on his ass. We yelled to Bob, "What's the matter, Bob, afraid of a little girl?" He yelled back, still at a full gallop, "She stinks badly!" Now, where was I in my book?

Many times I would have to stay out late and entertain some of the buyers. Dinner, drinks, and an occasionally a hooker. To be honest with you, I can't remember how many orders I had written on a white tablecloth napkin and took it home with me at two in the morning. This became almost regular. Not that I really wanted it that way, but that was the way you got orders then, and today, I don't think anything has changed. It's just more expensive today! Orders were written, and money was being made, a lot of money. Other things became part of the menu as well. Late at night and drunk not only with buyers but later on in my life with my friends, women started to pop into my life. Was I looking for them, no! I was making a lot of money, and it was nothing to buy some ladies a couple of drinks a table away while out with the buyers. Kind of showing off! Hell, it was even a write off on my taxes. But the money making, the drinking, the late nights, and the showing off as well as getting the buyers laid, had become a regular part of the program, and I started to participate as well. Actually, later in years, my friends and I had competitions involving other women. I am not going to labor over something like that, because now, today, it's certainly nothing to brag about. As I think back on it, back then it was fun, and I never really thought anything of it. It wasn't cheating in my eyes. It was just fun. I am sure it was just a major chunk of immaturity. But it did go on for years, on an occasional basis.

I had mentioned a while back that I hired a manufactures' representative. He had talked me into joining the manufactures' representatives association. I had been a member for a year or so. The powers that be had asked me to help them with their annual show in San Diego that year. It was a huge conference that lasted for four days. Reps came from all over and displayed their company's wares and went to lectures and got laid. Tijuana was only twenty miles away from San Diego. You know how that place is with donkeys and such. I asked them what they wanted me to do. They said, "We need someone to organize the all star show." "What's that?" I retorted. "We give you a budget, and you hire people to sing, dance or play instruments, but you need to hire a draw act first." "What's a draw act?" "It's a name that everybody knows." "You want me to ask Frank Sanatra?" "Now you got it. But Frankie is out of our budget." "What do you think about Sandra Dee?" (Christ, once again, I need to explain who these people are for the young ones. Frank Sanatra was the guy who started Mo Town Records and finally made a name for himself when he discovered Z Z Top. Sandra Dee was his gay daughter's ex-mother-in-law.) I told them that I have no idea how to go about it. They told me it is a snap and would give me guidelines, names, numbers, and the guy who did it last year to work with. I asked them that if I didn't use the entire budget, can I keep the rest for all the work I will be doing. They said, "No." I would be doing it for free but will certainly get some recognition in the next monthly edition of Rep News. I took the high-paying job. I am not going to get into a long dissertation about all I did and how long it took and all that kind of boring crap, mainly because I forgot most of it myself. I am going to tell you that I was a big hit, had a great write up in the rep newsletter, and wound up hiring, I think, Bobby Rydel or was it Bobby Vinton? It was one of those two bobby's or somebody close to that type of entertainer. Frankie S. NO!

Business just kept on getting better and better. In nineteen seventy-two, I opened a waterbed store. How and why I really don't remember, but it was all the rage at that time. I am sure someone probably suggested it. I am not bright enough to think of something like that on my own. So it is written, and so it will be done. I opened the first store in Upland, California in early March of seventy-two. It is the same town where I had Pacific Cable in. This was on the main drag, Foothill Blvd, about three miles from my home. Pacific Cable was about fifteen miles away. A far cry from the drive I use to make for Mike to L.A. and no traffic. The first person I hired was Karen. Pretty? Yes. Married? Yes. Sales oriented? Yes. We were off and running. Once, again, I made a profit the first month and again, never looked back. I opened with total newspaper coverage in the area. I still have all the articles in my scrap book. I know you won't believe this, but my opening special was, (remember the twenty cent a gallon for gas I had talked about ten years ago or so) a waterbed, twin or full size, the liner and (get this) a padded vinyl frame for only thirty-four dollars and ninety-five cents. King or Queen, for another seven bucks! Eventually, I became a distributor for the newest rages like deco art, lava lamps and even put in bean bag chairs. A month or so later I bought into a wrought iron manufacturing company. Now I was on a roll. I was busting my ass at Pacific Cable nine to five and then checking out the "Water Bed" (that was the name of my water bed stores) in the evening, and, of course, my new investment, the steel mill as I called it. I opened a second Water Bed store in Pomona, the home of the Los County Fair and my old house! By this time I had hired more people to work for me. One of them was from Visalia, California. Nice lady but I had to watch her on a regular basis. I figured anyone from a city named Visalia was going to be a problem. The original lady I hired, Karen, had a husband who had been out of work for a couple of years. He was a carpenter by trade. I asked her to ask him if he would like to make water bed frames for me. He said, "Yes." Now I was not only buying frames cheaper to add to the margin but also doing a little designing as well. I asked him to make a special bed frame for me, nine feet wide and nine feet long. It would be kind of the king of the king size beds. He made it, and I designed a manta out of wrought iron for the headboard from my company. I had it delivered to my house. I assembled the head board to the frame. I had made special silk sheets and pillow cases from one of my suppliers that I bought linen from for the stores. They alone cost me three hundred dollars and change. Add three down king-size pillows and a bed spread and now you are talking a grand plus. With such a bed I figured we should have a party before we put in the mattress, water, and of course, the two heaters. Nine by nine! This bed was big. Heather and I invited some friends over and supplied them with alcohol and sandwiches. Put on some music and had a minimum of six couples dancing inside the frame. Pictures on request! This all happened about late April or middle May. Now that I was becoming an entrepreneur, I had to open a bank account for each and every company. I banked with Wells Fargo at that time. Because of the amount of money I was depositing now, well over two hundred thousand just from Pacific Cable, they assigned me a special person who would take care of me personally. (If they had only known!) Her name was Deborah. We met and had lunch on the bank. She was a very pretty chick in my eyes. Great body (that means she had big tits) and when she walked, she bounced. Not her tits but her hair. It was nice to look at and very different.

August first I opened my third water bed store in Chino. (Chino, now famous for selling badly rotted cows.) This was the largest store of all. I had to have a great big special. Hmmm, summer time and what better to do but to give away watermelons. So mister "I always have a better idea" called a farm and had delivered a truckload of watermelons to each of the three stores. My ad ran like this, Grand opening of the third Water Bed store. Just come in and say hi. We will give you a free watermelon, nothing to buy and no obligation. However, you must say hi. I went through a plethora of watermelons and sold a bed or two at the same time. One day one of the girls who worked for me called me at Pacific Cable (that's where my main office was) and said we have a problem. I said, "What is it?" She said, "It really smells bad like dead rats or something." I said, "I will be right over." That was at the Pomona store. Before I got into the car, I received another call from the Chino store with the same problem. As soon as I walked in the Pomona store, I almost died. The smell was horrid. What had happened was that some of the watermelons had been cracked open when they were delivered, and they were starting to rot. It was really sickening. I called the garbage guy. He was a black man who lived next to my mom and Dad. He got the name "Garbage Guy" by looking into his own garage. This guy had so much shit in his garage that you couldn't get a stick match in it. He worked cheap and would do anything for a buck. He had a really nice kid maybe ten or eleven. No wife. In three hours we were back to almost normal.

So much had happened in such a short period of time that I said to Heather, "Let's take a three-day weekend drive to San Francisco and Napa and have a little fun." Heather was always ready for a little fun. We left Friday morning and drove to San Francisco, spent the night, hit a bar or two, woke up and bought about fifty loaves of San Francisco Sourdough bread, twenty pounds of assorted cheese, and headed off to Napa Valley. We hit winery after winery after winery. Shit faced sourdough, wine, cheese and driving. Really a great combination! Now, I really considered myself up on just about anything sexually. (I read the Playboy Adviser.) We happened into the vineyard of Pat Paulson's. The name may ring a bell from the show "Laugh In." Remember, he even ran for president? He got just about as many votes as I would have if I had run. We spent a lot of time in there, as the bar tender, counter guy, or whatever he was called kept talking to me and trying to sell me wine. Finally, Heather and I left. As we were getting into the car, Heather said to me, "Do you like him?" I said, "Who?" She said, "The bar guy." I said, "Why?" She said, "If he hit on you any more, I was going to deck the Son of a Bitch." I said, "Are you nuts? He's a dude." She said, "I know." Hard to figure, the know it all guy, the sex guru guy, the nothing passes me that I don't know guy, completely missed me being hit on by a gay dude. Needless to say, I didn't vote for Pat. However, my wife started to be more sexually active.

I started a bowling team called "The Water Bed" and our team did well. Number one in the league! Every thing seems to be hitting on all fours.

Now we are about in September, nineteen hundred and seventy-two. I was so busy with my companies and understandably so, that I never notice there was a Farmers Insurance Company right next door to my water bed store in Pomona. It was operated by two brothers. It was so long ago that I don't have a clue of what their names were. It could have been Heckel and Jeckel for all I know. However, one day they saw me in the store and came over and introduced themselves to me. Now that I think about it, I think they were Ernie and Dick. We talked for a while, maybe ten minutes, and then I had to leave. About a week later they saw me in the store again and came over and told me they had a tip on a horse. They asked me to give them six dollars and they would bet it for me. I had no idea what the heck they were talking about. A tip! Horses! So they explained. The L. A. County fair was on now and they race horses there. Do you know what the fair is? I almost told them! Oh yeah, they race horses there, right? Right! So a friend of mine told me that his boss had a horse in a race today and it was going to win. So Dick (I think that was his name) and I are going out there and bet some money on it. Do you want to bet it with us? We will put two across the board for you. That's only six bucks! I said, "Sure, why not. It's only six bucks." Two across the board heh! Like I knew what the hell they were talking about. But, it was only six bucks. I handed them the six and figured that I, not only would never see my six bucks again but that they probably gave notice and won't ever be back again either. They said they won't be back today but will see me tomorrow when I come in. The next day when I came in to check up on things at the Pomona store, Ernie (I think that was his name) walked in and laid nineteen bucks and change in my hand. I said, "What is this for?" He said, "The horse won and that was my return." Nineteen for six, and I didn't have to do anything. Shit, I'm in the wrong business. Now that was about thirty-five years ago. If it wasn't for that stupid bet and return, I am sure I would not be writing this book. Out of all the things in my life I did that were honest, fair and normal, that was the worst of all of them and changed the course of my life forever and definitely not for the good. Probably, if I could do anything over again in my life, it would be that six dollar bet. Once, again, I was not looking for a place to make a bet. It just came into my life by chance. It wound up costing me millions. Literally! So for the balance of the fair I went out with the brothers (whatever their names were) and played the horses. Won a little and lost a little. But enjoyed myself!

There was a family restaurant on the way from my house to work at Pacific Cable. It was called Brigham's Family Restaurant. I would stop in there a couple of times a week on the way to work for a little breakfast. After a few months I got friendly with most of the waitresses. So much so that when I walked in, there was my cup of coffee waiting at my table before I got there. As time went by, I eventually got friendly with the owner, Norm. Norman Ansara. (He recently died from cancer, I was told.) If the name sounds familiar, his cousin Michael Ansara played Cochise in the movies. I didn't find that out until a year or so later when Norm's older brother Ed came in and was talking about a bit role he just got because of Michael Ansara (Cochise). Now, in the many times that I had eaten there, I found out that Norm was a horse player. I told him I was into it as well. I had been to the fair at least five times with what's there a name. A big horse player was I! Norman even had his own bookie, named Cal. Ok, Norm, what's a bookie? I had heard the term before but I thought it had something to do with prostitution. One day Cal walked in as I had just sat down for breakfast. Norm came over which was rare at breakfast time. (Norm carried a whip and a chair when he was on the floor. His waitresses and bussers worked their asses off or they had to find another job. He was a tyrant, but he had the best service in California. You walked in and got greeted, served fast and politely and never rushed to leave. It was about thirty-five years ago, and I have never had the constant great service since.) He introduced me to Cal. This guy looked like he came right out of a Damon Runyon movie. Not especially attractive, unshaven, extremely rude and wore a sports car cap. Probably fifty years old. This guy was a trip. When you listened to him talk, you would think he invented the Mafia. Connected! Well, let me tell you, he did have his moments. Italian, you bet. Then, I never gave it a thought, but after knowing more about my dad now then I did then, it may have been the second coming of a problem. But who knew. Actually, my dad must have known, but he never conveyed it to me. Although he did join me for breakfast often at Norm's place, Brighams, he never got real friendly with anyone. It was kind of like he knew something that no one else did and didn't want to let on. He probably did! Now, there was Cal the bookie and Norm the restaurant owner and cousin of a movie star. The next person to meet was Andy. Andy was a huge Pollock about six feet four inches tall, a mustache, pitch black hair, and a twitch in his face that seemed to go off about every three or four minutes. He was a drug salesperson. Oh wait, I can say salesman because there was no "politically correct" then. Huh? However, after three or four years of being his friend, most of us guys tried to get him to steal some of the drugs he was selling and use it for his twitch. But I really think he thought he looked like Elvis Presley when Elvis did his thing with his lip. (I wonder if he knew Roger?) Only Elvis did it intentionally and Andy just couldn't stop. It must have been hell when he was young and dating. Obviously, it was not a problem in marriage, as kissing just didn't seem to have happened that much then, at least with his wife. Now, you have Norm the crucifier and consumed horse player, Cal the crude bookie, and Andy the twitch druggy. As it turned out, I needed an attorney for Pacific Cable, my wire and cable distributorship. I wanted to incorporate for liability purposes. I would have thought Cal (the bookie) would know someone because of the business he was in, but it was Norm who recommended Richard Anderson who frequented the restaurant. His office was right across the street from it. Norm arranged a meeting right here in the restaurant one morning. (If there was a way to make a buck, Norm knew how. Keep them buying food!) Norman was from Lebanon. Now, there is a good friend for me, the Jew. In fact, sometimes when we walked into his restaurant in mid-summer, the air conditioning was on in the restaurant but not in his office, which was the size of sleeping quarters for a Chinese family. Roughly eight foot by eight foot square with a desk that held twenty-seven thousand used race forms. It had to be about one hundred and thirty degrees in his office. He would sit there and handicap the horses in his suit and tie. (He always wore a suit and tie like most of us did except for Cal) and not a drop of sweat seen anywhere. Me, Cal, Andy and anyone else would have died in three minutes. Cal, you know the crude bookie, would call him, "You camel driving Arab Mother—r. (As I said, Cal had a way with words.) Norm would just sit there and say nothing, just handicap. We, Richard and I, met and to my surprise, with someone I would have thought to be normal within this group because he was an attorney, the first thing he did was to gulp down three or four spoonfuls of "A One Sauce" straight out of the bottle that was sitting next to the Sweet and Low container. I didn't even comment. He is an attorney, and I am sure he would have had a great answer. So the plot builds. Oh, wait, I would be remiss if I didn't mention Frenchy. This was a guy whose self esteem was so low (it could have been found under whale shit) that he had to be a self-made comic and errand boy and stooge. He was not really very funny. He would do stupid stuff like taking off his wig and tipping it when he was introduced to someone. He was very nervous and jerky, but he would do anything you asked him to do. He was really Norm's friend more than the rest of us. Norm would have him do errands for free. Frenchy always bragged about the beautiful wife he KEPT at home. I doubt it! So now you have the whole crew for the next fifteen years or so.

Pacific Cable got bigger, and I kept on adding to my companies. As I have mentioned, I became a distributor for the newest in lamps. Lava Lamps! Also, another new thing came out, Decoupage. Strange looking pictures on awkward looking wood frames covered in heavy clear resin. They were pretty cool. I also bought into a wrought iron company as I have said, and all three items were displayed in my water bed stores. When I had some extra time, instead of going home, I would go to Brigham's and play the horses with Norm. However, the six dollars did not reap the same harvest that it did a year ago or so with those other guys. (What were their names?) I would win some and lose some. But the losses were bigger then the wins but never over-bearing. But what the hell, I'm rolling in the dough, so what's a few bucks here and there.

In my spare time, which was getting non-existent, I took on managing (the bookie) Cal's kid's rock group. (Go figure, a bookie with a band. Next thing you know he will have me selling weed to elementary kids.) Weed, for you older guys, awe never mind. Most of the managing was at night, trying to get them gigs, and working with them on arrangements. After all, I was a madrigal so I did know something about music. However, I had to go to most of their performances to handle the money and the set ups as well as giving them information as to how they were being received after the first set. The performances were all at night, and Heather was not happy. Notice you have not heard her name lately? It was because she was becoming non-existent. I was starting to get consumed by work and gambling. One supported the other and a few other activities I have mentioned as well.

Late in December of that year, I was whipped and went to a bar not far from home. Just to have a couple of drinks, relax, and then go home for the night. They had a band there with dancing and the group was pretty good. At the break we started talking about Cal's kid's band and it went on for a couple of hours. I was pretty drunk and noticed the girl from the bank that now had my corporate account, Pacific Cable. She also had the others as well so we saw each other often at the bank. She came over, and we yakked a bit. Then, she asked me to dance. The night turned into, "We need to get out of here. The manager wants to lock up." Two-thirty A.M. We both being annihilated by now, left and I said, "Let's go to my Water Bed Store and sober up." We walked about four blocks or so. I opened the door, and we stumbled in. One thing led to another, and we found ourselves making Love in the front display window (I guess that is why they call it a display window) where anyone could have walked by, like a cop walking the beat. I had an octagon shaped bed as the display with red velvet inlays on a multi-angled wrought iron headboard along with a red velvet bed spread and matching pillows. It was a beautiful piece of work that I designed and later sold to a gynecologist who worked in Upland and had a second home in Palm Springs as well, where it eventually was delivered. The irony of the bed is that Deborah, my unintential date for the evening, wound up screwing him (the GYN) on the very same bed about three years later in Palm Springs. Go figure!

I started to fall into a kind of routine. Get up at seven or so, go to Brigham's for breakfast with the guys (sometimes dad would join me there), kill a couple of hours there, go to Pacific Cable Corporation for a couple of hours, then meet Norm, Andy and Cal at Brigham's again, and go to Santa Anita Race Track for lunch which just happened to be about the daily double time (The daily double is a special type of bet called a proposition bet), kill another couple of hours or so there, and then drop all off at Brigham's so Norm could be there for the dinner crowd, Andy could make a call to his home office so that they think he's working and me, check in with the rest of my businesses, pick up any money from the cash resisters, and make the appropriate deposits. Also say hi to Deborah at the bank, which in my spare time, I would see her about as much as I was seeing my wife.

About the only thing that kept me from gambling was the time that I spent with my two boys in little league and my daughter in Miss American soft ball. I not only coached but I managed David's teams as well, from six years old to twelve; I also did the same with Sean from age six. That was nine years total in little league. I mostly managed. It was one of the most rewarding nine years of my life. I never won a championship in all nine years. I never had that killer instinct that some of the fathers had. That NEED to win! I was always concerned with the comraderey and teaching the fundamentals of the game along with good sportsmanship. As I said, I never won a championship, but I always had many more kids ask me if they could be on my team again next year than any of the other father's. I guess the free pizza after the games didn't hurt either.

I might have been the only father who was fired as a coach from Miss American Softball. Not that I wasn't a help with my daughters team mind you, but when I would get excited when one of the girls did something really good or hit a home run, and when she crossed the plate, I would give them a hug or a pat on the butt just like I would do with the boys on my little league team. It was just a normal, natural thing to do. Remember, they need appreciation, support and an acknowledgement for the good things they do. After four or five warnings I no longer coached my daughter's team. I pleaded my case but they said I needed to learn to keep my hands off the girls! Go figure!

There was a restaurant named Rueben's. It was part of a large chain of restaurants, some with different names. They would have a happy hour from four o' clock to seven or so. A happy hour is when the restaurant discounts their drinks and puts out free food. (Unless you are in Utah.) In Utah they are not allowed to have a "happy hour" because of the really dumb laws they have there. So, some of the restaurants or bars have an "appy hour." Go figure. That's ok, but they are not allowed to discount drinks for a short period of time. You know, "appy hour" is usually just two or three hours. But get this. It's OK if they discount it for the whole day. This is just one of the reasons China is moving ahead of the United States. We have way too many stupid rules and regulations. Anyway, a lot of the guys met there (Reubens) after work for a drink. Ok, two drinks, all right, a few hours or more. I can't tell you how many times i called Heather and said I was on the way home and never showed up. Nothing ever happened there. We were all just getting drunk with the guys. Sometimes some of the wives would show up but not too often. Heather couldn't because she had three kids to watch. So I was there for the night sometimes. However, the guys who were there were not the gambling guys. They were married couples that I had met in the past year or two. They were the friends that Heather and I would pal around with whenever I thought about taking her somewhere. So, now we have two sets of people. Gamblers and drinkers! Boy is my life forever getting better!

In between work and play without you know who (Heather) and drinking without you know who (Heather) and gambling with the guys without you know who (Heather), I took Heather to Carmel and San Francisco (Northern California) one weekend up Highway One. Highway One is probably one of the most beautiful drives in these United States. I may have mentioned it before. Now, this in itself is no big deal, but something she and I will remember for a lifetime was a question she asked me on the way there. Now, let me set the stage. Heather is Mensa with a one hundred and fifty-six I Q. (Give or take a few.) The only thing stupid she ever did in her life was to marry me. But all women do that. They all think they are so smart and constantly bitch about men. Then, why do they marry them? Anyway, we were driving for a couple of hours. We had the ocean on our left, not more than twenty feet from the road. If I stopped and got out, we would be in the Pacific Ocean. On the right of this one lane narrow beautiful road is the start of mountains that travel up to a three thousand foot height. I am on the left driving and almost have my hand dragging in the ocean. Heather is on the right looking at how high up the mountain goes. She turned to me and as serious as anyone can be, asked, "How high up do you think we are?" I looked at her, turned and looked at the ocean on my left, turned back to her and about that time, she realized what she said. I think we both laughed about it for a total of ten hours that weekend and did for years after. Maybe you had to be there. For the smartest woman I have ever known, I just thought it should be in this book of truth.

So, for the next years to come, my life took to nothing but gambling and gambling and more gambling. I started to go to Las Vegas and started to build up a line of credit so I could take out markers (A marker is where the casino gives you money to gamble with and you don't have to pay it back for thirty days and it is interest free.) and use their money for gambling. Or, at least that was the way it was suppose to be. The drinking guys started an every Tuesday night poker game. They were the drinkers and not the gamblers so it was just a lot of fun. We played a penny, nickel, dime game. It was dealer's choice. We really played a lot of really stupid games, some with ten wild cards. No self-respecting gambler would admit to things like that. It was all just in fun. We would rotate houses every week. Most of the women (wives and girlfriends) would encourage it. They knew where we were and on top of it, the guys would give the lady of the house a hundred dollars to buy chips, soda and beer. That would cost, in those days, about thirty bucks. The lady of the house got to keep the difference for cleaning up after the game. This went on for at least thirteen years or so. It was just fun. I know many men do this and enjoy it as much as I did. Why is it in this book of nut stuff? It plays a large role in later years so I had to set the stage.

Gambling had become an obsession with me. It didn't matter what it was as long as I had some action. It got to a point that my routine started to change. Instead of going to breakfast at Brigham's and then to work and then to the race track and then home, I would and whoever wanted to join me, would go from Santa Anita after a full day of racing, not only the daily double, and then would go to Los Alamitos in Orange County for the harness races until eleven or so. Sometimes, if we were not too tired, we would go to the Los Angles airport right from the race track and catch a red eye to Las Vegas for a few hours and then head back, get in the car, and drive home. Shit, shave, and shower and then start the day again at Brigham's. This went on for years. The only good thing was that I was making good money with my companies to support my habit. If you could say that was a good thing. It even got so bad that when I happened to show up at work and the guys knew it, they would come down and we would play Gin Rummy for hours. Once again, Heather would call me at work and ask me when I was to be home for dinner. Once again, I would tell her a time, and once again, I would play until midnight and never make it home for dinner. Heather may have been the best cook in the world but would never have known it. At Brigham's when eating, if I saw two flies on a table or on a door I would bet which one would fly away first. It didn't matter where or when or what. I gambled.

I don't know why but I bought a Jaguar, nineteen sixty-eight XKE roadster, burgundy. This car was so cool. I fell in Love with it. It was fast and looked very sexy, if a car can look sexy? Now, I'm not the best looking guy now, and I wasn't a ten like my wife was back then, but if I was stopped at a stop light, no matter who or what age chick walked by in a crosswalk, she gave me a nod or a smile. If I acknowledged it, with some of them, I got a phone number. After awhile I kind of thought it was me. Of course, years later when I did not have it, no one looked at me and smiled. In fact, when they would walk by me, I would smile at them, and they would just flip me off.

One day, one of my best friends (and I know this is going to be hard to believe) Jack, who did not gamble, who did not drink, who did not cheat on his wife and yes, you heard me correctly, does not gamble, had a cabinet shop right across the alley from Pacific Cable in Upland at Ninth and Mountain. We met at the lunch truck one day and were inseparable for years (when I was not gambling Of course.) Heather and I became really good friends with him and his wife, Jean. They were my wife's only salvation for eating dinner out. (I actually made it to most of the dinners.) Jack was one of those guys who we all have known in our life time that Loved to show a big bank roll in his pocket at all times. Why, I don't know. Not only didn't he gamble, he was as tight as a flea's ass stretched over a rain barrel and that's waterproof. One day I decided to do a quick day trip to Vegas. I asked Jack if he would like to go to keep me company. He answered me just like a woman, with a question. "Are you paying for lunch and dinner?" I said, "Of course. If I waited for you to buy, I would starve to death and put two bookies out of business." Off we went. We hit the Nevada border where at that time there was no speed limit. Once again, for the youth who may be reading this, no speed limit means you can go as fast as you want and not receive a citation for speeding. That's hard to believe, huh kids? But as the infamous Lilly Tomlin would say, "And that's the truth", using, of course, her nationally acclaimed tongue razz. However, I will not get into who Lilly Tomlin is. Then, I would have to explain what a phone is that you have to dial and sometimes is found in a booth and that would open another can of worms (unless you are a superman fan), and I do have a book to write. So, simultaneously, as I hit the boarder of Nevada and leave California, I hit the gas. Pedal to the medal as they say. In what seemed to be seconds, my speedometer was tracking one twenty-three and climbing. It is approximately forty miles to down town Las Vegas from the state line. I was determined to make it in twenty minutes. Now, as solid as Jack was with his money and conservative, he was adventurous and not afraid of most things. He had a spirit of adventure as long as someone was willing to pay for it. But at a hundred and twenty plus, he got a little worried. My XKE, like I said, was a roadster, rag top, soft top, you know a convertible. So, about a couple of minutes into the speed dual with the wind, he started holding on for dear life. He had his hand outside his window with a death grip on the top. Holding it as tight as he could, as not to let the wind rip it off the car and suck him and me out of course. I told him to relax, but he wouldn't hear it. I was waiting for his cheeks to be pushed back against the car seat like there was a G force of eight. Then, about five or six more minutes into Mr. Toad's wild ride, I looked into the rear view mirror and guess what I saw with flashing lights bearing down on me? Right, the Gestapo! I checked my speedometer. It read one hundred and twenty-seven, but I could not understand why I was being pulled over as there is no speed limit. Anyway, most speedometers at that rate of speed are not that accurate. I probably wasn't doing more than one twenty. In those days you could just reach over and get your license and registration from the glove box and wait for the officer to approach the car. Today, you are suppose to put your hands on the wheel so they can see you don't have a gun and wait until they ask you for your license instead of having it ready when they come over. Today, you reach into the glove box when they are on there way to the car, you're a dead man. They shoot first and ask questions later. So, as he approached my Jaguar, he first noticed my friend Jack and asked, "What's wrong with your friend? He looks as white as a sheet." I said, "He doesn't like the wind and is feeling ill." "Drivers license and registration please," was the next thing I heard from the lips of Sheriff John. As I was reaching over to get my registration, I asked, "I thought there was no speed limit in Nevada?" He said, "You are right. There is none on the highways." Then why, sir, have you pulled me over? He said, "I will be right back." He was with another officer, and I saw him give my license to him. I guess to run it and see if I am a crook or whatever they check for. Once again, in those days, there were no budget problems in the U.S.A. and especially in Nevada. There was a chicken in every pot two cars in every garage, and two cops in every car. It was much safer that way. The one officer came back and answered my question. He said, "That although there was no speed limit, there was a safety requirement that had to be met to do those high speeds. We are going to check out your automobile to see if it passes our requirements. OK?" Like I had a choice! They asked us to get out of the car and by now the white knuckles on jack's hand had returned to normal, and he was able to unfold his fingers and exit the car. He looked at the officers and said, "Arrest him!" The officers looked perplexed. We were there for twenty minutes if a second. These guys gave my car a better inspection than a Jewish mother checking out a kosher chicken in a market before buying it. They checked the tires for the proper amount of air and worn spots, if any. Then, they got into the car and put on the emergency brake and tried to push it. The regular brakes were tested as well as the temperature of the engine and for scratches on the windshield. They started to check the top, but Jack told them it was fine. They thanked him and checked the side hooks anyway. They checked the car for irregular admissions and excessive smoking and how it handled by turning the wheel from side to side. I am telling you, they gave it one hell of a work over. All said and done, they gave me my license and registration back, wished me luck in Vegas, and said to drive safely and sped off before I got back into the car. I said, "Nice car, heh Jack?" Jack wasn't much into talking. He got into the car, and I kept it under eighty the rest of the way.

 Jack and I did a lot of things together. Sometimes I just forgot I had a wife and a business, in the early days, and Jack just didn't care. He did what he wanted to do, and that was that. Not long after my wife and I had split up (I am talking years later but while I am on the trials and tribulations of my friend, Jack, I might as well throw this in). Jack and

I decided to go to Mexico. Why Mexico I don't know. You know how I Love that place and its people. But we wanted to get some of that cheap lobster and crab we often heard about. This time we got into Jack's mini truck and headed out. (If those people stole my forty-nine Ford, I can't imagine how quickly my Jag would have disappeared.) It was only for a long weekend. Friday, Saturday and head home Sunday or Monday, depending. We got to the border, and Jack insisted on getting insurance in case we have an accident. Like it would do us any good if we had it. On the way to jail we would be yelling, "We have insurance, we have insurance!" but no one would understand our English. So Mister Safe buys the piece of paper that really says sucker in Mexican, and we are ready to proceed into the realm of brown. Again, Jack says, "Wait." "Now what?" I moan. Jack says, "Why don't we get Mexican money before we go over the border so we can wheel and deal better. They might not have change when we buy something and get cheated. (As if Jack was going to spend anything anyway.) We went to the money exchange place. We both gave them a fifty dollar bill, and they gave us a billion dollars back or at least what seemed like a billion. If memory serves me right, I think the exchange rate at that time was a hundred and thirty pesos to one U. S. dollar. I finally realized why Jack was set on changing the money. Instead of having one fifty dollar bill in his pocket, he now has three pockets full of cash. We actually laid out the money on a small grassy mound before going across the border and took pictures of it. It did look like we were millionaires. Now, you may be asking yourself, "What is so special about going to Mexico for a day or two to be put into this book?" Well, I'll tell you. Jack and I drove about four hours past Tijuana and Rosarita Beach and just kept on going much further until we found a place that advertised lobster for four or five dollars or something like that in a little town that was right on the water. The price for the lobster was about the normal price it was in the states, but we were tired. It was getting dark, and we needed a place to stay the night. We went to a couple of hotels to see if we could better the price that we had been told by the first hotel where we stopped. Six dollars for the night, and Jack thought it was too much. We wound up going back to the original hotel at the six buck rate. Paid the six and a gentleman (Poncho villa I think) showed us to the room. He pointed out the two luxurious beds and the bathroom. He showed us that there was a toilet, like there may have been some rooms that didn't have one. He smiled, pointed out the restaurant that we wanted to go to from our bathroom window, then left. Was it the Stardust in Las Vegas? No! Was it a real dump? Yes! It was in Jack's price range and that was all that mattered. I have slept in some pretty strange, unusual as well as just plain bad places, but this one took the prize. The beds, I swear, were made out of sea shells. Not only hard but noisy when you turned while sleeping and they stunk. I kept asking Jack how he liked the beds and he kept saying, "What do you expect for three bucks each." I decided to use the toilet for a few minutes before we went to dinner and closed the door. After a minute or so Jack yelled to me that he was going to go "walk about." That's Chinese for take a hike. Ya think? So, after a couple of minutes, I finished my business and washed my hands. Something I normally don't do, but in this case, I made an exception. The bathroom was very small so I didn't have to move much to open the door. Just turn one half turn. I tried to open the door and it seemed stuck. I pulled and pushed and then pulled again and nothing. The door just wouldn't open. It was about ninety-five degrees in the room. The more I tried to open the door, the hotter it got. I swear I tried for ten minutes and nothing. I had already yelled for Jack even though I knew he was gone for a walk. Then, I had a brilliant idea. Start screaming out the little window and maybe Jack would hear me and go for help. I was up on the third floor which was scary in itself. Who knows what the walls were made of? Paper Mache for all I know. One small tremor and I was a goner. I stared to scream for Jack. I saw no one anywhere. After five minutes I saw a Mexican guy and tried to get him to help me and go get the manager. Can you see me asking a Mexican for help? Even if he did help me can you see me thanking him? Not a chance. So I kept on screaming. Fifteen minutes went by. I heard Jack from the bedroom say, "How long does it take you to take a shit? Christ, Rome was built quicker." If I could have gotten through the door, he would have been a dead man. I told him what was happening so he tried to pull the door open from that side. He was pulling, and I was pushing and nada, nothing. We worked on the door for another couple of minutes. Finally, Jack said he was going to get the manager. Here I was, left alone again, only this time with hope. I had been in this freaking bathroom now for thirty minutes, not including the time I needed it for myself. I really wanted out. Another ten minutes went by. I heard some voices. With my luck it is probably the cops to arrest me for fucking up the bathroom door. I heard Jack explaining the problem. The manager started to work on the door. He and Jack were pulling and I was pushing. He was talking about something and all of a sudden I did not hear any voices. I yelled for Jack and he answered, "What do you want this time?" This time I could have choked him to death if I could have gotten my hands his neck. I started to yell back, "Six dollars huh, six dollars." Where is the manager? Where did he go? Jack said, "He went to get some tools so he can unscrew the bolts and free you." Jesus Christ, how long is this going to take! About now, I have been in this damn toilet for at least an hour, and if it wasn't for the stench, I would be starving by now. Finally, this dildo comes back and starts to unscrew the screws that hold the door on. Finally, I was free. Jack wouldn't look me straight in the eyes. He knew what I was thinking. Murder! I really needed a shower, but I was so hungry, not to mention I was afraid that frogs would come out of the showers holes or something like that, so we just went down to the restaurant and had our lobster. We went for a walk on the beach after. It was getting a little cooler but still quite warm. Midnight came and went. We headed for our luxury suite for a good nights sleep on my coffin made of sea shells. Seven o'clock came and there was a knock on the door. It woke me up. Jack was an early riser and already had his shower. (No frogs!) It was the manager with a bill for the removal of one bathroom door and accompanying labor charge. We both couldn't believe it. Jack came unglued! It had to do with money. I asked to speak with the owner. He said that he was not around. Then, I said, "You need to send the bill to my home because I don't have this much money with me. We are on our way home and need what little money we have for gas." I said, "If you will bring a cop here, I will sign a paper that we will pay for it." Normally, I would have tried to get the hell out of there as quickly as possible, but this is Mexico. Even the women are tough. They screw donkeys. He took my address that I gave him. (Jack's address and Jack never knew.) We were out of there. Jack never heard from anyone. I guess it was just a way to try and fleece some extra money from a couple of jerks. With the exception of a bar where we stopped at sometime later on and saw a dog up on a bar stool bellied up to the bar drinking tequila out of a bowl, all was normal the rest of the way home.

While we are on the subject of Jack right now, I do remember one time that Jack jumped out there with a bet. Jack never had a problem going places where gambling took place and he knew what betting was all about. He just never stepped out and made a wager. No matter with whom he was and where he was and how much one of us tried to get him to bet. To be honest with you, he had more money than the rest of us because of it. But one night, I, with another guy, and Jack went to the harness races at Los Alamitos in Orange County. It was always night racing. This particular evening there was an international handicap race by invitation only. The best harness horses in the world. We went out to watch this great race and make a wager or two. My friend and I are betting each and every race and having a good time. I never bet a lot on harness racing because I was told a lot of them were fixed. I was touting Jack to make a bet on a horse called Superbowl in the feature race. This horse was the favorite and his home track was right here. There was another USA horse in the race but nowhere the credentials that Superbowl had. Superbowl had run eighteen races here and won all of them. Eighteen straight! That's very hard to believe and very difficult to do. But this horse was a super horse. Los Alamitos was a half mile race track and the horses would have to go around twice. That was how far they would normally race. Today, because it was an international race, they made the race one mile and an eighth. Just a little longer than normal for the American horses. I guess that is how far they race overseas, and most of the horses were from there. I was showing Superbowl's race form to Jack. He basically knew how to read a race form. I showed him the eighteen wins in a row. I also told him that Superbowl was such a big favorite that he would win just as much if he bet to show as he would bet to win. That would be even more comfortable for Jack. For you betters and gamblers he was at one to nine as we spoke. In those days the minimum return on your bet was ten percent. Now, I am starting to appeal to Jack's innermost feelings. Ten percent return on his investment in less then two minutes. Jack questioned me, "Are you sure they payout ten percent?" Yep, they do, minimum. "There are ten horses in the race and all Superbowl has to do is run third, right?" Jack said. Hell, he has never lost a race so why would he do it today when there is such a large purse at stake. Even if he blew it and got beat for first and, of course, the unheard of, beat for second and ran third, I still get my ten percent, right?" Right Jack, it's like a sure thing. I knew I was getting to him, way too many questions. Now, I know he will make a bet because I have seen him do it before in Vegas. In fact, I probably should tell you about it.

One time Andy, Jack, I and our wives all went to Las Vegas. The line was very long at the check-in window. So, Jack, Andy and I went to the crap table and left the girls in line to get us checked in. Within ten minutes, both Andy and I were broke. Nothing left. No money! And we now had to tell the girls who were still in the check-in line and take the hit. Well, let me tell you what happened and why Jack was able to lend us the money we needed to stay. It won't take long. When Andy and I were on the crap table losing our asses, Jack was on the same table betting two dollars on the field. (A sucker bet as any self respecting dice throwing gambling sicko will tell you.) Jack put two dollars on the field and practically turned white from fear as it was such a large bet for him. The number twelve came up. Jack thought he had lost because he was harassing Andy and me about us being losers and not paying attention to the game. Jack said, "I will double up and catch up." He threw a five on the field not knowing he all ready had six dollars from the previous win. Then, just before the roll of the dice, he yelled, "No, wait; put it on the eleven instead." The dealer moved the whole eleven dollars to the eleven. The eleven came out and Jack won but started to harass Andy again because he lost again. The dealer rushed the dice thrower so Jack didn't have time to take his money off the eleven, figuring that way he would be a loser and give back the money he just won. Jack really got upset, but it was too late. The roll came out, eleven again. Jack went from really being upset with the stick man to yelling, "Give me my money, take it down, and that'll teach you for rushing me." In a very short time, Jack turned two bucks into six and then added five which made eleven. The eleven turned into one hundred and sixty-five (I don't think jack really realized how much he had bet this time.) The one sixty-five turned into twenty-four hundred and seventy-five dollars, just about by accident in just three rolls of the dice. It was all we could do to keep him there for the weekend. He wanted to take Jean (his wife) and go home to put the money in the savings account. We said, "Tip the dealer and let's get out of here." Jack's response was, "Tip who? I don't even know him." So, Andy and I borrowed some money from Jack (At a special low rate of interest. What a friend), and never had to tell the girls what had happened. The trip went well. Now, where was I?

Oh yea. So, the horses came out as they normally do for what is called, "The Post Parade". The horses strut in front of you for about ten minutes so you can look at them up close and personal, not to mention they loosen up as well. Jack said, "Are you going to bet him?" I said, "Does a bear shit in the woods? But not for show. I will bet him to win just in case the odds go up a little before the race starts. That way I will make a small amount more. I went to the window and dumped a bunch on him. Jack just watched and watched and watched. One minute to race time and Jack started to walk towards the window. Remember, I told you that Jack liked to carry a wad of cash, not to spend but to flash it. He did have a bunch on him. He made his move and reached into his pocket where he kept, what he called the vault, turned towards the window a second later, turned and put something into his pocket, put his wallet away and walked towards me. I said, "Did you bet him?" He said, "Yes." I said, "How much?" Just about then the race was on. Superbowl was a front runner and just as normal, he went to the front, a length ahead and now two. A half a mile under his belt and he was in front by six lengths and still running easily. He started to stretch his lead, now in front by eight and now eleven. Eleven Jack, eleven, as I smacked him on the back! I looked at Jack turn and he was headed towards the betting window to be the first one to cash his ticket before the track ran out of money from all the winners. The horses turned for home with just an eighth of a mile to go. Superbowl at this point was in front by eight and should have been able to cruise home and win by that much if not more. But wait (I think Billie Mays used to say that a lot. I'd explain who he was, but we are in the middle of a horse race here.) Superbowl quit running. Just quit. Quit!!! Stopped in the middle of the track, I tell you, just stopped. Every single horse went past him except for one, the other USA horse that was in the race. What could have happened? What?? I'll tell you what happened. He and the other USA horse had run so many one mile races and knew nothing else, just a mile race. When Superbowl got to the mile marker, he thought it was all over and done with and had won the race. Wrong! The only other time I have ever seen or heard of such a thing was some old jockey named Bill (Willie) Shoemaker. He stood up in the saddle in a major stakes race because he thought he had hit the wire but was about a hundred feet short, just like a horse I knew. Bill, I heard, got many more chances, but I never heard from Superbowl again. Not the same from Jack. He came unglued. I thought he had rabies or something. I didn't do it, Jack, I swear I didn't. We all thought he would win, honestly, we did. There was no stopping him. He was yelling and screaming, swearing and throwing stuff and kicking trash on the ground. All I could think of was that I had to ride back home with him. Now, I never found out how much he had bet on Superbowl. But knowing Jack and how he is normally, I would have guessed maybe twenty bucks to show. Not to take away the possibility it could have been much, much more however, if it had been, I think he would have gone to look for the horse and killed him. Believe me, all of what you have just read is true, and like this entire book, all is the truth. Just sometimes, it is hard for me to believe some of it. Next!

As I had mentioned in the past, I had that beautiful nineteen sixty-eight XKE Jaguar roadster. You know, the white fingers Jack car. The cop special! The lady stopper! Well, I had a guy who wanted to trade me for it. This was like asking me to cut off my right hand. But being a Jew, everything I own is for sale at the right price. I asked him, "What do you want to trade for it?" He said, "An XKE roadster." "Am I looking into a mirror here? *What* are you talking about?" He said, "I have a nineteen seventy-seven twelve cylinder I do not like. It's too expensive, too big, and I think the sixty-eight you have is much sexier looking. I am willing to trade you straight across." Well, I Love my little car and would have a real problem getting rid of it, but dollar for dollar, I think I am getting a hell of a deal. I checked out the dollar value. I would be about seven thousand better at that time. I told him I need to have it checked out and if all was ok, it was a deal. So it is written and so it will be done! I now own a bigger and faster and more expensive and newer Jaguar than I had. This thing had twelve cylinders and couldn't wait to take Jack to Vegas with me. No speed limit! About six months went by and my new Jag was in need of a tune up. I went to my regular foreign car mechanic and asked him how much and how soon it would be? He looked it up and told me twelve hundred dollars and about six months. I thought he was joking. I said, "Come on, how much and how soon?" He said, "Twelve hundred and six months. Do you want me to put you on the waiting list?" I said, "You're kidding, right?" He said, "No." I put my name on the list and walked away. Three days later I was thinking. Actually, I hadn't been thinking. I was actually talking to myself. I said to myself, "Self, are you Jewish or not?" I answered, "Yep!" If you put two and two together, you can see this guy has a goldmine here with this foreign car shit. How about you get a piece of it? I answered like a guy from the show "Laugh In" (never mind kids.) Why not! I followed the guy who usually does my work on my old Jag out to his car after work one day. I asked him if he would like to own his own shop some day. He said, "It would be nice, but it takes a lot of money. But in ten years or so it will happen." I said, "How about now if you had the chance?" He said, "Who do I have to kill?" I told him seventy-thirty my way, but he gets the same salary he is getting at the shop where he works at, and he uses he tools. We only buy what we need and that you don't already own. We shook hands but before I let go of his hand, I said, "There is a catch." He said, "What?" The first car you work on is mine and at no charge except for parts and they come out of the business. He said, "Deal." He gave notice and in three weeks I had secured a garage, drawn up the contract, had the lights on and were ready for business. (Sounds just like the way I opened up Pacific Cable. Not looking to start another business, it just happened.) Now, as luck would have it, the day we opened the doors we were busy and got backed up. Being Jewish, I put my Jag on the back burner in place of making an immediate profit. Believe it or not, six months later I got my tune up. A year later I caught my partner helping himself to side jobs on his own and pocking the loot. Thus ended a very profitable relationship. I might have kept doing it by myself as I had auto shop in high school. But the thought of a Jewish guy getting his hands dirty just wasn't for me. Anyway, I could have not found the time. I was still going to the races just about every day and Vegas, often. In fact by now, I had established a credit line in ten casinos for ten grand each. I was becoming a big time player and mostly losing my butt, only I didn't realize it. It was kind of creeping up on me.

Cal the bookie had asked me to work for him a little bit, like I needed something else to do in my life. It had to be somewhere around nineteen eighty, around mid summer. He wanted me to hand out football betting cards. They were a big profit maker for bookies. I would get thirty percent of what the bookie made. All I had to do was hand out the little cards in the begging of the week, Tuesday and Wednesday, and then at the end of the week, Friday, go and see the guys that I gave them to and pick up the money they wanted to wager on the football games that week. I started to make a bunch of money. Like I needed more. Cal even let me work the phones in his office part time. I would take bets on the games, write them down on a scratch pad say thanks and hang up and get another line. Cal would yell at me when he heard me say thank you, but that just came natural to me. The more I made, no matter how I made it, the more I gambled. It was just in one ear and out the other. This money was tax free by the way. (I am sure the IRS will never read this book. Hell, even Al Capone got caught.) After the football season was over, I gave some thought to going into the bookie business myself. I could work out of the house on weekends.

There was a guy named Frank. He had been stopping in Brigham's kind of regular lately. We'd see him mostly in the afternoon. Norm got friendly with him and found out he had just retired and bought an automobile generator and starter rebuilding company. Just to keep his hands in something. He was only forty or so. He would go into work, see that every one showed up, screw around a little bit, and head for lunch at Norm's place. This guy was very much like Jack. No gambling, tight with the money but did have a weakness. The opposite sex! Speaking of weaknesses, among the many things I had learned from Cal, who I think never got past the eighth grade was, if you can find a person's weakness, you have him for life. So, our Norm found franks, women. Now I know Frank really doesn't fit into the big picture with our little gambling group, as we had women occasionally by some goofy luck, but never went looking for them. They only got in the way of our gambling, but Frank had something Norm wanted. I didn't even find out until Frank got really friendly later on. Frank was a pilot and had his own little airplane. A Cessna one seventy-two, four seater! Hmmmm, airplane! You mean like one that can make it to Las Vegas at any time you want to go and don't have to make a reservation or stand in line and wait forever. That kind of an airplane? So, we all started to buy Frank's food at Brigham's and try to convince him that Las Vegas was a place with so many women that he could not be able to make a choice if they were throwing themselves at him. But we were bucking a lot of problems. He does not gamble, and he is tight. So we made a deal with him. We pay for all the gas and will get him hooker for an hour, but he has to wait for us even if we want to stay for five or six hours. Frank thought about it for eight seconds and said any hooker I want? Anyone, Frank. You the man! So, we gassed up and Frank, Norm and I were the first to make the trip. We left at nine pm and were back at three am. Total cost, gas one hundred two dollars, food twelve dollars, hooker, fifty dollars; profit or loss, down three grand. BUT FUN! This became a regular habit. It didn't matter, morning, noon or night. When someone wanted to go, we went. It got to be so often that Frank taught me how to fly the plane. But I stunk. You have to stay in-between a certain flight plan called the VIR that has a twenty mile variance. Frank would start me in the middle so I would have ten miles on both sides of the plane. I could not keep it in that twenty mile lane. I would fly out on one side or the other. (I never could stay inside the lines. Ask Arnold!) However, Frank was a good pilot but every once in a while, he would unsuspectingly put us into a nose dive. Scary, you bet! I would be yelling pull up, and Frank would be having a great time scaring the crap out of me. Just about puke time he would pull up. He did this often. It never was fun or funny, just scary and pukish. However, on one flight, I finally got back at him. I may have mentioned that his aircraft had a wheel in both front seats. We were flying at about six hundred million miles above sea level (or there about), and Frank does his thing. We headed into a nose dive at mock fifty. My lips were in back of my ears. My nose was blocking the airway in my throat. Eyes reversed and tongue somewhere on the floor. With what was left of my vision, I spotted Frank changing the position of his hands on the wheel to pull up. As he started to pull up on the wheel, I barely put my thumb on it, on my side, and kept him from pulling up. I am sixty-eight years old as I write this part. I have never in all my years seen such panic and terror on the face of anyone in my life. It only lasted a few seconds but I Loved it. I don't remember ever nose diving again.

Now to change the subject a little, my daughter, Holly, was coming home from school one day. There was the proverbial short cut through the woods. I think we've all seen this on T. V. at one time or another. She was about thirteen or so. As the story goes, according to her, she saw a gallon jug of something lying up against a tree. She tried it and drank most of it. (Kids will be kids). By the time she wobbled home, she was wasted. Drunk on her ass! Incoherent! A combination of laughing her ass off, drunk as a skunk, and sick as a human can be. We asked her what she had drank and could not get a decent reasonable answer out of her that Heather and I could believe. We took her to the hospital and had her stomach pumped. We just could not take the chance not knowing what she drank. We explained all to the doctor and he agreed. She thought she was in bad shape the way she was until she had her stomach pumped. That was a killer. Hard to believe, Holly never drank to excess again.

Later on, in just a few years, Holly got very close to and involved with a girl friend name Bugsy. She was having a really bad time at home. I am really not sure what was going on but it obviously wasn't good. Holly and Bugsy were friends for quite a long time. Why Heather and I didn't notice it was beyond me, but Holly's personally was changing. The closeness got so great between Bugsy and Holly that Holly (in her mind) became Bugsy and was having a major problem handling Bugsy's situation. It's funny how in such a major situation I can't remember who found her and who called whom, but Holly had taken a bunch of pills and tried to commit suicide. She was found unconscious and rushed to the hospital. The doctor informed us that the pills she took, if she was to live, would have a major affect on her brain. It is possible that she may never be the same as she was. The fear, the helplessness, the anxiety, the wondering of what we have done (at this point not knowing it was the involvement with Bugsy) being absolutely scared to death of what will happen or how it would turn out. In two days, as luck would have it, she pulled through the death part. We were so thankful for that. It was a waiting game to see if she would be a vegetable or whatever. As the good lord would have it, she returned to us as good as new. Not only as good as new, but she has rivaled her mother, in the realm of Mensa.

While we are on the path of suicide, not long after Holly's attempt, Heather decided to do the same. I just don't know what is or was going on, but I started wondering if it was me that was going on. Heather, I believe, about three years later took a bunch of pills. I found her on the bed, out! I called the paramedics and they rushed her to the hospital. Fortunately, she hadn't taken enough to do herself in. She had taken enough to certainly let me know that something was wrong. What I didn't know, as the person I was then, was that i probably didn't try to figure it out or even recognize that there was a problem.

Now, all of this with Heather was probably not me alone. David, our oldest son, was becoming more of a major problem. He started as a child of maybe two. You know, the terrible two's. We at that time disregarded it. But he would, in his walker, go over to lamps and just knock them over and stuff like that. As he progressed to school age, he would beat up on the others and so on. You've heard this before. Not unusual. It was that David was just a little different than the run of the mill ruffian. As he got older, things got worse and then a lot worse. One day, I think David was about twelve or thirteen, I came home from work and Heather said, "Sit down." She said to me that some doctor's wife had come over and told her that David had gotten their daughter pregnant. They were not going to do anything about it, but thought we should know. To this day, I have no idea if any of it was true. If it was true, did the girl have an abortion or does David have a kid walking around with no father? I let Heather handle it. Not because she would be better at it, but I couldn't. I, to this day, don't know if Heather even told David about it. The bottom line is that nothing was ever brought up about it at any time again. This was just the start of my David.

In the late seventies or so, Heather's cousin came to the U.S.A. from Australia. Job related, I think he worked for a big cement company. I believe it was the same one that Vice President Chaney was involved with. He, Heather's cousin, (I can't remember his name right now) and his wife and their very young children were all on the way for about three or four months. They were here in the U.S.A for a few weeks or so and after they got settled in, they came to visit us for a long weekend. They came in a huge Winnebago. It had all the tricks and toys you would want. It was better equipped than my home. At that time I was living in a twenty-three hundred square foot, five bedroom three bath house, in Alta Loma. I believed I had mentioned it before. In fact, we had just recently moved in ourselves. We had made the first couple of payments, and the builder went broke. For the next six or seven months we did not have to pay the house payment. There was no one to make it to. When the shit hit the fan between the builder and, I guess the bank, we had to scram out of there in a month and that was not fun, but definitely worth the savings. I guess the cousins were living in the Winnebago and kept it in a R.V. park somewhere. They were only going to be here until the job was finished. They had a very young child who never stopped crying or yelling from the minute they arrived until the second they left some four days later. Most of their waking hours, the cousins spent their time in our home. Both Heather and I couldn't wait until they left. Now, I know you are saying to yourself, self, we all have had something like that happen in our lives so what is so different or unusual about it? As you must know by now, with the exception of setting up of a situation to describe another one, you probably have never been in any of these situations or even heard of someone that has. That's what makes me different than others and being able to write this book. We will skip forward about four or five months. Heather's cousin's work is now completed. It's time to go home to Australia, taking screaming Mimi and the rest of the family with. God bless Australia. They call and say they would like to see us before they leave. I gave argument but Heather being Heather (little miss goody goody) said sure, not a problem. In a few days or so, in walk the Aussies, Winnebago and all. They spent a couple of days with us again, and the screamer lived up to his or her reputation. The couple of days spent were pleasant as they actually were nice people (except for you know who.) He told us that the Winnebago had been paid for in advance for another few months (or at least that is what I remember) or so and if we'd drive them to the airport, we could have it as they obviously won't be needing it anymore. This sounded great (with the exception of being stuck in a car with you know who), and I, of course, said OK. I had plenty of room to park it at one of my company's parking lot, Pacific Cable Corp. We took them to the airport and drove home. The next few months we used the Winnebago at least twice a month. We went to Bishop, Big Bear, Mammoth and Palm Springs just to name a few. One day, when I was at work, (rare) Heather called me and said there were two men at the door that were looking for Lloyd, (now that I think about it his name may have been Lloyd but don't bet on it) and the Winnebago. They told her that he was back on the payments about four months. He had given Heather's name and address as a contact when he rented it. I immediately went home. Heather for some reason told them nothing. Not like her but maybe she was learning something from me after being married to me for years. I got home in ten minutes.

Heather and the two guys in suits were having coffee. They asked me a bunch of questions about Lloyd and the motor home. I told them that we had taken them to the airport some four months ago, and they never mentioned anything about a Winnebago. They were polite but in a round about way were firm as to what could happen to anyone that was harboring them or the motor home. They gave us their cards and left. It could not have been two seconds after the door shut behind them that Heather broke out in major tears and frantically screaming, "We are going to jail and the kids will starve to death." "Starve to death, what are you talking about?" I said. She couldn't talk. The tears were flowing so much and the tormented expression on her face meant I better do something about it and soon. I finally calmed her down and said, "I will handle it, now! Don't worry." Fortunately, the R. V. was parked at my office, but I figured it wouldn't be long until they figured out where that was. I didn't want to leave right then and there because they might be hanging around waiting to follow me. I called Cal the bookie and asked him to meet me at Brigham's restaurant to have a cup of coffee with me. If they were lurking around, it would look like there was no problem or anxiousness with me. Cal met me, and we hung around for a couple of hours. During that time I called Heather a few times to make sure she was ok. I went home and had dinner. I called Robert, my warehouse man, who worked for me at Pacific Cable and asked him to meet me very early the next morning at the office. He usually came in about eight, but I asked him to meet me at five. He said no problem. I got up early and triple s'ed (shit, shaved and showered) left the house, drove around for a half hour or so, and finally made my way to the office being careful that I was not followed. Robert was there and I told him what had happened. I told him to get a friend, follow him, drive the Winnebago to the Mojave Desert, and drive it into the sand as far as he could drive without looking suspicious. Do the best to wipe all of the fingerprints off of everything, leave the keys in the ignition, get the hell out of there as quickly as possible, and there will be a nice bonus waiting for him when he gets back. So it is written and so it will be done! Robert returned late in the day and said, "Boss, it all went well, but I had to give my friend twenty-five dollars out of my pocket." I said, "Good job" and handed Robert three hundred bucks. That's when the expression, "Show me your pearly whites" started, I think. I went home and told Heather that all was well and not to worry. She smiled a little and left the room. About two or three weeks later we did get another call asking if we had heard anything from the Aussie's and of course told them no. That was the last we ever heard. Not sure whatever happened to the Winnebago, but I do believe Heather wrote to the Aussie's and gave them a piece of her mind.

Soon after that episode we had to move out of the free house and bought a brand new home in Cucamonga. Yes there is a Cucamonga! When we moved there, it was just Cucamonga, but not long after, the city fathers chose to merge three cities, Alta Loma, Quasti and Cucamonga and called it, "Rancho Cucamonga". Why they did it was not my business, but if I had a voice in it, my guess would be that, that way there was only one stupid name for a city and not two. I really Loved our home. Heather and I did a lot of things to it. We built a huge barbecue and made it look like a wishing well. It had three hundred and sixty-four welds on the grill. It had three different cooking areas, could cook twelve full chickens at once, and an area that was just for a large flame that was used for marshmallow roasting or a romantic setting after the kids went to bed. I designed the cement patio that was kind of circular and huge, with strategic holes placed in it for tree or shrub planting. The backyard was my favorite place to be. After all these years, I still Love backyards. I even wrote a poem about one, my old one, that was not mine anymore.

However, I was told recently that they divided them back to the three original cities. Why they did it was not my business, but if I had a voice in it, my guess I would be that Rancho Cucamonga is too long and hindered the official stationery when writing legal stuff.

Now we are in a new house, and things are still going pretty good for me. Businesses were making money. Our bowling team was still hanging in, and summer was only a few months away. The only things that were not good were my gambling and David's behavior. They both were getting worse and, in fact, out of control. I remember one evening (probably after a large gambling loss) I walked into David's bedroom and saw at least twenty dirty dishes from the week all around the room. It made me sick. I saw partial marijuana joints all over and bugs crawling around. He was just laying there watching T. V. I told him to get the room cleaned up and now. Everything clean and don't stop until it was finished. He just turned and looked up at me with some shit-eating look and a dare in his eyes, then turned away and didn't move. If this had been the only thing that had happened, I probably would have handled it a little differently. There were so many things that had happened and led up to it in the recent past, like cutting school, beating up on others at school when he did attend, not being a part of the family functions, dumping a beer in Sean's (our youngest son) fish tank just to do it and killing all of his fish. Even one night when Heather and I were at the bowling alley, we got a call from the police that David was up in the attic and was threatening to kill himself with a razor blade if they didn't leave him alone. At that point, alone, I couldn't handle anymore and asked Heather if she would go home and try to take care of it. She did. I stayed and bowled like there was nothing happening. I don't know if I ever thanked her for that, but if she is reading this book, I would like to thank her now for being so strong. How the police knew he was in our attic and or what he had done to get the police at our house, was and still is a mystery to me. All of these things and more that I need not elaborate on had built up in me. I picked up the T. V. that he was watching and threw it at him. He just blocked it from hitting him which, of course, now I am glad. I took off my belt and unleashed a beating that as I had mentioned in the front of this book, lasted for I don't know how long. It seemed like fifteen minutes. One thing I do remember as I was beating him with the belt, and I guess, waiting for some response from him. Somewhere in the middle he turned his head and looked at me with this look, like he was the devil, or I was. That look will stay with me until I die. He was six foot three inches and over two hundred pounds at that time and still growing. He just laid there until I was done. Never a whimper or a cry was heard. I was sick to my stomach for a week, and I think I lost five pounds. Today, if I could take it back, I would. He did deserve the reprimand, but I could have been more human and fatherly about it.

Chapter Eighteen

Heather and I talked about doing something with the family that might bring us a little closer to David and with the kids, in general. Holly was growing up fast, and you never knew how soon she would be leaving and going into the world to seek her fame and fortune. So, we decided to take a trip. Not a normal trip, but a Chuck-type trip. Heather and I took painstaking time and planned this great trip. I was going to close Pacific Cable for the summer as soon as school was out. We were going to travel the United States. I would pay my secretary to stay there and answer the phones and let any customer that called know that we were not out of business but just closed for the summer. The Water Bed stores could run themselves as I had a manager that was quite capable of doing what had to be done. Would I lose a lot of money doing this? Yes, but it had to be done. So, we laid out the plan to the kids. Sean was elated. Holly was ok with it, but she had a boyfriend that she would not see for a couple of months. David thought it was terrible. He was probably thinking that he could not get into trouble for a while. No drugs! No alcohol! No way! This trip was going to start the week that school let out. I made all the business arrangements I could in advance. Heather paid all the bills in advance so that they didn't take our house back while we were gone.

I gave the kids the best thing to do while they anticipated the trip. I asked them to pick ten places that they heard of or wanted to go to or see as we drove across country. They all gave me fifteen. I went to AAA and got a trip-tik that hooked up all the points of interest, starting out with a southern route, and going back with a northern route, as one long drive up and back. I promised my a fore-mentioned cousins, Sandy and Arnold, that we would like to stay with them for a couple of weeks or so before we turned around and headed back through the northern route home. The trip looked like we were going to spend about nine to eleven weeks on the road, including the two or so with the cousins. The distance from the west coast to the east coast and back is approximately fifty-two hundred miles round trip. Our trip was twelve thousand, give or take. I had my Jaguar for my personal use and a family car for Heather, a Gremlin or something like that, but no way were we going to travel twelve thousand miles in that. I needed to get a large car or even a van. As it turned out, one of my friends owned a van conversion company that was real big in the seventies and eighties along with C.B. radios. I went over to his shop and told him what I was doing in a month or two. He said he had a new Ford that he used as a demo that he could let me have for cheap. It had three thousand miles on it and was equipped with four captain chairs, two in front and two right behind them, a table that the captain chairs swiveled around to and a rear air conditioner as well as a rear bench seat that unfolded to a bed. It also had curtains all around and cup holders in every place that there was a place. It even had extra lighting inside so you had plenty of light at night if you needed it and a luggage rack on top for clothes trunks to make sure there was plenty of room inside to stretch when you needed to. I asked him if he could install a coffee maker in front. "Not a problem," he retorted. That was a done deal. I even asked him to buy and install a C. B. radio which he did. The only thing left to do was for Heather to work on clothes for the trip. Let's see, shorts and tee shirts should do it. Well, close anyway. We all got together and agreed on a handle for the C. B. radio. You had to have a registered handle (name) with the FCC as I remember correctly. The Ford van I bought was a big square green looking box-type van. The handle became, "Green Box."

At some point in time, I had wondered from time to time if I was doing the right thing. Closing businesses, kind of forcing the kids to do something out of their norm, and a thing or two like that that came into my head on an occasion or two. I was rewarded with the conformation I needed, by a huge firework show just prior to leaving. I took it as a yes; go for it, from the good Lord above. It was called Mt. St. Helens in May. I decided to include it on one of our stops on the way home. So, with that conformation, I was ready. I think I was about thirty-eight or thereabouts and about to age ten years in twenty-four hours. All was a go. Heather and I decided to leave at night and drive straight through the desert when it was a little cooler. Heather and Holly are very fair skinned and didn't handle heat very well. And no way was I to do the puke, cop thing again. There was nothing to see on the first leg of our trip anyway, so, it was no big deal. (I could have said, "tzores", but I would have had to go through, I am sure, a Hebrew lesson again.) We packed and strapped the entire luggage on top of the van and all the food and drinks inside. At seven o'clock or so I put the key in the slot, turned on the engine, and the Griswolds were off to Wally World.

But wait; in all of our excitement, we were leaving without David. He was yet to get into the car. I sent Sean in the house to get him. Sean came out saying, "He's not there." What do you mean, he's not there? I got out and went in myself and looked for him. I couldn't find him either. We all got out and searched the whole house, closets, garage, attic, under the beds, and left no place untouched. He was gone, just gone. How could he do this? He was disappointing the whole family. We waited for hours and hours and called all of his known friends. No one had a clue where he was. It's now midnight, and we started to call the hospital and police stations. No David. It was like he disappeared. We knew he didn't want to go with us but I didn't think it would ever come to this. Holly and Sean said let's just go without him. Heather and I said we couldn't. He's only fourteen and has no money for food. It's against the law to just leave a juvenile. Not to mention he's our son, we just can't leave without him. Christ, what to do! Heather couldn't stop crying and the kids making their loud mouth statements. He's not worth us losing this long planned great vacation. Let's just go! Let's go!

After a long and exhausting night, we all agreed that we needed to sacrifice one for the good of the all. Sun coming up and no sleep, facing the heat of the desert in front of us, we left. I started to drive. To get where we were going we had to go through San Bernardino. That was about twenty-five miles from our house and I have driven it many times to go elsewhere. Sun barely up, no sleep and a tear in my eye, I got lost. We drove for an hour or so with Heather saying you need to turn here or turn there. I, of course, being the ultimate driver that I was, I just kept looking at the map as I ignored her and kept getting more lost until Heather said, "No" and yelled to me, "Give me the fucken map, and from now on I will tell you where to turn and when to go, got it?" So it is written and so it will be done! We, in the whole twelve thousand miles of our trip, never got lost again. Women!

If I would tell you about everything that went on during our adventure, I would be writing until two thousand and forty. However, there are some things that have to go on the books. One thing that sticks out in my mind was when we finally got to El Paso, Texas. There was a hell hole! We checked into a motel with a swimming pool. The kids were in heaven. We let them swim a bit while we took a shower to get the sticky off our bodies. Heather and I were getting hungry so we rounded up the kids (note the cowboy talk) and made for the restaurant at the motel. We went in. There were a few tables that were attended by others so we figured we were not going to be poisoned. The hostess seated us, and a waitress came over and asked something. She was speaking in Mexican, and we had no idea what she was asking. I said, "Agua" and pointed to all four of us. She smiled and left. We perused the menu and noticed that the prices were very inexpensive. Very! It was like the old saying, "Where a dollar is still a dollar." I happened to look out the window and saw donkeys along with some cows grazing. Some chickens and a sheep or two. The waitress came with our water and stood there waiting for our order. When we left the house and was talking as we drove, I said to all, "No matter what you want as far as food goes, you can have whatever you want because this is a vacation. You should be able to experience the different foods all over the U. S A. Just try to eat what you order." Sean never had shrimp before in his short-lived life and ordered an appetizer of shrimp along with his pasta. Don't remember what Holly ordered but as Sean did, pointed to something on the menu. Heather and I both pointed to the steak. The words, "How would you like it?" never came out. We both figured what we get we eat. Sean got his shrimp and from that day on, he never passed up the opportunity to have his shrimp, if it was on the menu. He was like a whale to krill. Our steak arrived. Heather looked at me and I looked at her. We both tasted our steaks and then looked at each other again while trying to swallow. This may have been a city where a dollar is still a dollar, but a steak was definitely a burrow, or worse. I kept looking out the window and trying to figure out which one of the animals out there was the relative of what we were trying to eat. Did you ever sit down with friends or family and something struck you funny and every time you looked at each other you would laugh and laugh and laugh and couldn't stop? That's what happened to Heather and me. The kids didn't understand what was happening but after a while, they joined in. I think we laughed for a half hour. Maybe it was Heather's and my way, subconsciously, of letting out some of the pain because of what David did or maybe what Heather and I did by leaving him behind.

We woke up and continued on the trek of a life time. We got up early and put on coffee pot. (In the car) We were in the car at six and ready to roll to our next adventure. Although we hit many interesting places, they are the things that everyone hits while on a trip. I think it is just how you as an individual sees and enjoys them. However, one place that will stick in my mine forever was New Orleans. First of all, we were told, if we stop there, don't miss a place called Brenigan's for breakfast. Through the whole trip we never made a reservation to sleep somewhere. My thinking was if we had to be someplace at a certain time, we might have to miss something that we may never get the chance to see again. If worse comes to worse, we could sleep in the van. So, as luck would have it, there wasn't a place to stay downtown anywhere. However, I stopped at the last place on Bourbon Street. The lady at the desk told me she was sorry but they were all sold out. Begrudgingly, I turned slowly and started to walk out when I heard her say, "Sir, I do have one suite left, but that's all." I said, "How much?" Now, let me set the stage for you. As I had walked into this hotel, I was kind of hoping that there were no rooms available. There were beautiful cotton curtains draped everywhere from floor to ceiling. All the men were in tuxedos, and all the ladies were in beautiful long white gowns that went to their shoes and they wore their hair up and heads back. There were full-grown trees, and I mean a bunch of them, growing in the entrée way and at the check-in desk area and all through the hall ways. I know in my mind I said to myself, "I will pay what I have to on this trip", but there is a drawing line. She kind of looked at me and, with her head hung a little low, whispered (now, don't hold me to this as it has been a long time) eighteen dollars. I almost passed out! "Eighteen dollars" I repeated, "For a suite? Eighteen dollars?" The very next thing out of my mouth was, "I'll take it and do you take credit cards?" The desk lady asked if we needed help with our luggage. I told her, "No, but do you have a dining room where we could eat?" She pointed to a, beautiful elegant, linen-covered tables, with real silverware, crystal-laden glasses, dining room. I said, "That won't work." We are all in shorts and tank tops and very dirty from our road trip. Maybe something a little simpler would be better?" She said, "That's not a problem. Many of our guests are just like you, and we have no problem with it. Enjoy!" I went out and got Heather and the kids. We stuffed a bunch of clean clothes in one suitcase and had a guy park the car. From the looks of that area, he may have had to drive back to California to park. I told Heather we lucked out and got the last room they had, but it was suite. Heather looked at me with that look only a wife could have as to say, "Are we broke now?" I said, "No, I negotiated a great price so don't worry. It was their last room." Once again, the hero and proof that a little white lie here and there doesn't hurt!

We started to walk up to our room as it hits me. Just because it was a suite doesn't mean that it is a beautiful-looking suite. Then I gave thought to the whole hotel itself and again, I smiled. We opened the door and walked in. One look and we knew we were in the wrong room. I immediately called to the front desk and asked them what my room number was. The desk lady confirmed we were in the right room. She said that the owner of the hotel was supposed to use it today, but she had just called and said that the storm in Corpus Cristi had stopped, and she would not be coming up. That's when I called you back and offered you her suite. I said, "Thanks" and hung up. This room was as big as my house, well, almost and much more beautiful. There was a bouquet as big as a Volkswagen on the center table. Heather walked over to it and read the card. It read, "Hope you have a wonderful stay with us, Mrs. Helmsly." It was a hotel that Leona Helmsly owned. Go figure! But with my lifestyle and hers, not a surprise! What do they say? Great minds think alike. So I remembered that Heather and the kids were hungry, and I was starving myself. We washed our faces and combed our hair and headed to the dining room for a burger or two, if they even serve them there. We walked down and passed twenty thousand waiters and waitresses dressed as I mentioned before. A ton of trees that made me keep an eye out for dogs! You would have thought I was at a presidential wedding. I walked up to the front desk and asked for a table for four. The Maitre d' said, "It would be about an hour and a half." I was decimated. I said, "Nothing in a dark corner or outside on the street?" He said, "I'm sorry. Shall I put your name on the waiting list?" I was thinking, we are not waiting an hour and a half, but just in case, I said, "Yes", and gave it to him and said our room number. He said, "You are a guest at our fine hotel?" I said, "Yes." He said, "Right this way sir." We looked like paupers and sat amongst all the elegance. It was not as bad as I would have thought. There were others who looked as bad as us. We finished dinner and I asked the waiter if he had heard about a place called "Brennigan's?" He said, "Yes it is a fine restaurant" and told us how to get there. We left, bellies full, and a smile on all our faces. We started to walk to Brennigan's, the place where my friend told me to have breakfast. We figured we would eat there in the morning before we hit the road. We did find it. It was closed as it was only open for breakfast and lunch. But the breakfast menu was posted in the window. Coffee $7.50, toast $6.50, two eggs 18.95 and so on. Obviously, my friend had played a joke on us. Needless to say, we ate on the road as usual. However, on the way back to our room, a bat, as in A BAT, flew into Heather's hair and got caught in it. It was a good thing that Heather went number two in the room before we went to dinner. I am talking, panic, panic, panic! Sean crackin up, and Holly looking all around to make sure none were diving at her. All the while, Heather was crying and dying and screaming. I shooe shooed the bat away, and we ran to the hotel for a good night's sleep. Now, what do you think about New Orleans?

There was another stop somewhere in the southern states, (Virginia, Georgia, wherever) that was a little old converted house, where we stopped for breakfast. I remember it well. I paid a buck twenty-nine for a ham steak, grits, toast, coffee, and a muffin to go. The whole meal in itself was great, and the price was worth more than a dollar and change. The ham steak was then and still to this day, the best ham steak I have ever had. In fact, I thought about it a lot. To the extent that I gave thought, but not a lot, that, was it a four legged animal I had eaten? They say that,,,, *well never mind.*

We headed on to Philadelphia where my cousins lived and as before, hitting place after place that was on the list. At that point, the only place we missed that was on our list to see was the Blue Ridge Mountains. When we got there, there was so much rain that the roads were closed and had to take a round about detour and missed them completely. But when we got to, I think West Virginia; we stopped in Williamsburg and then went on to the Smithsonian Institute and the Reflecting Pond, the Treasury, and a few other places in Washington D. C. When we went through the Treasury, there were signs everywhere that read, "Absolutely no photographs or filming." Guess what? I put my video camera about my stomach level and walked through the whole place filming it all! I still have the pictures. Once again, I beat the system. Even my wife and kids didn't know I was filming. However, later on, I don't remember what building it was, but I was still taking still shots of pictures on the walls and got caught and was kicked out. Hell, I didn't even use a flash!

It was on to the cousins in Philadelphia or was it New Jersey? I don't think there is a difference anyway, is there? Bruce Willis might! Pretty much was as you would think, visiting relatives with the exception of going to New York. Now, there is a place that taught the Mexicans in Tijuana how to drive. Maybe the Asians as well! We went to New York with all intentions of seeing the Empire State Building and the bitch in the water with the fire in her hand. Some people call her the "Statue of Liberty." Well, let me tell you. We left Philadelphia and drove directly to New York with my two cousins and their youngest daughter, Marla. Marla was about one then. Great kid, but ugly! Their three other hooligans, Pam, Elaina, and Tara went also. (By the way, Marla is getting married in October two thousand ten. My brother and I are going to the wedding. It will be held in Caesars Palace at Atlantic City, New Jersey on a brand new pier overlooking the water. How could I not go! This has nothing to do with my book but sometimes you just have to get in a plug for the family. And by the way, she is much more beautiful now then when she was a baby.)

We got to New York and started driving around looking for a parking place. There were places available but not for vans. Every place we went there were signs reading "NO VANS." Not sure why, and I was surprised because you never see anything like that in California. Not to mention the parking places for cars in the car lots were priced ridiculous. They were like five or six bucks an hour with a minimum of four hours or something like that. Remember, this was back in the early eighties. We drove around, literally, for over an hour looking for a parking space. Finally, I made my move. I pulled into a parking lot that read "NO VANS" and said to the attendant, "Why can't I park here?" He, like a true New Yorker answered, "Because the signs say so." Go figure! I again asked in a different way, "There must be a reason for that. Do you know what it is?" He said, "They take up too much room." I said, "If I was a car, how much would it cost me to park here for three or four hours?" He said, "You are not a car, laughed a little, and finished by saying about twenty bucks." I reached into my pocket and pulled out two twenties. Handed it to him and said, "You're paid up front for the four hours and the rest is yours." The gate opened up just like the Red Sea parted for Moses and we pulled in, parked, got out, and started to walk to the edge of the water to get the boat to take us to the Statue of Liberty. We caught the water shuttle to the statue and got in line. The wait was about a half hour but not bad. We finally got to go up and at that time, it was a very long and hard walk up a very narrow twisting stairway to the top. We had just started up; when Sandy said she had to stay with Elaina. She is terrified and won't walk another inch. Elaina had to be at least ten or so. Sandy stayed with her, and Arnold, Heather, our two kids, Marla and the other two hooligans, Pam and Tara, and I did the whole route together. It was a tough walk but fun and very memorable. All the way up through Miss Liberty's arm and back down to earth. (We got so close we practically felt the heat from her torch.) When we got back down, Elaina seemed to be just fine. We finished sightseeing New York and drove back to Philadelphia. Years later, in fact maybe just a couple of years ago, when I was back visiting them, the real story came out about the frightening horror in the Statue of Liberty. Elaina was not really scared. She had a tremendous amount of gas and could not let loose with us around. She was in so much pain she couldn't walk. Sandy just stayed with her so she could do what she had to do with us not around. As the tail goes, (pardon the pun) she finally let loose, and no one else could go up the stairs for at least fifteen minutes and even then, they had to go quickly. Women!

The two weeks went fast (Bruce Willis would say it was like an eternity being that long in Philadelphia), and we got ready to start back to California via the northern route. Before we left, I made my daily call to my secretary to see if she was having any problems with work and/ or any customers. I also wanted to know if she had heard anything from David as I had her check each and every day at my house to see if David was there or anywhere around. The normal answer was, "No." This time she said she had run into David and absolutely will not check back to the house anymore. I asked what happened and if he seemed to be OK. She said it was not him that had to be checked out to see if anyone was ok, it was her. "What happened?" I asked. She said the last time she stopped over, David asked her to come in because he had something he wanted to tell her. She entered our house, and there were about five or six guys having a lugi spitting contest on the living room wall. She said, "That's disgusting" and started to leave. Before she could make it to the door, David threw a rattle snake at her. She panicked and started to scream and yell and jump around. All the guys sat there laughing. She finally made it to the door and ran out safely. I said, "Don't worry about going to the house anymore," and she was very relieved. I hung up and turned around. There was Heather standing there looking at me. She asked, "How's David?" I said, "Fine." We gassed up and were out of there.

The northern route home, although a little more beautiful than the southern route, was just as great only different. One of the stops we made was through Glacier National Park. I think it was somewhere in August. We got out of the car and made snow angels. Just wasn't sure if it was snow or dust from Mt. St. Helens? It did seem cold though. Washington, Oregon and then good ole California were in our cross hairs.

As I think back, Heather and I had a lot of time to talk in the two months we were vacationing, while in the van. Although I was a big asshole for the way I was in my marriage with her, I always thought of myself as a good father and taking care of my family, in spite of my whoring around, excessive working, gambling, and a bunch of other crap I was involved in, *including being way too much into myself.* Heather had mentioned that my brother (Who I sometimes didn't like because he would not let me smoke in his house.) had gotten Melanoma. I never knew it or I just didn't listen to anyone when they talked about it. After he survived that hospital crap early in the year, he went on to run a marathon race in Greece and then one in Honolulu and coming out in the top ten percent in his age category. He should have done well; he was a lot lighter with all his lymph nodes taken out, earlier in the year.

Home sweet home! Like any time away, no matter how great it is, there's no place like home. We unpacked, and still had a few more weeks until school started. I had a huge task in front of me with re-opening Pacific Cable and taking control of the Water Bed stores, not to mention the auto shop and a plethora of other things.

David was nowhere to be seen. But the house cost me thirty-two hundred dollars in repairs. It was thrashed. We had a cleaning lady there for three days, eight hours a day, and there was still stuff that had to be done. Occasionally, David would drift in and out, but no one would talk to him, and he seemed okay with that.

Holly's favorite group was the Osmonds. To be honest with you, Marie wasn't too bad without the family of singers. It was Holly's sixteenth birthday coming up in October, and Heather and I got tickets for the Osmonds show, including dinner in Las Vegas, for five. We just told Holly, and the boys, that we were going to take her and them to Vegas for the special birthday. Out of all the traumas we have had with her in the past, it's nice to be able to hark back and say that this is the one time that truly sticks out in my mind when I think about her as a younger person. We got to Vegas and had our dinner right in the theater where the Osmonds were playing. We somehow kept Holly and the boys from seeing who was playing at the show. We finished eating, and were waiting for the start of the show. To be honest with you, Holly wasn't real crazy about going to Vegas. I guess it seemed like an adult place to go and not for a child. But David and Sean were all for it. Bragging rights I guess for when they go back to school or something like that. Heather and I were sitting across from the kids, and we were about a couple of tables from the stage. Holly and the kids still had no clue as to who we were going to see, but of course Holly knew that we were there for her special night. The lights dimmed and from the back of the curtains in back of the stage in a loud boisterous voice came the announcement, "Ladies and gentlemen, the Osmonds." Holly looked at me and at Heather and tears started coming out of her eyes just like they are coming out of mine right now. She tried to talk but nothing came from her lips. I seriously thought there might be something wrong. But Heather touched me, and I knew all was well. In all my life I have never seen anything like that. From the first note to the last, there was nothing but tears and not a sound. Nothing, just nothing! It was an hour and a half or there about and nothing but tears. Just like I keep dripping tears on my keyboard as I type. Some things defy description and can only be felt. I am sure this is one of them. Hopefully, you have had such an experience and know what I am feeling and saying. NEXT!

Chapter Nineteen

It was early in nineteen eighty-one and as much as I tried to avoid my thirty-ninth, (Doing just about everything short of playing frog.) it did come and go and now some dumb holiday was on the horizon. Valentine's Day! I may have had a lot of problems in my life, but I never forget holidays, birthdays or anniversaries. So, being the ever-Loving dude that I was and still am, flowers were on the shopping list.

    I walked into a flower shop named "Aaron's Flowers." As I was talking to the owner, his wife was making up an arrangement for my wife and daughter. He mentioned that he was packing up and getting out of California right after this holiday. I asked, "Why?" He said in a whisper, "My wife is having problems breathing here and the doctor wants us to move to Arizona." I said, "Have you tried to sell the shop? It seems like a good location, and you look like you are busy." He said, "Yes, but no takers as of yet and really, we can't stay much longer." I asked, "How much do you want for it?" He told me and I said, "That doesn't sound like a lot." He said, "There is not a lot of inventory except for some ribbon and a few vases. The rest will be dead in a short time so you don't really put a lot of flowers in with the exception of days like this one." "Do you have a worker other than your wife?" I asked. He said, "Yes, and a very capable one. In fact, he pretty much runs this place, but on holidays my wife and I both come in and help out. It keeps the payroll down." I asked, "Any chance of talking to him?" "Not today but anytime tomorrow. He's doing drop offs and will be very busy all day." I said, "Thanks" and picked up my two bouquets and said, "I will be in tomorrow, and you might mention it to what's his name." Bouquets delivered and kisses exchanged. The next day I went to Aarons Flowers and talked to Dave, the helper. We spent a couple of hours yakking as he did mostly clean up from all the business that was done a day before. The bottom line was that he said if he had the money, he would jump on it in a hot New York minute. "This place makes a bunch of money." That was the straw that broke the camel's back. I said, "Would you like to be a minor partner?" He said, "Let's talk." We talked and in two days we were partners.

Heather and I finally got her "Aaron" that we had to name Sean because of my mothers complaining. Heather really wanted to name Sean, "Aaron." So now I have another business to worry about; a wire and cable distributorship, a chain of water bed stores, a wrought iron manufacturing company, a foreign car repair garage, and now a retail flower store. No wonder I had a heart attack some years later. But the money kept pouring in, and I somehow found a way to gamble it all away. Summer came and the cable company was doing just fine as always but the water bed stores, the flower shop and the garage went crazy. I almost didn't have time to gamble.

Somewhere in the middle of eighty-one, around late summer, I started to realize that betting the horses was breaking me. When I wagered on sports, I sometimes got back a bunch. Never what I lost, but it was kind of a kiss now and then. I never got that kiss with the nags. So I figured if you can't beat them, join them. If I owned a race horse, I would know the ins and outs of racing better and maybe even stop betting them or at least have better knowledge of when to bet on them. I certainly knew how to read a racing form, thanks to Norman of Brigham's and Cal, the bookie. The L. A. County fair was approaching (We all know how much that fair has played a part in my life, so why stop now?), and they have racing there. I decided to buy a horse and race it. The first thing I needed was a trainer. As I found out later, he does all the work. I just sign a check for a million dollars to him each and every year. It's that easy! That would be cheaper than what I had been losing every year. I went to the fairgrounds in Pomona after I did my homework on picking a trainer. I learned a lot reading the racing forms, both past and present, and a lot by talking to people who owned race horses and many bettors who were losers like I was. We all seemed to get along just fine. With the exception of the trainers, to whom the checks were made out, the rest of us were just a bunch of losers, only we didn't realize it. In choosing a trainer I boiled it down to two: Mel Stute or Ted West. Both of these trainers would be the top trainers year after year at Pomona, and far in front of the rest of the other trainers that trained there. I made a coin flip, and Ted West became my trainer. Mel Stute went on to be named in the Trainer's Hall of Fame. That figures! I need to stop here as I have a dilemma. I don't know if I should put in all my special stories about my race horses at one time or insert them in the order as we go from year to year. Hmmmm. I'll ask some friends and see what they think. They won't talk to me because I own race horses! Thoroughbreds, as a matter of fact! Ok, decision made. I will put them in, all at once, so anyone who is not interested in horse race stories can skip this part of my adventures, involving Sea Biscuit the movie, and the world's winningist jockeys and so on. Hmmmm, I may have gotten someone's interest. And so the horse racing tales begin.

I made some decisions before I bought a horse and later was made aware that you don't buy a horse, you claim one. (for the most part) But one of my decisions was that I would always pick the horse I wanted to buy, oops, I mean claim. That way, I will always be the hero or the goat. That way there would be no one to blame or pat on the back but myself. It was my money, and I felt I could spend it the way I wanted to. The first horse I claimed was a nag called Skipping Hill. My trainer strongly advised not to as he was a come-from-behind horse and the Pomona race track lended itself to front runners as the stretch run was very short. Skipping Hill went off at a long price but came in second. However, I did claim him for twenty-five hundred dollars. I will try to not get into the rules of the horse racing game as I would have to write another book. You'll have to trust me as I go, and not ask questions. I raised Skipping Hill to a thirty-two hundred dollar claimer in the next two weeks or so. He ran second again in the race but got claimed (bought) from me for thirty-two hundred dollars. In two weeks I made seven hundred dollars by buying him for twenty-five hundred and having him claimed for thirty-two hundred. I received an extra seven hundred dollars for my share of the race track's purse money. I made fourteen hundred dollars in two weeks! I knew I was onto something. Okay, as much as I don't want to admit it, this was not only fun, but it was the start of another business. Once again, I am not going to bore you with my horse racing career, but there are a few exceptional things that have happened in those early years.

In the racing business you move from track to track as one horse race meet closes, another one opens, and you wind up traveling all over California or if you choose, the United States and the world, if you are so inclined. I chose to stay in California with rare exceptions.

In late eighty-two I claimed a horse at Bay Meadows Race Track in Northern California and had him shipped to Santa Anita Race Track in Southern California. His name was "Farouk." (Probably would have not clamed a horse with that name today. Can a horse be profiled?) I bought him for twelve thousand five hundred dollars (a notch or two above what I had started with a few years ago).Ted, my trainer, said, "I think you made a good claim." Knowing Ted, he doesn't say things like that very often so I got a lot of confidence and said to Ted, "Then I double, no triple dog dare you to ask Chris Mc Caron to ride for me. For those of you who are not well versed in the horse racing game, at that time Chris Mc Carron was just about the best and hottest jockey in the world and wouldn't ride just any old mount. He had to have the best and only the best.

We entered Farouk into a sixteen thousand dollar contest and to my surprise; Chris said he would ride for me. Just about every time I race a horse in a race, it is a big thrill to me no matter what the outcome, but I have had probably six or seven great thrills in my thirty year career that exceptionally stick out. This was probably the third greatest. The race went off, and we won easily by two horse lengths. I still have the picture with Chris Mc Carron. But, as usual, we had to race again in two or three weeks. That was about the beginning of eighty-three. I, of course, had thought about once again asking Chris to ride for me. Is that pressing my luck? That was just about the time when the second greatest thrill came to me in my racing career. My trainer, Ted West, came to me and said, "Chris has asked me if he could ride Farouk again." I almost came to tears. I couldn't speak. I just nodded and kind of shook my head (as I remember) in agreement and walked away. I wasn't right for the next few days. I can tell you this. Every person whom I knew and a whole bunch that I didn't know knew that the one and the only "Chris Mc Carron" actually asked if he could ride for me again. It's amazing how the older I get; the more easily the tears come. That race ended up in a two-horse race from the top of the stretch, nose to nose, all the way to the finish line. A photo finish for sure! You couldn't put a hair between the two horses. After a long wait, Chris and Farouk and I, placed second and that was certainly nothing to be ashamed of. Now, that's where Chris Mc Carron, Chuck Gerson and the Farouk story ends, but not entirely. This may interest those of you who are not race enthusiasts. Later in years, a much attended movie called "Seabiscuit" came to the theater. The movie was not just great for us race guys but great in its context for any movie goers. If you were fortunate enough to have seen it and can remember, late in the movie, the match race between Seabiscut and the harrowed hero "War Admiral." The jockey on War Admiral was played by the one and the only "Chris Mc Carron." War Admiral with Chris Mc Carron lost the race. He ran second just like he did with my horse, Farouk, only different!

As I became more involved, I started to watch certain jockeys and what they would ride and when they would ride them. I figured that it could give me an edge as to what horses to claim. Something jumped out at me. Bill Shoemaker, one of the greatest jockeys in the world, was riding in a cheap ten thousand claimer in the last race at Santa Anita race track. Bill had no reason to ride in the last race. He didn't need the money. Usually, the soundest horses were not in the ten thousand dollar ranks. It is always taking a little bigger chance to get hurt, and Bill didn't have to do that. I figured Bill was just riding as a favor for a trainer or an owner. You would think that the horse, although not a whirl beater, was probably sound so Bill was not taking too big of a chance. The horse's name was "Ready to Go." Three weeks later I noticed that Bill Shoemaker was going to ride, in the last race, and again was on "Ready to Go". I figured that if Shoemaker could ride him, I can claim him. I told Ted West, still my trainer, to look him over as I wanted to claim him that day out of the last race. Come post time (post time is when the horses start to go to the track to race in about ten minutes or so, and you can take a good look at them as they walk by.), Ted said he didn't see anything obviously wrong so why not claim him. So it is written, so it shall be done. Thus I added another horse to my stable. The really good thing about the horses was that the more horses I had in my stable, the fewer ladies were in it. I think it was the eyes!

To make a long story longer, it was race time in about another two weeks. I claimed Ready to Go for ten thousand dollars and raced him back for a twelve thousand five hundred dollar race. They were all in the gate. I was sitting with my youngest son, Sean, as we watched the race. The gates opened and they were off! Ready to Go was in a great position to attack at the start of the far turn. Just about when the attack was to start, Ready to Go started to moon walk. (my brother's term for going backwards in a horse race) Ready to Go not only moon walked, he fell down. I knew I was in trouble. (Ya think!) The race was over and the horse van came out to pick him up. He obviously never finished the race. Not only that, I was out the ten thousand I paid for him and the appropriate tax to the state and another thousand to my trainer for training him for the last two weeks. At this point I was not feeling too good. In fact, not good at all! All I could see was about twelve thousand dollars disappear from my wallet. Twelve thousand in two weeks, shit! And I mean SHIT! All of a sudden my son, Sean, says, "Dad, they just put a red flag on Ready to Go's nose." I said, "No, they didn't?" He said, "Yep they did." (From that day on, I used binoculars for every race that I was in.) In a claiming race when they put a red flag on the horse's nose, it means that someone bought or claimed that horse out of the race. Let me tell you, I went from twelve thousand down to fifteen hundred up. That's about a twenty four thousand dollar swing in my favor. Instead of losing the ten thousand that I paid for him and the one thousand in sales taxes, I got twelve thousand for him. But I did learn a lesson. Never buy a horse that is named, *"Ready to Go."* Because he might!

There is always a lesson to learn, not just in general. If you look hard enough; even in horse racing as you will see. In fact, sometimes you don't have to look very hard at all. A few years later I learned a real big lesson. You may have heard the expression, "If it looks too good to be true, it probably is." Ted West, my trainer, was given three million dollars from one of his owners to go to England and buy some horses. (To you novice horse people, that probably sounds like a lot of money, but when you compare that to spending ten million dollars for one unborn foal, (baby horse) with no guarantee of a live birth, I guess it is not so bad. Not me, but a Sheik somewhere in Arabia.) Ted came back with five horses. One was called "Interco," who later became "Horse of the Year" and I am sure made millions for the owner racing, and then breeding. Another one was a stakes winner and certainly held his own money wise. Two of the others were just so and so but made a couple of bucks for the owner. The last one was called, "Forlore!" Forlore had broken his maiden (won his first race) in an allowance race in England by five lengths. He ran second in a stakes race the next time out, and then won two in a row before coming over to the U. S. A. in the package deal of five horses Ted bought. Now, you would have thought this horse was a terror, but as it turned out, he couldn't get out of his own way here. He ran in a stakes race. Finished last! He ran in an allowance race at Santa Anita. Finished last! He ran in a fifty thousand dollar claimer. Finished last! He was shipped to Golden Gate fields up north and ran in a twenty thousand dollar claimer and beat one horse.

This horse was, in my mind, one of the biggest and most beautiful Chestnut horses I had ever seen in my whole racing career. He stood seventeen plus hands and had a chest that equaled the size of a Volkswagen Bug. Just gorgeous! One morning I happened to walk into Ted's office and overheard a conversation Ted was having on the phone. Of course, I could only hear one side, but it went something like this. "Sell it for how much? Five hundred? One hundred? Just get rid of it? I guess a tax right off is better than an expense. Got it!" And he hung up. I said, "Who was that?" He told me, and I asked what horse he was referring to? Ted said, "Forlore." I said, "He wants to sell Forlore for anything?" Ted said, "Anything." I said, "How much for me?" Ted said, "You really don't him." (Mistake number one was that I should have listened to my trainer.), I said, "How much?" Ted said, "If you really want him, I'll take a dollar." I pulled out a buck and handed it to him. Ted said, "Put your dollar away, he's yours." (Mistake number two.) Now, about a page or two before I mentioned you never get something for nothing, right? So here is the saga of me and the something for nothing, deal. I basically had no money invested in him and basically he had been running (semantics) recently so my training fees were probably about two thousand a month or less. All I would have to do is run second once and third once each month, and it would have paid for all my costs. After running last in almost all of the starts for me at the lowest level he could possibly run in, and only beating two horses in all those races, not to mention I am now stuck about six or seven thousand dollars, I shipped him to Calente, Mexico. Not my first choice. However, it was my only choice. You know me and Mexicans. Well, after racing there for five months or so at a cost of another four thousand dollars and only beating a couple of horses there, I was about to have the horse executed. In the states it is against the law, but what happens in Mexico stays in Mexico. I have already learned three lessons. One, you never get something for nothing; two, there is a time when you have to cut the expenses like the previous owner did, and three, when you trust a trainer and he practically begs you to not buy a horse, listen to him and don't buy the fuckin horse. It's race time again and as usual, I am heading to Mexico to watch my horse race. (If you can call it that.) I have also made up my mind to tell my trainer there, after this race, sell Forlore for whatever he can get for hm. I arrived at the race track and it's close to race time. My trainer says to me very quietly, "Bet your horse today." I gave him a look like he had lost his mind. I said, "WHAT, are you nuts?" He looked at me and said, "Bet your horse today" and kind of gave me a wink-nod. I still looked at him with the look like I should have had when Ted told me that Forlore was for sale. Once again, he told me to make sure I bet Forlore. We went down to the paddock to saddle my horse. I looked up at the tote board and couldn't believe my eyes. We were always, from forty to one to ninety to one on the tote board. Now we are sitting at eight to one. Same horses to face, same distance and same jockey as usual. Nothing changed except the tote board. We finished saddling. I went to sit with my family who had come with me at the races. When my horses raced, if possible, my family was with me. Great support! However, when I told them to comb their hair as we were just about to be in the winning photo, they fell apart laughing. Well, the support was there most of the time! I told them that the trainer said to bet him and don't worry. Forlore's price now had drifted up a little to eleven to one. I went and made a substantial bet on him and wheeled him in the exacta, as well. (An exacta is a proposition bet, and if it wins it pays a very high return.) They were all in the gate. I heard the announcer say, "Abierto." They got out of the gate, but I didn't see Forlore. He was always the last one out of the gate so I was looking at the back of the breaking horses. Then I heard the announcer saying, "It's Forlore in front by two lengths." I looked to the front, and he was right! Forlore was in front. Or maybe he was just coming in last from the previous race. I couldn't believe my eyes. It was now Forlore in front by three, and now by five. At the wire Forlore had prevailed by seven lengths. SEVEN! I hot tailed it to the winners circle and the photo session so fast that I almost forgot I had a family with me. It was so exciting. When all the hoopla was over and done dollars and cents wise, I was within a thousand of getting even for the whole time since I had bought this great horse that won by seven lengths. After the race I told my family to wait; I would be right back. I high-tailed it to the stable and with a smirk on my face, asked the trainer if we had gotten claimed. He just smiled and shook his head. I said, "What are the chances of us winning again in the near future?" He just smiled and shook his head. I said, "Sell him, ok?" "Not a problem," he said. I shook his hand and gave a little hug and I was gone.

Last, but not least, (at least for this section of my horses), there was a horse named Incursion. I claimed him for sixteen thousand dollars against Ted's better judgment. (Well, maybe I didn't learn lesson number three as well as I thought.) But this time Ted was not emphatic about it. It turned out that Incursion had a chronic shin problem. Her normal racing distance was a mile and a sixteenth. When the race began, she would be at least twenty to twenty-five lengths behind all the other horses and looked like she had no chance at all. I would bring friends out to watch her run and have them bet on her. About twenty seconds after the race started, they were on my case big time. Why did you have me bet that pig? Gerson, you suck! I also heard, why would you keep that nag in your barn or something said along those lines? But half way down the back stretch, you could see her starting to get a little closer with every stride. It took that much racing (half a mile) to work out the pain from her shins. As she got pain free going into the top of the stretch, she started flying. Sometimes I would wonder how the jockey could hang on, she was going so fast. She was like a freight train down the stretch and just about always got in the photo at the wire if she just didn't win out right. The tunes were a little different from my friends after the race.

In one race she got a little hurt. Ted suggested we send her to Mexico for a little R & R. It was cheaper there, just for resting, and the hurt was not a big problem. I sent her to trainer Howard Fourzon, a friend of Ted's. About five months or so went by and it was time to bring Incursion home to Santa Anita Race Track. She had plenty of R & R and was in training by Howard. Incursion should be ready for a race at Santa Anita shortly. It just so happened that just before she was to ship up to California (yes they ship horses and not ride them home), there was a race that fit Incursion's M O perfectly. Howard asked me if I cared if we entered for that race. I said, "Let me check with Ted. I don't want to step on anyone's toes." Ted said, "No problem." (Howard would have said, "No-prob-lame-o, Mexician you know!") We entered the race. As it turned out, the top rated horse in Mexico was also entered in that race. Because it was Incursion's returning race I wanted to be there early and talk to Howard. We had our parley. Howard asked me if I would like to go half with him on the "Five Ten?" The Five Ten is just about the same as the pick six we have here in the U. S. A. You bet very little money and have the chance to win very big money. All you have to do is pick the winners in six specified races in a row. So, I said, "Sure, why not." So I gave Howard my picks and my money and he took his picks and his share of the loot and together we spent about a hundred bucks total. We had a few different horses covered in a few different races. In the last race we had three horses, Incursion, the best horse in Mexico (can't remember her name) and one other. We really didn't think we had a chance to win with Incursion as it was just a practice kind of a race. A tuner up kind of thing! Not that she couldn't run with this type, it's just that she needed a few races under her belt before she could get into her best stride. As it turned out, she was the second favorite at three to one, second only, to the Mexican champion at three to five. I told Heather if we win the Five—Ten, she could buy a brand new washer and dryer. I knew we really didn't have a chance to win, so why not promise her the world.) She was thrilled. What I didn't tell her was that if I win the Five Ten I could buy myself a new car. (See, I even lie to myself.) All the racing started, and I was winning pretty well. In fact, by the time Incursions race was to start, we had the first five in, of the Five Ten we had marked on our ticket. That pretty much insured we were going to win it. We had the big time favorite, the Mexican Champion, who pretty much would lock up the win. We went down to the paddock, saddled Incursion, and went back to our seats. The race was on! I heard the announcer say that word again. "Abierto!" The champion went to the front as she usually did. I looked for Incursion and as usual, she was way in back. I could hear the announcer call the field. The last words you would hear were, "And Incursion trails." It looked like the R & R did not do so well. Again, I could hear the announcer make the calls and again and again I heard, "Incursion trails." As the horses were in the back stretch, I could see Incursion starting to move up a little. A very little! The horses started to make the far turn. I could not only see, but I could hear the announcer saying, "Here comes Incursion eating up the horses on the outside." I couldn't believe my eyes. I had seen this mare run them down before, but not like this. I just hoped the jockey wouldn't fall off. By the top of the stretch, Incursion had put away every horse in the race except the Champ. And as a great announcer once said, "And down the stretch they come." It was Incursion in front by a head and then the champ in front by a nose. It was a head, a neck, a nose, a head. You really didn't know which of the parts belonged to whom he was calling, it was so close. That was the way the whole stretch run was run and at the wire, it was way too close to call. Either one could have won it. In any case, Incursion ran her eyeballs out. I couldn't have been prouder. The photo sign came down and the numbers went up. Incursion by a nostril hair! Winning pictures were in order. Now that the race is over, and you are all happy for me, and Heather gets her new washer and dryer that was not why I had this particular great race in my book. Although hair-raising and great, and in my top ten thrills of racing, it was what followed that we need to address. As I just mentioned, Heather got her washer and dryer. That means we won the Five-Ten. Forty thousand dollars! FORTY THOUSAND!!!! Twenty of that was mine, and twenty belonged to Howard, my trainer. I told Heather and the kids I would be right back. I needed to get the money. There were two more races yet to be run, I told them to order food. Lots of food and anything they wanted. Sean yelled as I walked away, "Shrimp?" I yelled back, "All you can eat." This may take a little more visual then you may be used to, but we walked to a stairway, a spiral stairway that was very narrow. So narrow that there would be no way two people could walk up it, side by side, no matter how thin they were. At the bottom of this stairway, blocking the entire entrance was Poncho Villa. I mean a three hundred and fifty pounder, unbelievably huge, with a machine gun on his lap and bullet belts crossed on his chest. Torn and dirty tee shirt and a hat only Poncho Villa could wear. I looked at Howard and he said, "No problem." My eyes opened real wide, and I looked at him again with terror in my face and again he said, "No problem." He walked up to Poncho and said, "We have to go and get our money. We had won the Five Ten." (That would have been the last thing I would have said.) Poncho said, "Let me see the ticket." Right then and there I knew that he was going to take it and all was for not. I wasn't going to put up an argument even though he was Mexican. This guy was huge, and the machine gun made him look even that much bigger. (I guess I will have to buy the washer and dryer out of my own pocket.) He looked at the ticket, nodded his head, and tried to get up. It took him thirty seconds to move his huge body, but finally he moved aside and we passed by him. Single file, we went up this very narrow spiral stairway to a room that blocked us from entering it by a wall of glass. Through the glass we could see a ton of money stacked up against the back wall. A woman let us in and said in the native language, "What do you want?" Howard said, in that same language, "We won the Five ten and want our money." (I wonder why Howard didn't say, "no-prob-lame—o" before to me, instead of no problem. Awe, because he never saw The Terminator with Arnold Schwarzenegger.) I don't think I would have been as forceful as he was. She asked for the ticket, and Howard handed it to her. Up against the wall were stacks of twenties, all with rubber bands around them in five hundred dollar increments. She handed both of us a paper, Von's grocery bag, and filled them with equal stacks of twenty thousand each. I said to Howard, "How do we know that there are five hundred dollars in each and every stack?" He said, "Do you want to stay here much longer and have the stacks counted?" This was the first time a man answered me like a female. My question with a question and it worked. We picked up the paper bags and walked out. It was bad enough that we now had to walk by Poncho again, the money sticking out of the top of the bag, and if Poncho wants to grab a stack, what am I going to do? Let him, I guess! Finally, we made it past Poncho. When I got back to my family, the first thing the kids said was, "Let me see the money" at the top of their lungs. I'm under a panic now. "Shut up," I'm yelling, "shut up." They finally get the idea and calm down. We finished watching the last race, paid the food bill and left. We kept looking over our shoulders for an attack, but nothing ever happened, thank God! We all got into the car and think that we all made it and all was well. Until the party pooper, Heather, says, "What if we get stopped at the boarded?" (For those of you who have never been to Mexico, via Tijuana, there are about a two hour line to get across the boarded into the USA, and they spot check many vehicles.) Great, just fucking great! Another obstacle to hurdle! Winning twenty thousand is getting way too much to handle. (And when I get back, with or without the money, I still have to buy the washer and dryer.) We can't go through the border check point with thousands popping out of the shopping bag. We thought about shoving the thousands in our pants but if they asked us to step out of the car we would be dead. I was driving a Cadillac at the time, and it had great big arm rests in the back seat with an ash tray on the top. I wondered what was inside the arm rest. I pried up the ashtray and low and behold, it was hollow underneath! Just a few wires were there. Probably for the ashtray and the light that went on at night, so you could see the tray and not flip ashes on the floor. We dumped the cash (as if we were criminals and had stolen it) into the arm rests, never thinking that there could be a fire from the wires that went to the lighter. I told the kids to look innocent as we crossed the border check point. That was the worst thing I could have said. When we got to the check point, they all had this look like little angels. In fact, I thought I saw halos on top of their heads. If that wasn't a tip off, there was something wrong. Nothing would have been. Fortunately, we made it through and got home safely. Not only with the cash, but with a great memory how my horse had beaten the best horse in Mexico. (Well, maybe Mexico isn't that bad.)

One other quick tale and we are done for now with the horses. It really has nothing to do with my horses or for that matter, any other horse. But it is a horse story. I used to go to Hollywood Park very early in the morning to watch my horses work out. It is a thing some horse owners do. Not all, just some. A lot of the horse owners are in television and the movies and sometimes you would find yourself standing next to one that was watching their horse working out as well. As faith would have it, Jack Klugman (I am sure you know him from The Odd Couple, Quinsey and a plethora of other works) had a horse call "Jacklyn Klugman" no one that I knew, knew why, but Jacklyn Klugmn was a male. Go figure! Every once in awhile I would be at the track watching one of my horse's work out around five or six AM and Jack was there doing the same. We were not friends by any stretch of the imagination, but we would talk a little bit about horses. He couldn't have been friendlier. Just a real nice guy! To make a long story a little shorter, what I noticed was, if you saw Jack in The Odd Couple on T. V., playing the Oscar roll, in my opinion, he never had to act for that part. He was a natural. I would see him at the track at six AM, leave in a little while, and then when I came back to watch my horse race in the afternoon,

Jack would still be there. Not too unusual to stay for the races but he would have his shirt tail out, a beard starting to grow, mustard on his shirt and pants, a race form sticking out of his back pocket, a hot dog in his face, and his hair all messed up under his tattered hat. *Just like Oscar!*

I just promised you that I would stop with the horse stories, for now, after the Klugman stuff. Well, I lied! Something just happened in real time that I would like you to know.

Today is around April two thousand and ten. I have recently claimed (bought) a six year old mare, and she was in my trainer's, Ted West's, barn. I called Ted up and said that I was headed his way and told him that I was going to stop by and see her, Fiona Freud. Ted said, "She's not in my barn and won't be for a month or so. In fact, none of my horses will be there for a while." I asked, "What's going on?" He said, "They are filming a movie here at Santa Anita, and they chose to use my barn in the film." I asked Ted who the star was and what the name of the film was? He said, "I don't know and could care less. I just want my barn back as soon as possible." He'd only been in that barn for thirty years and probably felt like a fish out of water. His nonchalant answer to me was really the way that he is in real life. He is and never was into the big time front page stuff. Just a good ole, down to earth, regular kind of guy who just wants a quiet life with his work, his church, his wife, Mary Ellen, and kid, little Ted. So, that was the way the story went. I never mentioned it again, and he never did either. A month or so later the horses were returned to the barn and all was back to normal. About another month later, as I was reading a horse publication, I noticed an article that caught my eye. It read, "HBO Pilot "LUCK" Being Filmed at Santa Anita." I read on, and this is a short synopsis of what I read. *Dustin Hoffman is on site in the filming of "Luck", an HBO pilot written and produced by David Milch and directed by Michael Mann. It's about a career criminal heavily involved in horse racing.* It also features Nick Nolte, Dennis Farina, and John Ortiz. Once again, I am indirectly involved in something unusual. Who knows, my horse, Fiona Freud, might even be in the movie. I just hope they change her name to protect the innocent. That is a good thing, involving me. The bad thing is that by the time I finish this book and get it on the shelves book stores, the film will probably be on tape at the local level or at the swap meets. (Flea Markets) Now where was I? Oh yea!

Chapter Twenty

Early in '82 business was going gang busters. Actually, I had thought about selling one or two of the businesses while they were making money. But, I figured I would just piss the proceeds away at the track or through my buddy, Cal, the bookie.

One of the manufacturers where I bought my electronic wire from had an argument, or something happened and the head of production got canned. He called me because he was looking for a sales job. He did know a lot of the customers from the company he got canned from. I made a lunch appointment with him for a few days later. I had been dealing with this guy for a few years now, and in my mind he was not a salesman. He was a factory/warehouse kinda guy. Very good what he did: it just wasn't sales. For the sake of conversation, let's call him Vic. Probably because that was his name. We went to lunch and in a nice way I told him he would stink as a salesperson. Actually, now that I think about it, those were my exact words. But I did have an idea. Actually, I had thought about this idea a day or so before when he made the appointment with me for the job. I said, "Vic (I always called him that because it was his name) how would you like to own your own manufacturing company?" He said, "I'm all ears." He actually was. They were way too big for his head. Anyway, I said, "I had been thinking about you for the last couple of days and about me as well. If I owned my own factory, I, Pacific Cable, could buy some of my wire at a cheaper price than I could buy from other factories. I would be the one that sets the price structure. I could make more sales and a larger margin in my distributorship, and at the same time, make a buck or two from the sales from the factory. When I place an order with the factory, let's say for a million feet of a particular type of wire, I could make a few calls and sell another million feet of the same type, making our cost cheaper and, therefore, making a greater margin for the factory as well. What do you think?" "Chuck, I have known you for a few years now and know you don't have time to shit. How the hell are you going to have the time to start a factory? Not to mention the money it takes. Did you even mention this to your wife?" "Let me handle all of the above. But that is where you come in, partner. I do the financing and all the sales and paperwork. You set up the factory and run it." We need an extruder." "Ok." "We need a couple of respoolers." "Ok." "We need to set up an account with the copper factories, and with the plastic companies." "Ok." "I will need a slave to work for me." "Ok." (Little did he know that I planned to do some of the work so I could learn what was going on). "We need a bunch of stuff." "Ok." "So, are you in?" "I need a job, what's the deal?" I said, "Fifty-fifty. I put in all the money and you put in all the work. Deal!" I really didn't know what I was getting into. But that's me. It did sound good though. The main expense was the extruder. That is the huge machine that lets the bare copper wire go through it and squeezes the plastic covering on it in a very symmetrical way. The one we needed cost about two hundred and fifty thousand dollars new. Vic found one that the government had rebuilt and was just sitting around doing nothing. (How unusual.) It was up for bid in a government auction. We got it for seventeen thousand five hundred dollars. Hell, it cost four thousand to ship it and another four thousand to switch the one twenty voltage in my new warehouse to two twenty or was it four forty?

Anyway, in sixty days we were in business. (Hell, being Jewish, I could have fought a war in that short of a time. Putting together a business was nothing!) And were we ever in business! (*I am sure that Heather was thrilled, also.*) From the day we opened the doors, between me buying for Pacific Cable and the customers I hustled, we had to run two shifts. And months later, three around the clock. I actually did work there quite a bit. My routine was to leave Pacific Cable at four P.M. or so and go home, catch a meal and four hours sleep, then go to work at the factory. I was running the third shift. Like I knew what I was doing. Then, I would leave around six A.M. or so when Vic came in. It was just me and a worker at night. It had to be a hundred and fifteen in the factory. I think I lost twenty pounds the first month or so that I worked there. It made me think of my dad in the Armour factory fifty years ago. We were making a lot of money. Then, one day, Vic said, "I have to make more money then I am getting now." I said, "A deal is a deal." You are making plenty, aren't you and if you get more, I have to take more. We are fift-fifty partners right? He said his wife thinks it's not fair. She said that I work much harder then you and get the same pay. So, I should get more. I said, "Vic, what do you think?" He said, "She's my wife." I said, "Then we need to end the partnership." Do you want to talk to your wife anymore about this? Maybe explain that greed is not good. We are a good match the way we have been working. Why screw it up? We are both making a nice living this way. He said he already talked himself blue in the face, and she won't budge. I said, "Okay, give me a couple of days. I will come up with a buy-out plan." I submitted a plan to them where either of us could buy the other out on the same terms. It was the same for either one of us. I buy him out or he buys me out. He accepted the deal after conferring with the boss. He was to buy me out. There was to be a three month delay before any money exchanged hands. This would give either of us time to change our mind or to help get things working on our own. The three months went by. When he was to give me some cash for the buy out, he couldn't. Two months later he folded the doors for lack of business. I got nothing for my half. He filed bankruptcy and started looking for a job again. I never talked or saw him again. A few years later I heard he played frog.

With all this new time on my hands, I thought about booking horses and sports on my own. It was coming close to football season so I started to round up some sickos, a lot like myself. Bettors! I rented a small office and had a couple of phones installed. I hooked up a tape recorder to each so I could record all conversations. You never know who will say they did one thing and not something else because they lost a bet. This way I had proof. That way the Feds did also when they busted you. Live and learn. The hard way! So, I started booking bets on my own. On Sunday, when all the bets were placed, I would go home and watch the games on the tube. One Sunday, I was a basket case all day. Heather, the kids and any friend who knew what I was doing, knew not to talk to or call between ten A.M. and five P.M. during football season and later at night if it was baseball season. If they did, I would put a contract out on them. I did have the means and they knew it.

It just so happened that in the beginning of the week, I decided to quit smoking. (The seven hundred and eighth time that year.) This time I had quit from Monday all the way to Sunday. Seven days. Almost! After the morning games were over, I was stuck for sixty thousand dollars. I was starting to panic. Sixty grand was a lot of money. A lot! I reached for a cigarette at least fifty times. None around, none! So, I asked Sean, my youngest son, if he wanted to make a couple of bucks. Being an offspring of mine, he would probably kill, even at his young age of maybe twelve, to make a couple of bucks. His answer was, "Who do I have to kill?" "That's my boy!" I said. "Go outside and find some cigarette butts in the gutter and bring them to me. I'll give you a buck a piece." He said, "That's all?" I said, "Yep, easy street." He went out and in ten minutes was back with twenty of them. I crossed his palm with the cash and proceeded to light up. You, who don't smoke and never have, have already gotten sick just thinking about me and those nasty butts in my mouth. No telling what I could have caught from them, and I am sure there are a few other things you have thought about that I haven't. But, you who do smoke or have smoked before, can imagine the pain, not only in lighting them so close to my lips and nose, but the burning sensation I felt as the smoke went down my throat from twenty-day old tobacco. As I looked at them when I was lighting them, I could see tire tracks and water spots on them. Maybe not water spots but cat urine. Who knows? But when you are down sixty thousand dollars, it is unbelievable what a person will do.

Later in the year I was hustling customers as football season was approaching. That was the big money time for bookies. I was at a bar in the early afternoon talking to some friends. Some guy in his fifty's kind of joined in the conversation. Nothing unusual! He was sitting close and could hear us. We got friendly after a few weeks. I asked him if he bets football. He said he did but was a very-small time dude. I gave him my phone number and a code, and then told him to call when he wanted to make a bet. That is the way you do it. You always need a code. Just like in the movies. He made a few bets each week and as he said, was a small better. But a lot of small betters make a large amount bet total. One afternoon as I was ready to pack it in for the day and go home. The doors in my office flew open with a crash. Three Federal agents came in with guns drawn, badges flashing, yelling, "Don't move, don't move! Put your hands in the air and don't move!" I almost shit my pants. Needless to say, I was fucked. They cuffed me, read me my rights, which at this moment I felt I had none, and carted me off to the calaboose. They took all of my phone recorders and a ton of bet slips. They even took the pencils I used. They booked me and let me go home on my own recognizance. After all, I was a substantial businessman in the community and had even donated to the policemen's ball! Assholes!

A month later I went to court and pleaded guilty to misdemeanor bookmaking. I was fined five hundred dollars and was told never to do it again. I went back to the office to see if they had left anything for me to salvage. It was like Hannibal Letcher alone with a skull. All was licked clean. I went home and told Heather what happened. She was appalled. She said, "We don't need the money, why do you do it?" (I believe, that in much later years from now, I said the same thing to Sean for something he did.) I really didn't have an answer for her at that time. Much later in life I think I just really need the action as I do now. She asked me if I was going to stop and I told her probably not. However, I did check into it and found out that if I get caught three times, it becomes a felony. I promised her that if I get caught again, I would not do it again. No jail time for Chuckie. None! I had seen the inside of one years ago. Feh! About a month later I started back again. It was still football season and a lot of money to be made. I got another office and begged forgiveness from all my players. I had no records from their past bets so I couldn't pay them or collect from them. Most understood. A few of them wanted to kill me because they thought they had won a lot of money and got nothing. *I just shot them first.* That way I didn't have to watch over my back all the time. Oh, by the way, did I mention that I was just joking about killing anyone? I didn't? Well, it was a joke. I didn't kill them! However, the thought, ... well never mind!

Right about play-off time I was at the new office and things had been going quite well. I locked up and went downstairs to head on home. It was dark. As I got into my car, I felt a punch on the back of my head and then again on my back. I was lying across the front seat, not knowing what the heck was happening. I thought someone was trying to rob me or whatever. As I lay prone across the front seat trying to get up, I saw a figure leaning in and trying to punch me again. I coiled my leg and kicked him in the chest. I heard him yell and fall down on the ground. He got up and ran away. (I'll tell you it was a good thing he wasn't Mexican or I would have killed him.) I kind of saw his profile but it didn't ring a bell. I was bleeding a little so I went to a friend's house to clean up a bit. Then I went home. I was perplexed about what had happened and couldn't reason it out. A year or so later I was in a friend/customer's house. He said, "Do you remember one night a guy attacked you at your office at night?" I said, "How the hell did you know about it?" He said, "I sent my son to beat you up just in case you ever got busted again. You would know that we can find you anywhere and anytime to get my money. So don't ever fuck with me, ever!" (Soon to be my ex-friend!) He had told me, more then once, that he was connected. I never really believed him, but this type of threat would be something that the boys would do. So, who knows? You thought you just answer a phone and go collect the money from the bettor. Wrong!

A few days later that guy I had met in the bar showed up again and said, "I heard you had some trouble a month ago. Is that why no one answers the phone anymore?" I said, "You heard right." He said, "Does that mean I can't bet the playoffs?" I said, "No. I have a new number for you and a code." He said, "Great. I really like the playoffs and even bet a little more on them." So, as luck would have it, a few days later I heard the door of the new office crash open again and heard the Feds yell, "Put your hands in the air and don't move." "Jesus Christ, I said, don't you guys have anything else to do?" They said in a very unbecoming way, "We like you and wanted to keep you company." Bastards! So, we went through the same routine as before. This time they asked me if they had to cuff me and I said, "No. I am starting to like you guys so why would I run when I can hang with you?" We all went to the station again. As I started to walk through the front door, my buddies asked me to put my hands behind my back so it would look like I was cuffed. I did so, walked in, and did the picture thing again, the finger print thing again, twenty minutes in the holding room again, and then they released me. Court date was attended by all. I was given a two-year probation, a thousand dollar fine, and told the next time would be a little different. I already knew that. So being, for once, true to Heather, I quit the bookmaking. However, I started betting again and much much more than before. Now that nineteen eighty-two and the bookmaking is behind me, it is back to the businesses that supports my habit.

I started to go to Vegas and increase my marker credit with some of the casinos. I looked great on paper because of the money I was making. Nothing shows the losses that are gone each and every day to bookmakers. I wound up with about ten thousand dollars in marker credit at about ten different casinos. For you novices, marker credit is when you go to Las Vegas and sit at a table and ask the pit boss for money, and he gives it to you. If I was approved for ten thousand dollars, then I could be given up to that much. If I lose whatever I had asked for gambling, I would have thirty days to pay it back with no interest. If I failed to pay it back in the thirty days, they just break my legs. It's just that simple! (I may have touched on that a few pages back.) So where were we? Oh, yes! I was losing so badly at home with the bookies I was betting with that I had to go to Vegas almost every week to get my marker money and bring it back home so I could pay off the bookies at home and then have the thirty-day grace period to pay back Vegas. It gave me a little breathing room. Now, here is the kicker with the markers in Vegas. When I go there and get my ten thousand dollars, I play for a while. Then I leave the table. I am supposed to give back whatever I haven't lost against what I had borrowed. So, if I did that, I wouldn't be able to go home any money, right? What I do is "rat hole" as much as I can without anyone seeing me do it. I know, what is "rat holing?" Shit! Don't you know anything? Rat holing is when you slip the money, a little bit at a time, into your pockets when no one is looking. You play a five dollar chip and slip a hundred dollar chip into your pocket. After a while it looks like you have been losing your ass betting. Then you get up with virtually nothing visibly left in chips, walk to the men's room, kill a little time there, and then casually walk to the casino's cage and cash out the nine thousand that was rat holed. Get into the car and drive as fast as I can home so I can now pay the bookies that will be on my door step Monday morning to collect the money I had lost to them. I hand them the money and with a smile on my face, say, "What's the line on the Lakers game today?" I would hope to hit them for a bunch in the next few weeks so I can take the winnings to Vegas and pay off my marker so I can keep walking. Now, all this in itself has to be new to most of you. I could end this segment here. But, as my life is, (As I keep saying) much different from yours (If you haven't noticed it by now, you should probably put the book down, put on your coat, head back to the book store where you purchased it from, and get a refund.) I would like to add to this tale.

My Lovely wife, Heather is starting to wonder about all those late night trips, practically, each and every Sunday night. I didn't exactly have a great track record of accounting for my time for many reasons. Some of them were working, cheating and more of both, not to mention gambling and gambling and gambling. In fact, sometimes I stayed at my office for hours after work playing gin rummy with a few guys. It was like sometimes I was non-existent as a husband. After a few arguments about my Sunday night runs to Sin City, I said, "Do you want to go with me this Sunday and see that I am telling you the truth?" It may be boring for you as I need to spend time on the tables gambling, and there will be nothing for you to do. She said, "I really want and need to go." I said, "Fine." So Sunday night approached and we were off. It was about a four hour drive there, and we left about six P.M. I figured I needed about three hours at the tables and then home by five o'clock ish. Just enough time to shit, shave and shower (Triple S) and make it to Brigham's for breakfast around seven and start my day and see whatever it brings. My days and weeks were always a surprise to me, whether good or bad.

We got to Las Vegas about eleven. I believe it was the Hacienda Hotel and casino I stopped at. I gave Heather twenty bucks in case she wanted anything. I told her she shouldn't bother me at any time. Just keep a watch on me and when I went to the bathroom, be ready to leave. I sat down and got a marker for five thousand dollars. In less than two hours I had lost it. Well, it wasn't on the table anymore. I asked for another five thousand dollars and received it. I proceed to play and rathole the chips. Once again, I was broke. I got up and went to the men's room. I checked my pockets and had just fewer than nine thousand dollars rat holed. I went to the casino cage, gave the lady my chips, and she gave me the cash. I put it in my pocket and nodded to Heather. She started to walk towards the front door, and I was headed there as well. I was just about fifty feet from her and about another twenty more to the front door when I heard someone call to me. "Mister Gerson, oh Mister Gerson!" I took a glance trying not to let anyone know that I heard anyone call to me. I saw two guys wearing suits walking towards me. I started to walk a little faster. Heather heard them call as well. She started to walk faster, also. By this time they were yelling my name, and they were walking faster as to try and intercept me at the front door. I wasn't but ten feet from Heather and yelled to her, "Hurry up, they are catching up to us." About this time we both met at the front door with the two guys hot on our trail. Heather, of course in heels, stopped at the front door and took them off. We were now at a full gallop. I busted through the front door and screamed to Heather, "Hurry, hurry."

Don't look back just run." My van was about fifty feet from the front door. There were no buttons to push on my key ring at that time so I stopped, unlocked my side of the door, reached over and unlocked the shotgun side, started the car, Heather jumped in, and we were off. The two guys had to be within ten or twenty feet from us but I didn't look back, just drove. I got out of the parking lot, looked at Heather and said, "Fun?" She looked at me and crocodile size tears started to roll out from her eyes. All I could hear was crying. Loud crying! Me being the normal asshole that I was, asked her, "Did you break a heel?" We drove home and not more then ten words were spoken the whole drive home by either of us. In fact, I was the one who spoke. If memory serves me correctly, I believe I said, "Hope you are happy now. Want to go next week?" *If looks could kill!*

My dad had finally passed away. Mom was one of those moms (like so many wives from that era) who never did or knew anything because Dad had done everything for her and the family. Always! He even bought my mom's underwear for her. Mom's job was to cook, clean and take care of the dog now that the kids were gone. Now we (my brother and I) had to do all of this for her. This was not working out very well. We had our own lives and were not just around the corner from her. For her birthday I got her driving lessons. She had the car that Dad drove. Well, let me stop here for a second and change the word, "drove". My dad, may he rest in peace, never in his later years drove a car. He usually aimed it. That is, if he was not falling asleep as he drove. More then once I heard tales about him driving on the sidewalk. He was not ever aware of it until Mom yelled at him, "Mike you are on the sidewalk." He would hit cars on a regular basis when parking and side swipe them as well. With all of this erratic car crap going on, the one that really takes the cake, in my eyes, was one day he fell asleep doing forty miles an hour in traffic. Mom, riding shotgun, and under a panic, gave him a smack and yelled, "Mike, wake up, wake up." He awoke and yelled back, "Shut up, I'm driving!" (I think in reality that in another life, he taught the Asians and the Mexicans, in Tijuana as well as New Yorkers how to drive.) Now where was I? Oh yea. Mom was very reluctant to learn how to drive. In fact, she refused. It was much better for her that we did everything for her. She didn't even know how to write a check so she could pay her bills. In fact, I don't even think she knew what bills were. As time passed we were not able to do what she wanted us to do for her when she wanted us to do it at the drop of a hat. (You know a Jap, a Jewish American Princess.) We finally convinced her to take driving lessons. I just prayed she didn't learn anything from Dad's driving. However, she actually did well. But it took years for her to become independent.

One day Heather and I decided to spend a weekend in Las Vegas. Not the Hacienda! I made reservations and we drove up. I had a convertible as well as my Ford van. I had the top down. It had to be one hundred degrees heading through Barstow. Barstow, now that's a chapter in itself. Anyway, I had the top down and was doing about eighty five miles an hour in a sixty-five mile an hour stretch of the freeway, running neck and neck with another car and had been for some miles. He was in the fast lane, and I in the slow, right lane. Heather was probably the fairest-skinned person I have ever known. Milk white! No, milk white, white! Heather was starting to get sick from the heat and repeatedly ask me to pull over and put the top up or to pull off so she could get a coke or some water. The all-American asshole knew better. "You are just fine," I said. (You would have thought I would have remembered the Holly puke thing a few years back.) "Not to mention honey, if we pull over, it will impede our time getting there." She kept nagging me over and over that she felt terrible and may have to throw up. "Please," she said, "please. I'm really sick." After twenty minutes more of that infernal nagging, I gave in and pulled off at the next ramp. All this time the guy in the car on my left was still neck and neck with me at eighty-five miles per hour. As I pulled off the freeway onto the off ramp, I noticed a police car behind me with his red lights on. (That's the only color they had then. Now, they look like a Christmas tree on wheels.) I pulled over. The cop came up to me and asked, "Do you know how fast you were going?" I answered like any idiot speeding, "No officer but probably about sixty-five. That is the speed limit on this section of the freeway, isn't it?" He said, "That's correct, but I clocked you (they didn't have radar yet either) at eighty-five." "Eighty-five!" I exclaimed "That car next to me was doing the same speed as I was doing for a long time. Why didn't you pull him over instead of me?" "I had intended to," the officer said, "but as I was going to put my lights on him, you started to pull off. It made it easier for me to cite you. I couldn't do both." That was the last thing I needed to hear. It was all Heathers fault that I was going to get the ticket. If she hadn't been nagging me for all those miles to pull off, this wouldn't have happened. I looked at her. She looked at me and immediately knew that she was in big trouble. She knew me like a book. We sat there in the hundred degree heat while the cop wrote the ticket. She was getting sicker, and I was getting hotter and not in degrees. She knew not to say anything. It would be just better to puke. The more I sat there, the more I was getting more pissed off. I was thinking of a way to get back at her. After all, it was all her fault. The cop came back and with a smile, handed me the citation and asked me to sign it and pointed to the appropriate line. I took the ticket holder and the pen, looked at the citation and said, "I am not going to sign it." The cop said, "It is not an admission of guilt, but just a promise to appear at court." I said, "I don't deserve this ticket so I am not going to sign it. Find that other guy and give it to him. I was only following the flow of traffic from someone in the fast lane. I am not signing it." The cop said that if I didn't sign it, he would have to take me into the station and have me talk to the captain or something like that. I said, "Bring the captain here. I'm not going anywhere." About this time Heather started crying. She did a lot of that when we were together. I said, "You are upsetting my wife." He said, "You both will have to go to the station with me. Get in my car, please." I said, "I am not going anywhere." Heather said, "Please sign the ticket, please. I don't want to go to jail. Please do what the officer tells you to do." "No!" I yelled. It's your entire fault so if you go to jail, it's not my problem." The cop said I was being unreasonable. What does he know? He doesn't know my wife. Either sign the ticket or get in the squad car. I am going to call my chief right now and tell him we are coming in or that he may have to come out here. Heather, taking all of about a half of a minute to say, "Please do what the officer says," in between crying and the flood of her tears. At this point it all started to seem very funny to me. Not realizing it at the time, I was getting even with Heather for causing all of this crap. She's panicked, stressed out, and was emotionally very upset. Seems I got what I wanted. "Ok, give me the ticket." I signed it, and we were on our merry little way to have a great time in Las Vegas. Yea, right! As we were driving, one of the very few words that were spoken was when I asked her if she would like to come to Barstow with me in a month to fight the ticket. She just looked at me.

Chapter Twenty-One

We had a dog named Chloe. Chloe was the runt of a litter that her mom had, which was our dog also. Mom got hit by a car so we kept the runt. This in itself is not big deal, and certainly not unusual, but it is a good segue to the turning of the downside of my life for a while. All of my life, for some reason, I never laughed at jokes or thought that things were funny that everyone else laughed at and thought was funny. In fact, I really never laughed much, period. The exception was when my dad or my brother said stuff. They made me crack up. Them and only them! Why, I have no idea. It was just that way. To this day, my brother is still the only one who makes me laugh, especially when we talk about our dad. The tears just roll down our cheeks and our stomachs hurt for hours. Now that I have all of that crap out of the way, it brings me to Chloe, our dog. One day Heather and I were sitting around and the radio was on. A song called "Baker Street" came on. Chloe sat down, raised her head to the ceiling, and started to howl and howl. She did it for the whole length of the song and when it was over, she stopped with the last note. I can't tell you how much we laughed and laughed. It was really funny. I bought the record and whenever we needed a laugh, we played it and Chloe did her thing, over and over and over each and every time. When we had gotten back from Vegas after the ticket deal, I put it on and it relieved the tension a bit. So now I have a dog in my life.

In nineteen eighty a guy named Ronald Regan, actor turned president, (basically no difference) got into office and put his financial plan together to heal the United States of America economically. It was affectionately called, "Reganomics." By nineteen eighty-four, bankruptcies were up about five hundred percent, I was told. In nineteen eighty I was, on paper, worth about a million dollars plus. Even with my huge gambling losses, I was still making a dollar or two. Pacific Cable, the wire distributorship, was the bulk of my profits and towered over the other businesses I owned in sales. However, my smaller customers were falling like ducks in hunting season. They were buying from me but couldn't pay their bills. My sales were sky rocketing but my receivables were not being paid. So, one by one, I was getting stuck with no payments from them. Eventually, they took me down with them, and I had to file bankruptcy. I had a few dollars tucked away, but it could have been a million or two had I not gambled. From a millionaire to busted in a matter of a year or so.

If you hark back a bunch of pages, you should recall that one of the reasons we took our trip of the United States was because we felt the kids would be leaving the home nest soon, and we, Heather and I, wanted to be a little closer to them before they left, especially Holly, our oldest. She actually did move to Orange County a year or two after high school with her boyfriend. Heather and I were not real crazy about the arrangement, not because Geoff was not a nice person, but he was almost three years younger than Holly. They seemed to be doing well, but we hadn't seen her for about three months or so. One day Heather and I were sitting around, and she was opening the mail. I heard a yell, and she came running into the living room where I was sitting. Jumping, screaming, and totally irrational, pointing to a paper she had in her hand. Now, with the exception of me and cop things, she was pretty solid emotionally. This was out of character for her. I calmed her down and she said to me, "Holly is about to give birth, if she hasn't already, because of the time the mail took to get the letter here, She and Geoff have given the baby away already to the new adoption parents. (The original letter is in the following pages). I said, "Do you know what hospital she is in?" Heather said, "Yes." I said, "Get in the car." We were off not more then ten minutes after Heather opened the mail. We got to the hospital and found the room that Holly was in. She hadn't delivered yet but was due the seventeenth of May. Hugs, kisses and tears abounded. We talked for hours and hours about the adoption. We finally talked Holly and Geoff into keeping the baby. I am not going to speculate on what the real reasons were to give up the baby, but at this point nothing really mattered. Heather called the nurse and told her of the change in decision about the adoption. The nurse said she would tell the appropriate people and after the baby arrived, someone would be in contact with her and Geoff. Not long after, a beautiful little girl arrived and was named Heidi. (Personally, I thought she should have been named Chuckelet after me. After all, I did drive Heather and myself to the hospital like Mighty Mouse, to save the situation.) So, now I am forty-two (double blackjack for you gamblers) and a grandfather. Great just great! By the way, the kid didn't pop out until the second of June.

3152 Pleasant St #1 5/18/84
G.G. 94602 Fri.

Dear Mom,
 This letter is way over due & the hardest one I'll ever write. I've wanted to do this for a long time, but I just couldn't bring myself to do it. I've finally come to the realization that I have to.

At first, I thought by keeping silent, I would keep you from being hurt, but now I realize that I've been hurting you all along by letting you wonder & worry. So I decided I better get the whole thing out in the open once & for all. So here it goes:

 You asked me quite a few times if I was pregnant & I always denied it or didn't →

(2)

answer. Well as you probably figured out by now that last. Believe it or not I didn't know (or maybe just wouldn't admit it to myself) untill I was 6 months along. I had a sonogram done, that's how I knew for sure how long I was. When I found out, I almost had a nervous breakdown. I was so scared, I didn't know what to do. I did know that I didn't want to be like Ilana. Then I remember the talk you, dad & I had on last birthday at the Arbor about being a single mother & what a mistake Ilana was making. I can also tell by the way Ilana was when I saw her that she was not really as happy as she wanted everyone to believe. I also know sooner or later it will reflect

(3)

and thought the whole situation through very carefully. I know that deep down inside I am definately not ready to be a mother. I know by my biological age I should be ready, but I'd be lying to myself if I thought that I was ready emotionally. So taking all this into consideration I decided that my baby deserves a better mother than I could ever be for it right now. It deserves to have a happy family that's ready to take care of a child properly and give it everything it needs, everything I can't give it. Obviously this is not something I'm taking lightly, it causes me great pain & stress everyday & I don't want to put you th

(4)

through any of this, but it's too late now. I also didn't want you to hate me. Anyway here comes the hard part. I've decided with all things considered to put the baby up for adoption. I know that sounds horrible, but I feel that it's the right thing to do for the baby's sake. Next to writing you this letter, this is going to be the hardest thing I'll ever have to do. Be reassured that I'm doing it all the right way. The adoption is being done through an agency called "Holy Family Services", they work through the County of Orange. I was able to pick out the family for the baby. They also have been giving Counseling + set me up with a very good O.B who I have been seeing at work... I'm going to have the baby at

(5)

Fountain Valley Hospital. It was due yesterday (17th), so now I'm just waiting.

So here it is. I've told you everything. I'm really sorry. I know that you + dad have been through enough pain in your life already and I hate myself for puttin you through more. I know all of this is my own fault, I caused my own pain, I just wish I could have kept you from feelin it too. I really don't know how you are going to react to this, but if you decide that I've hurt you too much + you want me out of your life for good. I'll understand. Just remember I do love you both more than anything else in the world + I always will.

> (6)
> Again I'm truly sorry. I hope you can find it in your heart to forgive me, but if not, it's my fault I know.
>
> I love you,
> Dolly

A few days after the new arrival, maybe a week, Heather was still in a great mood. We were home and went out to eat at Vince's Spaghetti. It seemed like every time we ate there, we came home and were both very romantic. I am sure it had nothing to do with the two bottles of Chianti we drank. Certainly not what I would drink now, but Heather is not here either. (Actually, I wanted to go to Vince's every night, but Heather had some special sitcoms she wanted to watch on T. V.) This one night we got home and Heather, a little shit-faced, changed into something very special. Once again, you need to use your imagination. I was in the living room sitting in MY easy chair. We had a couch that separated the living room from the hall which Heather had to walk through from the bedroom. She walked down the hallway and made the turn into the living room. As she approached the couch, she put her hand on the top of it and then threw both her legs up into the air as to fling herself over the top of the couch and land onto the seats. Kind of like you might see in a movie. Little Miss Coordination completely missed the seats, and, in fact, she completely missed coming over the back of the couch and landed flat on her side in back of the couch on the floor. She was in pain or maybe just embarrassment. I rushed over to her while laughing my ass off, to see if she was still alive. It really looked funny. She bobbed up and was laughing also. We both laughed for a while. It was quite a sight to see. The next day she couldn't walk!

Now that I am on to really stupid stuff, I will add two things that completely do not make sense. So, I guess that would be normal in this book. But, in a way, will somehow link up with something much later in my years that also doesn't make sense. First, I have always believed that I had an older sister. I have and had asked for the truth many times. The answer was always, an emphatic, "No." The other thing that doesn't make sense is that I have always thought I was or should have been in World War Two. Crazy? Maybe not! Now for some very serious stuff! This is something that not only many of our close friends at that time didn't know but some of our relatives didn't either. I filed for divorce in eighty-four. Oh wait! Now that I think about it, Heather did the filing. Sometimes I really think it was me that filed. How could anyone file for divorce against me? It must have been me! Right? Well, whatever. I was never home. I only cheated on her a few times a month. I gambled away all our money. I only played cards each and every Tuesday with the guys and always got home before three or four o'clock in the morning. I controlled my male companionship to only three or four times a week and tried to be home before two A.M. I only went to Vegas without her maybe three times a month. I could go on and on about what a great husband I was, but you can already see I am a great husband by the above. Hell, I even bought a flower shop just because she liked the name "Aaron." In those days it took six months to have the divorce final. Nowadays, I haven't a clue and hope I never find out. I moved out and got an apartment not far away. We worked out a deal with the kids. As a matter of fact, no matter how mad we were at each other or no matter what might have happened in the week, we both Loved and always supported the kids, all three of them. Even though David had been in and out of detention until he was eighteen and now jail a bunch, he was no less Loved than Holly and Sean. If one of the kids had a game they were in or a play or even a dinner to go to, Heather and I would always go hand in hand, sit together, and try to be as natural as possible so not to embarrass any of them. They were always our focus. So, the deal we worked out for the divorce was, that I could have custody any time I wanted them as long as they were not already scheduled for something. And in return, at any time, Heather needed money for them, no matter what is was, the cash would be there. I trusted her in that the money would be for the kids and not to be spent on her or some suitor. I think she knew better. She was a better person than that.

It's kind of funny how things change after some years. Then I was happy to live alone. Today, I am not really happy to live alone, but I don't think I could live with anyone and I never have in all these years. Well, I really don't know what Heather did in those six months before our divorce was final but, if I had to bet on it, I would say she did very little dating and spent most of her time with the kids. To be honest with you, I really don't want to know. A lot of really strange stuff happened in those six months as we did haunt the same places and basically did have the same friends. One thing I did know was that at least two of my closest buddies kept asking Heather to go out with them. She had told me she said no, but I moved from those buddies to others. I had trouble believing my close friends would turn on me that quickly. Maybe it was just the way I perceived it, but I was pissed. One time in the summer we bumped into each other at Reuben's restaurant. I believe I have mentioned that place before. Heather had a pretty good rack. Oh wait, bust. The word rack still has not been invented. She, herself, had a really large bust, but after all that baby stuff, gravity became the boss. So, I laid the money out and had her (them) reconstructed. When I saw her at Reuben's she had been wearing a tube top. A tube top is a kind of a large rubber band around her chest. No bra and was looking great. As she turned the corner, she almost bumped into a guy. However, it wasn't an accident. It was planned by the guy. As they ran into each other, his hand grabbed the top of her tube top, pulled it down, and held it there for a few seconds. Heather was unbelievably embarrassed and humiliated. Hell, I wanted to deck the guy myself. I had to control my emotions because I was being divorced from her and was Joe macho as well. I was probably the first one that said, "Did you see that set?" The real me felt really bad for her and made me horny at the same time. I had seen them before but now, they were not mine. I started to think that maybe I was still in Love with her, even though we were getting divorced. Naw, can't be.

Another time in the same bar, she was dancing with some dude I didn't know. I got very jealous. When they were done dancing, I walked up to the guy and said, "Nice set of tits she has, huh!" He said, "Yea." I said, "I bought them for her. Want to see them?" He said, "No" but that was not good enough for me. I walked over to Heather and said, no, screamed, "He wants to see your tits that I bought for you. Show him ok?" Everyone in the place stopped talking and dancing. I thought they were waiting for her to show them her tits, but they had all been looking at the major asshole that was doing screaming. I walked out. Still in Love?

I did have to give Heather a monthly check that the court decided. Because Heather and I had decided how we were going to handle it before hand, it was a small amount. But I did have to send it monthly. On the fifth day of the month, five days after I was suppose to have sent it. I would put the check in an eight and a half by eleven size manila envelope and fill half of it with sand, address it to Heather in small print and then the letter "L" which was her middle initial very large in the middle of the envelope and then Gerson again in small print. On the bottom line of the very large "L" I would write "Louse" and then put it in the mail without a stamp. When she went to pick it up, because the postman would not deliver it without postage, she would not only get it days late but have to pay postage for an overweight parcel. It really made me happy and Loved to brag about it to my friends.

Now, while I was having a hell of a time whenever I ran into Heather, when I was back at my apartment or was out with my guy friends, I was getting laid on a regular basis. A lot of the chicks I didn't even know their names or had forgotten them as soon they walked out of my apartment. I had what I called an open door policy. No matter what time it was, morning, noon or night, if the door was unlocked, just walk in. If the door was locked, don't even bother to knock. Now, I need to tell you something, today, I know I was a sick son of a bitch for what I had been doing to Heather and believe it or not, myself, but then it was a game and was fun playing. I was still seeing Debbie from the bank on a regular basis. I guess if I had been paying her way, she would have been labeled my mistress. But I wasn't so I guess she would be called my whatever. One night I was in bed with Debbi, and there was a knocking at the door. I jumped out of bed and looked through the little hole in the door and saw it was Heather. She probably saw me look though the hole. She kept on knocking for five minutes or more. The banging got louder and louder. I talked to Debbie. She said to open the door and see what Heather wanted. I did so and the first thing out of Heather's mouth was, "Is she here with you?" I said, "Yes". I could see

Heather's fury and the pain in her eyes. She said, "I want to talk to her." I said, "That's not a good idea." Just about that time Debbie walked out of the bedroom. Naked! At least I had put a robe on. But that was Debbie and probably one of the reasons I liked her. Maybe in my own way, Loved her. I told Debbie to put something on. She went into the bedroom and didn't come out. Heather and I talked for a bit and it wasn't a fun talk. I said, "Let's go into the bedroom and have Debbie in the conversation." We sashayed in (Yea right!), and Debbie was in bed and had put nothing on. She sat up with her tits out of the covers. We talked for an hour or so about our (ALL three of us) situation. I am not really sure how it happened, but I probably talked myself blue in the face. I was a good salesman, but I got them both to agree to a threesome. Right then and there! Heather got undressed and got into bed. I already had my robe off and was in between them both. It's not necessary to go into any details, but within a half hour, Heather got up, put her clothes on, and left. She never joined in. Not really sure what was in her head when she agreed to it, but today she is still a class act. Well, at least since I have seen her last.

The six months to the divorce went fast. I had taken a job with a firm that sold things you use only once. It was a great job. You always knew that they had to reorder. The products were diversified like syringes, latex gloves, a similar product to Sterno, and the sort. Not to mention that outside sales and cold calling was my meat! Car allowance, small expense account and commission, just my bag! Most people don't care for that type of sales. It's my meat! To this day I Love outside sales.

It was nineteen eighty-five and I was, *shit*, forty-three. How old can you get? Not to change the subject, but when my dad turned forty and had a really big party, I took my little brother Mark aside and said, "Dad really doesn't have much more time left. I will be the head of the family soon. So let's be nice to Dad because he only has a few years left." Where was I? Oh yea. It was that time when all good men get divorced, legally. I took off my wedding band. Heather had taken hers off months ago. In fact, I think it was six months ago to date. Anyway, I called her on the phone and said, "Do you know what day this is?" That may have been the most stupid thing I have said in all my life. She said, "Yes, of course." I said, "Do you want to celebrate it?" She said, "What do you have in mind?" I said, "You know our favorite Mexican restaurant off the corner of Foothill and Garey. Let's meet there for dinner and toast to our demise." I'll buy! She said, "What time?" I said, "How about six?" She said, "Okay." Now, I have to set the stage for you. This particular Mexican restaurant was a little more up scale than most. It had the usual tables on the floor but also had tiers of booths, each tier a little higher than the others and they were deep brown leather and would accommodate six people. The tier area was dimly lit and sexy red lights for background. At this point in my life, I had smoked only one joint, ever. (Joint, for you younger readers, it is a marijuana cigarette. Yuk, Yuk. Like you don't know! For you older readers, it could mean prison as well.) A few years ago I decided to try one. I had a buddy get me one. I told Heather what I was going to do and asked her to watch over me and didn't know how I would react. I sat down in the living room against the wall and smoked away. In fifteen minutes I fell asleep and was cloud walking for the next two hours after I woke up. Nothing, nada! I thought I would smoke one before I met with Heather so I would be very calm and relaxed and not cause any problems. Good idea, yes. No! I got my joint, smoked it and drove to the restaurant at six. We met, gave a very little kiss on the lips, and sat at our favorite table. Menus in hand, I asked her if she would like a glass of wine. She said, "Fine," so I got a bottle. We drank all of it and surprisingly, we were enjoying each others company. The bottle was empty. "Would you like some more wine?" I asked?" "Sure," was the answer, "Why not?" Bottle number two was almost gone and we ordered our Burritos or whatever. After the ordering we kinda kissed and then kissed a little more. The joint I smoked, that I remembered from a few years ago, must have been grown in different soil. This joint was a mother f—r. I was groping and she was groping and the only thing that tore us apart was a little voice that said, "Who gets the Chulapa?" We stopped and ate, in between touching. We kept looking at each other and smiling. If there had been a blackout, she would have been done right there on the Corinthian leather. I was wet, she was wet. We certainly didn't need any hot sauce. We finished eating. I said, "How about us going home?" She said, "Okay." Home we went and we made Love for the whole weekend. I never left. I really don't know how many people know the whole story. Well, not the Chulapa part, but the final divorce part. We lived in sin for a long time. Although I tried to change in many ways, I pretty much failed in most.

Chapter Twenty-Two

Although Dad passed a while back, he had lived much longer than anyone ever thought. He would go into the hospital and the doctors said, "There is a chance that he may not come out." We heard that so many times that it became second nature. But my dad was strong, really strong. He beat cancer. He beat diabetes. He beat living with a Jewish woman all those years. When he could no longer work for Bond Clothing, he started to work at the flea markets (Swap meets.) Selling anything he could get his hands on, but mostly electronics like stereos, speakers and the like. (He did stay away from T. V.'s.-Not a Gerson thing.) He would stray from his usual products if he could get a deal on something else.

One day he bought a thousand pair of woman's nylons. These were no ordinary nylons. These nylons had no feet in them. A thousand pair of nylons with the feet cut off! The cutter in the manufacturing process had been set wrong, and the first thousand pair came out with no feet before it was noticed. "Dad, what the hell are you going to do with nylons with no feet?" my brother and I asked. He said, "Sell them." He had paid about five cents a pair if memory serves me correctly. I went out with him to the swap meet one day, and he was hustling them at fifty cents a pair. I swear he was touting them as masks for the Mexicans when they were to hold up a bank! I could hear him yelling, "Crook masks, rape a chick, and don't get caught." The Mexicans were buying them for their hair, and Dad thought they were all bank robbers. He sold out in three weeks! What a guy. My hero! Dad actually opened a "Wholesale to the public warehouse" in Pomona. (I actually should have sat him down and explained to him, for three hours, why he could not afford to open it. Not to mention, he has no prior experience and should take a few years to plan it.) My daughter worked for him part-time as did my oldest son, David. David refused to take money from his Zada. He probably just stole what he wanted and made a living that way. My dad, David's Zada, I am sure he turned a blind eye. Although he had never mentioned it, I am pretty sure that Dad's favorite was David. I know because Dad was the one that David called to be bailed out. Not me! (I was not supposed to know that it had happened.) They both had this kinda nomad, deceitful, great smile and gift of gab that would and could turn anything into money. Dad filled the warehouse with stereos and all types of electronic equipment. I looked for the nylons but there were none. Not long after, may be a year or so, Dad went into the hospital and never came out of the hospital. I threw a big party for him. He would have wanted it that way. Many were at his funeral, and many more were at the house for the party. David, my alcoholic son, tended bar. Dad would have wanted it that way, too.

One day in eighty-eight, I came home from my outside sales job and noticed there were some papers on the table. I picked them up and started to read them. The first two words were, "Hey Bucko" I'm thinking who the hell is Bucko? I read on and found out. It was a farewell letter to me. After the classic title the next few words were, "If you are reading this, I am already on a ship going to Australia." I'm thinking, this is a joke, right? I called the bank that Heather worked for and asked for her. Whoever answered the phone said, "Heather hasn't worked here for some three weeks." I hung up and called to where Holly was. I asked her if she knew anything about Mom going to Australia to visit her mother, nana. She said, "No." I asked her to come home. I needed to talk to her. I had the boys come in. When Holly got home, I sat them down and broke the news to them. This was not an easy thing to do, but there was no option. No one had a clue, no one. Holly was the most devastated. She had just announced, a month ago, that she and Geoff were finally to get married. About time! Heidi, the new baby (not to be confused with the name Chuckellet), was going to be thirty-seven years of age already. Well, two years anyway. Heather and Holly had started looking at colors, invitations, places, and so forth for a month already. She was in a bad way. In the letter to me, Heather said, "Tell the kids that I will call them as soon as I could."

A lot of things changed that day. A lot! As I recall, it was in early June. Emotions ran wild with all of us. We each had a different take on it. But, devastation is devastation. Of course, I could not get over that the kids were thinking all the time that it was my fault that their mother was gone. Unfortunately, I had to agree with them. It was my fault. One hundred percent my fault! I weighed, at that time, two hundred and thirty-seven pounds and was a mess. Holly had a wedding coming and with her shaky past, I was very concerned. The boys still had to finish school. Sean, my youngest, had a pretty straight head on his shoulders but David, my alcoholic oldest, could go off in any direction. Heather had done probably what she wanted to do. She got back at me big time and caused me about as much shit and pain as I had caused her. She may have gotten ahead. It took me years to screw her up, and she did it to me all in a day.

I used to play poker with the guys each and every Tuesday night. On Wednesdays I would notice that there seemed to be a lot a hangers lying around. I should have suspected something right then and there. She was shipping her clothes overseas little by little. DUH! Where do I start? Where?

We Holly, David, Sean and myself, all got together and formed a partnership. We designated chores and responsibilities for all. Of course, chores which David seemed to forget to do almost all the time! I had been so used to being taken care of; I didn't know how to run a washer or dryer. Sean had to show me how. This all may be the way other dads had to deal with having the kids and Mom being was gone, for whatever reason. Normal. Then why is it in this book? Well, are you ready? I'm gona tell ya. I may not get all this stuff in the right order, but you probably would not notice, anyway. It was just after the fourth of July. David had been at a friend's place. He got drunk or stoned or both. I got a call from a hospital that David had been burnt. By the time I got there, he was in surgery. Surgery! What for? You said he got burnt. He got very much burnt. He had his head down right on top of a dud firework when he realized it wasn't a dud. It exploded an inch or two from his face. David was in pain and in the hospital for weeks. He was really a great looking guy. Very handsome! I thought he would look like a monster from here on out. God and a very good hospital worked their magic. When he was finally released, he was none the worse for wear. *Although he looked fine, his attitude did not change and was constantly in trouble!*

This kind of started a bunch of things that could have been digging his grave, and I mean literally. He got drunk and robbed a bank for five bucks, went next door and bought a six-pack of beer. Then he sat down up against the banks wall that he had just robbed and proceeded to drink the beer. I am sure he had been already drunk at the time of the robbery. David, by now, was six foot six, bright orange red hair, and had a smile that knocked over the ladies. He wasn't hard to find. He did time again. Only this time it was in a penitentiary. David was in and out of jail and/ or the penitentiary many times in the next fifteen years for a plethora of things. There was robbery, probation violation, wife abuse, driving a car without a license, not knowing whose car it was and many, many more. By the time he was forty, he had spent half of his years behind bars. One time when he was out of jail, he met a shiksa (non-Jewish girl). I would have used the word lady, but she wasn't. David fell in Love with her. She already had two children and did not know who the fathers were. Both kids had different ones. I, personally, I fell in Love with the two kids. (that happens to me a lot) I spent a lot of time with them as I was soon to be a grand-dad again. Anyway, David had done something wrong again and was in Soledad Prison. He had asked me if I would bring his "lady" to the prison for a conjugal visit. I said, "Sure." On Friday morning I would get up at five o'clock A.M., pick her up, take her to the train depot three hours away, drop her off, pick her up late Sunday night, and bring her home. This went on for months. I am glad someone was getting laid, because I wasn't.

I spent most of my weekends either picking up and delivering or driving to Orange County to watch a beautiful six-year-old sit on a bench at a softball game. That went on for years.

David decided to get married. Why, I have absolutely no fucking idea. He couldn't give me a reason either. It seemed to me that his bride to be had nothing to gain from it, either. She would be married to a professional jail bird. David had nothing to gain from it, either. Hell, he was getting laid on a regular basis, already. (Hopefully, from outside the walls only) Of course, when he gets married, that would stop, right guys? So, it looks like the only one who benefitted from it is me. I get to tell you that I was a best man at a wedding in Soledad Prison! I dare you to tell me you stood up for someone at a wedding in a prison. I triple dog dare you! When I received letters from David, he kept repeating that I needed to stop bad-mouthing him to her and the kids. I never had said anything. She was making up lies, and he was buying them. Finally, he realized that she was lying so we would not be as close as we were. (Years later, I realized that we weren't as close as I thought we were.) When he finally got out, it wasn't a long time after that he filed for a divorce. She then told the cops he was beating her. He went back for a few more years for wife beating. Was he? No, but who are the cops going to believe, a lifer or a trollop? Next!

David wrote me one time and asked if I would pay for schooling for him to be in a water management program. Aw, I thought, school? I sent the money and according to him, he went and graduated in a year or so. He told me that there were openings at a few water plants and that he had high grades so he was to be a shoe in. I guess when he finally got out; he felt that water didn't need to be managed.

I regularly sent him money for tooth paste, cigarettes, and the like. I did it year after year after year. He was my son and responsibility. To my knowledge, his brother, sister or his mother never sent him a thing. Not only that, they never visited him in the twenty some years he was in and out of prison. Ever! There is plenty more to tell about my oldest son, but I banged on him enough already. I just thought the jail stuff was a little different from what most men have had to endure with a kid of theirs.

Sean, my youngest, was the very best son a dad could ever have. He went to school! Next! Just kidding! Sean had a Love for the good things. He saw what his mom and dad went through with David. I feel he didn't want himself to do it. He not only finished high school, but he had intended to become a veterinarian. The reason he decided that was, one day he was at the race track with me very early in the morning. I had a horse racing that day. I had asked him if he wanted to go and give the horse a kiss for luck. We were talking to Ted West, my trainer, and the track vet stopped by. He asked Ted which horse had to get the lasix shot. That's a medication they give some horses the day of the race. Ted said, "This one." The vet shot him in less than thirty seconds. I said, "There goes thirty bucks." Sean said, "Thirty bucks in that short a time? I'm going to become a vet." It's amazing what will inspire a nice, little Jewish boy. Money! Sean not only finished high school but three years prior, I had told him that when he graduates junior high, I would get a limo for him and all his buddies to be picked up and dropped off at the school for the graduation. David said, "You never told me that." I would have told David that if he graduates, I would have him picked up and delivered him with a helicopter. The only problem with that was he would probably figure that he had to steal it himself.

Sean was working for a vet and met this very cute girl. He would tell me that when he picked her up and dropped her off, her dad was standing there with a loaded rifle. Curfews were imposed, and certain values and rules were installed. Sean was made aware of all of them. Sean was a very smart fellow. He had great grades and good street sense. I saw red flags all over the place. Sean, against my better judgment decided to marry her. (Maybe, I should have voiced my opinion to him, but he was in Love. You know what that is like being a male in heat!) What was he thinking? She did the whole wedding. Made the dresses, supplied the food, made and sent the invitations, and told Sean who was to come and who was not to come. Later, I found out that the rifleman (her father) was seventy-five years old, military, and all was done his way. The divorce came within a year or two. A time after the divorce she, at one time, found Sean with a gun to his head. Fortunately, the trigger wasn't pulled, I think, to her credit. (Had it been me who found him, I am not so sure, well . . .) We never spoke about it much. A little later in his life, he met a really nice lady. She was a couple of years older, but very lady-like and proper. She had been married once, also. We all liked her. Except Heather! Heather didn't know her just like she didn't know Sean's first wife. Heather was in Australia. That Love affair went on. The marriage happened and her mother and I sent them both to Hawaii for their honeymoon. I actually missed the wedding. I was stuck in traffic because of an over-turned truck and had all lanes blocked for eight hours. No cell phones then, either. I can't imagine what they were thinking.

I picked them up at the airport as they came home from Hawaii. Sean and she gave me a kiss and a hug. Then Sean leaned over to me and said, "I am filing for divorce next week." I didn't ask! That was many, many years ago. I still don't know! There's just nothing normal in my life. Sean muddled through his personal life for a while. Sometime later, Sean hooked up with a guy who was in the sports world. (Sean's favorite sport was basketball. He always said he was mad at me because he was only six foot three and white. Sorry! I told him to stand closer to the hoop and yell mother words. That is probably as close to what he wanted, and that he is going to get.) Sean would do things like go to sport shows and have big name players sign basketballs and things like that and then sell them for a huge price for this guy. Sean was paid well for this. If the boss really knew, Sean probably would have done it for free, just to be near some of those guys.

Sean met a cheerleader and they became close friends. Just friends! She would invite him to different events. One of those events was the wedding of the daughter of Jerry Buss. He was the owner of the Lakers. My son, Sean, was at the height of his glory. He went and had a great time. The story he told most often and was so very proud of, was when he was in the bathroom taking a leak and Magic Johnson and Kareem Abdul Jabbar were standing next to him doing the same. Now that's bragging rights! Right? Pissin partners!! I just guess there is no accounting for the thoughts of youth. (I need to put in a disclaimer right here. I am guessing that the name of the Lakers' owner is that of Jerry Buss at that time and to be perfectly honest with you, it might have been Pat Riley's daughter, and not that of Jerry's, whom got married." Hell, for all I know and remember, it may have been Michael Spinks' kid.) Let me tell you, Sean seemed to have the job that he really wanted. One day I got a call from him to bail him out of jail. I said, "Are you sure you are Sean and not David?" He said, "Please come and get me." So, I did just that. For some stupid reason, something that I will never understand, he took and cashed a customer's check for fifteen hundred dollars that was to his boss. Sean didn't need the money. I guess he thought he could get away with it because of the shabby way his boss kept the books. Or in fact, maybe didn't keep them. The bottom line was that Sean did time in prison. Now, I have two jail birds. One that I am now used to and one that was a shock!

The months kept coming. I now am playing mother to the coming bride. I was going with my daughter to all the wedding shows at the malls and wherever she wanted me to go. It had to be funny, as I am sure, when we would walk into a store to sign a register or get some free stuff that the people there were trying to guess if I was the groom-to-be or her mother in drag. This went on for months. When all was said and done of that stuff, I think I had won five bouquets of flowers, a couple of dinners, at least two pedicures, and a bunch of women's phone numbers to call for help on colors and flowers, food and gifts. So all was not a loss! Well, the date of July twenty-second comes around and that happened to be the exact date of my beautiful daughter's wedding. And how beautiful she was!

Now, this is where the fun starts. It had been over a year since Heather had left us. She had been in touch with the kids on a regular basis and pretty much all was as good as possible with them. What she had said and the reasons she gave them for leaving were never shared with me. (I didn't realize that that would become a habit with them in later years.) And I never asked. That was between them. I did what I had and wanted to do and all seemed to be working just fine. Heather was invited to the wedding, of course. She is the mother. Heather came over from Australia for the wedding with her mother and an aunt if memory serves me correctly. They stayed at the Disney Hotel, I believe. We had a rehearsal and a dinner followed. Of course, I paid. Not unlike Heathers and my wedding. The rehearsal went great, and Heather and I got along just fine. (We were not exactly kissing cousins, but fine.) As I believe I have mentioned before, no matter how bad things were between her and me, we were always the best of friends when we were with the kids and for any and all functions. This was no different. The next day was the wedding and reception. The wedding was held in Dana Point, on the top of the harbor, overlooking the world, a harbor filled with multi-colored boats and loaded with friends and family, it seemed. It was a beautiful day as my God had seemed fit to make it great for me and mine. We all were dressed to the nines. Heather was, as always, beautiful and so were my boys. Thank God all my family was there and not in jail somewhere. We were running a little behind time waiting for the bride to show up and waiting for the bride to show up and waiting for the bride to show up. Finally, the limo drove up on to the grass and stops. The bride's maids pour out of it and then we were waiting for Holly to pour out. No Holly. I went to the limo and saw her stuck in the back corner in the limo and very drunk. She could not get out by herself. I reached in and grabbed her arm and gently pulled. She made it out and had this huge, super big grin on her face and said, "We were drinking some champagne." I said, "Yea, I can see that." I really don't think she was as drunk as it seemed. I think she was just nervous with all of the things that were happening: the wedding, her mom and dad together for the first time in over a year, and not knowing how things were to go. The wedding was just beautiful. We all went to the reception. I had rented a hall not far from the wedding site that was a great big hexagon building with huge glass windows that was built for such occasions. There was an open bar, live band, and a full sit-down catered dinner of steak or fish and all the trimmings for well over one hundred people. We waited for all to show up and then some. The music played, a lot of drinking and dancing was going on, and all were having a great time. All of a sudden we heard the best man on the PA system ask us to be seated. The seating was arranged so that Heather and her mom and aunt and a friend or two of Heathers were at one table just below and to the right of the head table where the bride and her entourage were to be seated. I, my brother, and my mom were right across from Heathers table on the left with a friend or two. All were seated. The best man stood up and made a toast to the bride and groom. Then he said, "Let the eating begin." He sat down and just before the food was to be served, my daughter Holly stood up and said, "I would like to say something." All was quiet again, and this is what came out of my daughter's mouth. (Unfortunately, I can't remember it exactly, but this is the crux of it." "I need to pay special thanks to my dad. In the past year, he not only endured all the trials and tribulations that goes on with a wedding, like taking me places and helping with the colors, invitations, and the flowers and all the things like that, that I could have not done alone in the planning of my wedding. Unbeknownst to anyone, but Geoff and myself, I wanted to cancel it all a month ago, but because of my dad's support and inspiration, we are all here today, and I Love him dearly for it." I want you to know that the reason this dissertation from my daughter about me is in this book is not for bragging rights by any means. But, to tell you that as the speech from my daughter's lips stopped, Heather, her mother and aunt got up, walked out and never returned. Not a word of goodbye or have a great life the two of you or anything. Just left and went back to Australia never to be heard from for a year or so. The only good thing that came of it was that the caterers gave me credit for three dinners. Daughter married off, David probably going to spend the rest of his life being protected by our men in blue, and Sean back on track. (I thought.) Maybe it's time to move and get my head on straight. I started to make plans to leave at the end of the year. Thought I'd hang around for awhile and see that all is going hot straight and true before I make my move.

One night I was with a buddy, and we went to a night club that had a really great entertainer. He sang and played the piano while putting on wigs, face masks, and many other things to act out the songs that he sang and played. Don't remember his name but the club was in Pomona and usually packed. Pomona, at that time, was not really the safest place to be at night. We were having a drink and my buddy, an Italian with a huge ego, said, "Look at that chick over there. She's reading a book while everyone else is either dancing or laughing and having a great time." He said, "She's got to be easy. She's either bored or having husband problems." I said, "Go for it." I really couldn't see what she looked like from where I was sitting. It was too far away. He talked to her for about fifteen or twenty minutes and then returned empty handed. "What," I said, "No number?" He said she was married and from out of town and really not interested. She was here to meet someone on business. I said, "Good story. She really just told you to fuck off, didn't she?" I didn't get an answer. I asked him what she looked like and he said, "Not bad." I could see she had long, kind of dirty blonde hair and seemed tall and thin. I watched her for a little while and when the music stopped for the entertainer's break, she walked over to the entertainer and started a conversation. Assuming that it was her husband, I told my buddy to look and see who she was talking to. Of course, I had my tongue in my cheek and a smile from ear to ear. "She's just a groupie trying to get laid by an entertainer, nothing different, right?" I said. Again, he just looked at me. The music started, and she went back to her table and to her book. It was driving me crazy. I didn't really know or believe what was what. So, it was my turn. I sashayed over and sat down at her table and said, "Hi." She immediately said, "Did your friend send you over to help out?" I said, "No, as a matter of fact he didn't. I just wanted to know what kind of book seemed to be more important than a good entertainer. But then, again, you seem to know him so he probably plays for you personally." "Why don't you go sit with your friend?" she said. I said something to the effect, "Because I am really happier looking at your pretty face and beautiful long hair, if that makes any sense." She looked at me. I knew that some smartass remark was to be shot at me by the look on her face. Instead, she said, "Not bad and a lot better than your friend." I said, "Does that mean I get your phone number?" She said, "I'm married." I said, "I think I have heard that somewhere." She said, "It's true and I am here to talk to the piano man." I said, "Why?" She said, "He's a member of a P.O.W. and an M.I.A. group." I said, "Why?" She just wanted to meet more people with the same feelings and beliefs that she had. I was kind of hoping she was getting the same feeling and beliefs that I was getting. We talked for a very long time. The show was over, and I gave her my phone number. She had told me a few things that she didn't tell Ron, my Italian stallion buddy (Sorry Rocky.) Mainly, that she was really having a rough time with her marriage and that she was starting to get scared of him. I think she meant physically. He had been scaring her for a while on a mental level. The night was over, and we all went our separate ways. She never did give me her phone number but did say she lived in Simi Valley and her name was Bonnie. That's about two hours away from my house. I never heard the end of it from Ron, how I spent the whole night courting a chick who wouldn't even give me her phone number, forget a kiss. Actually, it did seem like a waste of a night. There could have been someone else out there that could have floated my boat and I never would have known. But, I am a salesman and have a lot of patience.

    I still had a pretty bad habit gambling. Only this time I didn't have enough money to cover my losses when I lost. There was one bookie name Paul. He was a kin to my friend, Cal the bookie. Only this guy, not only thought he was part of the mob, he thought he was the mob. I had lost to him big time one week and just like you see in the movies, he sent over to my house, the bone crushers to collect. I didn't have all of my losses but gave them a small portion. They took it and said they would be back in a few days for the balance. There was not going to be a payment when they came back. I was broke, but I didn't let them know that. I figured I could skate for a while because Cal was my friend and would put in a good word for me. Cal did, and I skated for a couple of weeks. I was playing with a couple other bookies and hoping that I would hit it big so I could pay off Paul. It didn't happen. Too many days went by, and Cal could not hold them off any longer. One afternoon, in broad daylight, a car pulled up across the street. Three guys got out and walked up to my house. One of my friends, Marty, and neighbor happened to be outside and saw what was going down. Marty knew that I had been a bookie and that I had a bad habit of betting. The three jack offs broke through the door with guns pulled and threw me against the wall, hit me a couple of times, and said, "Where's my money? No excuses this time. Where's the money?" (It was good they were not Mexicans, or I would have killed them!) I said, "I am waiting for the loan to go through for a second trust deed on my home. As soon as they funded me the money, it's yours. I can't rush it. It's been approved so it's just a waiting game. I should know in a day or so when to pick up the money." They smacked me around a few more times and called me a liar. (I'm telling you, they're lucky that they weren't Mexicans or I would have exploded and beat the shit out of them.) They didn't believe me. I said, "It's the truth." Just about that time Marty knocked on the screen door. He yelled, "I saw the guys with the guns come over and I called the cops. Are you ok?" The three gun wielders went to the door and pushed over Marty, ran to the car, and drove off. Marty and I both said at the same time, "Are you ok?" He laughed. I kind of choked and I said, "Thanks!" He nodded and went home. Just a few doors down, as he walked away, in the back of his belt I saw that he was packin also. This was kind of a wakeup call for me. I had been around some of this stuff a bit. The gang I was in, and I saw some of it in Vegas a long, long time ago. I didn't like it then and certainty don't like it now. Who would be next, my kids? Well, I guess I could sacrifice David! I called Paul after talking to Cal. We worked something out so I wouldn't be harassed anymore. It was just about then I stopped gambling with bookies and pretty much in general. It was as hard as quitting cocaine, I guess. One of the few habits I never got into. I started to work harder at selling product for the company I was with. After all, I now had a fourth child (my bookie bill) I had to pay off. I started to live off credit cards. My credit was very good because of my being in business for so long. I always kept up my credit status.

One day, about two or three weeks after I had met Bonnie at the night club, I got a call from her. She said she was going to be at the club again and would I like to meet her. Needless to say, I said, "Sure." Meet her I did. But first I called Ron and said, "Guess who called me?" Bonnie was a totally different kind of lady than I had ever met, probably a lot like my ex-wife. The difference now was that I was open to change. However, at this point, not a lot. We talked for hours. She gave me her number and said, "If a man answers, hang up." (Why do I keep playing parts from movies?) I called her. In a day or two I drove up to a place near her area for lunch. As it turned out, it was fifty miles from her home. Guess she didn't want to be seen with a stranger. We talked for a very long time. A very long time! The more she talked, the easier it was to say more. By the time I left to go home, maybe six or seven hours later, I may have known more about her than anyone else that knew her, including her husband, sister or parents. When we left the restaurant, I walked her to her Dodge van. I had never kissed her before, but she seemed very venerable right now so I tried. She still backed away and said, "No. I am still married." BITCH! So, it was about a week or two later. We got together at my place in Rancho Cucamonga. She had no problem driving to see me. Nobody knew her there. Bonnie didn't drink, and she didn't cuss or seem to do anything normal that I did and still probably do. She was just like Heather when I met her. There was one big difference, though. After so many long conversations I couldn't but notice that she and her family had money. Right at this time in my life that was just about all I really wanted. Cash! It would help me out in a plethora of ways. That was my goal with her. Not that I didn't really like her, because I did. I just had a larger goal right then and there. I mentioned before that up until now we hadn't even kissed. Although I was her confident, sounding board, life line to the human race, it hadn't happened. Not as much as a peck on the cheek.

Several days later, there was a knock on the door. I opened it and it was her. Before I could say, "Hi," she put a lip lock on me for so long that I had to push her away so as to catch my breath. I wasn't expecting it. I asked, "What the heck was that for?" She said, "I asked my husband for a divorce and now I feel I am not cheating." I said, "No shit!" (I always had a knack with words.) For the next couple of months we saw each other as often as we could. She was in Love and that made the drive much easier when she came down to see me which was the better decision at this point. I had asked her how she got up the courage to ask for the divorce. She said she had been thinking about it for a couple of years, if memory serves me correctly. She said, "You gave me the strength to do it because I knew that you'd be there for me always." I had only one word going through my mind at that time. FUCK! She didn't have an easy time with the divorce and the child custody situation. Although both of their children had been adopted, they both wanted custody. I pretty much stayed out of the custody stuff. Only giving support to Bonnie when she asked for it or I felt she needed it. I personally thought that he didn't deserve shit on a stick. Certainty didn't deserve the boys. But this book isn't about Bonnie and her divorce.

My house had so many seconds, thirds and fourths on it (from refinancing it to pay off bookies) (Hmmm, can't be one of the reasons Heather left me, can it? Naw), that I let it go back to the bank when I moved. Hell, they didn't want it either. I had planned to move at the end of December/first of January to the central coast of California. A small town called Morro Bay. It housed about six thousand people right on the ocean. The population signs said about ten thousand, but as I started living there, I realized that many of the people there were transients with second summer homes and Cal Poly students who went to college there and left at summer time. Soon, I found a place to live. A lady named Diane was renting a four-bedroom house from a doctor (a block from the ocean), and she was sub-letting the rooms. She didn't have any rooms left, but there was a garage that she'd let me have really cheap. It wasn't really set up as a room, but I twisted and turned a few things and seemed to make it work. There are a few stories I could tell about her, but one really sticks in my mind today and fits in this book perfectly. She was really into animals. Whoa Nellie, don't let your mind go wondering in the wrong direction. Let me finish. She was into bringing them back to health. She would take in all kinds of wounded critters and then fix them up and let them go outside so they could be hit by a car or shot by a hunter. But she had a good heart. She had a goose that had a broken wing or something like that. Every time I would open the garage door to go to bed at night or leave for work in the day, the damn goose would run into my room (the garage.) I would spend a ton of time chasing that damn oversized duck trying to get it out. This happened just about every time I opened the door for months. It got very tiring. One time I opened the door to retire for the night. I was very careful not to let the freaking hen in. Somehow it managed to slip into the garage without my noticing it. I don't know if you ever saw, had, or played with a goose, but they have a really big bad habit of shitting all day and all night long with the biggest slimy squirts ever. (Hope you're not eating as you read.) I got out of bed that night to go to the bathroom which is in the house. That means I had to walk to the front end of the garage, as my bed was at the back of it, to open the big overhead door. As I started walking, I kept stepping in stuff and knew not what it was. It was not pleasant. I changed direction and turned on the light. I guess I don't have to go any further. You guessed it. I was tramping through goose shit from one end of the garage to the other. What made it worse; I had to go into the house to wash it off. There was no way to get into the bathroom without trappsing the shit all over the carpet in the living room. I slept with it on my feet until the morning and it had dried. This was one of my first of many pleasant experiences in Morro Bay.

It was a Friday night, the sixteenth of December, and I was going to spend the weekend in Morro Bay. It was roughly a four-hour drive from Rancho Cucamonga. I was just finishing a cocktail at Reuben's Restaurant and Bar with my bartending friend, Mike. I had promised myself to give up smoking for good this time. I believe I alluded to it a time or two in the past that I had tried it, and it just wound up costing me a dollar a butt found in the street. At least there was no extra charge for the truck tracks on them. This time I had made a plan that started way back in September. It was to end the last day of December. Finally, free of that terrible habit! That was just another reason that my wife of many years should have left me. I probably not only stunk from them, as I today smell people who smoke, but I was a dirty smoker. I would have the balls to not get up and move the ashtray closer. I would try to flick the ash from my cigarette all the way across to the ashtray on the closet table. If I got lucky to make it, there still was a fine trail of ash on the floor and if not, a bigger bunch on the floor which, of course, I left for the maid to pick up. Heather. Where was I? Oh yea. What I did was, I started to decrease the amount of nicotine intake. I had been smoking three packs of Marlboro red packs every day. Most of the time, I had to tear the filter off as they were just not strong enough for me. I first started to poke tiny pin holes in the cigarette so when I took a drag, I was getting a little more air and a little less tobacco. I did that for a couple of weeks. Each day poking a couple more holes in it. After a month I went to a lighter cigarette. I think it was a Lark. (Pardon the pun.) Did that for a week or so and then started to poke holes in them. Slowly, I wound up with those cigarettes that women smoke and are real skinny and about a foot and a half long. When you take a drag, you practically suck your kishkas out (Kishka, guts or insides in Yiddish.) After awhile, I had to go back to smoking Larks. I was starting to get bigger lips and eyes from all the sucking. About this time I had so many holes poked in the Lark cigarette that you could see the person sitting next to you through it. So, like I said, I was just about to leave Ruben's and the bar tender, Mike, said, "Before you leave, will you loan me a cigarette? I'm out and don't get off for an hour or so." I paid my tab, took out a cigarette and handed it to him. I noticed that I only had a couple left in the pack so I said, "Here Mike, take them all. I have to stop and get a pack anyway." He took them and I left. I started to drive to Morro Bay and was driving on the freeway. I started to reach for a cigarette and realized that I had forgotten to stop and buy a pack. I said to myself, "Self, you can wait until you get to Santa Barbara." Santa Barbara came and went, and I said to myself, "Self, try to make it all the way to Morro Bay." I replied, "Are you nuts? That's another two hours." I never bought another pack in my life. I was supposed to quit by the thirty-first of December and quit on the sixteenth. Two weeks early. Although about ten days later, at home in Rancho Cucamonga, I did have a fit. I suppose it was similar to a heroin addicts fit when they can't get what they want. It lasted about ten minutes. Even though I had a half a carton of Larks in the cupboard, I didn't take a puff. I fought it and prevailed. Now, I can't stand people who smoke. They usually stink.

Chapter Twenty-Three

As it turned out, I was to move sometime in January and decided to have a garage sale. So much crap and I am moving into a garage. The only thing that is going to be garaged is me, so how apropos to have a garage sale. Bonnie said she would help me. She drove down and we spent the weekend putting out shit and selling it. Bonnie kind of got upset with me every once in awhile. There would be something that may have originally cost, at some time in my life, fifty bucks, and I would ask a buck for it or something along those lines. She would yell. (Bonnie did not have a quiet voice anyway. In fact, her family called her the fish wife.) "You are going to have to buy that at some time later on. Don't sell it so cheaply." I said, "Don't worry. I am never going to buy that kind of item again in my life." Once again, I should have listened to a female. Somehow, they seem to know what the hell they are talking about more often than not. I just hate to admit it.

Not sure what day it was or even if it was in January, but I finally got out of Dodge and made it to Morro Bay. I am finally tucked away cozily, in my little garage, with the chickens, geese, birds, a seal and a bunch of other living things that usually kept me awake at night if I wasn't stepping in their shit, as well. But happy!

Now, what do I do for a living? I was still working outside sales for that disposable goods company but I really needed to be working for myself. I have always been more comfortable that way. I just promised myself that I would not get into retail, only wholesale. I just had to keep my eyes and ears open and see what will befall me.

Morro Bay was, and still is, a beautiful city. It is right on the water (Pacific Ocean), and Highway One runs right through it. Highway One is sometimes called the most beautiful short drive you can take. You have probably seen it in movies and commercials and don't even know it.

I didn't work real hard right away. I had a few bucks left on my credit cards and was really living off them, and I was earning a few bucks from the company for which I was working for.

Bonnie and I were hitting it off really well. She had two boys as I have mentioned. Chad was about three or four (about the same age as Holly was when I met Heather), and Evan, his brother, about four or five years older. Just like I did with Holly, I did with Chad. I fell in Love with him long before I fell in Love with Bonnie. I guess I am a sucker for three year olds. (Hey, watch it. I know what you are thinking. Get those thoughts out of your mind.) As nice and cute as Chad was, that's how evil and nasty Evan seemed to be. It was almost like my Sean and David scenario. Or even me and my brother. I just can't seem to shake that kind of thing, I guess. However, as time passed, my relationship did improve with Evan. In fact, somewhere in the years to come, Evan joined the Boy Scouts. They were to do a canoe trip down the Colorado River. Ten days all self-contained. That means we would see no one, talk to no one, and receive help from no one. Everything we needed we would bring with us. The food, cooking equipment, toilet paper, sun block, etc. etc. etc. will all be packed in and put onto the canoes. We, the scout leaders, of which I was one (Go figure. I wanted no part of Boy Scouts when I was younger. It interfered with my stealing and corrupted life that I led at that time. Now I am a Boy Scout leader!), took the boys to a lake and taught them how to row a canoe, swim, if need be, make a shelter from the canoes and anything else that needed to be taught. I, myself, was very good with a canoe. I had bought one when I moved to Morro Bay and used it a lot. It was a four man canoe, just like the ones we were going to rent for the trip. There would be just two people in each canoe. The other area was for the stuff that would be brought along. This is not an over-nighter. This is a major outing! Ten days on the water! We had planned to canoe twelve miles per day for ten days. The trip was obviously one hundred and twenty miles from where we would be dropped off and then picked up. There are land marks at certain places along the river (approximately every twelve miles) where we were to make camp each night as this is a regular route for water trips. All the boys were stoked as well as the leaders. Most of us leaders had never done anything like this, so it was really something exciting to look forward to. Canoe time came, and we were ready for anything. Well, so we thought. We were dropped off by six thousand very worried mothers whom I am sure went directly to the pick-up spot and waited the ten days so they wouldn't be late to pick up their adorable, Loving, caring, missing children. They probably waited with pizzas and soda in ice. The pizzas would be hot just by putting them on the roof of their cars. It had to be well over one hundred at the time of our departure. Well over! We once, again, double checked for everything, even for the maps that the leader had for all of our stops. There were about twenty-five scouts and six or seven parents who were the leaders. So, the trip begins. Once again, please don't hold me to times, as it was a long time ago. We put in about ten A. M, to start the first leg of the first twelve miles. The first couple of hours were great. We were splashing and frolicking in the waterways. About two o' clock came and we pulled over at a clearing on the edge of the river and disembarked. The leaders were to do absolutely nothing but lead, direct and answer questions. The scouts were to do it all. They had designated who would cook on each day as well as who would do the clean up and who would do the packing, and the unpacking and so on and so forth. Our first lunch was to be a sandwich, potato chips and soda. We also had two five-gallon drums of salted peanuts that would be opened at all meals for snacking. With all the energy that the kids had, there was more running and horse playing than sandwich making. So, when we finally got fed, the sandwiches were thirty percent sand. Hopefully, the scouts had the same and would try to correct it later on. Feeding time at the zoo was over. We packed everything, even the trash, back into the canoes and were on our way again. Five o' clock came and went. Seven o' clock came and went. We all were getting tired from paddling and hungry, as well. It was about eight o' clock, and the scout leader said there is the route marker. We all started yelling hooray! We pulled over. While the boys started to unload the boats and make dinner, the scout leader called us men over and explained how he screwed up. "We completely missed the first route marker. This one was the second one," he said. "We did twenty-four miles and not twelve." No wonder the kids, and us men, were beat. Dinner was slow to come, but nothing was holding the night back. As the food started to arrive, the sun started to set. With the dusk came the mosquitoes and the mosquitoes and more mosquitoes. It got horrible. We did not bring tents as we would take shelter under the over-turned canoes. Great for rain, if it rained, but the bugs could just fly under with us. Very few of us brought anything long sleeved. By nine o' clock some of the scouts were crying, being bitten at an alarming rate. We let the clean up go until morning. By ten o'clock we, the leaders, were very concerned. Mosquitoes can spread disease, and this was no normal amount of bugs. The scout leader was looking on the map for some area where there might be a phone. We were ready to call the parents to come and pick the kids up. This was just the first night, and there was panic with all of us. No phone to be found anywhere until the forty-eighth mile. Around eleven o'clock or so, the bugs went home to mate and to make more bugs, I guess. They all disappeared. We all huddled around and tried to console the kids who had really been bitten badly. We, as leaders, knew that now there was really not much of a problem left tonight and we could move on tomorrow. What about tomorrow, the same thing? Not to mention the scratching that would start in about twenty-four hours and the infection that might happen. We had brought medication with us but for this magnitude, I don't think so. We leaders even went so far as to discuss potential law suits from the parents. When day broke and we got up, we realized we actually did get a fair amount of sleep.

As the kids started to make breakfast, we leaders told them that we could have a really fun play day today because we had overshot the first marker and that we were a day ahead of schedule. Not to mention that you were very brave last night and deserve it. There was a lot of cheering at that point. We went around and checked the bites on all the kids. These facts are really one of the reasons why this event is in this book. There were some scouts that had no less than three hundred bites. Three hundred! I know, as I counted them. There were some with as few as twenty and up to a hundred. There were one or two kids who had none. The water in the Colorado River was pretty low that year, and that may be the reason for the mosquitoes. We ate our ration of sand and eggs, loaded the canoes, and were on our way again. A couple of kids wanted to know where the showers were. Twenty-three kids just looked at them. Hell, no showers. That's what this trip was all about. About an hour had passed and we had to stop and carry the boats over a sand barge. The sand was protruding through the water in some places, an inch or two, and it was way too shallow to row. The shallow area was probably a couple of hundred yards long (about the length of two football fields.) We picked up the canoes and started to carry them past the sand. It took us about three hours to get past it. Water fights, sand fights and even a wedgie or two. Not to mention a swimsuit pancing party. The boys even opened the five-gallon cans and threw peanuts at each other. After the extra twelve miles and the mass attack of mosquitoes last night, we decided to let them have their fun. What the hell, they are only twelve year old kids. The next few days, in fact most of the rest of the trip, went just great. Rowing, eating food, eating sand, no more mosquitoes for some reason (Maybe they got their fill the first day), and playing in the river. We even did a couple of hikes off shore. We did hit an area where there were some small rapids. The kids thought the rapids were great. I was afraid that we could lose our food if the canoes turned over. These were not flat-bottom boats, you know. We started on the last leg of the trip. Only twelve miles to go, spend the night, and in the morning the mothers with their pizza and soda would be waiting with open arms. Well, at least until they smelled their kids. When we were into the last leg, it started to rain. No, pour! No, really pour. I am talking rain drops as big as your eye balls. No let up, just rain and then some. Although we did do some bailing as we rowed, it got so bad we had to stop every hour or so to tip the canoes over a little and to empty them. Our destination was in sight. The bank we were looking for.

We pulled over and emptied the canoes of all food stuffs and whatever, lifted the boats back a little further off shore, and turned them over for shelter. The bank had a slight downhill grade which was lucky for us. That way the rain water would go into the river and not back into the camping area. Some canoes had two kids under them, but most had three or four under them. Safety in numbers, I guess. We put the remaining food under the empty canoes, as well. It would be dinner time soon. The cooks for this last night were heard offering money for someone to take their turn. No takers. It was really raining bad and had been for hours now with no let up. Don't remember what we were supposed to have that night, but it was to be cooked over an open fire. No way, not in this downpour. It was to be sandwiches and peanuts. By the way, our troop gave new meaning to the word, *sand* wich! We finished eating and the clean up went fast. It was about eight ish as I recollect, and the sun was starting to fade. As the sun started to disappear, it was being replaced by another form illumination, lightning! The strikes were far and few in between and in a distance. Certainly tolerable! As it got darker the strikes became more frequent and closer. The rain, if possible, got worse. Much worse! The strikes became more frequent and much closer and lasted longer. It was about eleven o'clock and not a kid was asleep. In fact, some were starting to cry. The leaders pulled everything that was metal far from the boats. (Peanut cans and the like.) Some kids were looking out from beneath the canoes but most were huddled together towards the back of them. It got really bad. The strikes were getting very close. You could see them hitting on the top of the hill that we were right under. The booming of thunder was deafening! It had to be around midnight and most of the kids were now crying. It was so scary that we adults were starting to be intimidated. It was just way too close and way too intense. One o'clock came and went. Not an eye was closed. By now, we adults were afraid and way past intimidation. For some reason I decided to have a talk with God. Now, I am not by any stretch of the imagination real religious, but there is a time and place for everything. I told whomever I was rooming with at that time, that I'd be right back. It was raining as hard as I have ever seen it rain and then some. It was hard to see ten feet in front of me. It was about ninety-five degrees outside so I didn't need a jacket. However, I should have taken one because the more I walked, the harder I was getting hit by the rain drops, and they hurt. It took me about ten minutes to climb to the top of the hill that we were under (maybe one hundred feet high.) I got to the top, and with some kind of authority that came somewhere from within, and to this day I really know not where, with some abandon recklessness, I shouted to my God, "You need to stop this rain now! Right now! You are scaring the shit out of all these kids. So stop, it! You understand? Stop it!" I turned around and started to climb back down the hill. Before I got to the bottom, the rain had just stopped. Just like that, it stopped. No rain. No thunder. No lightning. I got back to the canoes and a couple of adults came over to me and said, "I don't know where you were, but you should have been here when the rain stopped. The kids all cheered and said they were going to pray and thank God that they were safe." I just looked at him and smiled. My life and mind seemed to change a little at that time, in a kind of weird way. I really felt that I had talked directly to God and that he had listened to me (Moses, I am not.) and that that may not be the last time. It wasn't! As I have mentioned before, I have never been a real religious person. As I have grown older and have been introduced to the scientific reasons for life and the being of our planet, I am now even less religious. However, I do believe in God as the Supreme Being and controller of us all. To not ask for his help in extreme cases is not real smart. I have never asked him to help me personally. Even when I was getting a ticket! (I hate getting tickets.) So, the dawn broke and the kids, no matter how much fun they had, were ready to go home with mommy. Some actually brought breakfast for us. Pizza, no! Coffee, milk, O. J. and a plethora of Winchell's and Dolly donuts.

You have to take the good with the bad. Bonnie and I dated for a long time. It started costing me way more money than I was making. The original thoughts I had when I first met Bonnie had slipped away the more I dated her. I seemed to be spending all of my money on her and myself, and that was OK. When I first met her, it was the exact opposite. I thought she would be taking care of me. That's why I kept on dating her. Isn't it funny how things work out sometimes? However, she did spend some bucks on me once. She invited me to go to Cancun with her to a singles club called "Club Med". We had a super time. Snorkeling, swimming, drinking, tanning, and it was the first time that I had gone para sailing. We did go to Hawaii once with her kids, but I don't remember who paid for it. The bottom line was that I finally had to file bankruptcy again. I don't think Bonnie ever knew it. The only good thing about this BK was that I had spent the money on things I liked and not gambling. As I searched my inner mind, I think I was having trouble living off what I was making. Remember, at one time I was a millionaire. It's not that easy to come down. I think this BK opened my eyes to reality. One day I was sitting in a restaurant called Rose's in Morro Bay. I met a couple called Bonnie and Vic. (Not to be confused with the other Bonnie, or Bonnie and Clyde.) Vic was a little off. Dementia, I think, and Bonnie was one of the nicest persons I had ever known. (It must have something to do with the name.) Vic had served in World War Two as a pilot and was really hard of hearing. Bonnie's family, as I found out later, was one of the five land barons that were given huge acreage in San Luis Obispo County before the turn of the nineteenth century. There was even a street named after the family name. Quintana! Between the two of them (Bonnie and Vic), I heard many stories. Vic passed away in the early two thousands but Bonnie is still pitter pattering around and nearing one hundred, I would think.

Bonnie introduced me to two important people in my life. One was named Martha whom I later dated for a while and am still close friends with today. The other was a gentleman whose name I can't remember right now, maybe Mr. Duncan or something like that, and he had a boat. A sail boat and he wanted to, in some way, have a picture of it put on a sweatshirt for him and his wife. They were members of the Morro Bay Yacht club. We talked for a while and soon it came to me. I said, "Do you have a picture of it?" He said, "Many." I said, "Get me the one you want on the shirt and give me a day or so." He said, "What are you going to do?" I said, "Not sure yet but I do have an idea." I met with him in a couple of days and got the picture. It just so happened that I had seen a sweatshirt not long before on someone in town (Morro Bay is a tourist town. Tourism is its second largest income.) that read, "Here today, gone to Maui." So why not, "Here today and gone to Morro?" (Personally, I thought it sounded even better.)I took the picture to a screen printer in Atascadero, a neighboring town fifteen miles away, and asked him if he could put that picture on a sweatshirt and if so, how much? He said, "It would be a lot if you wanted just one. But if you could buy six dozen, it would be a lot cheaper." I thought, "That is just what I wanted, six dozen sweat shirts of a sail boat I don't even care for. Maybe I could get him to take six or so for family but six dozen? That's nuts." I got the price from the screen printer on six dozen. I got in touch with the sail boat owner and told him that I needed to make six dozen or it would be a ridiculous price for him. "But," I said, "I do have a thought." His eyes opened wide. I asked him if it would be ok if I wrote on it, "Here Today and Gone to Morro"? He said, "That would be fine." In fact, he said he liked it. Question number two. Would you care if I made a bunch and tried to sell them in Morro Bay? That way your boat would be everywhere you looked. You could say, "Dat's a my boat." You would be famous. (Yea, if I could sell the little fuckers.) He said, "That's a fine idea. Let's do it. But how much would it be for the two sweat shirts for me and my wife?" I said, "Because you are letting me do it and use your great sailboat on it, it is no charge for yours and the misses. The first two off the press are yours." His eyes lit up. No charge! He was probably worth fifty million, but that's probably how he got that way. By getting things for free. I should have them to you in a couple of weeks.

I had the screen printer make up six dozen and in two weeks another six dozen and in another three weeks twenty four dozen. I am now officially a screen printer to anyone who asks. So, my lively hood that I was concerned about, as usual, got started by accident. This had to be the best job any single person could have. I went to the mountains in winter and sold the ski lift gift shops my winter designs, staying at the resorts and watching the snow bunnies as they came down the slopes. I would go to the beaches in the summer. Hard to concentrate and especially draw designs with all those bikinis running around.

Now, speaking of drawing designs, if you can hark back a few hundred years when I was a child and I lived with my cousin, Arnold, do you remember the lines? Remember the lines! How I could not stay within the lines in the coloring book. Well, in the next fifty years from then, nothing had changed. In fact, I could not even draw stick people. I needed to find someone who could not only draw but also decipher my stick people. I found him in Cayucus, a little town five miles north of Morro Bay. This guy was the proverbial starving artist. (There were many of them I found as time went on, in the whole area.) But he was good. I would sketch stuff when I had an idea and he could see what I was seeing. To be honest with you, sometimes I couldn't see what I saw after I was done with my stick people. I was really bad. As time went by, I started to do okay stick people. But just ok! One time I had to do a very hot sun scène. I think I was doing a Saddam desert tee shirt. It took me three days to do it. But when it was done, I was so proud of myself. I really drew a great sun. You could see the heat radiating off of it. At that point I could see what artists strive for. That self-proclamation that says, "I have done it, and it is perfect." Not just great, but perfect. It's a great feeling. I got so involved in my sketching and found that I got my best ideas as I was driving. And God only knows how much I do of that! Oh yea, my friends know as well. It must be because I am at rest when I drive. If I am not very careful, I will be I laid to rest while I drive. Most people hate to drive and are tense. Not I. Sometimes I would be sketching and get caught up in it. It is supposed to be a quick look down at what I am sketching and then raise my head to see if I was ok. Sometimes that didn't happen. Sometimes I would get so caught up in a particular thing I was sketching and forget to look up. Many times, and I say many times, I would finally look up and I would either be in the wrong lane and a truck would be heading for me or something like that would be occurring. Not good! More than once I faced death that way. I escaped death only by the hair of my chinny-chin-chin.

I was getting pretty good at designing tees and sweats. Not to mention pretty good at selling them as well. I had been doing it for a year or two now. Customers were calling me instead of my calling them to see if they were ready to buy. I really think, in the life of a sales person, you know when you are successful, when they do the calling. Once again, I was on my own to making a buck or two and enjoying it.

Now, just about this time my granddaughter, Heidi, was about six or maybe seven. She entered into Miss America soft ball. Maybe it was another league, but it was softball. She played every Saturday. Let me rephrase that. She *sat* every Saturday, even though she was very good at soft ball. She must have been. She had the shiniest butt for *being at every game.* (I know, I was there too) This went on for years. I guess someone has to sit out once in a while. But not all the time! Here's the kicker to that scenario. I drove down from Morro Bay at least three Saturdays a month, if not all four, to watch her sit on her butt. FOR YEARS! It was five hundred miles round trip. For years! The good thing that did come from it was that she turned out to be the third best catcher in the United States around age sixteen. So, when she gets her punim (face in Yiddish) on the front page of Sports Illustrated, I hope she can see fit to repay me for my gas money. No charge for the time spent. She's family.

You know it's funny. All of the times that I spent going down to see my granddaughter sit, and then maybe play some ball for an inning or two. I drove down to the beach area in southern California, where she lived year after year. And all the time I have been my daughter's father and my granddaughter's grandfather. I drove down there to watch her and her little brother, later on in life, go trick or treating at Halloween. All those years being a part of the family and doing the best that I could do as both a parent and grandparent. Doing it alone as my spouse had left years ago. All of this and I never, not once in my whole existence, was invited to my daughter and son in-laws house for anything. Never, anything! Nothing! Nada! Well, there were two exceptions.

One time I was on my way down from Morro Bay to go trick or treating with the two grandchildren. My daughter said if I came early enough, I could have some soup if there is any left. There was and I did.

The other time was my when daughter had invited a couple to an Angel game at Anaheim Stadium, and they had to cancel. Holly, my darling little daughter, thought of me. She called me and told me she had two extra tickets for the Angel game that night. It was now two o'clockish and I was in Morro Bay, some two hundred and fifty miles away. I said, "I would Love to go." I really do not like to watch baseball. It was nice that she invited me. When I was there, I could play with Heidi, my granddaughter. I hot tailed it to the game. It turned out that I had a blow out somewhere near Anaheim Stadium. I thought, maybe fifteen miles from there. I didn't have a spare but I did have AAA. I was about twenty miles from Holly's house. I called her to see if they could help. I didn't ask them. I only told them that I had a blow out and that I didn't have a spare. "What do you think I should do?" She said, "When you get the car fixed, come to the game. I will leave the ticket at will call." (Not exactly what I would have done.) I got to the game just before the seventh inning. I said, "Hi" and sat down. Just about that time it was the seventh inning stretch time. I thought I could spend some time with Heidi, but she was racing all around the place and playing as kids would do. I would have thought that in this situation, my daughter, Holly, would have said to sit with Zada (me), a little bit. It has been such a long time since he has seen you. But that did not happen. Less than an hour passed and the game was over. Holly thanked me for coming. I thanked her for the invite and proceeded to get in my car and drive the two hundred and fifty miles home and as usual, no mention of how about we all go and get a soft drink or a pizza? Nada! I got home about three in the morning wondered why?

My screen printing business was doing very well. I was starting to make a buck or two. But the drive to see Bonnie just about every weekend was becoming a problem. I wanted to be with her more regularly. She was about a three hour drive from me. Among the many reasons I wanted to be with her was that she was teaching me how to be a human being. I was learning morals (WHAT!), family closeness (WHAT!) manners, (WHAT!), cleanliness (WHAT!) and a bunch of good things that I never realized or noticed before that had been missing from my life. Maybe I just didn't want to see them. She taught me to snow ski, water ski and to camp outdoors in a tent of which I still do as of this writing. She taught me how to cut down a live Christmas tree (not too Jewish and lots of WORK!) and many other things that normal people do with their lives. To be a human being was the greatest asset I could have learned from her. The experience was enormous. I couldn't get enough. Without too much thought, I decided to close shop and move to Simi Valley where Bonnie lived. No job there. No income there. No place to live there. Obviously, no brains here! I drove to Simi Valley and found a room for rent. Plunked down the deposit and told the landlord I would be moving in at the beginning of the month. I went back to Morro Bay, gave notice and prepared to move. This had to have been about May of '93. Love, isn't it nice? I gave up a business! I gave up my friends! A week after I had moved to Simi, I got a job selling cars. New and used! Okay, now that I am settled in with an abode and a job, it's time to tell Bonnie, "Guess who is coming to dinner?" Yea, you're right; I had not told her what I was doing. I took her to dinner and told her about a week after I was settled in. She was happy, as I remember. I went to work for a dealership called William L. Morris. I stayed there until the beginning of December. I read an ad about a salary plus commission job selling cars. I applied, got the job and started in December right after the two week notice I gave.

One night, maybe six months after I had moved to Simi, Bonnie and I went to dinner in Oxnard. It was a very romantic place on the water. I think it was called the "Lobster Trap" or something like that. After dining there was dancing. The song, "I'll Always Love You" by Whitney Houston was playing, and we were dancing. Bonnie pulled her head off my shoulder as I motioned to kiss her. Instead of a kiss she said, "I think it's time we break up and move on with our lives" or something to that effect. To be honest, I can't remember what I said, but I still, today, remember how I felt. Total devastation! It felt like my guts fell out on the floor. We went together for three and a half years (just about as long as I had to go to the shrink after our split.) I was really in Love with her. Hell, I gave up my friends and my business to be close to her. Did you ever hear of the expression "What goes around comes around?" Years later, I realized how Heather, my ex wife, must have felt when I cheated on her. As much as I was in Love with Bonnie, I think Heather was in Love with me more. I never moved into Bonnie's house. (In fact, to date, I have had three long relationships and have never lived with anyone but Heather.) For the first year I pleaded, begged to get back, and drove down her street a bizillion times wondering if I should go in or what I would do if I saw another guy at the door and all of those stupid "Mel Gibson" things that we men do when things like this happen to us.

The new job lasted about a month. They told all the new guys who were hired that the salary was no longer. I gave notice, and in two weeks I was gone from the Simi Valley area and back in Morro Bay. I applied at a couple of car dealerships and got hired at one. I looked into the mirror one morning, as I was shaving, and said to myself, "Self, you are not a car salesman." I called the car dealership and said, "Thanks, but no thanks." Unemployed again!

For the next year I spent pining and doing more stupid stuff. I remember once, I spent so much time driving to Simi Valley from Morro Bay and back, that I got a bunch of stay awake pills from my friends and was living off them. No time to eat or sleep. Just drive to see if I could catch a glimpse of Bonnie or see who was at her door. This one time I had been up for forty or fifty hours straight. On the trip back home to Morro Bay, I fell asleep at the wheel as I was traveling through Nipomo (a small town fifty miles south of Morro Bay) while on the freeway. I actually remembered starting to drive off the freeway and down a grade but could do nothing about it. Then the lights went out. I was rudely awakened by a highway patrolman banging on the window and yelling, "Are you OK?" I had the doors locked and my belt on. I opened the window with the automatic window opener. The car was still running, I guess. The car was wedged between a thousand trees so I couldn't get out. As I looked back, there were a few trees that were sheared off that I must have taken out as I went down the slope. The chippie called AAA for me (no cell phones in those days.) I don't think he wrote me for anything, as I recall. AAA pulled me out and the tow truck driver said, "How are you still alive and not even a scratch?" That was when I started to realize that I was blessed and destined for bigger and better things. I started thinking church. That lasted two days, if that.

I left Simi Valley in January, on the tenth, nineteen hundred and ninety-four. Exactly to the day, one week later, the North Ridge Earthquake hit. The epicenter was six miles from where I had worked. Blessed again! Upstairs watching out for me? Maybe, but I don't even remember him saying move! Church? Naw! Not yet. If memory serves me correctly, Bonnie's house sustained about two hundred thousand dollars in damages and she had to live in a trailer for a few months. (The exact same type of thing happened later in my life, at Yosemite, as you will read later in this work of art.) However, there are certain things that Bonnie left with me and some that I cherished regularly, I just took. One of those things is a saying, and it goes something like this. *"What I do today is important because I am paying a day of my life for it. What I accomplish must be worthwhile because the price is high."*

I started to work for a furniture company in Morro Bay. My mind wasn't really ready to take on the world so I had asked a friend in Morro Bay if he would hire me. Not in the sales department but doing deliveries. He knew me and really wanted me in sales, but because of our friendship, he put me into grunt labor. I worked for him for a while until we had a disagreement and then I left. I went to work for a Seven Eleven, doing the graveyard shift. It was an ok job. The real ball buster was that the manager was a gay guy half my age, if that. He hired me and after working there for a few weeks, I realized that he liked me. I am not talking as a worker but as a partner. With the shit I have gone through in the last seven years or so, with Heather leaving me and now Bonnie dumping my ass, if it was going to happen at all this would be the time. But, I told him I wasn't there yet. Actually, I could never be there. That's just me. (Who would I have to bitch at? No female to take the blame!) As time went on, he hooked up with another older guy who had just got dumped by his wife for another female. (This is soap opera stuff.) To top it all off, they both moved in with me at my rented abode. With the exception of a pinch on the ass occasionally, we all stayed there as friends for a couple of years. One very cold and rainy night I came home about midnight and walked in on them. They were on the bear skin rug in front of the fire place, doing it. They had been back on their rent for a couple of months, and this was a great excuse to get them out. They wouldn't leave so I gave notice and left a month later. Shame! It had a huge bay window that overlooked the Bay and right off the sixth hole at the Morro Bay golf course. Not long after, I quit the job as well. It was starting to be a problem.

One day I just wanted to get away for a long weekend. Just get away! I loaded my tree trimmer, aka car, with my camping gear. I headed off to Death Valley to see the lowest place in United States. If memory serves me correctly (you know how that goes) it is somewhere around two hundred and fifty feet below sea level. Death Valley also has seven hundred pound rocks that move by themselves, but that's another story. Chapter ninety-three I believe. It's about a six hour drive to Death Valley. When I got there, it was one o'clock ish as I recall. I drove to "Scotty Junction," known for not much, but everyone goes there, and then to find my goal. I found it and didn't even know I was there. It is a gradual drive on a slope for miles. The way I knew I was there was because there was a sign saying, "You are here." With the day just about dead and night almost upon on me, I looked for a place to set up camp, like a camp ground with a shower and a flush toilet. I kept looking and looking and looking until it was pitch black. Maybe even darker! It was so dark out I couldn't even see the road. It was winding and just dirt. I was in an area that had no electricity for the last forty miles. (Maybe that's why they go to Scotty's Junction. Air conditioning!) It had to be at least ninety-five out and by now, midnight. I could tell I was going uphill for quite a while. My water heater gauge was starting to show signs of overheating. Where is this "blessed shit" now? I finely got to the top where there was supposed to be a camp site. I couldn't see ten feet in front of me. It was as black as I have ever been in. I saw a light about fifty feet in front of me. I drove towards it, and it was a camper with a small fire going. I got out of the car and was almost blown back in. The wind had to be blowing fifty miles an hour. I asked him if there was a spot where I could set up my tent. He said, "All the spots were taken. I have been here for two days, and there is nothing available. There's only room for fifteen tents total." I said, "Thanks" opened the door of the car and let the wind blow me back into it. I backed up a little, turned around and crept away. Driving about two miles per hour, I saw what looked like a flat spot right in front of my car some fifty feet further. The head lights did not go very far in the pitch blackness. I stopped and checked it out. It was a flat spot. Though I had no reservation, I also had no other place to go. It was late, and I could leave early if need be. I pulled out my tent and tried to set it up. The wind was overbearing. I would put in a pole and when I went to get the other pole, the wind would practically blow the tent over. I wrestled with it for a half hour. Finally, a light bulb went off. I got my ice cooler and put it inside the un-set-up-tent. It was heavy enough to hold the tent in one place as I set it up. Doing all of this in, as I said, pitch blackness and what seemed like fifty mile an hour winds. I literally, could not see one side of the tent from the other side of it. After an hour (normally not fifteen minutes), it was set up. Not the way I really like it but sleep-able. I walked, really blown, to the correct side of the tent, took a leak and went to bed. Right about now, all you campers are saying to yourself, "That's no big and unusual deal to be in this book of rarities. We have all had to set up a tent in strong wind at one time or another." Well, here's the difference. When I got up in the morning, the edge of my tent was exactly three feet from a four thousand foot cliff. Thank God I set it up with the back side facing the cliff. Had I gone the wrong way to pee that night or just slipped while setting up the tent, I would have been having breakfast in Pahrump, Nevada. Not to mention that was the way I was driving when I stopped, right towards the edge. The flat area I had seen was the edge of the cliff. It looked flat but was air. Once again, help from above? Now where was I? Oh yea!

Still longing for Bonnie and not really having a romantic life in any respect, I joined a club called "ADAPT" somewhere late in 1994. **Adapt is an acronym for, "A**id in **D**ivorce **A**djustment **P**roblems of **T**oday." It had four steps of programming. Using a very short description of this club, so not to bore you, the first step is when you first got divorced, separated or even suffered a loss by death. You would go into group number one. In this group you could call your ex anything you would like to. Foul language was accepted. Get all the anger and frustration out. You could stay in group one as long as you felt you were not ready to move on. Some people stayed for a week or two and some for a year. It was always your choice whether you were ready to move on. Group number two was for rebuilding your own life. It was for building self-confidence, self-respect and such. You moved on to group number three which was teaching you about what is out there for you now and how to go about it. Remember, some of these people had not dated for ten, twenty, thirty, forty and even fifty years. I guess it would be like being in jail for a life time and then getting out and seeing T. V., cell phones, and microwave ovens for the first time. At least the criminal can commit another crime and go back in to be comfortable. Not so the divorced. They are now stuck out there and are all by themselves. We taught them to try and have first dates in lighted places like Denny's restaurants (Do people still go to Denny's?) and things like that. The fourth group was for those who have finally ventured out and need some help on the next step. "Fucking!" (See, now you know why I am divorced and haven't been lucky enough to have remarried. I just ruined a really good thing and it could have been avoided.) Actually, there is a problem with getting into the romance part after you have met someone you really like. That lack of confidence seems to rear its ugly head again. Not to mention the AIDS thing, etc.

When I first joined ADAPT, I started in group two as I had already called Heather and now Bonnie (the main reason I joined) just about all that you could call anyone, not to mention some names I made up. I put in about five months until I felt I was ready to face the world again. ADAPT was a non-paid functioning group that is held together by those who had received help and wished to give back what they got. My nights were not taken at that time so why not? I thought it would be good for me and maybe I can help others break free from, (in most cases) their own bondage. There were some rules you had to abide by, and you also had to have a position even if it was just running a group (a facilitator.) I had to go to an attorney and to a psychologist for training. They offered the training for free to anyone who was in training for ADAPT. After that was done, the head of ADAPT asked me what, if anything, I would like to spearhead. As a facilitator we had to lead, lecture, chaperone, conduct the regular Friday night meeting, collect any monies, watch out for possible problems and council all groups and were assigned different nights to do so. That way we did not have the same people all of the time. I opted to take the responsibility of social coordinator. (I would be in charge of group planning!) One of the rules in ADAPT was that there was to be absolutely no dating within the group. The more advanced ones in the group could easily prey on the newer ones. Another reason was that you were trying to rebuild your own life, and not to get involved before you are ready to do so and screw it up again. (See, I could have said fucked it up but didn't.) You would be surprised how vulnerable you are at the beginning of a divorce. Planning group socials was a little tougher than it would be with a normal group. Our meetings were every Friday night for an hour and a half. A dollar donation was asked for at the door. There were always fifty-fifty raffles and a speaker of some sort. Anyone who would like to bring cookies or some kind of sweets to be put on the entrance desk was always welcome. However, we did have to watch out for "Alice B. Toklas" cookies! The meetings went on regularly and I arranged many socials. We really had a lot of fun. One place we would go almost on a regular basis after the meetings was to the Graduate. It was a place with a huge dance floor and food if you got there early enough. When we got there, the facilitators would stand guard over the girls to make sure that they said, "No thanks," when someone, outside of our group, asks them to dance. We were only to dance with members of our own group. This made for a very safe environment for all in the group, especially the females! We also encouraged no slow dancing. If they had to, keep your distance. This place was so much fun that after I had left the group years later, I still went there to dance and socialize with friends. There were two events that I had put together out of literally hundreds that I thought were extra special.

Before I get into that, I need to tell you about a lady I met in ADAPT. Her name is Cathy. Cathy, for some reason, when she entered ADAPT as a lady in need of help, I was attracted to her immediately. She looked a little like Betty Boop, just not so cartoon-character looking. I did the best to be in her group sessions. In doing so, it seemed to me that she didn't need as much divorce support help as she was looking for friends and a safe environment to be in. After four or five months or so I asked her out to dinner. She accepted. I picked her up in a city called Paso Robles and drove to Cambria at a very nice and romantic restaurant. As we were perusing the menu, we ordered a drink from the waitress. Cathy ordered a glass of white wine, and me, the usual scotch on the rocks. J&B of course! The meal came and I ordered another scotch. My drink arrived and two minutes into the eating Cathy said, "Will you take me home?" I just looked at her and smiled. Again she said, "Would you please take me home?" I asked if she was joking. She said, "No." I said, "You must be kidding, right?" She was very adamant about it and insisted. I said, "Ok." I dropped some cash on the table, and we left. The whole way home I nagged her; I kept asking her what I did or said at the table. Knowing me, it could have been anything as I am sure you must know by now. Anything can come from my lips and half the time I don't even know what I may have said or done. A thirty minute drive to her house was filled with twenty-eight minutes of asking. Begging! Not only did I want to know what happened but I said, "It might help me at some time in the future with someone else in a similar situation." But nada came from her lips. Just an appeasing, "Don't worry about it. It really isn't that big of a deal." We made it to her house and with one last deep breath came one more begging plea. I asked again. She said, "Well, is it that important to you?" I answered, "It is." She told me that after I had a second sip or two from my second scotch, I got a different look on my face and a change of voice when I spoke. She said, "I had an alcoholic husband for years. I promised myself that I would never put myself in that position again. When you had that second drink, you changed just like he did so many times in my life. You are probably a very nice man, but I am not willing to take that chance again to find out." She got out of my car and I drove off. I, for years, had been a big drinker and never even gave it a thought or had a problem with anybody. Even with the cops. Very lucky! A few weeks went by and her words echoed in my mind over and over. Now that I thought about it, Bonnie came from a non-drinking family. I wonder if that had anything to do with our break up. I always had a bunch to drink at her house. Scotch of course. Straight! Hmmmmm! On just about any given Tuesday, a male friend of mine and I would have dinner and finish the night drinking. He drank scotch as well. He had his with water. I drank mine over ice. This one night, I decided to abstain from the one-hundred-proof stuff, and have a diet drink with my sushi. We usually met at a sushi bar, nailed a few rounds of sake before our meal, and then we would start on the hard stuff. He ordered the sake and me a diet. He looked at me in disgust. "What the hell is that all about?" he asked. I said, "I was not feeling well and thought I'd go easy tonight." We ordered the food and then he ordered his scotch. I always sat across from him. After his first scotch his face started to droop and a little drool formed in the corner of his mouth. After another one, his words started to slur a bit. Why didn't I see all of this all the times before when we drank ourselves to oblivion? Got it! I was the same. Right! Cathy, right! Need to think! And think I did. In a couple of weeks, I told all of my friends (Yes, I had more than one in Morro Bay. Hard to believe I know.) I was going to quit drinking. I also told them that before I did, there were a few things that I needed to experience about drinking so I never needed to go back to drinking because I never experienced them. Some of the things were certain drinks that I had heard of and never tried. Between the sheets, a blow job, etc. But the main two things I wanted to experience were a hangover and getting sick. I know it's hard to believe that after all the drinking I did in my life, and, remember, it started when I was thirteen or fourteen with the tequila drinking contests with my dad, to drinking to oblivion with my buddy just a few weeks ago, that I never got a hangover or got sick. That's a pretty long run. I asked some of my friends to help me out. I gave myself three weeks to stop, but only after I had a hangover and puked really well. Sick, I know! I can't tell you how many drinks my friends bought for me all in one night. Night after night after night! Starting with a beer and then a Long Island ice tea and then a shot of scotch and a glass of wine and a between the sheets and then a rum and coke etc. etc, etc. etc. Night after night! Did I get drunk? Damn straight I did. Did I puke? No! Did I ever have a hangover? No! Was I sluggish many mornings and needed a couple of hours to put on my best face? Yes! Well, two weeks into this, I was killing my liver if it wasn't dead already and financially breaking my buddies. So without any hesitation I stopped and didn't have a drink for years and years. Like fifteen or so. Not even a glass of champagne at a wedding. Nada! Nothing! Life really sucked from then on. Not really. I am joking, but there was really no difference that I could tell or remember. So why drink? It wasn't until the early two thousands that I started again and that was on a doctor's advice. But that's another chapter. Now, where was I? Getting old sucks!! OH Yea! Special events!

It was in January of ninety-six. I had a brainstorm for the lonely of ADAPT. Something we all could take part in. It would be very healthy, lots of togetherness and great fun. So, at the very next meeting, I told everyone there that I was going to hike Half Dome in Yosemite. Anyone was welcome to do it with me. We would start training this weekend. We would do long walks at first and increase the intensity and difficulty each and every weekend. If you are overweight, this will definitely help you lose weight. (I was overweight.) We had six months to get into shape. Who's in? The first thing I heard from someone was, "What the hell is Half Dome?" (Surprised that someone didn't ask what the hell Yosemite is. I actually know someone who lives in Fresno and has never been to Yosemite, forty miles away.) The Half Dome hike is a seventeen mile round-trip hike with a five thousand foot elevation gain. Half Dome is a frequently photographed mountain in Yosemite that we all have seen in magazines and pictures. We are just not aware we've seen it. Not that I was any big hiker, because I am not, but I did see it in a National Geographic magazine one day. It looked like something great to do. Not to mention the beauty. Little did I know what I was getting into? The first weekend there were about ten out for the hike. After whatever we did, and depending on how long it took us to do it, we then went to an optional lunch or dinner after. I tried to make it fun because it was a lot of work for most of us. I alone lost eighteen pounds when all was done. Week after week and month after month the attendance increased and so did the challenges. I had everyone doing fifteen mile hikes, and we climbed a lot of mountains in the Montana De Ora area. I encouraged everyone to challenge themselves. I got to a point where I carried four plastic pop bottles filled with water in a backpack just to increase the weight I was carrying. There were times when some did not make it in the later stages. When all was said and done, I had to make reservations for thirty-six of us at Yosemite. It had been ok to invite any friends or relatives who would like to go with us as well. It was going to be too much fun to leave out anyone. I invited my brother, Mark, and his son, Michael. I also invited Bonnie as she was the one who got me started into hiking and camping. (Now I can't get a date. No one my age wants to sleep on the ground and in a tent. In a bear infested wilderness.) In fact, now that I think about it, maybe that was why I did all of this, just to prove that I was still the same guy she originally liked. Hmmmm, and dumped! Now, June twenty-ninth came around. We all had made our arrangements to get to Yosemite. I am not sure what the actual day was, probably Friday. The day is not real important but the date is. Friday we all met and set up camp. Saturday was the day of the hike so most went to bed early. The real good hikers, and there were a few, stayed up and did the camp fire things. You know, singing stupid songs and pretending they were bears for those with less experience. Saturday was upon us. We were up at five-thirty, maybe six, just before sunrise. Most of us had to put something in our stomachs before we were off. The Half Dome hike is anywhere from a six hour round trip for the very experienced and fit Park Rangers to a two-day affair with a second camp site a little more than half way there. Most do the two day trip and spend the extra time camping and enjoying themselves. Not us! We were on a mission! We worked very hard, and the morale was very high. All were anxious to get going. Out of the thirty-six that actually went to Yosemite, only thirty were going to attempt the hike. We all met at the trail head to Half Dome. We had to scale Vernal Falls and then Nevada Falls before we started the assent to much higher ground. In my mind, if you could scale *both falls* (The first two falls were covered with heavy mist from the falls. You were going to get wet.), you were probably a shoe-in to finish the hike. The falls were really tough. There were lots of two foot high stepping stones and lots of water from the falls to make every step a slippery one. There were a couple of us, as I remember, that did turn around half way through the falls. This group was an assembly of all walks of life. About the only thing most of us had in common was ADAPT. I will skip the little incidents and get to the meat of the story. There was a lady named Roberta. A school teacher as I remember. She was like the Librarian in so many movies. She was probably a little miss prissy, in school. But out with the crowd and away from work, she was a hoot. Non-stop jokes and she could dance like a cross between a voodoo obsessed tango dancer, and a meshuganah. (Meshuganah, Yiddish for a crazy person.) She could shake parts that I didn't even know a female had while lowering herself to the ground and back up. She was so much fun to be around. She had made it all the way up, and I met her there like so many others that made it to the top. Most of us stayed on top for a while before heading back to the camp site. We were all taking pictures, hugging each other and were so proud of ourselves. As I recall, some of us had trouble getting out of our cars at first. Now, we are on the top of the world! The view was not only breath-taking, but scary as well. The last five hundred feet was done by holding a rope and going up almost vertically. There were a plethora of old beat up gloves lying on the ground, that you would put on before you started up and leave them when you came down. After a bit, Roberta went down, like we all did, at some time. That was the last I saw of her for some time. I had gauged myself to do the trip in about ten to twelve hours. I was right on schedule when one lady, who was having a pretty bad time of it, asked if I would walk with her. I was the leader so it was a given. Pretty soon another lady with blisters the size of my palm on the sides of both ankles was walking with us. Now it's me and two. I looked at my watch and it was about three-thirty. I had been hiking for nine hours. I really would have liked to make it in the twelve hours max that I had set for myself. It was still possible. Later, I found out that my brother and nephew finished in seven hours. I had expected that they would do great. My brother is a marathon, runner and my nephew has a lot of experience running from the law!

Shortly after I hooked up with the aching ladies, one of the others in our group saw us and said that Roberta was not far from here. She thinks Roberta broke her ankle. Being the leader, once again I was interrupted from my twelve hour target. We walked over to her maybe a hundred yards away. Yep! It was broken. I am no doctor, but I do know which way a foot is supposed to extend. She had been walking and talking with four others from our group. They said she was being Roberta and did not see a root sticking out of the ground. Walla! Broken foot! Now, you need to realize the importance of where we were and the seriousness of the situation. The wilderness! Miles from our camp! No cell reception! Two women who can hardly walk! The three of the four hikers who were hiking with Roberta left, as soon as we got there. The one that was left was one of the walking wounded just like the two ladies I was already with. Fortunately, I watch westerns. I remember seeing one of the good guys make a travois. I think that is what they called it. Two poles and a couple of shirts stretched over them. Plop Roberta on it and we are out of there dragging Roberta. After fifteen minutes or so we had to abandon the idea. We would have needed four travois's. One for Roberta and three for the almost standing other ladies I was with. Did you ever have a car break down, and you were right in front of a garage? You say to yourself, "Damn! Why do I have to break down? Why does this always happen to me? I am so unlucky." But, what you should be saying is, "How lucky I am breaking down right in front of a garage." Right? So, as if that garage was on horse shoes, four rangers appear out of nowhere and ask, "Is everything alright?" I just looked up to the sky and probably said something very clever and then answered the rangers, "No, she broke her leg, and we have no way to get her out of here. Can you take her out on your horses?" They said, "No, but we will call for a helicopter and all will be just fine." Roberta, hearing all of this, could see nothing but was smiling like she just got a new BMW for her birthday. We stayed until the chopper arrived. It had to land about a hundred feet away from us where it was flatter with fewer trees. The four horsemen got a plank from the chopper, lifted her onto it, and carried her to the rescue vehicle. However, what she hadn't realized in her painful situation was that the horsemen where all young hunks. Once Roberta realized she was being carried by the Chippendale guys, she was in seventh heaven and somehow the pain, during the trip from the ground to the helicopter, disappeared. We heard about it for the next four years about how great it is to break a leg! I left her in good hands. Now the four of us started down the hill again. I looked at my watch, and it was nearly six o' clock. That already puts me over the twelve hours that I had set for myself. If you have ever been to Yosemite, you know it gets dark fast, especially if you are on the wrong side of a mountain. I am now looking at six-thirty and feel I should be ok with two hours of light left. If Mother Nature is shining (pardon the pun) down on me, I may be on the correct side of the mountain and will have some moonlight for another hour or two. Not that it will take that long, but, just in case. The trek down continues, and I really have no idea how far I have gone from the top or how far we have to go to get to camp. One of the ladies was really in pain. Her foot is so swollen that she has to take off her shoe to stop the pain. The other two are not much better but can walk on their own. Minutes go by and now an hour. We didn't see anyone for about thirty minutes. The good thing is that there was an easier way to get down. Rather than going down the same way we came up, by the two falls route, with the prolonged very high steps. (I had asked the rangers and they told me about the Mist Trail. I was sure that none of the ladies could make the high step trail that we came up. So, I took the Mist Trail instead. Longer but easier and if memory serves me correctly, they said it's an all dirt trail so no big obstacles to climb. Another hour goes by and our pace has lessened. This is not good. Fortunately, we had water and some trail mix to eat. We kept on trucking. The ladies were all now in great pain but hard knocken troopers. Not much complaining about the pain, but I was hearing some talk about what if it gets much darker and we have to slow down even more! We didn't have any flashlights, and there are bears out here! (If anyone knows anything about Yosemite, they know there are many, many bears there and I had the same thoughts running through my mind.) It's now nine o' clock and pitch black. Mother Nature did not smile on us. There was barely any moonlight illuminating our way. I could see that we were heading away from what little moonlight there was. Ten o' clock and now I can't read my watch any more. We were still headed downhill but that was about all I can tell you. No light at all! Pitch black! Pitch black! No one thought to bring a flashlight because the estimated time of camp arrival was six o'clock at the worst. Go figure! Now, if you remember back a few hundred pages ago, my brother was the Boy Scout while I was stealing tee shirts. It could have been flashlights I stole, right, but no, it was tee shirts. So where is the Boy Scout, my brother, now that we need help? I remember when there was a little light, that the mountain was on my right and the cliff, the CLIFF, OH SHIT, was on my left. My hand to my God, there was no, NO LIGHT. None! Pitch black! I knew that we were still heading down so I moved very slowly as far right as I could possibly go and told the ladies it's everyman for himself! No, I am just joking. I can joke about it now. Then, there was no joking. I told one of them to put their right hand on my (get you mind out of the gutter) left shoulder and the next one to do the same with the lady that was in front of her. This way it would be single file. I said, "If I fall, just stop walking." It was easy to stumble because there were roots sticking up and rocks on the trail that no one could see. That is if we were still on the trail. Now, we were starting to hear sounds that were very scary. Probably, was nothing, but if you let your mind wonder, I am sure they're bears. The dark made your mind wonder. According to the ladies it was bears. Hungry bears! If there was one and it attacked one of us, I could not have seen it anyway. But, if for some goofy reason I did see one, my only defense was to out run one of the slower ladies. The women wanted to sit many times and rest, but I would not let them. Not only would we get back later but, not to mention, more apt to be dinner for a bear. Also, their muscles would tighten up, and they might not even be able to get up again. So we kept on. They were not happy.

All of a sudden we all heard a noise. All at the same time! I felt a hand tighten up on my shoulder. I said. "That's not a bear." Three guys on bicycles were riding down the hill with head lights on their helmets. I could see them coming and stopped them. I told them our plight and one of them gave me his light from his helmet. They said we were only about a mile from the bottom but would tell the rangers that we need help. We thanked them and they rode off. Not quite as fast as they came. They were one light short. And I may have mentioned it was PITCH BLACK out here. We all breathed a sigh of relief but then realized that they said it's only a mile to go. SHIT! It might have well been fifty.

We started down again at least this time with a light. No knife for bears but we could all see, a little at least. SHIT! I was just getting used to having a female hand on me all the time. We never saw a ranger but made it all the way back to camp. It was one o'clock in the morning and just about all were waiting for us. The word must have spread about how close we were. In fact, it was only about another twenty minutes until we saw lights and humans. Hell, even Roberta was back. She was on a chase lounge with a cast on leg and was wiped out celebrating the climb with wine. (I knew I liked that chick!) The ladies I was with came unglued as I remember. The crying started and the tales of almost being eaten by wild animals spread through the camp. I would be lying if I said my ass wasn't dragging as well. I wasn't drinking at that time in my life. But a shot of Jose Cuervo Gold would have been a welcome pleasure. My climb time turned out to be nineteen hours and not ten or twelve. I promised myself that I would return and try again. Just another promise I have broken in my life.

Now, the real kicker to this story is that exactly to the day and hour, one week later, the place that we all met to start the hike and were all jazzed up and raring to go, a huge earth slide happened and millions of tons of the mountain came crashing down and killed two people and injured few as I remember. If I had scheduled our hike one week later, I probably would not be writing this book and many of my friends would be having dinner with Jesus right now. Once again, divine intervention? It seems like a pattern is forming. Or something else?

So, that was the first of the two special events I mentioned. The second one was not so tense or hair raising. A trip to Hawaii! Doesn't sound too different so far, right? I had been working on it for awhile; I had to stop on it for a bit to do the Yosemite hike. When I got back from that trip and was still alive (Thank God!) (Pardon the pun!), I started back on the Hawaii trip again. It was set for September tenth, nineteen ninety-six. I got a pretty good deal through a company called ABC

Travel, out of Sacramento. It included the flight on an L-1011 wide body Tri-Star leaving from SFO and included a room (double occupancy) at the newly remolded Hawaiian Monarch Hotel, three blocks from world renowned "Waikiki Beach." There wound up being forty-three of us that went, and why not? The total price including air and the room for eight days and seven nights was only (believe this!) four hundred and twenty-five dollars. TOTAL! I tried to get them to include all meals at the hotel but was unsuccessful. I really laid this whole trip out great. I had an event scheduled for every day and some nights. You had a choice to go with any of us, from the group that decided to go. Nothing was mandatory. You could do whatever you wanted to do at anytime you wanted to do it. We did many things that everyone does when on Oahu, like snorkeling, shopping, the Polynesian Cultural Center, the Mormon Temple, Waimea Bay, Botanical Gardens and even ate at "Chuck's Steak House." We even rode mopeds around the island. But I am not going to bore you with the whole trip and most of the details, just the highlights. We did, although, hike Diamond Head and saw the gun emplacements from WW II and the unbelievable breathtaking views from the top. We also did the Pearl Harbor Cruise which is a must for all Americans. Well, at least the ones in my age group. The younger ones probably think that it is a Carnival cruise, that stops in a harbor and you dive for pearls. At the end of the Pearl Harbor Cruise, I had scheduled our luau at Paradise Cove on the other end of the island. It was the thirteenth day of September on Friday. All who went were picked up by limo and transported to the other side on the island, about an hour car ride away. Don't remember how many attended but it was most of us. The luau was spectacular in every way. The food, the games, the beach, the music, and, of course the company! Remembering that we are, for the most part, from ADAPT and a non-dating group. All just good friends! There were two sisters. Both were very pretty. One was an ADAPT member, and she had invited her sister along. Needless to say, I was interested in the sister. I spent as much time with them as possible. Remembering I am the leader of the group, and not only had to be available to all but, had to set a good example as well.

    Now, I don't know if any of you who are reading this book have ever heard of the "Green Flash?" The Green Flash has to do with certain atmospheric conditions as the sun sets in the distance, only on the ocean. Just as the top of the sun disappears from the horizon, if the conditions are right, there will be a green, almost emerald colored flash. Not many of us have ever seen or heard of it that live inland. I had heard of it but never had the luck to see it. A bunch of us were talking about it earlier when we arrived at the luau. There were two people who said they had seen it, but most had never even heard of it and thought that we were fu-fuing them. However, the two sisters said they had seen it not once but three times. Even I quietly questioned that in my own mind. As the day turned into evening, I was walking and talking with one of my favorite, and probably the nicest guy I had ever met in my life, Leo Corona. Yea, I know, a Mexican. (Not to be confused with Jose Cuervo. Although, probably a distant relative.) What can I say! Shit happens! We were kneeling down on the water's edge. I saw a piece of white coral and reached to pick it up. Just about then Leo said, "There goes the sun." I looked up and lo and behold, I saw the flash. We both saw the flash. We looked at each other in disbelief. Smiled! We turned to tell and ask if anyone else had seen it besides us and guess who was standing close by? Yep, the sisters! They looked at us, and in unison, stuck out their arms and put up their thumbs. And they smiled! As it turned out, about ten of us caught it. For the rest of the night, it was like we ten could walk on water. I have never seen it since, even living on the ocean in Morro Bay for twenty-years. My good friend Leo died a few years later from cancer. I still have that piece of coral and think of the Green Flash and Leo often.

    There is one thing that I did not plan that turned out great for everyone but me. It was either Saturday or Sunday after a day swimming at Waimea Bay and hiking at Sacred Falls. I had set up a dinner at a very nice restaurant for anyone who would like to spend a little extra for one real nice dinner in Hawaii. As it happened (I tried to take credit for it but failed miserably) "Charo, of Cuchi-Cuchi fame" was the entertainment that night. If you have never seen her entertain, it is a must. She not only plays the mandolin the best I have ever heard but moves through the whole audience singing and sitting on all the guy's laps for picture taking. She had the audience mesmerized. Especially the men! She is as great and young looking as the day she came on the scene, some forty years ago, I would guess. She is still very shapely and was popping out of the top of her very short dress. Got my attention!

So here's the kicker! She sat on just about every guy's lap in our group and a picture with them. Only one guy who was in our group did not get that lucky. And that one guy probably would have appreciated it more than most, just because of her gorgeous body and almost out of her dress knockers. Need I say who?

Like I said earlier, I am not going to bore you with the rest of the stuff that took place and was common, if there is anything about Hawaii that is common. There was just one more thing that happened while on the plane home. We were returning on that same L-1011, wide body, that held probably upwards to three hundred and was full. Most of us were worn out and tired from such a good time. Although there were about forty of us traveling together, we were not all sitting together. Some got lucky and switched with other passengers on the plane, but, for the most part, we were scattered. I was trying to get someone's attention for some reason which slips my mind right now. I didn't want to yell and disturb anyone or embarrass myself either. After a few attempts at using a loud voice with no luck, I threw a pillow at him. He was only a few rows in front of me and a half a dozen seats to the right. Now, for you youngsters that now fly in a commercial aircraft and go from one place to another, I want you to know that in my days, we not only got pillows for our heads and blankets to keep us warm all at no charge, but free food on most flights and ear phones as well so we could watch movies. If memory serves me right, I even remember the flight stewardess being cute and smiled. Now where was I? Oh yes! So, I threw the pillow at him to get his attention and just missed and hit the guy sitting next to him. (I didn't go out for basketball either.) Fortunately, the person sitting next to him was a nice person and just threw the pillow back to me. I tried to tell him to shake the guy next to him to let him know that I was trying to get his attention, but he could not understand me. So, I threw the pillow again, missed again, and hit the same guy again. This time he was not so nice and threw the pillow back at me a little harder with a nasty look. However, he missed me by a bunch but did hit one of our group who happened to be watching all of this. He picked up the pillow and tossed it to one of the girls from our group who, in turn, tossed it to another in our group. Then I asked the person sitting next to me if she was using her pillow and if not, if I could borrow it? She said. "No and yes" and gave it to me. I tossed it to someone in back of me, only I didn't look at who it was I threw it to. That person, whoever it was, in turn threw it at someone else. Are you getting the drift here? Pretty soon just about everyone in the plane was throwing pillows at someone. The stewardesses tried to stop it, but no one would listen. Way too much fun! Pillows flying everywhere! Everywhere! We were laughing our heads off. Not only our group was tossing but just about everyone on the plane was. It was a riot. Try to imagine two hundred and fifty pillows flying everywhere. Two hundred and fifty of them all airborne going right, left, up, down, sailing, tumbling, and bouncing off things. All of a sudden we heard over the speaker system the captain saying something. You couldn't understand what he was saying (way too much yelling and laughter) but you know it was not good. Some of the tossing slowed down but the die-hards kept it going until we saw the captain walking around. He was not a happy camper. We finally knocked it off and most of us went to sleep. Even me! But what great memories!

I seemed to be very active with everything going on in my life right now. In fact, from the middle of ninety-five through the years of nineteen ninety-six, seven and eight, I was doing everything for and with the ADAPT singles. I was writing affirmations in their monthly publications, doing trips, and just about anything and everything you could imagine that goes hand and hand with a group of singles that were mostly in need. One way or another!

One day I was approached by a guy in the singles world who knew of me through a previous function I had done for singles only and who were not in ADAPT. Yes, I was branching out. His name was Bill. Not sure what he had been doing for a living at that time, but he told me that he had been an editor for a couple of well recognized publications. He was thinking about starting up a singles magazine for this area and wanted to know if I would be interested in being a partner in it? Hell, this sounded like there might be a pay check in it. Of course I was interested. I had been working for a printing and advertising company, based in Arroyo Grande, for the past few years, and it was commission a job for the most part. (Don't work, don't get paid.) That meant I really had time to do it as I had been doing things for and with ADAPT. Only this time I might get a pay check. As it turned out, he wanted me to do the sales and get advertisers. The publication would be a freebe to all who wanted it. I was to spread thousands of copies out all over the county. I was to get the paying advertisers to advertise in it. Hell that could have been many of the accounts I had already been calling on for advertising for Slow Co Data that I already worked for. This is going to be a piece of cake! I was to get doctors, psychiatrists, social workers, police, councilmen, etc. to write an article that would pertain to singles, no matter what it was about, as long as it had to do with singles. Their articles were put in for free so all singles might have some help solving some of their problems. The articles would include things like whom to call if your child is arrested or what to do if you are having a drug problem, who to date or not to date and why. All types of articles as long as it was constructive for the single world. I worked on it feverishly for three months and got many advertisers and a lot of open arms from the singles world. They, we were all looking forward to it being published. Everyone seemed to be in favor of it and couldn't wait until it came out. Bill and I worked hard on its design. We had a page for dining and entertainment, support groups, a singles' calendar for the month, a job seeker page, and a matchmaker column where you could put your ad in. There was a fitness section, an investor section, and Bill plus other professionals would write editorials. It seemed to me to be an all inclusive Bible for the singles. I got many advertisers like travel agencies, hair cutters, clothing companies, party supply houses, condom manufactures and houses of ill repute (just joking), massage centers, jewelers, and investment firms, just to mention a few. We spent a lot of time on the front cover, trying not to be too sexually oriented but letting people know that this was for singles. We came up with a very simple name, "Central Coast Singles Magazine." Finally, we had the first issue in the can, as "they" say. (I don't think I will ever know who "they" are. Do you) Anyway, we printed about five thousand and as soon as they were off the press, I loaded up my car and went to drop them off. I had previously made arraignments with stores and businesses to take them. These were to last a month, and being the first issue, of course, that was a guess.

    I immediately started working on issue number two. Bill could do nothing until I got the advertisers and the articles from the professionals. It wasn't three days before some of the stores were calling for more copies. We didn't have any, but I ran around stealing from one store and giving to another. Service is always a big part of the game. After a week, I knew we had a winner. Just about that time Bill called me into the office and sat me down. He said he needed to talk to me. I sat down and his words went something like this. "I finally met a woman that I am in Love with and we are probably going to get married. She doesn't want me to continue with the SINGLES magazine; so, therefore I am out of it. I guess you will have to find another editor. Sorry and good bye."

Now, how's that for a pink slip! Find another editor! Yea, right! Ninety percent of all the people I know can't spell their own names. The other ten percent don't know their names! For the last two months, single after single would walk up to me and ask, "How's it coming?" and for the last week, as it made it to the stores, they were thumbs up-ing me and high fiving me with huge smiles of appreciation. Now, I was sure they wouldn't even talk to me. Hell, I didn't want to talk to me either. The only thing I could do was tell the truth for once in my life and point the finger at Bill. I didn't use my index finger. So, what can I do to make amends to and for all my friends? I think I knew. By the way, I still have a few copies of the original issue if you would like one. Just let me know.

Now that I am into the singles thing and have been for some time now one way or another, I might as well make it work for me. Sometimes I make myself think of the saying, "Worker of all trades and master of none." (Hell, I am starting to amaze *my*self with all the shit I have either done or been involved with.) Know, I have experience in social settings for singles, and God knows, I know plenty of singles from ADAPT and some I have not met with the recent undertaking in the literary world. Why not start a singles club that I can make a buck on? Or at least get laid once in a while. So, as I think it was Jon Lovitz who said, "Yeah! That's the ticket!"

Now, how should I go about it? I needed a catchy, cutesy name for this club. I already had a lot of names and addresses from all the past events I had done in the last two or so years. I came up with the name, "Single Adults Sharing and Socializing" and a great acronym of "SASS." I wrote a short blurb and mailed it to all on my mailing list. It said that I am forming a new club for singles. No partners this time to screw things up. It would be nice if anyone who would like to join the first meeting, at no charge, to give me some ideas of what you would like to do. Whether specifics or generalizations, all would help.

I found a restaurant in the area that was willing to give me the conference room at no charge as long as I encouraged the people who attended to belly up to the bar. I struck a bargain with them that if they would put out some cheap appetizers, I would physically push them to the bar myself. Deal! It's been a long time so I really don't remember how many invites I sent out or how many attended, but I can attest that the club was formed that night. I informed all of those who were in attendance that within a month, there would be our first event and a sign up for membership. I had my work to do. How much should I charge to be a member and how much for each event and what should be the first event and should there be monthly dues and, and, and? It was late in September when I think as all of this started. For my first event I scheduled the, "Wine, cheese and bread walk to the whales." Well, that was what I called it anyway. I knew of a great place to whale watch that was not far. It was up on a small hill in Montana De Ora. I told all who would attend that they were to bring wine, cheese, bread, a blanket, and jacket just in case. We all met at a grocery parking lot and car pooled from there. All in all there were about thirty-five people. When we arrived at Montana De Ora, I had everyone gather around and told them the dues amount for the year. I also said that each and every event would have its own price tag that would be determined as each of the events unfolded. Today was a "freebe" and thank you all for coming. It was a half mile walk to the hill and just about three to five minutes' walk up it. We got to the top and spread out our blankets and started pouring and eating and sharing food and conversation. Some even brought hot chicken from you know who. I was the official lookout for the whales. Being a non-drinker, after a half hour, I would still be able to see. I passed out invitations to join the club and many paid me right there and some sent it in by mail. All but two joined from the initial group. Within two months the club had a hundred and twenty members paid in full. We did everything from wine tasting at wineries to a trip to Catalina and house parties. I thought about Hawaii, but there would be too much trouble explaining the Green Flash. Anyway, the price had gone up substantially.

However, I do need to tell you about one major thing that had happened on that first meeting, for whale watching. Two of the people who came were my friend Gregg and a lady I didn't know, Marge. I met Marge as she signed in for the walk and to get the membership paper to join. As we were walking up the hill to spread our blankies, I introduced them to each other. That was many years ago and they, still today, are married and enjoying life just because of me. Ain't I great?

Many members from ADAPT, when they left, joined SASS for their kicks. I was still involved with ADAPT so I kind of knew who should be and should not be going to SASS. I wound up dating the NO BOOZE Cathy for a while. I hadn't drunk for quite a while. Somehow she heard about it and made herself available to me. The relationship lasted about nine months or so and then she moved to Florida for some reason I didn't understand. (She said something like, "If Heather can do it, so can I." Just joking!) She turned out to be the best kisser I have ever kissed.

With all that was going on, I still did some hiking. Not so much with SASS but more with friends and small groups from ADAPT.

In San Luis Obispo County (where I lived), there are seven mountains called the Seven Sisters. Five of them stretch from the shallow waters of Morro Bay (where I lived) to about fifteen miles inland towards the town of San Luis Obispo. They are what are left of in-active volcanoes, sometimes called the neck or plug. Some were great for hiking. They were not Mt. Everest by any means, but they would give you a good workout. I have hiked five of them. (Of the remaining two mountains that I hadn't hiked, one was way out in the Pacific Ocean and the other one was way inland and quite a bit off line with the other six.) There was one that I particularly liked. Its name eludes me right now. Oh yea! Hollister. One day I was hiking it with three or four people, one of whom was a female. It was probably a small group from ADAPT. We got to the top and hung around for a bit, taking in the view. On the way up we thought we heard someone yelling at us, but knew not from where it was coming or what was being said. We joked about it being someone stuck in a tree and couldn't get down and really just shined it on. As we started down the trail for home, a guy jumped in front of us yelling, "Didn't you hear me telling you to go away?" He was branding a rifle and waving it around as he yelled. I said, "Slow down, dude."

Apparently, that was not the correct thing to say at that moment. He shoved the gun in my face and said, "This is my mountain and if you don't leave right now, I will blow you away for trespassing. Didn't you see the sign as you were hiking up here?" I said, "I didn't see any sign, and you have no right telling me to leave." The people with me said, "Let's just get out of here. It's no big deal. Let's just go. OK?" I was getting pissed, but the gang was getting scared. I told him that we were going but I was going to report him to the police when I get down. He said he owned the mountain, and he could do whatever he wanted to, and wanted us out. We left. Actually, we had seen a no trespassing sign on the way up. But nobody obeys things like that unless there is a crocodile on the other side of it. We left! About three or four weeks later, a couple of buddies and I went hiking. Guess where? Yep! I had told them what had happened, and they wanted to meet this guy. No female this time so I could use a little different wording this time. We made it to the top and sure as shooting, (pardon the pun) guess who? He came running at us with the rifle aiming at us. I don't think he recognized me, but it was the same routine. "Didn't you see the no-trespassing sign? I own this mountain and you are trespassing, get out!" My buddy said, "What sign?" He kept yelling and screaming. Then he got behind us and told us to start moving towards the edge. He shoved the rifle in my buddy's gut and said next time it won't be the barrel you will feel. We slowly started towards the edge of the mountain. He said, "Look down." We looked down and saw nothing. I said, "What do you want me to see?" About this time I saw one of my friends slowly moving towards the rear of all of us. The guy said, "Look, way down there. Do you see a house?" I said, "Yes." He said, "That is my house and yard and my kids playing in it. If you were the wrong kind of guy, you would have a perfect bead on my kids with a rifle, so get the hell out of here and if I ever see you again, I am shooting first and not even going to ask any questions. Get it?" We turned around and started walking down the hill. He followed us back, about a couple of hundred yards, for a good half hour or so and then we didn't see him anymore. The three of us just shook our heads and concluded that this guy was a loony, or something had happened to him and his family at some time in the past. Either way we never hiked that mountain again. However, I did check with the police. They told me that we were not the only ones who had a problem with that guy.

They also said that he did buy the mountain and does have the right to blow our heads off for trespassing. End of story! NEXT!

During the past few years I had been going to a restaurant and bar called Branigan's, in Morro Bay. They had karaoke a few nights a week in the bar area. Not that I sang, or for a matter of fact drank, but a lot of my friends were there on a regular basis because they sang and drank. I would usually sit by myself or with a friend or two and sing along with whoever was singing. Most of the songs sung were "Oldies but Goodies," and I pretty much knew how they went. So to me, even though I was not on stage, I enjoyed it. This went on for years. It got to the point that the KJ (karaoke jockey) would try to slip another microphone under my nose when I wasn't looking as another person was singing. I would even go to other bars where my friends were singing, just to be with them. Although I did not use a microphone, I sang loud enough with the music that most people could hear me singing along. They would always tell me that I had a great voice so why not try it? They also said to people who were terrible that they were great. It's called moral support. They would always say that the applause was for having the guts to get up on stage and not necessarily for how good you sang. So I kept on sitting.

One evening at a karaoke bar, a friend of mine, as she was singing, walked over to me and tried to put the mic under my nose while she was still singing. I, as usual, was singing along with the music. She sat down next to me, at my table, and finished her song right there. Every once in a while she would lean over and put the mic under my nose. I would sing with her but very quietly. This started a regular kind of thing and always with the same song, Bobby Darin's "Dream Lover." It got to the point that when she did that song, she handed me another mic, and I sang along at full strength with her. It might have been over a period of ten to twelve times until I had reached this milestone. Now, if you can hark back a few hundred pages, you will remember I was in glee club, then choir, and then madrigals. Not to mention a duet and a trio. So I know I had a decent voice. But, if you have harked back to those pages, you will also note that when asked to do a solo in madrigals, I said no and Gene took the part. So singing alone (solo) was just not for me. Now, every time that she would do that song, I was handed the other mic and sang along with her. I always stayed in my comfort zone, the table, as she walked all around the bar singing. This one time, after she finished the song, just about everyone in the bar came over and congratulated me. I didn't know what the hell was going on. They were yelling, "You did it, you did it." "I did what?" I said. Apparently, my friend, after we sang the first word or two never sang another note and I did it all by myself! I couldn't believe it. Needless to say, although it took me a little bit longer than evolution, that created a karaoke monster. Move over Elvis! Well, during the next year I really got pretty good. So good, in fact, that a guy named Roger (however, all called him R.J.) asked me if I would like to join his little traveling musical group called, "Joe Cruisers Legends of Rock and Roll?" They did all songs that dated before nineteen sixty-seven. I accepted and now I had to buy larger hats. My Love life had been non-existent. Most of all of what I was doing was for others to enjoy themselves, so why not do something for myself. I always liked singing and being in a group sounded great. There were five of us: RJ (Roger); his girl friend, Brenda Sue, (a native Indian); Alex; his girlfriend, Penny; and now me. We would practice at Alex's most of the time in Cambria.

My first show with the group was in Morro Bay at the Harvest festival, (AKA Fish Fair) on October fourth nineteen ninety-seven. The Harvest Festival was an annual affair. It was Morro Bay's largest money maker. It had wine tasting, fish tasting, and outdoor music. (This year, Joe Cruiser's Legend of Rock and Roll was one of the groups that would be there.) There were a hundred kiosks's selling everything from art to hot dogs and many games for the kids to play. It was just a real fun couple of days. They even had a couple of trolley's that takes you from all over the town to the fair so you don't have to walk very far. There were many stops all over the city where you could catch the trolley. In fact, when I first moved to Morro Bay, I donated my time on the trolley. There was a driver, of course, (hard to believe it wasn't me!) and there was also a narrator with a microphone in the back, who told all who rode the trolley to the fair, all about our town and some of the special features of it. That be me!

Now back to the Harvest Festival and my performance. Was I scared? I was scared! There were no monitors in front of me with the words. No color changing words that told me when I was supposed to start singing. Just some pre recorded music that if I needed to stop and start again, it would just keep on playing with no regard for me. (Sounds like some of the women I have dated.) I remember it was over ninety degrees outside, and that is very hot for Morro Bay. But, I was sweating (wearing a suit and tie) like it was a hundred and fifty. I did two songs and they were, guess what, Bobby Darin's "Dream Lover" and "Sealed with a Kiss," originally done by Brian Hyland. The boss anchored his eight millimeter camera on a tri-pod and recorded the whole show. I have the copy, and for a few thousand dollars, I will autograph it for you upon purchase. We finished the show, and I was congratulated by all. *I* even thought I did a good job, and I am usually my worst critic.

It was late in the year so we kept busy performing for weddings, Thanksgiving's Day parties, Christmas and some New Years parties.

It was the end of the year. I had no place to go for Christmas or New Years. (Awe!) Our gigs were done, and I was now free for a few weeks. I had dated a lady for a while and had broken up, maybe a couple of years earlier but kept in touch with her. Just about everyone I have dated I have pretty much kept in touch with. This one was no different. In fact, she had a problem daughter and I was always concerned. I also send out Christmas cards to all I know. Ex-dates included. However, this one lived in Morro Bay. I would stop over every once in a while to say hello and to see how the daughter was doing. Let's call this lady Joan. So being single and nothing to hold me back, I decided to drive to San Francisco for the holiday and just crash a party or two. What would be the worst that could happen? Maybe get a hummer from a queer, right? So, a day or two before I left, I went to Joan's house to give her her X-mas card. (Saved twenty-two cents) She put up a pot of coffee and we yakked for awhile. She asked me what I was doing for New Year's Eve. I said, "I am going to San Francisco and party crash." She said she had nothing to do either so would I mind if she tagged along. I said, "Fine, but no strings. You go your way and do your own thing, and I'll do the same, OK?" We are brother and sister, right? Right!

On the thirtieth I picked her up and we started up the Coast Highway, Highway One. As i have mentioned, probably one of the most beautiful drives in America. We drove for about two hours or so and came up to one of my favorite restaurants. It is the Rocky Point Restaurant, about a half hour before you get to Carmel. It has a cove second to none for beauty. I said, "Let's get out and spend a few minutes here and hike down to the cove." She said, "Fine." We drove in and parked in the parking lot. It was a short hike to the cove. Maybe seven or eight minutes, that's all. There is a ledge I usually hike down to and stand on. It's right on the edge, but there are small outcroppings that you can hold onto. The ledge itself was a good eighteen inches wide. You would just hike down to it, hold on in back of you, and shinny out. Once there, you could see the waves come in and crash twenty/twenty-five feet below you. The water was always four or five shades of blue and made me think of the Caribbean. It was a little nippy out so I had put on my jacket and she her sweater.

As we were standing there and looking at the water crashing below our feet, in the center of the cove there were huge rocks which made the water swirl all around. We were enjoying the moment and the beauty. The waves were crashing twenty feet below us. Joan said, "Look at that wave. It is so big it might even get us wet." Talk about a black cat putting the eye on us! As the wave got closer and closer, I knew we were in for trouble. I put my right arm around Joan and held on for dear life to the cliff with my left hand as the wave swept completely over our heads, by at least ten feet. The water started to push us off by being in back of us and in between us and the cliff as it fell back to the sea. The pressure was too great for us. We started to slide down the thirty foot drop to the ocean. When we hit the bottom, I didn't know what to do. I seemed fine and thought we had better get out of the water and on higher ground before another wave came. I looked at Joan and she was head-first stuck between two rocks, face in the water with blood all around us. I pulled her face out of the water and checked for breathing. She started to cough so I know that part was ok. She said, "My back hurts." I could not see anything because she had this huge bulky sweater jacket on. I said, "Get up." I was afraid there would be another wave any minute. Much later on as I ran this exciting event over and over in my mind, had her head not gotten stuck between the rocks, I am sure we would have been swept out to sea and never heard from again. I started to lift her up. As I did, I noticed my two fingers on my left hand were pointing the wrong way. Not pretty. Not thinking, I just pulled them straight with the good hand (the one I use, well, never mind), and they seemed to pop in place. They must have broken when I was holding on so tight to the cliff to keep us from falling. They, I guess, just bent backwards. I would think, had they not broken, I may have been able to hold on. I just didn't realize they broke. I guess, because of the adrenalin rush, I didn't feel them break. However, that obviously was not the case. Again, I tried to get Joan up. She didn't want to move. I was still afraid of a second wave. I forced her, and she got to her feet. I had her by the arm and with baby steps she put one foot in front of the other and we started up the hill. She was obviously in pain and was crying. I made it about ten or twelve steps. A young guy's hand was extended in front of me. He said that he and his girlfriend saw the whole thing, and she was in the restaurant calling the paramedics. "Can I help you with her?" I said, "Sure." As I started to pull on her again, I noticed my fingers again. They had taken up the reverse positioning once more. Again, I just yanked on them, and they popped straight forward again. We made it up the hill and into the restaurant in fifteen minutes or thereabouts.

The manager had cordoned off the women's restroom for us. He said, "Is there anything I can do for you?" Right then and there, I was ready for a really stiff scotch. But I said, "Maybe some water for her?" I took some toilet paper and wrapped three of my fingers together and hoped that they would stay straight. Joan was crying. Not loud, but crying. It sounded more like whimpering from shock instead of pain. We were waiting for the paramedics to arrive. They had to come from Monterey, a half hour or so. The restaurant staff couldn't do enough for us. I thanked the girl and her boyfriend for their help. He left and she stayed for a bit. I was talking with the manager. He said that they lose at least one person a year to the rogue waves. He said, "That's why we have the signs posted everywhere. It's terrible. But it happens and no one can tell you when and where they are going to hit. They just do. You were very lucky." Joan slowly looked up for a quick glimpse and then down again. I think she was disagreeing with the management.

I couldn't tell what was wrong with Joan. She said she was hurting on her back. I tried to take the sweater off but as I did, she was in more pain so I left her alone. I am not a paramedic by any stretch of the imagination. I was starting to feel a little pain in my legs, myself. I went into the men's room and took down my pants. Shit! I was all cut up from my knees down to my shoes. The bleeding had stopped but there were long scrapes up and down my legs. I started to wipe the blood off with paper towels and hot water. I went through twenty paper towels and came out clean as a whistle, as long as the wounds did not start bleeding again. I went back to Joan. The paramedics had just arrived. They loaded her into the ambulance and drove to Monterey Community Hospital. Fortunately, Joan had insurance from her previous job, as a nurse for the Atascadero State Hospital for the mentally disturbed and criminals in general. (That was probably why she liked me in the first place.) She was on a work related leave. One of the inmates had broken a mop handle in half and stabbed her in the neck with it. (I had hoped it would have kept her from talking, but no luck!) I followed in the car. By the time we got to the hospital, they had already taken off Joan's sweater and blouse. They laid her on her stomach and started picking sweater out of a hundred very long scratches that were on her back. It looked like someone had taken a huge comb and started on top of her back and scraped it down, all the way to the small of her back. When she fell off the ledge, she must have had her back to the cliff all the way down, and it just cut into her the whole trip down. I had asked them if they could do anything for my fingers. They answered just like a woman. They said, "Do you have any insurance?" (They answered my question with a question.) I said, "No." They said, "NO." I asked if I could buy some tape from them. They said, "No." So, as I waited around for the better part of four hours waiting for the sweater pickers to finish, I snooped around and found some medical tape. I said to me, "Bill would be proud of me," and copped the fuckin tape and taped my fingers together with a Popsicle stick I had kept from my, not so long ago dinner.

Today, the wedding ring finger seems to be just fine, but the pinkie has a little crook in it. My legs healed up fine also. Finally, they put Joan into the car, told me she has a shot for pain, but try to keep her back away from the car seat if possible. So, I put a rope around her neck and tied it to the sun visor to keep her bending forward. She didn't like that very much so instead I put a couple of shirts towards her lower back and told her to lean towards the front of the car, if possible, and we were off. Right before I started the car, I leaned over and asked her if she wanted to continue to San Francisco or go home. I didn't get an answer. But I did get a look!

I started the car and headed for home. It had to be somewhere around ten o'clock. We hadn't had anything to eat since before we left Morro Bay. I asked her if she was hungry. This time I got an answer.

The only place I could think of that would be still open was Rocky Point Restaurant from where we just came. I pulled up to the front door and ran in to get a menu and brought it out for her to peruse. We only ordered a couple of appetizers each. I went in, put in the order and waited. The food came. As I was reaching for my wallet, I had mentioned that we were here earlier. The hostess recognized me and called the manager. It was a different manager, but he knew all about the ordeal. He said, "Is all ok and is there anything I can do?" This guy, just like the other manager, bent over backwards for me. (Where was my ex-boss now?) He wouldn't even let me pay for the food. He walked out to the car with me and gave his condolences to Joan and we drove off. Later, as the days wore on, I finally realized why the management was so great to us. So we wouldn't sue them! Needless to say, I never made it to San Francisco or got my blow job from a queer. Guess I'll live. And that may be the reason why!

Nineteen ninety-eight was upon us and it was well into February. One night I was in a karaoke bar. It was my time to sing. I gave myself some applause (Joking!), and then grabbed the mic. Not sure what I was singing, but all through the song I had noticed a good looking young blonde who couldn't take her eyes off of me. (I would have expected nothing less. (Joking!) After my song and for the next hour or so, she kept looking at me. She sang a song about a half hour after I had and was very good. Again, it was my turn to sing and still a glance from her came every ten seconds. Our eyes hooked many times until I would turn my head out of embarrassment. Most people who know me know I am gregarious and a big mouth when amongst friends. They also know that I am tongue tied and anything but outward going when I am not. So to just walk up to her and say something was not easy for me. She was alone and that did help. My best offense is usually some kind of joking; I finally walked up to her and said, "I noticed you looking at me. Would you like my autograph?" She smiled, handed me her drink napkin and said, "Do you have a pen?" That broke the ice, and we talked for a while. I am not going to drag this very short relationship on and on and through the rest of my book, but there are some things that do need to be said. She was great looking and about fifteen years my junior. I had been without romance for quite some time and pretty much realized that there was no more passion in me. What was worse was, I really didn't care. I was so involved with other singles' problems with ADAPT and arranging their socials and putting on stuff for others in SASS that I had no time for myself. Not a good position for anyone. But, that is how my life had been unfolding. She had and did things with me, and they really got my juices going. I fell hook, line and sinker head over heels in Love with her in two weeks. Where was my ADAPT training now? We were inseparable, and it felt great. After a couple of weeks she joined "Legends" and was a big asset. Now, all three of us guys had girlfriends in the group. That worked out well. Even with all of my activities, I found time to spend with Lyn. So much so, that I would go over to her house, uninvited sometimes, to surprise her and bring flowers, candy, condoms and the usual shit that an idiot brings when in Love. All of a sudden she disappeared out of my life. Never home! Never answering the phone! She did show up to a rehearsal. I asked her what was going on. She said very coldly, "It's time for me to move on." "That's it?" I said "That's it," she said. I was devastated! I will not take this any further, but about three weeks later R. J. "our leader of Legedns", had a heart attack and played frog. The group broke up, and I never saw or heard from Lyn again for ten years. My reign in pro singing lasted for a couple of years until R.J. croaked. It was a great experience, and I will never forget it. There always seems to be lessons to be learned in all we do if you look for them. Lyn showed up in my life when I had given up, basically, on my life. I had lost all passion and the need to improve myself in any way. Just give myself to others until I reached a place when it was time to just give it all up. Lyn renewed my passion not only physically, but in my life in general. The timing was right for Lyn to be there, even with the pain I had when she left. People come into our lives for a reason and go out that way also. Thanks, Lyn, for being there for me.

 I did continue my karaoke career for a while, and even today I still do a song or two a few times a year. In fact, not too long after Legends broke up, I went from karaoke bar to karaoke bar with a cassette. As I did a song, I had the KJ tape it. I made twenty duplicates of it and sent them to all of my relatives for Christmas. I now, only have only three relatives left that will even talk to me!

 This will be short and sweet, but I have to stick it in because it is something I will never forget. My brother and I were invited back east to my cousins daughter's wedding. All went great. While we were there, we, my brother and I, had to take a ride with my other cousin, Sharon who was five years younger than I was. Now Sharon is a bit over-weight, and her eyes seem to be squinted a bit. I don't know if that was the reason this happened, but if it isn't, she needs to have her driver's license revoked. We got into her car; I believe it was one of those real expensive ones, like a five-year old Comet. As we got in to this beauty, my brother said to me, "Did you see all of those dents on all four corners of her car?" Actually, I hadn't noticed. I was taking in all of the missing paint from the hood and the missing head light. We were on the seventh floor of a parking garage. It was one way only (Thank God!), and very narrow. She started the car and started down. Up until then, I have never hooked a seat belt. After the first turn I grabbed for the seat belt. The turns were sharp and like I said, very narrow. I would think you should be doing no more than five or six miles an hour. I glanced at her speedometer, and it was showing twenty-three. Now this speed, of course, won't kill us, but there were so many sparks coming from the corners of the car that I was afraid of a fire and burning to death. After passing the third floor my brother and I looked at each other and started to laugh. And laugh we did. It was like Mr. Toad's wild ride in Disneyland, only worse! We were hysterical. She just kept on hitting each and every wall with every turn. The noise was screeching, and the sparks were flying. By that time we had tears rolling out of our eyes. We finally made it to the bottom where she turned to us and said, "What's so funny?" We blew it. I almost pissed my pants laughing so hard. She was oblivious to what she was doing. She must do it every day and doesn't have a clue! Just glad she never asked to use my car when we went somewhere!

When I got back to California, things were back to normal. It was late in the year. I had met a very pretty Jewish lady through my own club, SASS. We had coffee a time or two, and I really liked her. Now, she being Jewish, at that time, was OK. I have been circumcised myself, you know. Sometimes I think that Jewish women have that done also. I know a few who have bigger balls then most of the Jewish men I know. Anyway, my optometrist was in Simi Valley near where Bonnie lived. It was a long schlep from Morro Bay down to there. I had asked her if she would like to take the ride with me. I mentioned that my taste in things like this sucked, and it would be nice if she would help me select the proper frames. She said, "That would be great. I'd like to do it." So we headed for "THE VALLEY!" Our conversation all the way down there (a three hour drive) was stimulating, and her company was great. She picked two different frames for me. I paid the bill and left. On the way home we talked for hours and never had a lull in our conversation. The more we talked, the more I liked her. Later on in the conversation, some stuff came out. I am not a saint by any means, but she had mentioned that she had four children, and the youngest was eighteen months. I asked how many times she had been married. She said, "Four." I asked how long she had been divorced and she said, "It's in progress." I asked her how many children are from the same guy. She said, "One from each." A little in dismay, I said, "What do you think about sex? With all of your kids I guess you like it, right?" She said, "Yes it's great. But only after marriage." I said, "You don't believe in pre-marital sex?" She said, "That's right." "Then how do you know if you are compatible?" She said, "It doesn't matter if you both are in Love." I asked, "How firm are you on this subject?" She said, "Unwavering." I said, "OK." I dropped her off and spent the next five hours trying to analyze how I get involved with this kind of woman and how come she doesn't realize that the reason she has four husbands and four kids that it is her own doing. Not to mention idiot men. Not that I am right, but common sense has to tell you that, at some time, if you are in a relationship, you need to see if you are compatible sexually and not only in conversation. I really liked her so I called her just to make sure I understood all correctly. We talked for fifteen minutes. Next! The funny part is that a couple of years later while camping; I bumped into a male friend and guess who his wife was? They were *camping*. I knew I liked her.

To end this chapter, I will do it with a new beginning. As I had mentioned a few pages back, there is a dance place called "The Graduate." I was there one night stalking about a hundred chicks. Once again, I was the "Stalker of many and taker home of none." However, this time, as I was walking off the dance floor, I noticed someone who looked familiar to me. I got a little closer, and she had caught me looking at her. A huge smile came over her face, and I guess mine as well. It was Debbie, the girl from the bank where I used to bank when I was doing very well years ago. You know my mistress, or whatever you want to call her. I don't think that mistress would be appropriate as I never "kept" her. She was as much freelance as I was. Only she was not married. We talked for an hour or so catching up on years. Then we went out and had some coffee and talked more where it was quieter. I knew that she had gotten married to a guy named "Chuck," and they eventually got divorced. Apparently she had gotten into drugs and had gotten all screwed up because of him. She was up in this area and living in the house they had in Santa Maria somewhere. I think it was her grandmother's or something like that. We dated for a while. Nothing serious and eventually she moved to Santa Cruz where they have a college. The mascot of that college is the Banana Slug. (Not to mention that, my Niece, Marina, graduated from there with a masters in Marine Biology.) She became a minster of a church. Changed her name to Grace something or other. We kept in touch for years and then she almost died and in need of a liver transplant. I was there in the hospital when the doctors gave her just a few hours to live. It was that time that I would have another talk with my God. I had asked him to help her. I said that she was one of those persons that needed to be on this earth, if for no other reason, then that she is brilliant. I went back into the room and whispered in her non-hearing ear, that she will be just fine. Gave her a light kiss on her forehead and left the room. And just like in the movies, she got notice of a liver that had her name on it. Hours later she was smiling at me when she awoke. The new liver gave her another two years or thereabout and then she went to see her maker. I think it was about two thousand and five or six when she left us. Well, she left and I think I will also. Next chapter!

Chapter Twenty-Four

It was about the end of nineteen ninety-nine. It was late October, I think. I was walking downtown, in San Luis Obispo, Oh wait, just a quickie.

One night a couple of buddies and I were walking in downtown San Luis Obispo, looking for a place to have a little dinner and maybe a drink or two, when we saw this huge crowd gathering on the corner. We moseyed on over and asked some dude what was going on. He said, "Linsey Lohan was shooting a movie, and they want a big crowd to run across the street on cue. So, I guess everyone is waiting their chance to be a movie star." WE, I, Dion and James, looked at each other and decided that we wanted to be a big time movie star as well. We hung around for about an hour. We ran across the street two maybe three times and then it was all over. We never got to sign any autographs and to be totally honest with you, I never went to see the movie to see if my little face ever graced the screen. As I recall, the title of the movie was, "I think I know who killed me" or something like that. Now, where was I? Oh yea!

A lady stopped me and started to talk to me. We talked for fifteen or twenty minutes or so and then we went on our separate ways. As I continued on my way, I asked myself, "Who was that?" She didn't even look familiar. She obviously knew who I was. I had been doing so much for so many for so long now, that I didn't even know who I was and who anyone else was. All people just started to run together. My life was starting to be one big blur. After all, it had been about six years or so since I started to do singles things. It seemed that I did nothing for myself. Everything was for them. I went home and gave it a lot of thought. I opened some albums that I had made when on trips and this is how they went.

Number one: *I took a group* in May, nineteen ninety-five from SASS (The singles group I started) to Cancun and Chichenitza.

Number two: *I took a group* from SASS to Hawaii in September of nineteen ninety-six.

Number three: *I took a group* from SASS to Ensenada, Mexico in October of nineteen ninety-seven.

Number four: In September of nineteen ninety-eight, I drove for ninety-six hours *all by myself* to Mesa Verde National Park, Colorado, and Bryce Canyon National Park, Canyon Lands National Park, Arches National Park, and Zion National Park all in Utah. Just a quick day trip to get away from something, I guess.

Number five: I took a cruise September of nineteen ninety—eight to the Western Caribbean. Playa del Carmen, Cozumel, Grand Cayman and Jamaica in Ocho Rios. It was the first time I had ever had a roommate and when I came into the room, he was getting laid and said to me, "Don't worry, it's OK to stay." Oh yea, it was with the SASS group and not ADAPT!

Number six: *I took* a ten dayer in July of Nineteen ninety-nine, *alone*. (Might as well been with the SASS group.) Not in any order I went to Crater Lake in Oregon, Craters of the Moon National Monument in Idaho, along with Hagerman Fossil Beds, and then to Glacier National Park and taking the "Going to the Sun Road" in Montana. I also hit Yellowstone, Grand Tetons, and Chandelier, the drive through Tree, in Leggett California. I did about five thousand miles.

Number seven: Late, in the summer of nineteen ninety-nine, I drove to Arizona looking for the Dutchman's gold. *Alone, of course!* I not only made it to Superstition Mountain, but I saw Jerome, the gay motorcycle hang out (man, am I going to catch flack from that statement. It's a bunch of Harley guys antique shopping.), Sedona, one of the most beautiful cities I have ever seen, and then on to Meteor Crater Natural Landmark, the Petrified Forest and Sunset Crater Volcano at Wupatki National Monument where Easy Rider was made.

Number eight: Just about the middle of the month in September nineteen ninety-nine, *I did* a quick three thousand mile roundtrip to Roswell, New Mexico, to see if any aliens were hanging out. I did see some suspicious Mexicans, but that was not the kind I was looking for. On the way there and back I stopped at Casa Grande National Monument Prehistoric Ruins, Saguaro National Park, Tombstone, where the famous gun fight took place, the International Space Station Hall of Fame in Alamogordo, White Sands National Monument, and of course Roswell. Last, but certainly not least, Carlsbad Caverns National Park. (Just for your edification, did you know that when bats leave the caves to go feed at night, they always turn to the left coming out?) I have one other quick bit of information for you. Bats eat about two hundred and forty thousand tons (tons not pounds, tons) of mosquitoes and insects every night, worldwide. If we were to kill all of those nasty looking bats, we would be overrun with insects. They would eventually rule the world.

Number nine: In late September, nineteen ninety-nine, I *took a cruise to Alaska with SASS*. We went to Van Couver, Juneau, Glacier Bay, and Ketchikan.

I am sure that there are a few things that I did not log or just don't remember. So, when I look at all that I have done in the past five or six years, and of course, in ninety-nine, where it seems I started to do things alone, and never really gave it much thought, I need to say that I have done a lot more than the average guy, I would think. The difference is that I have either done it alone or for a group of which I was too busy making sure that all goes right, that there was no time to find someone for myself. This does not include anything I did for ADAPT, the non-dating group of which I was heavily involved. That included almost every Friday night every week for about the same period of time. I believe it had been Bonnie that taught me that Friday nights were special. Mine were, but not the right way. I needed a break. I needed some intimacy. I needed someone who would care for me or at least would go with me on a one to one basis. Someone, that when I would look at her, I could remember her name. I felt I needed to go and find myself. Once again, I find myself moving. My brother calls me a nomad. One of the few things we don't quarrel about.

When I moved to Morro Bay, it was a choice between there and South Shore Lake Tahoe, so why not there this time. I had a few bucks saved up so I could go to work for peanuts if I had to. I put an ad in the Tahoe newspaper for a room to rent for cheap or to house sit. I got a call from a couple who were both teachers. They told me they had a rental in Reno that was destroyed and that they needed some time to go there and repair it. They wanted to move into it and not have to drive from South Shore to Reno all the time. They needed someone to babysit their house in Tahoe. We settled on a figure (a very good figure for me), and then they dropped the kicker. They had a Sheppard who would stay home with me. All I had to do was feed it and walk it for ten minutes a day and the place was mine. We both needed to see each other and the dog. I drove up and met with them. The house was beautiful. A great big bay window looking out over the whole area with a huge fireplace next to it for those long, cold days with a woman. There was a jacuzzi in the backyard and a non-mowing front yard. I knew I wanted it and was ready to move in as soon as they made up their minds. I put in a few applications with some of the casinos while I was there, then left. About four or five days went by. I guess the time it takes to check me out. I received a phone call from the teachers and they said, "When do you want to move in?" I said, "In two weeks, if that would be OK?" Done deal! I can't tell you how many people wished me the best. There were many of them that were not real happy that I was going, however. How would they find something to do?

Tahoe bound!!

Once again I found myself moving from a bigger place to a smaller place. No time for a garage sale so what I didn't throw into the trash, I put into storage. In two weeks I was there. As luck would have it, I had just met a school teacher from the Morro Bay area named Lynne and had just started dating. I figured that was history. I needed to concentrate on my new life, at least for a while. I decided to spend a little time just relaxing and exploring this most beautiful area before I pursued a job with any seriousness. However, that lasted about two days when a small local casino where I had put in an application called me and asked if I would like to start to work. I lied a little and told them definitely yes, but that I could not start for at least ten days or so. I wasn't quite all moved in. That was fine with them, and they gave me a starting date for training. I started my exploration of this beautiful area with the security that I had a job. My life already seemed to be changing for the best.

As time passed, I found out there are so many great, beautiful, and different places in Tahoe. It had been snowing heavily for days. Fortunately, I had a four-wheel drive Jeep at the time. The four-wheel drive had given me a false sense of security. You can't do fifty in the snow, especially around curves. You just can't. It didn't take me long to find out. One day, one of my treks had led me to Carson City. Carson City is the capital of Nevada. It was only twenty miles from where I was living, but you had to go down a huge grade. From the summit of about seven thousand feet to maybe fifteen hundred feet, on a clear dry day in ten, twelve minutes. This day the snow was four or five inches deep on the road. There was a little snow fluttering down and the snow berms that the snow removal equipment made on the side of the road were eight to ten feet high on both sides of the road. So, happy Charlie started down the grade, slowly, as to get the feel of driving in the snow. I needed to learn as I would be doing it for a while. I started at twenty-five and then thirty. Piece of cake! Soon, I had kicked it up to forty-five. Right about then I started into my first significant turn. I just eased on the brake so to slow down but instead of slowing, I started to slide. Not only slide but by the time I realized what was really happening, I had done two three-sixties. Now, from the edge of the cliff it was five thousand feet straight down! I didn't have a clue what to do. Not a clue! Finally, by hitting the eight/ ten foot berms so many times, I stopped. I might as well have had no brakes in the Jeep. They did not help whatsoever. I was helpless with zero control. Had it not been for the berms keeping me from going over the cliff, I would have been a goner. Had this happened a week or two earlier when the berms were only a foot high, or not even existent, shit! It took about five minutes for my heart to stop pounding at five hundred beats per second. (Of course that is better than no beating.) That would be lesson number one in a series of lessons to come. To quote a phrase from a Dirty Harry movie with Clint Eastwood, "A man has to know his limitations." I just found one of mine. Thirty miles an hour! Tops!

I checked in at my appointed time with the "Lakeside Inn and Casino." It was about eight blocks from the major casinos at State Line. State Line divides California from Nevada. Training started and was an eight hour day for five days. They taught the ten of us in training to know where all of the bathrooms were, the garage was, the elevators and the customer service desk was, and things in general about the area in case a customer would ask, also how to spot a suspicious character, to counting cash and chips and where to get fed. There were written tests that had questions on it like, "What would you do if you found a bag of cash lying on the highway with no one around?" It was really a lot of training. There was stuff that the layman would never even think about.

I started real work that next week. I was given the position of cashier. (They may have noticed I was Jewish and figured I should be with the money.) This job was a kick. I started my first day and each and every day from there on with counting my cash draw. I started with fifty thousand dollars in cash. At the end of my shift, I was to have not a penny over or under the fifty thousand dollars that I had started with. Now I had checks, chips, I O U's and coupons. There were weekly rewards if we, the tellers, individually, were within twenty-five cents each day, as I recall. If our draw was perfect, we would get a free meal or a bunch of different rewards for different things. We all carried change just in case we were only short a small amount so that we could add a little to make our draws come out on the button. However, that was not allowed, and there was a bunch of cameras watching us all the time. Not just for the slipping in and out of small change but because of the fifty K in our cash drawers, and also because we all had access to the vault not more than ten feet behind us that held, I am sure, in access of ten million or thereabout. So, my new life begins. Now, I don't remember, if you remember, that I had a gambling problem? So, I had to make some kind of agreement with myself as to what to do. (Fifty thousand in cash each and every day. Hummm, I think I know!) I made a decision that I would gamble no more than forty dollars a week. If I was to lose forty or I would win forty, I would walk away. Hard to believe that I stuck to it and actually won money that year. Now, to work in a casino, you have to be approved by the sheriff's department. Not only a background check but for the use of drugs. (I told them I used them all the time. Not funny, right? They didn't think so either.) They charged me fifteen dollars for the finger prints and twenty-five for the paperwork. I had to pay forty dollars for my uniform for work, as well. The job was suppose to pay me. But, it was starting to get expensive. I went to get my drug test at the sheriff's department. I thought they would just extract some blood and it was all over. Not this sheriff's department. They wanted hair, my hair. I told them I can't afford to give up any, but they had other ideas. They lifted my hair in back and then snipped a bunch, if that was possible. I really would have rather given up my blood instead of my hair.

My first paycheck was for one hundred ninety-two dollars and eighty-nine cents, net. Thirty-nine and a half hours at six bucks per, less deductions of course. When I applied, they had asked me if I had a particular shift I would like. I told them, "Graveyard, because I had never done it before and I would like to try it." So, I would go to work at eleven ish with a slight beautiful snowfall and get off to go home at sevenish and had to dig my car out of the two-foot snowfall that occurred while I was working in a nice warm casino. In fact, sometimes I would have to wait a few hours for my door locks to unfreeze so I could unlock my car. As time went on, I just left it unlocked. On my days off I started to do little road trips to places like Virginia City, Truckee, Donner Pass, North Shore Tahoe, and many others. As I was working for the Lakeside Casino, all the cage employees, at least once or twice a week had to work a short shift at the small kiosk at the far end of the casino. That was there for customers who needed to cash in, get change, or do any other monetary things and did not want to walk all the way to the other end of the casino where the main cage was and where I worked.

One day I was in the kiosk and an employee I had never seen before got the shift with me. There were always two working it. He looked really bad. Not someone I would hire to meet and greet the customers. He looked like he had died and barely came back to life again. Frail, pimply, slurred speech, spotted hair loss, and that's just the start. He seemed pleasant enough and friendly. I worked the one day with him and didn't see him until the next week as I was in the kiosk again. Apparently, he was hired on a part-time basis. When the shift was over and I was changing clothes to go home, one of the other employees said, "I see you have met (for the sake of a name, let's call him Bill) Bill."

"Do you know him?" I asked. "Sure," he said, all of the old employees know him. He worked here for years and then got AIDS and was off for a couple of years. I guess they had to hire him back again. Not sure why, but I think it had something to do with pressure from the outside." "AIDS?" I asked. "Nobody told me anything about that. If he would have cut a finger at some time, I would have been the first one to help him with a bandage. Shit, this is not good." The next day before my shift, I went to my supervisor (a lesbian, I might add), and asked her about what I was told about Bill. She said that that was true. I asked her why I wasn't told about it and she said that it is against company policy. It would be considered discrimination. I asked her, "What about my safety? I have no problem working with him as long as I know what I am getting into. But keeping it a secret is just not right." I gave a two-week notice right there on the spot. I suppose they had to do what they had to do, but I just don't think it was right. Why should he be protected verbally and not me physically? Talk about discrimination! So, without further ado, I promptly put my application in the four major casinos at State Line. They are Harrah's, Harvey's, Caesar's and the Horizon. About that time the Horizon was having a major makeover, and they seemed to be a lot more aggressive. I thought that there might be a better chance for advancement there. So, that was who I was hoping would hire me. As it turned out, three of the four hired me. The one that did not was the Horizon. That figures, doesn't it? I can't remember why, right now, but I chose Harvey's. (As it turned out, Harrah's eventually bought Harvey's, and that made a monopoly because Harrah's already owned Caesar's. So Caesar's was sold and replaced with the Montbleu.) Not long ago, I was told that the Horizon was shut down for some reason, probably un-lawful gaming practices (my guess) and now has only slot machines and no table games.)

Just before I started working for Harvey's, I thought that I'd take a trip or two and see a thing or two that I had heard about. One of those places was Area Fifty One, the flying saucer area. I know it really doesn't exist. But, I thought I'd try anyway and if our government just happens to be wrong, maybe I would see a saucer or two. (In fact, later in life, I went to Area Fifty Two, and I know, it doesn't exist either. Just wait!) So, I started out for a small town called Rachel, not a stone's throw from my intended target. I soon approached the turn off to Rachel.

Now, here's the start of what our government says that there is no such place. As I turn onto the highway to Rachel, the green, government-manufactured highway sign that every single freeway and highway that our government puts on them for directions and our edification, in every state, this one reads, "Extraterrestrial Highway." Not only does it read the E. T Hwy, but it has pictures of flying saucers on it, at both ends of the highway. Now, I know some of you don't believe me, and, personally, I really don't care, it's not the first time I have not been believed, but I dare you to go see for yourself. As I am in the very little town of Rachel, Nevada, there is one very small restaurant, bar and motel all under one roof and it's still very small. Guess what the motel part is called? "The Little Ale'inn" and, of course, it has a picture of a large, black almond-shaped eyed space person, with the saying next to it that reads, "Earthlings welcome.".

It was just about that time I looked down at my speedometer and saw that it had three hundred thousand miles on it. That's a lot of miles to be taking long trips. I hope it doesn't break down in this area, I could be abducted!

Little did I know, later in my life, I would have a vehicle that would hit four hundred and eighty thousand mile on it and not use a drop of oil.

When I started at Harvey's, I kept the graveyard shift but chose to work in the slot machine department. I went through very little training. Maybe one hour, if that. The slot department was the best job that I have ever had. It was fun and because of the late shift, not much pressure from the bosses.

I started out as just a change guy and eventually did some slot tech stuff. The slot tech stuff was the best. It was nothing but accolades from the guests. There were three major things that would happen. First, if a guest would fail to get paid some coins (Yes, you children of the twenty-first century, there were actually coins that fell from the machines when you got your three little cherries) because the hopper was out. They would call for me. I would fill the machines hopper, and they would be so happy because they could continue to play, and, of course, they got the balance of coins that were due. Second, when the slot machine would malfunction (this has nothing to do, with Janet Jackson), they would call me over. I would open it and un-jam the coin slot. That was usually the problem. When the machine was open, and

I had fixed the problem (just before I shut the top down), I would look suspiciously (especially when I was with the older women) at them, then check both of my sides to make sure no one was looking, and turn the wheels so that there were three sevens looking straight up at her. I would give her a quick smile and shut the top. I can't tell you how many great big smiles I got from them. Some even broke out in a sweat. The bad part was that when I shut the glass top, the wheels would go back to whatever they were when I had opened the machine up, by that time I was gone. The third thing was if there was a Jackpot to be paid, I was the one who came over with the money and did the paying. Once again, the thank you's were deafening. Great job!

Harvey's had a suggestion box. Any employee who had put in a suggestion that the company implemented would get some kind of a bonus or gift. No matter what was decided, they would be called into the boss's office and told why or why not they were going to use the suggestion. I thought that was pretty kewl. I had seen so many things that I would have changed for the better that I was in the boss's office on a regular basis. They only used one of my ideas the whole time that I was employed. But, when I came back a year or two after I had left Harvey's I not only saw, but I was told by some friends, that a few of my ideas were in process. Guess the bosses wanted the credit for themselves. That's big business for you. However, there was one policy that I never did understand.

Harvey's had a foreign school program. If I had been a fly on the wall, I guess I would have known what was really going on. At summer time they would bring, just for the summer, a plethora of college kids from all countries to work in the casino. They would pay them more than us guys who were there from one day to fifty years. Ninety percent of them couldn't be understood by not only the Harvey's help, but the guests as well. I can't tell you how many guests would give us looks as to say, "What did he say?" Then to add insult to injury, at the end of the summer when all were to go back to their respective countries, Harvey's would offer them a thousand dollars to stay longer than Labor Day weekend. No regular employee that I had ever talked to was ever offered ten cents for anything, period! Big business, heh!

I finely had to move as the rental had finally gotten repaired and the owners wanted to move back in to their home. I rented an apartment near Heavenly Ski Run. I started to get my head together and gave thought about moving back to Morro Bay. I am an Aquarius and am supposed to be out-going and gregarious. In all the time that I lived in South Shore Lake Tahoe, I met no one to be close with, male or female, and only an employee or two to go have breakfast with on an occasion or two. You have heard the saying "It is a nice place to visit, but I don't want to live there." Well, that's Tahoe. Extremely transient and the only way to be befriended is to have grown up there.

My friend, Lynne, did come up a time or two. One thing that I think should be in this book that is nothing short of the Bible in pages is that we had gone hiking on a very hot day at Eagle Lake. Or was it Emerald Lake? Oh well. When we got to the end of the hike and just before we were to start back, Lynne said she wanted to take off her shoes and socks and wade in the water at least up to her mid thigh and cool off a bit. I told her that this is no ordinary lake; it was glacier fed and could not be much over thirty-five degrees. She said she has a pool and she went in often at very cold temperatures. I said, "OK, but don't go far." So little miss no-never-mind jumps in and in less than thirty seconds, she was gasping for air. She was reaching out as far as she could to try and to grab my outstretched hand to pull her in. I could see that she wasn't breathing well. Of course, being the gentleman that I am, I yelled, "Stretch farther, you can make it." She did and I pulled her out to shore. Of course, being the gentleman that I am and wanting to say "I told you so," I held her close and said, "I told you so." She didn't know whether to say thank you for saving my life or fuck off, you asshole. That was kind of the turning point that made me move back to Morro Bay. I was becoming the jerk that I used to be. I'm finally back. It's me! It wasn't long after that that I moved back to Morro Bay.

Chapter Twenty-Five

Morro Bay, oh, Morro Bay! What a beautiful place to be. It is just as beautiful as Lake Tahoe, only different! Now go figure. The reason I moved away from Morro Bay to Lake Tahoe was to clear my head from all the stuff that was and had been doing for others and start doing things for myself. So, the first thing I did when I got back to Morro Bay was to become a docent. "What is a docent?" you ask. A docent works for **no pay**. Stupid, right! "What does a docent do?" He **does things for others** without the pay. So, why did I take the hiatus to Lake Tahoe for the two years? Dumb? I guess *so*.

The Museum of Natural History in Morro Bay ran an ad, asking for help. To be a docent you had to go through a lot of training. Book studying, walks with other docents, tests on what you have been learning, and a psychological test to see why you want to work and train for no pay. It just so happened that I was in really great physical shape at this time. When in Tahoe I did a lot to keep in shape. I did bike riding, walking, and karaoke. (Even my voice was in good shape for doing lectures.) After many weeks of rigorous challenges, both mentally and physically, I got my little piece of paper to hang on my wall. Now, they asked me what I wanted to specialize in. In my past I had studied many aspects of nature, like geology, the sea, subduction zones, tectonic plates, the mountains, volcanoes, outer space, the moon and the sun and their relationship with us, fish, mammals, birds, flowers, Morro Bay's beginning, and even earthquakes. You know, speaking of earthquakes, let me side track for a page or two.

Remember my cousin, Arnold, the weakling, who beat the crap out of me when eleven years old or so, and could color waaaaay better than I, and his Lovely wife, Sandy? You know, the Sandy that I got in the cross hairs of turtles fucking. That Arnold and Sandy! By the way, I recently saw them, and they are doing just fine, thank you. Anyway, they came out to Las Vegas one weekend. As usual, they got a room on the seven hundredth and fifty-second floor like they usually do. I, as usual, was just below them, rooming with my brother Mark, on floor number *one*. About six A. M. in the morning (The "in the morning" is for you who are paying attention and could use a good laugh.), there was a seven point two earthquake. The epicenter was in a town about eighty miles away called Landers. Even though there is not much in the town of Landers, they still called it the "Lander's quake". I, personally, believe that they should have named it the "EMSoV" quake. "Eighty miles south of Vegas" quake for us locals. I woke with the rumbling and knew exactly what was happening. I have been in at least three biggies and a couple of smaller ones. Being from Philadelphia, and never having experienced an earthquake, I was fearful for my cousins. I started to go upstairs to where my cousins were. (My brother grabbed as many hats and tee shirts that he had brought with him and ran outside to save them. You really have to know and understand my brother better to get the full meaning of this last sentence.) Knowing that you are not supposed to take the elevator when something like this happens, and knowing that he is in the nose-bleed level of this hotel, I hit number fifty-seven and prayed. (No fucking way I am to climb some fifty plus stairways.) I got off and ran to their room, knocked loud, and the door opened. I said, "Sandy, are you two ok? There was an earthquake, and you must have been swaying up here." She said, "It was great. The toilet bowl water was sloshing all over the bathroom floor, and we could feel the swaying. How cool it was." "Where is Arnold?" I asked. Sandy said, "He's in the bedroom calling the kids and telling them how neat it all was." I hope my brother saved his hats and tee shirts!

Now, where the hell was I? Oh yea, specializing in something. I have always liked the earth, both the ground I walk on and the earth we live on. I learned so much geology in training. The more I learned, the more it made me think of more questions to ask. So, why not teach about the land all around us and mix in a little of the local animals, fauna, flora and a little about space and how things like the moon and sun affect us, as well. So, that was a done deal in my mind. Then, they asked us what age level we wanted to teach. For me, that was easy. I wanted the six to sixteen year age group of mixed boys and girls. I figured I should know more than they did. Well, at least, fifty-fifty. I put in my request and was approved. I immediately started doing my walks and accompanying lectures as we walked locally. Sometimes, we would have to car-pool to get to where my teaching and hiking needed to be. I was really Loving it. So were the kids. I tried to make it on their level by doing things like giving them M&M peanuts, having them bite one in half and then looking at it. It pretty much wraps up our earth. The in-side peanut was the middle or center core, and is divided into two parts. The outer part is spinning molten metal, and spins around the very center of the solid metal. The thin outer sugar coating was where we all live, called the outer crust, and is roughly, thirty-five miles thick. The chocolate in-between was the very thick layer of many types of rock, about two thousand miles thick, and surrounds the core, is called the mantle. They would Love it when we would see a fossil high up in the mountain and no water for miles. I might say something like this, "They were from the frog species and hopped up here." The only ones that didn't smile were some of the parents who may have been with us. As I got into this docent stuff more and more, I thought that I would take the hikes with other and much more experienced docents. How much more could I absorb? I think much more. I always did better hands on then with books. So, I started to do some hikes and walks a few days a week. I started to notice that some of the docents, where their geographical areas over-lapped, were saying different things about the same things. An example would be, "Morro Bay Rock is twenty-two million years old." While when I would be on a walk with another docent, he might have said, "Morro Bay Rock is thirty-million years old." Now, between you and me, eight million years, geologically speaking, is a blink of an eye. But what if it was on a test at our local high schools? One child would be marked wrong on his/her test and both would swear that they heard in from the mouth of a docent. I know this example may be a little far-fetched, but you get the idea. So, I being me, (not necessarily a good thing) decided to take matters in to my own hands. This, besides, the total abomination of my two submitted poems some years ago, is probably the start of my literary career. (I am sure that this book will be the end of it.) I did write some affirmations for the S.A.S.S. newsletter not too long ago. I decided to look into the discrepancies and write an article about them. Not naming anyone but just talking about the particular thing, the correct way. When the docents read my article in their monthly publication, I thought they would either look it up to see if I was correct or call me down on it. At that time I would show them pages and pages of notes, proving my claims. Then, the incorrect docent could change what he was saying without any egg on his face. I put it through to the board, and they thought it was a great idea. They approved it, realizing that many of the docents started with the museum when Jesus was a pup. Since then, many things that they had learned changed with new technology, and no one really kept up. The older guys were saying something different from the newer guys who learned it correctly. I needed to have a name for the column I was going to write. I remembered having a conversation with my youngest son, Sean. What we were discussing eludes me right now, but I do remember him saying something like, "Knowledge is Power." So it is written, and so it will be done. My very first article was very short. They all started out with, "Did you know?" It went something like this.

Did you know? When the Pacific plate and the North American Plates clash, the North American Plate slides on top of the Pacific Plate. And that's the truth! I always ended up with, "And that's the truth!" I don't remember what the discrepancies were at this time, but whoever read this should have corrected their lecture or at least checked it out or have come to see me. Just in case you are wondering what plates are, they are called tectonic plates. There are fourteen of them. Nine of them are very huge and five a lot smaller. They are constantly moving. They cover the entire world. In fact, the United States is on the North American plate and is sliding on to the top of the Pacific Ocean (Plate) at a rate of approximately one inch per year. Eventually, the Pacific Ocean will be gobbled up. By the way, this process is called subduction. Don't ask! Eventually, my column became columns. I pissed off many of the older guy and gal docents. (This was not my intention at all.) In fact, one of the most astute ladies, with many college years of teaching and a string of credentials behind her, left as a docent, because, I guess, she was embarrassed by her mistakes. It had to do with flowers. Go figure, me a grunt, correcting a professor in the field of pretty, dainty little flowers. Next!

Needless to say, with my return from Lake Tahoe, I opened a door to new friends, new acquaintances, and a few new areas of my life. Let's talk about the latter, new areas of my life. One day I went back to an ADAPT meeting. Just to sit in and say hi to some old friends. One of the speakers was a director of plays who had recently moved to the San Luis Obispo area. San Luis Obispo was the big town in the area. It was a town of old money, a very creditable college (Cal Poly), and was twelve miles from Morro Bay. It was where most of us went to have a little night life. Morro Bay had a little night life, also. Very little! Morro Bay was not a town of old money either, just old people. This director dude gave his little talk and after it was over, he asked if anyone would like to be in a play. He said he was just starting to recruit for his next play, "A Few Good Men." One of my old friends raised his hand and volunteered. Then, he looked at me as if to say, "Come on you chicken shit. I'm gonna do it, how about you?" "A play I thought. Can't hurt to find out a little about it, right?" Hand went up. After the meeting, we all went to the Graduate to dance. My friend and I walked over to talk to the director. "Okay, I said, "What's the scoop?" He said that there were to be tryouts for the different parts at the high school on Monday night. At that time you could pick the part you want to try out for, or I will assign you a tryout sheet to read from. READ FROM! Shit! I am the worst reader. As I think I have mentioned before, I am A D D in that subject. I'm dead!

The tryouts started and I had to look at the script. There were a billion words on it. You had to memorize them as well. SHIT! I read some lines like most others. It was obvious that many there were not novices at this. The bottom line is that I got the part of the sergeant. The black sergeant! At least, me being a Jew and a minority myself, I got the part of another minority. So, the practices started. We practiced three or four nights a week every week for six weeks. As it turned out, one guy quit later on, and I took his part. It was only seven or eight lines, but I did have a costume change to do for such a short role. I, also, was one of a few that from the back of the stage who had to scream out a few lines with others. But we could read those from the backside of the stage. About half way through the practices, the stage hand left for some reason. I picked up that job. So, for a guy who had never done or even thought about doing a play, I now had a small feature role, a small costume change to be a different guy, a back stage screaming guy, and a scenery change guy. Thank God there was no pay for this, or I would have had to ask for a raise!

Now, as I had mentioned before, my youngest son, Sean, had gotten into a lot of trouble with the law. As I have mentioned before, I not only continually backed my oldest son, David, while incarcerated, I did the same for Sean. Paid his bills, kept in contact regularly, and was constantly in touch with his parole agent to make sure things were going hot, straight and true for his release.

    I have added a letter that Sean had written to me on standard issue, prison stationary. I don't want you to think it is me bragging or anything like that. It is something that in the very near future will come into play. I know it is a little difficult to read, so I will highlight it for you. It was written on November eighteenth, two thousand, at a time when Sean was in prison. He started out by saying how he continually messes up. Not only with his life by being in jail but with his marriage also. How he is always looking for an edge (his big brother's trademark.), and blames himself only, not like his brother and sister who seems to find someone else to blame when they screw up. How he always tried to make me proud of him. (He has always made me proud of him. How could he not? He is just like me in so many different ways.) I am proud of not only him, but his brother and sister as well. God only knows that we (I especially) all have our bad moments, but we hopefully learn from them and move on to become a better person. Sometimes it takes more than one or two experiences. David, my oldest son, is a prime example. Twenty some years in and out of the calaboose and now is a terrific person and giving back to the world what he had extracted for so many years. Do you think I am not proud? Then take my daughter, Holly, who after a poor start with having her child out of wedlock and wanting to put her up for adoption, then not getting married for years after has made a great life for herself and her family. She now heads up the international division of a major insurance company.) Sean goes on to say that he is a regular kind of guy, clean cut and not extravagant by any means and now surrounded by thieves, rapists, drug addicts, and more. He made me think of the time that I walked through the jail door at a young and tender age and almost threw up when I peered in. He says how sick he was for not being able to see his mother for the holidays. (I guess she was coming over from Australia that year.) We had discussed when he gets out, and how we would get a race horse together. I think I was more anxious than he was about that subject. He also says that I have never led him to believe anything other than that I was proud of him and that I Loved him and have always been there for him. Then he signs off with these words. "If I don't tell you enough, I Love you. I am very proud to have you as my dad and my friend. Love, Sean"

I can't tell you how very difficult it is to read and write these words, as you will note later on in my writings.

After this letter I have enclosed a birthday card that Sean sent to me in late January. It basically says how he has been a screw-up for the past twelve months, and the only constant in his life was me. How he looks to me for guidance and I gave it. How he should have had listened to me more. He says that it is no secret that his role model is me, his father, and that anyone can ask any of his close friends, as they all know it to be true.

11-18-ω

Dad,

Well, here we go again. For some reason I can't just live the normal life. If I am not in jail I am messing up my married life. Weather or not you say it or not I have been quite the disappointment. I have been doing my own thing for years and it just doesn't seem to work. I think I am always looking for an edge. I blame only myself and never anyone else. Dave and Holly always have someone to blame, weather it was mom leaving or your alternate jobs, etc. I honestly can say I cause all my own problems.

You have always been there for me through thick & thin. I have always wanted to make you proud of my job, my wife and my life. I basically lead a good life. I don't drink, I don't smoke and I don't do drugs. I enjoy gambling, but that is merely recreational on special occasions. I know you feel it is an issue, but it is not.

I always wanted to finish school and

make you proud. I always enjoyed school but found other things to do. Like getting married or starting new jobs. It is not like I have negative influences or anything. All my friends are great and straight-laced. I do what I want to do. Maybe I need to do something else. I don't lead an extravagant lifestyle, but I am very happy with what I have. I never wanted a huge house or lots of cars or anything fancy. I don't know what the deal is. I think I need to stop looking for any angles and just do what I am supposed to.

    I am surrounded by drug addicts, strong-arm robbers and more drug addicts. It makes me ill to think that I am sleeping next to these guys. I am just a number to these people, but I am very different from all of them.

    I am really excited about the horse racing game with you and have always wanted to get involved. We will get a good one soon, I am sure.

You have never lead me to believe anything other than you love me and am proud of me. I just feel I let people down, especially myself. I really wanted to see mom this year and see how she was doing. I really screwed that one up.

Anyway, I just wanted to say I am very thankful that you have **ALWAYS** been there for me through all my "issues". I have always spoken very highly of you and always will.

It is always a good time when we get a chance to see each other and it will continue to be so. If I don't tell you enough, I Love you. I am very proud to have you as my dad and my friend.

Love, Sean

> *Returning Some of the Special Love You've Always Given Me*
>
> DAD,
>
> It has been a UERY bumpy road the last 12 months for me and the only constant in my life has been you. I know I may have disappointed you but I know you understand that things just happen. I look to you for guidance and you give it. I just wish I listened to you all the time. It is not a secret who my role model is and who I respect the most. Ask anyone close to me and they know it is you. Happy B'day. Love, Sean

Sean finally got out and for a short time we all got back together as a family. David, my oldest, has been sober for a couple of years. My daughter, Holly, was on her way to a great position with her company. Sean was moving forward, as well. Late in the year Sean had an argument or some kind of a situation like that with his boss. The one that he sold sports memorabilia for. They had been close friends, as well. But, I guess not that close. He, Sean's boss, told the police that Sean had guns at his home and that was a violation of his probation. Sean did have guns at home. He was holding them in storage for my brother, Mark. They were

World War II antique rifles. Don't even know if they worked or not. It didn't matter to the police. Sean had violated his parole. He was in jail for that violation when he wrote the aforementioned letter. His sentence was for a hundred and twenty days. He got out sooner for being a good little boy. Maybe a little of my begging to his parole officer might have helped as well.

So, once again all was going well. It was either late in two thousand and one or early two thousand and two when I got a call from Rachel, Sean's girlfriend of a year or two. Now, I am not one hundred percent sure of my facts on this one as I did not investigate it much. It happened so fast that I just walked away from it when it was over. Apparently, Sean had written a check to pay back a marker at a casino in Las Vegas for some six thousand dollars, and it bounced. (For you who don't know what a marker is, I'll explain once again in a little more detail. You can establish credit with the casinos and when you need money, all you have to do is call for a marker. The dealer gives you as much as you ask for or you have been approved for, credit wise. There is good and bad when it comes to markers. The good is that you usually don't have to pay it back for a month or two, interest free. The bad is, refer to Sean's immediate problem. If he bounced a check, why was he up there again? I have no idea, but he was. The cops got him. (Better than Vito, I guess) and put him into jail until he paid off the bad check. Sean made his one and only allowed phone call to Rachel. Don't know why not me? Maybe he was too scared to talk to me at that point. However, the first thing Rachel did was to call me. (Notice, when anything happens that is not good, I get the call!) Probably the last thing I really wanted to hear was shit like this. So many years with David's crap and now there seems to be no let up with Sean. You would think that one of my boys would have taken after Heather, my goody, goody wife. Someone! So, being a little strapped at the time for cash (I don't think they would take a check!), Rachel and I borrowed the money, I drove it up to Vegas. Bailed the little fucker out and left. Now that I think about it, I don't remember if he had said thank you or not. Guess this was starting to become the norm, the Gerson boys getting into trouble. Fortunately, that was the last time he did. Well, almost. You know, sometimes I often wonder if my ex-wife even knew that the "GOOD" son was a real pain in the ass as well, just like the "BAD" son??

About early summer two thousand and two, Sean and I decided to get into the race horse business together as we had talked. We wound up with a few shares in some and others we both owned together. That enterprise seemed to be going just fine. We also got into business together selling pet supplies and that was doing just fine also. So by late summer, I decided to go camping (tent camping of course) at Yellowstone National Park for a week or ten days. About a month or so before I left to go camping, I was contacted by phone from someone who had me put my name and number in one of those books that they have in places to show that someone traveled through at one time or another. You know how some places have a register to sign, showing that you were there. Now I found out what it was for. They wanted to sell me some land in Colorado. Some bare land. I told them that I would swing by on the way home from Yellowstone and take a look. As I was driving through Utah, on the way camping, I was listening to talk radio. When the hell did I make the switch from FM to AM? That is how old I am! I just can't remember a lot of things! I was listening to a program called "Tradio" which is a swap meet (flea market) on the radio. It was really pretty kewl. Someone would call and tell everybody listening what they wanted to buy or sell and give out their phone number. To buy or sell what you just heard, all you had to do is just make the call. Bam! Done deal! So, I was listening. I heard this guy say that he has an acre and a quarter lot for sale for this amount and a double-wide mobile home for that amount. Being from California I really thought he had made a mistake and was quoting the down payments. That couldn't be the selling price, as he suggested. Curious, I made the call. They were the selling prices! I immediately wondered how much a hooker would cost in Utah. Obviously, I knew nothing about Utah. I told him that I was headed for Yellowstone for a week or so and after was headed to Colorado to possibly buy some real expensive land (five acres of dessert). When I was all done and was ready to head home, I would give him a call. If all was still there, I would take a quick ride there and take a look. That was fine with him.

Yellowstone was beautiful, and I had a hard time leaving. But, the rangers helped out a lot. I had been chasing a grisly to take a picture up close and personal and for some reason, the rangers came unglued. They told me that if I was even out of the car to take a picture of a sparrow on a wire, they'll kick my ass out. Touchy, touchy! Geeeeesch! So, now I am on the way to Colorado to look at the desert. I really had to drive all the way to Colorado to look at the desert. Really! I lived fifty miles from the desert. Remember, Hesperia where the birds, lizards and rabbits use to run wild until my brother and I got that Red Rider B B gun? I finally arrived in Colorado. It was the San Luis Valley, Costilla County, and to be more specific, in the or should I say, near the town of Alamosa. I was taken to an area that had twenty-seven billion lots, all of which were five acres. The words "Gated Community" were not only not spoken, but I am sure they did not have any idea what that was. I looked at at least ten lots and not one was any different from the other. They were all five acres of sand. I never saw a Yucca, a rabbit, a lizard, a scorpion, or a bird. There was one trailer, however, and some people did live there. I could see a dog, a child (great environment to bring up a kid, unless, of course, he is soon to star on the SiFi channel), and a car. This wasn't really what I was looking for. So, I am sure the real-estate agent knew that I was not too interested. Just about then I said, "I don't think I am really interested." He said, "What if your lot was very close to the Rio Grande River?" I said, "We are close to the Rio Grande?" That was way too much emotion from me and a big mistake. He might not have known what a gated community is, but he is a real-estate agent and could smell blood further away than a shark could. So, as we drove closer to it, he was hooking me in inch by inch. He was telling me all about the movies that had taken place on and at the Rio Grande (not necessarily at this part), as well as the history, and what Indians were here and what the Mexicans did. (It probably would have helped sell the land to me if he had mentioned that many Mexicans had been slain by the rowdy Indians. But he had no knowledge of my past.) Well, you get the picture, right? We finally got there. The Rio Grande was less than six feet across. I could have jumped it. He did tell me they were in a drought and that it soon would be much much wider. Yeah, and the check is in the mail. (For you who know not what I speak, "the check is in the mail" is the first of two biggest lies that a man will tell you.) So, as I drove away the proud new owner of five acres on a corner lot overlooking the famous Rio Grande (well almost), I started to look for a phone booth to call my guy in Utah to see if the land and the mobile home were still available. (It was probably on a cliff overlooking a cemetery if I was lucky.) I made the call and much to my bad luck, it was still available. Let's see. Chased out of Yellowstone and couldn't wait to get out of Colorado. Can't wait to see what fate will become me in Utah. So, I made the drive.

Utah is a very beautiful state. Lots of mountains, made up of many different pastel colors and predominately different shades of reds. I believe mostly sedimentary rock. I drove for twenty-four hours and then got some sleep. I met the guy who owned both the land and the home. He had only one arm, was wearing black socks up to his knees, brown shoes and red shorts. (Remember the last time I had anything to do with a one armed person? My brother and I couldn't stop laughing. Little did I know that this time the tears will be of a different flavor.) He was either an L.D. S. Mormon or related to my brother. His name was Paul. We went and looked at the land first. It was one-fourth of a five acre parcel. Nothing good or bad that I could see except that it was five miles out of town. (Sounds like something someone would say in a western movie.) There were other homes (mobile homes or as they called them, also, modular or manufactured homes) on some of the parcels near the one was looking at. Not like my huge investment on the practically non-existent, Rio Grande. Some of the residents even had cows on their land behind their houses. (That should assure me of no visits from my brother.) So, in my mind, the price was right for the land. I wouldn't have known the difference anyway. The way I figured it, anything was better than the Rio Grande *plot*! We went over to where the manufactured home was. He didn't tell me that it was not on the land I was to look at. Now, this was a real piece of shit! It was in two pieces, just like you see being driven down the highway being escorted by a pickup truck in front and one in back with yellow blinking lights and a sign that reads, "Wide load." I am not sure this would make it down the highway. So, after a minimum of discussion, he agreed to move it on to the land that I had just seen. Then glue (or whatever you do to stick the two halves together) it together all at no extra charge. I am telling you that this piece of shit was really bad. I told him that he would have to guarantee that it would travel the five or six miles it had to go without falling apart. A money-back guarantee! Then we worked out a plan for fixing it up. If that was even at all possible. First, I had to pay for a cement slab to be put on the land so that the house had a place to sit. Even with all the work that had to be done, the price was so low that it was worth it. I thought! Of course, I now know why I never got into the real-estate business. To make a very long story as short as I can, I bought the house and commissioned him to do the repairs. Many repairs! A one-armed man! (Do I deserve what I got?) So, after he quit a year later or so, I hired at least five others in a four-year time span. At that time, I was still living in California and really did not have a way to check on who was doing what. I was now way over forty thousand dollars, and it was no better than it was when I bought it. One time, it somehow caught fire. One time, all the windows were broken out of it. One time I couldn't get into it for the grazing cows in front of my door. (I wonder if my brother would have helped me remove them.) One time I found a totaled car on the land. One time, I had to remove the homeless that had moved into it because they thought it was vacant. I am sure they were thinking that no one would live in it because of the way it looked. It was just one thing after another. I had to put in a septic tank and have trenches dug for electrical and water lines. I had put on all new siding and a new roof. It not only was a financial disaster, it became an albatross around my neck. My whole life was centered on, at first, fixing it up so I would have a nice place to retire to, to getting rid of it because it was that albatross around my neck. Finally, I hired a real estate agent and she sold it. I sold it for a pittance of my indebtedness and was happy as hell to see it go. Three months later I got a call from the guy who bought my house and land. He told me that when I had the house moved and set on the cement slab that I had put on my land, I had put the slab on the wrong land and the home as well. The one arm guy that had sold it to me (I am sure that you remember the black knee high socks, brown shoes, red shorts, one arm guy. Remember him? The guy who when I first saw him, I should have run. I should have never bought anything, in the first place from him. I guess I get what I deserve guy. That guy!), put the slab and the home on the wrong lot! So, I had sold land that was not mine and built a home on someone else's lot. Great! Just fuckin great! So, I had to buy the lot that I had the home put on and had sold to someone and then try to sell my vacant lot that I never knew was mine. The albatross just wouldn't let go of me. It was one loss after another. At that time, if I could have found that one arm guy; he would have had no arms. After paying through the nose, a bunch more, it all got worked out. In fact, after all the new necessary stuff that I now had to go through, I found out that neither the land nor the house was his to sell. Go figure! However, all that had been done legal. (I hope.) The moral of the story is, don't ever trust a one-armed man with long black socks, brown shoes and red shorts.

It just so happens that one of the guys who had done some work on my albatross was hurting for money and offered me a small mobile home (single wide) in the same area. That particular area was so lucky for me, how could I turn it down? I still live there now.

Chapter Twenty-Six

About the middle of October two thousand and two, just about the closest thing to the second coming of Christ happened. Besides my birth, and unbeknownst to me, my ex-wife, Heather, returned from Australia after a sixteen-year hiatus. She was planning on moving in with Sean, my youngest, and stay in these United States of America. As Dirty Harry (Clint Eastwood) would say, "Swell"! We may have seen each other, maybe twice, since she disappeared eons ago. We had talked several times on the phone, though. Was I surprised? I guess so.

Thanksgiving was rapidly approaching, and we had been celebrating it at Sean's, my youngest, house. (You can see where this is going, right?) Nothing changed for this year that I was aware of. I was told that, of course, Heather, my ex, was going to be there. That was not a problem for me. I went down the day before and stayed the night. All was fine then and the next day, Thanksgiving, went very well also. The whole family was there, both of my sons, their girl friends, my daughter, her husband, and my two grandkids. All in all, we all seemed to have a very nice time. Actually, it was nice to see Heather again. Now, some of you who may be reading this book and know me, know that I am into extraterrestrial stuff, ghosts, fortune tellers, and things like that. You know, stuff that a smaller percentage of humans on this earth are into. So, it would not be unusual that I occasionally go to a fortune teller to see what is going to be bestowed on me for the following year. This year was no different. I am very particular about whom I see. I feel that not all are honest and certainly not accurate. Most of the public feel that none are, and that's okay. They haven't experienced the real thing and probably won't, because they will not go to one for whatever their reasons are. I always have my reading taped, and this year was no different. My reader has me bring a picture of anyone whom I want to know anything about. I usually bring a photo of a family member, a girl I am dating, or even one of my race horses I am concerned about. This time I had brought a picture of my son, Sean, and his girlfriend, as well as a couple of others. Prior to my coming down to the Thanksgiving

Day dinner, I went to my reader. I was probably inquisitive about my ex-wife. However, one of the things my reader said, and of course it is on the tape, was that my son Sean, and his girlfriend were to have two children together. She never mentioned anything about marriage. Just that they were to have two children together. So, after dinner, I asked if anyone would like to listen to what my Fortune Teller had to say a few days ago. Of course, there was a lot of laughter and looks that might say, "Dad's nuts." However, I was humored. I put on the tape. There were a few things that I remember coming true at a later time. But, when the part came on that said that Sean and Rachel were to have two children, all laughter broke out. They all laughed for ten minutes. They talked and joked about. "If she is so good, why didn't she say what the date, month or year of marriage was to be?" they joked. The laughter stopped and then went on with the rest of the tape. Today, Sean has two children with Rachel. The oldest (I believe) is five. They are not, and I don't think they have any plans, of being married. I laughed.

As I recently mentioned, Sean and I did get into the racing game as we had planned. I had been out of racing for so long that I told Sean to make all the decisions, and I would go along with it. Sean had been interested in breeding for a long time and had kept up on horses much better than I had. We wound up with a few horses that were ok in the few months that we were partners. He was enjoying the game, and I was enjoying being a partner with my son. (We had also gotten into a different kind of business not too long ago. It was involving animals as well. These animals were dogs and cats. But that's another story.) We bought a horse (filly) called, "Pocketfullofpesos." Lots of horses have very funny names. I think that's the reason people don't get involved in owning them. They think they should have names like dogs and cats. Can't you just hear the race announcer calling the horses as they come runnig down the stretch, saying, "Here comes Spot and Meow Meow right behind him, just in front of Puggsy and Whiskers?" Sick! Very sick! Anyway, Pocketfullofpesos was a great horse. (Filly) If you can remember, in the front of the book, where I said my biggest thrill as an adult was winning the "Sunshine Millions Horse Race" in partnership with my son. Well this is that story.

I had been in and out of the horse racing game for over twenty years. I had some nice horses and a bunch more of some not so nice horses.

Anybody, in the game of horse racing, will tell you that you get one good one and twenty-five not so good ones. That's normal. We bought this one for forty thousand dollars out of a claiming race. (A claiming race is where anyone may buy any entrant for a specific and preset price.) She won that day. Now, she was ours, and we stepped her up in class. She won an allowance race. That is better than a claiming race with a much higher purse, awarded to the owners. She won so impressively that day that we decided to run her in a stakes race. The name of the stakes race was called, "The Sunshine Millions." It is a day of racing that was hosted one year in California and the next year in Florida at that time. It is a very prestigious group of races. The purse, for the race we entered in was one hundred and twenty-five thousand dollars. I didn't stutter. You heard right, one hundred and twenty-five thousand dollars. This is the real reason people own race horses. Not for the names. The day of the race was December twenty-seventh, two thousand and two. The whole family was there, and a bunch of our friends. There were somewhere around fifty, in all. After all the years of racing I have been through, I had never had a horse good enough to get into a stakes race. At this point, it was to me, the same as being in the most prestigious race in the world, "The Kentucky Derby." It would not be all about the thing of winning but just to have been entered into the Kentucky Derby would be the biggest thrill in my racing career. Winning the Derby is unimaginable.

    Sean and I went to the saddle area just before the race to talk to our filly. This is something I do at every single race I race in. We mentioned that there was to be a barbecue at Sean's house. If she doesn't win the race, guess who was to be barbecued? We went back to the stands to watch the race. I am always nervous before one of my horse's race but not like this. I had even made up tee-shirts with our special racing colors on them and handed them out to any and all who wanted to wear them for our race. They were bright red with a huge "V" for victory, spanning the whole front on them. The sweat was gushing down my forehead and neck. My glasses would not stay on my head. I was standing next to Sean and surrounded by family when the gates open. You could hear the announcer say, "There they go." I would Love to call the whole race for you, but you may not read any more of my book. So, I will just tell you the end result if you haven't already figured it out. We ran dead last!

Just joking! We won by an impressive three lengths, going away. (Going away is race talk for extending the lead further and further.) Had the race been another half a mile, she would have won by five thousand eight hundred and fifty-six lengths. That is better then Secretariat, if that is possible. So, the party was on! It was very hard for me to absorb that we had won. Like I had said before, just being entered in the race was enough. Winning was inconceivable. And we won! Again, the sweat ran fluidly. But this time, it was from the eyes. There was no doubt that that was the largest thrill in my adult life, and it was because I got to share it with my son, Sean. I will never, ever forget it. I also will never forget the dinner Sean and I paid for, at a very fancy restaurant afterwards. Many had gone to eat on us, and we Loved it. When all was over, I fought Sean hard for the bill, but he won. (Lost!) But, I did get the tip. $800.00! Unquestionably my biggest thrill! (And my largest tip.)

About a month later we entered Pocketfullofpesos into another stakes race. We were the favorite to win it. We lost that day, and Sean and I had very different opinions for the reason. That day in January was the beginning of a downfall between Sean and me. We also had a problem with the other business we had started, involving honesty. So, between the two problems that, in my eyes, were workable, but obviously not in Sean's eyes, by the first week in April two thousand and three, not only Sean but he had convinced his brother, David, his sister, Holly, and my two grandchildren, Daniel and Heidi, that no one was to ever talk to me ever again. Sean told David, my oldest son, to go tell my brother, Mark, that he was ousted from the family as well because he was my brother. (Guilt by association I guess) He too, has never talked to anyone, since. As of this day of my writing, March twenty-sixth two thousand and eleven, I have never heard from them. I call it the "Darth Vader syndrome in reverse." The best kid in the world, great looking, absolutely positive attitude, great sense of humor and smile, turned into a man in black with nothing but hate and destruction in mind for his dad. To this day I still don't understand it. I may be wrong, but I always thought I was better than the usual good, ole dad, especially when I had to deal with one child who tried to kill herself, her mother tried the same, and one kid that spent twenty years of his life in jail, and another son who was convicted of two felonies and did time in the penitentiary. After all of that, I never looked badly at them or was any less of a supportive dad. Then, and now!

Two thousand and three went by very slowly. I had been doing way too much thinking about family. I tried a few times to make contact, with no replies.

Sean had ripped me off with some of the horses that we had had together. He said that possession was ninety percent of the law. I was not going to argue with him. I didn't need any more reasons to be separated from my clan.

I was working the other company that Sean and I had been partners in involving dogs and cats. Sean took away all the accounts and supplier names when we split up and left me with really nowhere to go. I had some of his inventory and kept it so I could survive. I told him I would pay him back as soon as possible. For months I had continued to deposit thousands of dollars into his bank account, paying back what I had owed him. Obviously, that was not good enough for him. So, about eight months later he sued me for one hundred thousand dollars, plus punitive damages! Once again, his greed came out. Just like the time he stole money from one of his employers, and really didn't need the money. He got caught and went to prison. (I think they called it "Grand Larceny.") He must have thought that all the extra money he was receiving in his bank account (Thousands), was a gift from God. The bottom line was that I won the case, but it cost me twenty thousand dollars to defend myself. That was late in two thousand and four. That pretty much made the decision that there would be no reconciling with my family.

I struggled through the next few years building the business and playing a little bit to keep my sanity. Right around the summer of two thousand five, I had my heart attack, as noted in the front of the book. What I had said in the front of the book was really the truth. No family. The IRS was driving me nuts! No real relationship in my life to speak of. No real reason to live. I did tell them to pull the plug. I just didn't care anymore. As I have already said, the doctors were very convincing, and I am still alive with a battery propelled ticker. Now, not that there have been that many women in my life since. When I am naked and in bed with them and they ask, "What is that protrusion in your chest?" I simply tell them, "I am working on the hardening of my heart, because of my kids." A few months went by. The doctors told me that my heart attack was not from blocked arteries but from stress. They said I needed to retire. Yea, right! Retire. They are making millions a year as doctors so it's easy for them to say. Although I had plans to give my company to David, my oldest son, who now does not talk to me, I offered the company for sale. As faith would have it, my brother or my sister-in-law, (really can't remember.) asked me if I would give a job to their son, Michael. He was a nice kid. Just doing everything other nice kids do. When working, he was stealing from his employer and drinking as much as possible while on the job and staying drunk as long as possible when not working. Doing just the average amount of drugs that is normal for twenty-three year olds. Well, maybe a little more. He is my nephew, you know. So, with all of these great credentials, of course, I immediately hired him. Oh, did I mention that one time, years ago; I had gone on a cruise and left my car at my brother's house. I had asked my brother, Mark, if he would just start it up a couple of times while I was gone to keep the battery charged up. Not a problem with him. Michael, his son, my new hire nephew, offered to do it and told my brother it would be better if he took it around the block once or twice. He took it and crashed it into a telephone pole. He not only totaled my car, but it cost his dad a thousand for the replacement of the pole. He swears he was just tired and fell asleep. (I am sure that drugs or alcohol had nothing to do with it.) So, now with these extra credentials that I had forgotten about, as he will be making deliverers as well, was an asset to my company. Once his parents found him, somewhere in New Mexico, hiding from the cops, girlfriends, the job corps, and the credit card companies, and told him about the chance to go to work for his uncle, he showed up in a week or so, semi-sober in a (I think a Jeep or some kind of a four-wheel drive vehicle) broken-down car that sounded like a washing machine that was on its last leg and looking like it had hit more than one telephone pole. A hand grenade for the shifting knob, half the stuffing was coming out of the seats, and three of the windows were cracked or broken. I guess to shoot out of while driving or on the run. I sat him down and told him that I had planned to give this business to David, my son, as I have said. But, now that there is no son anymore and that I was supposed to retire, if things work out, we could work a deal for you to buy it from me at a very good price.

Right about now I was thinking that my heart attack not only stopped me from major activities but seriously affected my mind. I actually hear myself saying what I am saying, and can't believe what I am hearing. Michael says, "I don't have any money, how can I buy it?" I said, "Let's see if you work out, and then I will work on it some way."

Knowing what I know about Michael's past, and figuring that I probably don't know half about Michael's past, I told him this. "Here is the deal, Mike. I will bend over backwards for you and help in any way that I physically and mentally can to get you on the right track. I really want to sell this to you so I can go on-living as much as I get to with this metal in my chest. I will give you one and only one chance if you fuck up. One! Do you understand, one?" Michael replied, "I do, and I really appreciate you giving me this chance, Uncle Chuck." The next month or two went really well with the exception of my inventory counts, of which I let Michael do. It's part of the training process. The first month he was off by fifty thousand dollars. The next month he was off by much more. I can't tell how much I thought for sure that he was ripping me off to buy drugs. He certainly wasn't doing it to buy a new car. In fact, that fucken wreck he was driving broke down to the tune of a thousand dollars a month, of which I was the source of repairs. It even had to be towed in one time. I never asked him for the money. I just tried to get him another car. But, it was the Love of his life. His pride and joy, and it was not going to happen. I had no choice but to keep on fixing it so he could get to work. I decided to check out the inventory shortages myself. I was hoping that it was all there. It was! Now, I was concerned that this guy couldn't count from one to five without making a mistake. I was starting to wish that the inventory was stolen. At least then I could fire him and save face with his parents by having a good reason. Now, I thought I'd have to put up with an idiot. One morning he was late for work. The phone rang; I answered it and guess who it was? Yep, Mike. All I heard was, "Uncle Chuck, would you pick me up at the county jail?" I said, "I am on the way." I saw Mike sitting on a wall and drove over to him. He got in the car. I said, "What happened?" He said, "I was fishing off the pier and killed a six pack while doing so. Then I got in my car to drive home (I am sure the car was not a reason to stop him. With the broken windows, hand grenades, lack of paint that was originally camouflage colors, dents from going off roading and generally just looked like what a drunken, drug doing kid would be driving), and the cops stopped me and gave me a DUI." He added, "I guess that I am washed up with you and the job, heh?" I said, "Do you remember what I had told you at the very beginning of your employment about fucking up?" He said, "Yes, one and only one chance." I said, "You just used it. I will never bring it up to you or knock you down because of it. It never happened." To this day, at least five years later, he has been an asset to humanity and to himself. However, the statement that I had made about it never happening was constantly brought up to me by him having to go to driving school and the cost of it. Not to mention the rise in insurance costs, not to mention the "AA" meetings.

Today, as I am writing right now, I am very proud of him, not only with his work, but because he is a compassionate, productive, and bright human being. Hell, I can't even say that about myself!

Unfortunately, and because it is a passion of mine, I had stayed in the business of horse racing and some breeding as well. My business that we have just been talking about is in a small town called Morro Bay. Not far from there, maybe thirty miles or so is a town called Paso Robles. It just so happened that a horse called, "Miss Paso Robles" was for sale in a claiming race. So, I bought it. I took it up to Golden Gate Fields in northern California to race. I thought she was a pretty good horse. I asked the top jockey there, Russell Baze, if he would ride my new purchase. He said yes, and that made me very happy. The race took place on June sixteenth two thousand and six. We won the race by three lengths. I have the picture with him, Miss Paso Robles, O.J., my trainer, and myself in the winning circle. Standard procedure if you win the race. Just another way the race track makes money. You have to buy the pictures. Miss Paso Robles was claimed from me out of that race. So, I am horseless again, but not for long. (By the way, there is a point to all of this horse race stuff, and it is not about winning races.) About five months later my trainer, O. J. Jauregui, called me and said, "There is a horse I would like you to claim." He said the name was, "Bemuse." So, I claimed Bemuse not long after he asked me to. Our first race with him was on December twenty-eighth. Knowing that I had made a good claim and that the horse seemed physically fine, I asked Russell Baze to ride for me again. Once again, he said, "Ok." Once again we won, and the track made money off of my picture purchases. Now, the point of all this is that Russell Baze not only is and was the top jockey at Golden Gate Fields, in northern California, but he was now very close to being the all-time winnin'est jockey in the world, having won more races than any other human being in the world. That's quite a feat. If memory serves me correctly, not long ago, in this monstrosity of a book, I had bragged about having Chris McCarron ride for me and win and then became the biggest money winner in the world. Although I have never made any money with this business, I seemed to be blessed in certain areas. If nothing else, it makes for good reading! Once again, it was race time for me and Bemuse. Once again, I asked Russell Baze to ride for me. Once again, he said yes. The difference this time is that he had made the big-time list of miracle workers. He is now the number one jockey in the world. He has won more races than the great Willie "The Shoe" Shoemaker or Laffit "The Pirate" Pincay. Just to be mentioned in the ranks of those two names has to make any horse race enthusiast smile and tear at the same time. Certainly, now more than any other time, the win here is so much more important than the purse money award for winning the race. If I win this race, if I ever write a book, this will be in it. So it is written and so it will be done!

We won the race by a nose and only because Baze was the jockey. Any other jock, besides The Pirate, (who could hold an elephant's head up to cross the line first), would have lost in the photo finish. So, now the pictures were taken and the hugs were given, smacken hands, smacken backs and tears of joy were the choice of the hour. As it so happened, I had a date that day (Ironically, she lived in Paso Robles. However, she didn't look anything like a horse), and I had asked Russell if he would take a picture with the both of us. He did, and that picture stands proudly in my living room as we speak. Right next to a couple of other horse pictures, of great horses I used to own, named Sea Biscuit and Secretariat. (If you believe that, I have a couple of bridges I would like to sell you.) Three mounts with Baze, and three winners. The last was with his new credentials. Numero Uno. I am telling you, if I ever write a book, this is a chapter in itself. Oh yea! I made a buck or two as well.

About two years have now gone by, and it was time for me to retire. Believe you me, that, that was not what I wanted to do. I am, and have always been, a work-a-holic. I worked a deal with my nephew, Mike, to buy the company using the profits from it. No money down and about one third of what I should have sold it for. But, then again, he is of my blood. By this time he had gotten a mind, not only for and about the business, but of his own. Amazing what the lack of alcohol and drugs will do to you or for you. The way I figured it was, I was going to give it to my son, David, for free, so whatever I get for it now was a lot more than I was going to get for it. However, this guy, Michael, you know the one with the new mind, decided to get hardnosed on the terms of the sale. Unbeknownst to him, it got so hard to get what I thought I should get for it, considering I was basically giving the company to him (nothing out of pocket and payments from the profit and the sale price was about one-third of what it should have been), that I almost fired him and decided to work until I had my last heart attack. If he gets the company and he goes broke, he is twenty-six and can get a job anywhere. I am sixty-six and my social security check won't cover my back taxes that I owe. Hell, he wouldn't even be able to hire me, so I could make a buck if he lost the company. He would, at that time, have no company, nor would I. Talk about a backfire. Anyway, I gave in a little and so did he. So, now I am unemployed, and he is a big shot of his own company. I found myself hanging around the office and being in the way, I am sure. Months have now gone by and it seems like I am begging to help. Can I deliver something? Can I put out the trash? Can I? Can I? Can I? I needed to get away.

Chapter Twenty-Seven

With all of this time on my hands, I started to think about all the stupid and goofy things I have done and have been around and involved with all of my life. It was obvious to me that I am probably never to see any of my kids again and certainly not my two brand-new grandchildren (of whom I was told about by my cousins, Arnold and Sandy, in New Jersey), whatever their names are. Not even sure if they are male or female. So, since I have a pacemaker and I will assume an abbreviated life span, why not tell them who I am and what if anything they have missed by not ever knowing me, their grandfather. That is what this book is really all about. Not the sale of it. At the beginning of this writing, it was never a thought to sell it. Never! I figured I would have made about thirty or so copies and hand them out to my friends and any relatives (who were left and speaking to me), who wanted it. Just ask some of them to find a way to get one in to the hands of my grandchildren, in a few years, so they could have the chance to know me. That is the real reason why this book is one hundred percent the truth. At this point in my life after death, there would be no point to not tell the truth. I'm gone!

So, with this in my mind, I figured that staying around the Morro Bay and Los Angeles areas, where all of my friends are, would be a huge hindrance. In all of the transactions involving the properties in Utah, I wound up with a small mobile home. It was a single-wide trailer in a mobile home park. (I think I, may have touched on it earlier.) It was inexpensive to live there. I would be away from my friends and what was left of my family. I could have the quiet I need to write. No one saying, "Let's go to the movie, the dance, the party, the bar", and whatever else they could have figured out to distract me from writing. So, it is to Utah.

I figured it would take me a year, maybe a year and a half, to do the whole book and then figure out what I wanted to be when I grew up. I moved to Utah on March seventeenth two thousand and seven. I really didn't stay there all of the time. It took a while getting used to. It is (my guess) about ninety-five percent Mormons. At least that was the way I made it. They seemed like the nicest people in the world, on a howdy-do basis, but not very sociable to outsiders as far as going places and doing things together. I hark back to when my dad was ill and the Mormon elder would come over and leave money when he left. Never an invite to dinner! It took me a few months to totally move in both physically and mentally. Now, here I am in a non-drinking state and a non-drinker. Seems to fit well, right? So, what do you think happened? Right! I start drinking.

    I was with my brother for a weekend at Laughlin, Nevada. It is kinda like a very, very little Las Vegas. We were both sitting at a slot machine next to each other and playing our nickels when a very Lovely waitress came by and asked if we would like a drink. We always said, "Yes." I would order the same thing that my bro ordered. When the waitress came back with the beers, we'd tip a buck. I would give my beer to Mark, my brother. For some reason this time I looked at Mark and said, "You know, the doc said it would be good for me to drink a glass or two of red wine every day to benefit my heart, and I feel like having one. So, I think I will." I ordered and it tasted just fine. Now that I am a connoisseur of wine, six years later, I almost puke to drink the same wine they served me for free back then. How we do change with age! Now that I am a drinker in a non-drinking state, I have to join a private club to drink. There is only one in Cedar City where I live and they only serve beer. Great! Just Great! (I would have said, "Great, just fucken great, but I am now in Mormon country and need to watch what I say.) However, soon after I moved to Utah, they relaxed the non-drinking laws and eliminated the private club thing. All hard liquor is metered, and they pour only an ounce. The beer is three-two.

    I have been driving a nineteen-ninety-nine GMC Suburban. It had over three hundred and fifty thousand miles on it and never used a drop of oil from oil change to oil change. (I believe I had touched on this vehicle some pages earlier.) In fact, I can't remember having to fix anything on it. I called Chevrolet and asked them if they would like to use my SUV in a commercial. We talked a bit and the bottom line was that I really had to have about a half a million on it before they would talk to me about making a commercial. So, I decided to drive my SUV until it had the required amount of miles needed to get it on television. I am still driving it. It has four hundred and eighty thousand miles on it, but I did have to replace the heads on it because the engine overheated coming back from Lake Tahoe, Nevada, one day. I did not notice the over-heating until it was too late. I did the required work, but now I overheated myself out of the movie business. As we speak, it is for sale for three thousand and five hundred dollars or best offer. Today, April twenty-nine two thousand and eleven, I am still driving it. (I haven't had an offer!)

Now, living in Utah is not what you might say . . . . a very exciting place. It is really Mormon country. With the exception of every man having twenty-five to fifty-five wives or so (and not wanting to share with me), it sucks for adventure and female companionship. However, there are two exceptions in the adventure department. First, on Saturdays I would go to the Walmart store and count how many sixteen/seventeen year old girls were pushing a shopping cart with one or two kids either in it or helping push it. Not to mention with one usually in the oven. The other is going to the many National Parks that are near and around where I live. Believe me, I have taken advantage of that. As far as the romantic end of it goes, well it just does that. It goes!

I have found myself spending more time going back and forth to California to have a little fun and some adult conversation. One time I had a friend, Martha, come back with me and stay a few days or so. We had been friends for twenty plus years. On the way back to Utah from Morro Bay, California, you have to go through a place called Kramer's Corner. It is a large intersection with gas stations and fast food places. For about five or six miles before you get there, the road is just a two-lane highway. There is just one lane each way and no turn outs. You are stuck in your lane until you get past Kramer's Corner. As I was driving and about a few miles from Kramer's Corner, I noticed that there were about a bazillion trucks and cars all stacked up about a mile from where I was. Fortunately, they were in the other lane and heading towards me or possibly heading towards me but not moving. My lane was slowing but still moving. I turned to Martha and said, "Can you see what is going on way up there?" She said, "Not really." The closer I got to the oncoming traffic, the longer the line of vehicles was. This is a big truck route, so many of the vehicles were trucks. No exaggeration! There must have been no less than two hundred vehicles stacked up and coming my way, but very, very slow. There was a slight bend in the road, and as I made the lazy turn, I could see the first vehicle heading my way. It was a truck. Now, this is why I have included this scenario in my book. There were two Pit Bulls walking in front of that truck. They were right in the middle of the lane. The truck driver was honking his horn and flashing his headlights, but they could care less. They just strutted themselves as if they were in a funeral procession. Slow and steady. Martha and I just couldn't stop laughing. It was absolutely hilarious. Well, for us on this side of the road anyway. Try to imagine this. Anyone who was trying to see what the hell was holding up traffic could not see the two mutts walking and talking in front of the truck. All two hundred of the backed up vehicles had to be totally pissed off at the lead truck. That was all they could see, I am sure. We passed the dogs and started to count the vehicles. After the first fifty I pulled off at Kramer's Corner and relieved myself. (Probably more than you needed to know!) Got a cup of coffee and was back on track to Utah.

Now that we are on the subject of animals, it was a few months later, I was again on the way home from southern California to Utah. It was very late, maybe two A.M. and very foggy. This was sometime about late September. I was plugging along in my practically brand-new suburban. (You know the one with the four-hundred thousand plus miles on it.) I was going up a slight grade and around a right turn. I am sure I was not one hundred percent alert as I saw the ass-end of a deer right in front of me. (Normally, I would Love to see the ass end of a dear in front of me late at night.) I was probably doing seventy/seventy-five miles per hour. I started to swerve towards the left and then realized that I would be going into the oncoming traffic lane. So, being on a turn and it being a little foggy, I could not see what might be coming from that direction. I decided to try to avoid the deer by turning to the right and missing it that way. (Remembering this has all taken place in a split second or two.) The bad part of that decision was that there were about ten other deer next to the one that I could see, just a plodding along. Too late! The right turn was made. I became a deer hunter with a three hundred horse power weapon. As it turned out, I only hit one deer that I was aware of. Not that that was good, but it was better than it could have been. I live in a big game hunting city and state. Just about everyone has or carries a gun, rifle, bow, and arrow, and a hand grenade or two. (Mormons, I tell you, you can't figure them out!) Later on, I told my big game hunting story to the guys whom I know and kinda hang out with, at my local bar (The only bar in the city that serves real wine out if a bottle, and not out of a refrigerated box.), all of their comments were exactly the same. Novice! Just one deer since you have been here?1

I am sure on an occasion or two I have mentioned my cousin, Dottie. You know, if you can hark way back to the front of this instruction manual of insanity, she was, and is the one who thinks she is a poet. (Beatnik) Awe, now you remember! She was the one with the magician for a father. As it has turned out, in the last year or so, she had nine of her poems published in Poetry Magazine. It was in the March issue of two thousand and ten. Not to mention leaders at the University of Chicago asked her to summit a manuscript of her poems for their consideration to publish. Possibly as a whole book! Go figure! A beatnik!

Speaking of my cousin Dottie, she is also the opening act for a private jazz concert held in the very top of California, somewhere near Ukiah, in an area called Potter Valley. She has graciously invited me as a guest for the last four years. I have attended all but one. It actually is a lot of fun and I had a great time. All of the great food and music you can put into your ears and mouth. I understand everyone who plays, except for her. I still don't get it. But don't mention it to her, as she may not invite me anymore. However, the real reason why I am mentioning this is because the whole jazz festival is held in the original barn of the great and acclaimed horse, "Seabiscuit". The now owners of this barn had purchased it awhile back, and had it dismantled, and then shipped to their ranch in Potter Valley. They had it refurbished and re-assembled, in all of its grander, on their property. That is where the jazz festival is held. In Seabiscuit's barn! The food and socializing is on the bottom section where all of the pictures of Seabiscuit and his amazing feats are displayed and where the horses would have stood in the earlier days. Then if you take the stairs to the top, where the hay should be stored, and that is where the talent assembles and plays. I, being in the horse business, have an extra interest in the concert. Just sharing the stage with such a name like Seabiscuit is a giant thrill to me in itself.

I am sure that I have mentioned my brother, Mark, many times. I am sure that I have mentioned my nephew, Mike, many times. But, how many of you have ever heard me mention my niece, Marina? My brother's daughter! My nephew's sister! Rare! There is a reason for that. She graduated from girl scouts with the same degree as did her brother, Mike. An Eagle Scout! In girl scouts they call it "The Gold Award." Her name was sent to the White House and placed in a special section for that great job she had done. I guess it is quite rare that a female gets to that level. Her brother Mike's name is in the Post Office, along with his picture. Another rare feat! Unlike her brother Mike, as he was spending his time making a great attempt to get into the pen, she was spending time at Berkeley College after graduating from the University of Santa Cruz, majoring in marine biology. She then became a professor at Stanislaus State University in California. She is a little like her dad in that way. Bright! However, again like her dad, not too smart sometimes. However, there are many things that separate her from the normal human being. She became bi-lingual and was sent to Brazil on a grant from Stanislaus College to write her thesis on her major, Herpetology. She also had a yearning to do things by herself, like taking a drive across the USA, on her motorcycle for weeks on end. She also spent weeks all by herself in Joshua Tree National Monument, catching lizards, bugs and stuff like that. Not normal! Not normal at all!!

One day, my brother called me and said that Marina was going to get married. I believe it was July fifth two thousand and nine. I asked him when and he said, "Today." I said, "Today?" he said, "Yes, today." I said, "Where?" He said, "At the museum in San Francisco." I said, "WHAT?" He said, "Not only that, but the marriage service was to be held in front of the alligator tank." Nothing had ever been said about marriage. Not to Mark or her mother, Myra. No one was invited, like anyone would have gone anyway. Who would go to a wedding that takes place in front of an alligator tank in a museum? I am sure that the minister or whoever performed the service had to have second thoughts, as well. Now, you might think that the whole thing is nuts, and it is. But, it probably has something to do with her father's brother, and his way of thinking. (That's me by the way.) Great minds always think alike. The burning question that remains in my mind at that time was, would I have driven the fourteen-hundred miles round trip (in my practically new GMC Suburban that now had four hundred and seven thousand miles on it) to see the marriage vows, had I been invited? *I do know the answer!*

It was late in the summer and somewhere around mid-August, two thousand ten. I was at my watering hole, Toad's Bar" and sipping on some of Napa's finest when I started talking to the guy next to me. We were both bitching about how many times we have come in to have a drink and had wished there was a foot-rail on the bar, to rest our feet on. I had seen him in the bar a few times before but never had spoke. After bitching about no foot-rail the conversation somehow turned to my writing a book. I told him what it was about and he said he could add something to it. I said, "What?" He told me that his name was Bill Robertson, and he had had a car lot in Las Vegas, Nevada a long time ago. He said he had always been known as "Wild Bill" to all in the business and the area. He said he had done over four hundred T. V. commercials and had been a household name in the Vegas area. So, this is the story he told me. He said in late nineteen sixty-nine or early nineteen-seventy; Elvis Presley came in to his car lot and bought two brand new black Pontiacs. It was on a Saturday. He sat down and filled out the paperwork. Then Elvis wrote out a check for the total amount. All paperwork finished, Bill had Elvis's check in hand when Elvis said, "Please give me the keys as we need to get on the road." Bill said, "You will need to wait until the banks open on Monday to take possession of the vehicles." Elvis exploded and after an ensuing amount of yelling, *Elvis left the building.* He left with no cars. I tried to put myself in Bill's position and to have to make that decision. I would have let the shaker take the cars. If the check had been no good, at least I would have a bad check written by Elvis Presley that now would be worth a million dollars on E-Bay.

In November two thousand and ten my cousin's daughter got married. My brother and I were invited. It took place in New Jersey at a very Lovely place called Caesar's Palace. (You may have heard of it) It took place over the water on a brand new edition meant especially for special events. My cousin, Arnold, asked me if it was all right if Marla invited my son, Sean, (the son whom I feel started the whole, "don't talk to Dad, thing") as his daughter had a friendship established with Sean for years. She, Marla the bride-to-be, had asked her dad what to do knowing the problems between me and my children. I told Arnold it was fine if she invited him.

My brother and I were enjoying the dinner after the really great wedding when Rachel, Sean's girlfriend, and the mother of my two new grandchildren (I assume) that I have never seen or even know their names, came over to my table and started a conversation with me. The chat lasted roughly ten minutes, and then she left. Not much had been said that really mattered with the exception of her wanting to show me the pictures of my two new grandchildren. I said, "No thank you" while in a pool of tears. I just couldn't bear taking a quick glimpse and then never seeing them again. It just seemed easier to me at the time. My son never came over to say, "Hi". Later in the week, my cousin Arnold said that he went over to Sean and Rachel's table and had asked them to go over to my table and say hello to me. So, Rachel didn't even come over on her own volition. She was just being polite to my cousin's request. As of today, and as I am rapidly coming to a close with this book, I still do not and have not, had any communication with my children. To this day I still do not know why they hate me so much. It's been approximately eight years with no communication, period.

Not long after the wedding, I went on a cruise to Mexico. I believe it was in mid-December. I have done this cruise a few times and never seem to get tired of it. It's an inexpensive cruise as cruises go and to me, very relaxing. There were about fifty people in our group. We all joined together from all over the USA through a singles travel agent named Marcia, aka "Marsky." There are two formal nights on the cruise where the men dress up in tuxedos, and the ladies are dressed to the nines. On one of the nights they serve lobster! All you can eat lobster. This one evening I felt exceptionally hungry and said that I was going to try to beat my record. I had established a record of thirteen lobsters at one sitting on a Norwegian Cruise ship a year or so before. This time I was on a Carnival ship. This would have been my eighteenth cruise with Carnival. VIP with them, you know! So, I announced that I was going to try to beat my record of thirteen. Most of the people who didn't know me before this cruise, I am sure, thought that I was probably exaggerating about the thirteen that I had already bragged about. As the night and dinner progressed, I had my salad, appetizer, a little bread and butter, and a sip or two of wine. Then the main course was upon me. The lobster came with three very large shrimp and broccoli. The first two lobsters went down along with the shrimp and broccoli. The next five were, lobster ala cart, and so on and so on until I had eaten sixteen lobsters. I had eaten sixteen lobsters and with witnesses all around! Granted, the lobsters served were not, by any means, huge. In fact, they are fairly small. But to my knowledge, no one has ever come close to sixteen. I really could have eaten a few more but stopped because I didn't want the cruise line to go broke.

The next day as I was coming out of one of the rest rooms (hmmmm, I don't know why. Sixteen lobsters!), in the hallway on the ship. I saw one of the ladies from our group (Marline I think), heading into the men's room that I was just coming out of. Obviously, she was just off about five feet as the ladies room was just off to the right of the men's room. She looked up at me a little startled at first and then realized she was heading into the wrong room. I said, "Do you want to go into the men's room and see how it looks," just jokingly, of course. She said, "Not really." Before she had time to think, I grabbed her by the arm and led her into the men's room. Once in, I asked her if she had ever kissed anyone in a men's room before. She said, "No." I then planted a good one on her, led her out of the men's room, and pointed her in the direction of the ladies room and said, "You have just made my book." She looked at me like I was nuts. Dead on!

So, now we are at the end of my nutty novel. I guess I should mention a few things to sum up some of this story.

The first one being, in keeping you absolutely up-to-date on my life, about the middle of June two thousand eleven, my nephew Michael told me that I was invited to the families, Fourth of July party, a barbecue on Saturday, the second of July. Yes, the "FAMILY" whom I have not heard from for over eight very long, years. However, the invitation came from my nephew and not directly from my children. No one has asked me directly, and I am not sure why. So, I now have a lot to think about in the next week or so. The thinking is not so much about going to the barbecue as I would Love to go to the barbecue, and to see all of my children again, especially my two new grandkids and my brand-new great granddaughter. The thinking has many facets to be considered.

"A" is when the door opens and I walk into the house, do I kiss, hug, or shake my kids' hands? Or just deck all three of them for what I have had to endure over the last eight years? Remember, I have no clue as to whatever really happened, (Only speculation on my part.) and no one has ever told me. No one! Ever! Just eight years of silence.

"B" and the most important! What if things go poorly? I now have to not only re-kindle my feelings for my children but now have seen the faces and heard the sounds of the new babies, the two grand and one great-grand. Do I want to endure all of the pain all over again? It was literally torture these past eight years and with the new faces, it will be even more torture than before!

"C" would be the opposite of two. If all goes well, do I move back to California to be close to them? I couldn't stay in Utah any longer. It's a seven-hour drive one way and not to mention about two hundred and fifty dollars in gas round trip. What if I did move and then things don't work out? Do I move again? Etc. Etc. Etc.

"D" is would I not finish this book? It was to give to the ones whom I would never see and or talk to, you know, my grandkids, so that they would really know who I was. I honestly believe that they have not been getting the truth from anyone about me. In fact, I was told that when my grandkids ask why Grandpa Chuck is not coming to whatever, that they are told that I am really busy and can't make it. The truth is that I am not and never had been invited! I can't imagine what else they have been told.

"F" is when I asked, through my nephew Michael, what it was that I had done to cause the destruction of the relationship in the past eight years so that I would be aware of it and would make sure that I didn't do it again, the answer did not come. But, Michael said, "Just to be a nice human being and all should go well." I always thought I was!

"G" was that I was told I could never bring up the past. Let by-gone's be by-gone's! For me this is not an easy task. So many "Why's" dwell in the back of my mind that I really think I should know the answers, even if I don't like or agree with them. I can't tell you how much crap that was thrown at me by Sean in those past years, including the lawsuit for a hundred thousand dollars plus punitive damages! (I may have mentioned that before.) He lost the suit, but it cost me twenty thousand dollars in attorney fees to defend myself. Everyone asked me why I didn't sue him back. I just said, "He's my son."

I could go on and on, but I am sure you get the jist of things.

So, after ten days of agonizing thinking, I told Michael about the twenty-eighth or so of June, that I had decided to go. Take the chance. If all goes well, it would certainly be worth it, hands down. I had prepared myself for the worst and would hope for the best. Michael asked me if I wanted to ride with him and his. I thanked him, but I thought it would be better if I had my own car, just in case. He agreed. I asked him if he would arrive at the same time I did so I would feel more comfortable when I go in. He said, "Not a problem." He then relayed the acceptance to my family that I would be there. I also asked Mike if I was to bring anything with me. He said, "All was taken care of, and all I needed was me." The past ten days or so were loaded with telephone texts, computer emails and a phone call or two, to and from Mike. Talking, suggesting and planning! Michael was doing all he possibly could to try and get the family back together. He was very sure that it all would work out well for the future. I planned to drive to Huntington Beach on Friday morning and then stay overnight with my brother, Mark, and then go to the barbecue on Saturday from there. He was only a few miles away from the festivities that were to start at two P. M. As I was packing for the weekend, on Friday morning I received a call from Michael, the match-maker. He said, "I hate to tell you this, but your children have decided that they don't want you to come down after all." (I am still picking my heart off the floor today, the Fourth of July, as I am writing this.) I said, "Why?" He said that David (my oldest son) said there were going to be too many people there that he knew, and that he thought if there was an incident that he did not want them to be a part of it and bare the embarrassment. My youngest son Sean told Michael that he was afraid I would bring up old stuff and didn't want to go through with it. (You know the stuff that I agreed to not bring up.) You would have thought they would have given as much thought to inviting me as I did accepting. What did they think; it was just as we left it eight years ago? They knew how many guests and which ones they were going to invite, didn't they? I had promised that I would not bring up the past as they had asked. I did and accepted all the demands and requests on their terms. However, they did mention to Michael that maybe in the near future, we might meet for dinner sometime. But with that, of course, brings up the possibility of having to clear out the entire wait staff, as they might not quite understand our conversation if they were listening. So, I guess I just missed out on the barbecue. *A free one at that!*

The second is, if anyone reads this monstrosity of a book and they were in it or were just confused and need some clarification or would like to be in my next book, I can be reached at *chukegee@aol.com*. Or, I guess, just wait for my next book to come out with or without you in it.

Third, "I had a dream!" (Seems to me that I have heard that somewhere before. Don't know where that cliché` came from, but it fits today.) I awoke this morning, and my dream said to list all of the places that I have been. I will try my best, but I am sure I will miss some of them. Here goes, in alphabetical order:

Anza-Borrego Desert St. Pk.; Big Sur; Castle Crags, St. Pk.; Catalina Island; Chandelier Tree (drive through)in Leggett; Death Valley; Driven "America's Loneliest Hwy." (Hwy. 50); Klamath Basin Natl. Wildlife Reserve, (Ca. & Or.); Lake Shasta Caverns; Lake Tahoe, both (Ca. & NV.); Lassen Volcanic Natl. Pk.; Lava Beds Natl. Pk.; Monterey; Morro Bay; Obsidian Pillars (Volcanic Glass) at Mammoth Mtn.; Multiple Pony Express (and brothel) Stops; Yosemite National Pk. Ca; ** Arches Natl. Pk.; Bryce Canyon Natl. Pk.; Canyonlands Natl. Pk.; Monument Valley; and Zion National Pk. Ut; ** Aruba, Barbados, Dominica, Grand Cayman, Martinique, Ocho Rios, (Jamaica) Nassau, Playa del Carmen, Puerto Rico, St. Maarten, St. Thomas, and Tulum, all in the Caribbean; ** Badlands Natl. Pk.; Custer St. Pk.; Mt. Rushmore, and Wall Drug, SD; Carlsbad Caverns Natl. Pk.; Roswell, and White Sands Natl. Monument, NM; ** Casa Grande Ruins Natl. Monument; Grand Canyon; Lost Dutchman St. Pk.; (Superstition Mtn.) Meteor Crater; Petrified Forest Natl. Pk.; Saguaro Natl. Pk.; Sedona; Slot Canyons at Page; Sunset Crater Volcano Natl. Monument; Tombstone (O. K. Corral); and Walnut Canyon (cliff dwellings) Natl. Monument, Az; ** Cabo San Lucas, Cancun, Chichenitza, Cozumel, Ensenada, La Paz, Mazatlan, Puerto Vallarta, Tijuana, all in Mexico; ** Crater Lake Natl. Monument, OR; ** Continental Divide (at seven thousand nine hundred eighty-eight feet elevation Yellowstone Wy.); Craters of the Moon Natl. Monument, and Hagerman Fossil Beds Natl. Monument, ID; ** Donner Memorial St. Pk.; Fort Churchill St. Historic Pk.; Pyramid Lake;; Rachael (Area 51); Reno; Truckee, and Virginia City, NV; ** Glacier Bay, Juneau, Ketchikan, Skagway, all in Alaska; **

Glacier National Pk. MT; ** Devils Tower Natl. Monument, (Our first Natl. Monument, 09/24/06, and featured in the movie, "Close encounters of the Third Kind.); Grand Teton Natl. Monument; Jackson Hole; Yellowstone Natl. Pk. WY & Mt; Honolulu, Hawaii; (Also, five of the other seven islands; ** Mesa Verde Natl. Pk. Co. (Cliff dwellings; ** Mt. St. Helens, WA; ** And last but not least, Vancouver, Canada.

Fourth, how about all that I have done and seen that is not already in the book? Again, I am sure that I will miss many.

Anatone City, (entering either WA. or MT. I can't remember which one) I actually have seen the city road sign that read, People 67, Cats 31, Dogs 27, Horses 35. It did not have the elevation marked on it. (Probably no room); been on over twenty cruises and on five different cruise lines; been to an Island, in the Caribbean, owned and operated by Jimmy Buffett; been to, "Sutterville", where the California gold rush started; been to the Grand Canyon in AZ; been to the La Brea Tar Pit, in Los Angeles, Ca; climbed Walls Falls and had my hair braided and beads put in in Jamaica. I have been in every state but New Hampshire, Rhode Island & Vermont; I have never bought a brand new car; I have seen glaciers calve; have seen lava flowing; hiked Superstition Mtn. in AZ (Did not find the Dutchman's gold); parasailed; repelled down a huge tree; sailed through the locks at the Panama Canal; saw a street sign in Big Bear City, CA and on one side it read, "Michael" and on the other side it read, "Micheal"; skied both water and snow also snorkeled; started a multitude of different companies; stood on a glacier and on the newest ground in the world, only three weeks old. Swam with dolphins and with manta rays; took a helicopter over the active volcano, "Kilauea"; thrown (almost) out of Yellowstone for chasing a grizzly bear; I have walked through lava tunnels and white water rafted on many rivers; Zip Lined through the canopies of many trees over a hundred feet high in Mazatlan, Mex. I have been in four states all at the same time. It's called four Corners! AZ, CO, NM, and UT., I guess for the drinkers, we should add a, "fifth". If you don't get the pun, don't worry about it.

I still have the SUV with four hundred and eighty-three thousand miles on it. However, I have reduced the price from thirty-five hundred to three thousand. Interested!!

The last three pages with the two lists on it, completes my life from a pup to an age, of sixty-nine fully-lived years. (I would not have this book end on any other number.) I sincerely thank you for reading about my life and I truly hope that it did bring a smile to your face and an occasional tear in your heart.

I love my kids!

Yiddish Glossary

(As close as I can get)

Bar Mitzvah. This is a celebration of a boy when he becomes thirteen and becomes a man.
After that, his whole life flashes before his eyes, and marriage is in the future. However, he does lose a little weight and doesn't cry as much.

Bubba, or Bubbie. A grandmother.
Also, someone who bitches, moans and complains about everyone and everything all the time. Yet, everyone still Loves her.

Bupkus, Slang for shit or nothing at all.
Bupkus on toast. In the armed forces it was more commonly call S. O. S., shit on a shingle.

Cantor. A trained person who is in charge of leading and singing the liturgical parts of religious ceremonies, especially on holidays, in a synagogue, by singing.
Usually better than Neil Diamond (from the movie, "The Jazz Singer"), or at least as good.

Chanukah, or Hanukkah. A religious holiday, usually in December.
Celebrated by lighting candles to compete with Christmas Lights.

Chai cock. (Pronounced, "high cocked")
Slang for Big deal.
Not to be confused with an erection.

Dreck, Drecky, This is an easy one. Shit and Shitty!
Not to be confused with doggy doo. This is the real thing! SHIT!

Faygalah. A gay or lesbian.
Johnny Mathis or Ellen DeGeneres, for example!

Feh. Slang, for not good or don't like.
Example, "Is this all I get for all that money?" Feh!

Gelt. Money.
This word is used more abundantly than schlep in the Yiddish language. Because no Jew has any. Ask them! Or possibly, it could be a misprint and is meant to be guilt. Another word used more than schlep by most Jews.

Haftorah. A part of the Bar Mitzvah ritual that has to be sung or recited (usually by memory) by the boy who is to become a man.
Fortunately, it is done in Hebrew so no one can tell if you make a mistake or not.

Hasari. Usually used to describe a bunch of junk or same old crap. (But, literally means, "pig food" not kosher)
What an old Jewish woman really thinks about antiques and making Love with her husband of fifty-five years or so.

Kishka. Guts or insides.
What Jewish men lose when they get married.

Kosher. A very old set of laws that prohibit a Jew from eating shell fish and pork products because they are said to be unclean. Also, you may not mix meat products and dairy products.
Why these laws are still on the books is beyond me. Did you ever have a bad lobster or a bad steak with Hollandaise sauce on it? Hell, even the Catholics eat meat on Friday now!

Matzos. A large unleavened (non-rising) cracker-like bread. Usually tastes like shit!

Mench. A big hearted and giving man.
Aren't we all?

Meshuganah. A crazy person.
The true description of the author of this book.

Mikva. A Mikva is a ritual involving the total submersion of a person, in a special body of water, that finishes the conversion process and purifies the new-Jewish person spiritually.
This also can be confused with the collecting of insurance policies if done properly.

Mitzvah. A good deed.
I would have thought the BAR part of Mitzvah was the good thing!

Oi Vay, OiVai, Oi Vey, Oy Vey. (The choice is yours) Oh my gosh.
(Who the hell comes up with these words?)

Pipick. A belly button.
See, you don't have to be Jewish to have one.

Punim. A Face. Like the thing that holds your eyes, nose and ears together.
Not to be confused with pudding as when a child eats it and puts it all over his face to hold his eyes, nose and ears together.

Rabbi. A teacher and the head of the synagogue.
Unless you really know and understand Jews, no man is the head of anything. The women run the show.

Rebbitzen, The wife of a Rabbi.
Also known as, "The Boss"!

Schlep. To go far or a tough journey or to drag along.
Jews always use the word schlep when talking. But they rarely do it.

Schvartza. A Negro, black or Afro-American person, but literally means, "the color black."
How can they have so many names and all look alike?

Schmuck. Literally, a large penis. But used to describe a "dummy or idiot."
I am not going to touch that one. (Pardon the pun)

Schnaps. Liquor or booze.
Once you drink enough, you think you can whip a Mexican's ass.

Shiksa. A female non-Jew!
A Jewish female that has not been circumcised! Ya think!

Shul, Another word for Synagogue.
Geeeesch! Synagogue, Shul, Temple. So confusing! What's wrong with one word, "Church," like the normal people call it?

Shvitz or Shvitzing. Sweat or sweating!
Something women never do. Ask them!

Svelte. A slim body.
This is not a Yiddish word! Certainly nobody whom I know knows from it!

Synagogue. A Jewish house of worship.
Basically, the same as a church only the crucifix has been replaced with a star that was donated by the Highway Patrol. Do you get my (missing) point!

Tzores. A big deal, problem or literally meaning, "Trouble"!
Not to be confused with a bull (Toro) from Mexico or just plain bull from some of my friends.

Yarmulke. A small circular hat worn on the head, as a sign of respect to God, in a synagogue.
If you have noticed, I have not tried to pronounce any of the words for you so far. But this one even I don't understand. It is pronounced, Ya-mi-ca. I think it is a cross between a motorcycle and a small musical instrument played by the mouth.

Zada, Zeyde. Grandfather. If you will notice, just about the first word in this glossary is Bubba, "Grandmother." In the Jewish religion the women are always on top. With one exception, sex!

Zets, A light slap. Usually on or about the head.
Having nothing to do with a type of pimple.

www.ingramcontent.com/pod-product-compliance
Lightning Source LLC
Chambersburg PA
CBHW050146130526
44591CB00033B/701